ASSESSMENT TO ASSISTANCE: PROGRAMS FOR WOMEN IN COMMUNITY CORRECTIONS

THESE PAPERS INITIALLY WERE PRESENTED AT THE
1998 CONFERENCE OF THE INTERNATIONAL COMMUNITY
CORRECTIONS ASSOCIATION AND UPDATED FOR THIS VOLUME.

MAEVE McMAHON, PH.D.
DEPARTMENT OF LAW
CARLETON UNIVERSITY, ONTARIO, CANADA
EDITOR

Cover design by Michael Selby. Cover art from "Africa, Mandala" by Betty LaDuke, Ashland, Oregon, from the book: Multicultural Celebrations: the Paintings of Betty LaDuke, 1972-1992 by Gloria Orenstein, reprinted with permission from the artist. For more information see her website: www.bettyladuke.com.

Printed in the United States of America by Kirby Lithographic Company, Inc., Arlington, VA.

ISBN 1-56991-124-X

This publication may be ordered from:
American Correctional Association
4380 Forbes Boulevard
Lanham, MD 20706-4322
1-800-222-5646

For information on publications and videos available from ACA, contact our home page at: http://www.corrections.com/aca

Contact the ICCA home page at: http://www.ICCAWEB.org

Library of Congress Cataloging-in-Publication Data

McMahon, Maeve W. (Maeve Winifred), 1957-
    Assessment to assistance : programs for women in community corrections / Maeve McMahon, editor.
        p. cm.
    Includes bibliographical references.
    ISBN 1-56991-124-X
    1. Community-based corrections. 2. Female offenders–Rehabilitation. 3. Female juvenile delinquents–Rehabilitation. I. Title.

HV9279 .M35 2000
364.3'74–dc21   00-028859

TABLE OF CONTENTS

INTRODUCTION

Once again with the publication of these proceedings, we are proud to be working with the International Community Correctional Association (ICCA) as we both try to find and define what works in corrections.

With the increasing number of incarcerated women, the presentations from the 1998 ICCA conference are extremely timely. The presenters address issues that ICCA has not tackled so forthrightly before—women and how their needs differ from those of men. These essays offer some thoughtful ideas for further inquiry and research.

Policies on incarceration of women and assessment of their needs affect not only the individual woman but her children, of whom she often is the sole support. We know that children who have a parent in prison have a 50 percent greater risk of landing there themselves. Are there alternatives to "normal" prison? ICCA believes that often there are. Some of these alternatives include family programs and substance abuse programs with extensive aftercare components so that the concepts learned in treatment can be exercised in the real world.

And what kind of treatment is best? It depends on the gender of the offender. Often, single sex treatment groups are more effective with women while men claim greater benefits from co-ed treatment groups. There are other gender differences that those in corrections must be aware of and take into consideration when planning and evaluating any program. The authors of the essays in this book explore this concept and present some conclusions that should help reshape discussions in the future.

We look forward to a continued partnership with our affiliate, ICCA, as we endeavor to examine the issues, policies and programs in our corrections systems and promote positive change.

James A. Gondles, Jr., CAE
Executive Director
American Correctional Association

FOREWORD

I had been looking forward to coordinating the 1998 women's research conference for several years. Those of us involved in the planning process understood the need. There had never before been a research conference focusing exclusively on women and girls in community corrections. We believed the highly specialized agenda of the program would generate considerable interest from practitioners, policymakers, and academics from throughout North America. We were not wrong.

The International Community Corrections Association's elected board fully supported the conference. This is significant because associations make most of their income from conferences. Associations generally try to stay away from "specialized" topics because they tend to draw fewer registrants. In association business, registration equates to revenues. The ICCA Board supported the conference because they knew it was the right thing to do.

ICCA's conferences are distinctly different from other association programs. Most significantly, ICCA commissions researchers to examine the academic literature and then to write papers on specific topics. The goal of the research papers is to add to the knowledge base of what we know to work with offenders, hence, "What Works." The most valued aspect of ICCA programs is to have the researchers interpret their work in order that it have practical application to practitioners and policymakers.

ICCA also tries to offer a value added component to each of its research conferences. The 1998 Women's Research conference presented ICCA with an opportunity to sponsor complementary events that add value to the research papers and presentations that better meet the needs of members and conference delegates.

The ICCA conference as a package had three distinct sections. First, and most importantly, is the research conference. The papers and keynote presentations from this section of the conference are contained in this volume. Secondly, ICCA sponsored preconference intensive training featuring cognitive-behavioral curriculums. Finally, we sponsored a leadership forum.

The Women's Leadership Forum: On the weekend prior to the conference, ICCA sponsored a leadership forum. The Leadership Forum was a conference unto itself. A committee was assembled to identify a list of invitees throughout North America. The selection committee established criteria, knowing that it had to control the numbers in order to keep the meeting manageable. Academics, practitioners, policymakers, and governmental representatives were selected. Special care was given to selecting representatives from varied geographical areas. In total, more then eighty invitees attended the session.

The Leadership program began with a discussion titled "Fits and Starts." Evidently, there have been a number of attempts to establish a type of leadership initiative for women's programming in community corrections. The good news is that there was past and now current interest in establishing a "national advisory group," which could represent the field of community corrections. The bad news was that for whatever reasons, the leadership initiative had never been sustained.

Considerable attention was given to the planning of the weekend Leadership Forum. ICCA had found an excellent facilitator to lead the forum. An agenda was developed to give participants a history of past efforts to organize. The agenda then brought forward speakers to discuss an overview of what ICCA believed to be current best practice. Finally, the agenda offered a vision for the future.

The women's leadership forum was planned with the best of intentions. The strategic goals were as follows: to identify leaders who could lead with both style and substance; to establish a committee to represent the interests of programs that serve women offenders; to identify experts to advisors on policy issues; to identify authors and editors to assist with publications; to develop surveys to learn more about the needs of programs that serve women; and to analyze baseline data to gain a better understanding of what programs do and if what they do is effective in treating women offenders. Finally, we wanted the committee to lead with research and data as a guide.

I had envisioned the leadership group being comprised of individuals who could assimilate the research data to assist practitioners in developing gender-specific interventions that were grounded on sound and established theory. I had hoped the leadership group could establish a set of principles stating what was known to work and what was known not to work.

What we had planned to happen did not happen. Instead of moving towards the goals referenced above, the leadership forum ran amuck. There were fits and starts again. What is most upsetting to me is that gender politics derailed good intentions.

The Real Issues

The real issues involve the lives of tens of thousands of women and girls now in the justice system. What women and girl offenders need is a way to remain in the community surrounded by family, programs, and services that will promote their reintegration potential or their ability to be safe, productive, and contributing members of the community.

The real issues for women offenders were well articulated by conference and forum delegates. To summarize, the following is a partial list of issues that conference attendees brought forward:

- Lack of Research: Several delegates expressed their distress with the lack of research that has been conducted specific to programs for women and girls.

- Increased Populations: Delegates were justly upset with the dramatic increase of women in prison and jails.

- Health Care: A number of delegates expressed concern with the poor level of health care afforded to women while incarcerated.

- Institutional Abuse: Attendees were equally concerned with the abuses women experienced while incarcerated.

- Community Programs: Delegates vocalized their distress over the lack of community-based programming for women prior to and following incarceration.

- Child Care: There was concern over the care of their children while women were incarcerated.

- Substance Abuse Treatment: Delegates expressed their dismay over the lack of substance treatment funding and treatment specific to women both in institutions and in the community.

- Coed Programs: There was repeated concern that low populations of women in many jurisdictions forced women into programs for men, where women were once again forced to be subordinate to men, thereby minimizing their treatment needs.

- Abuse: There was almost universal agreement that women's physical and sexual abuse was not being attended to, nor understood by those responsible for building, designing, and operating programs for women.

- Medical Needs: There was vocalized concern that by the time a woman finds herself incarcerated, her physical health has deteriorated to the point where recovery would never be fully realized.

- Health Care: Health care is not being afforded to women in the justice system to the degree needed.

- Community Childcare: Childcare is not available to women upon release, making the transition back to community and family more difficult.

- Mental Health and Illness: There was frequent discussion that women's mental health diagnosis and psychotropic medications were generally not available to women in the justice system and that the justice system was not doing enough to meet the needs of women who may be dually diagnosed.

- Pathways to Crime: There was distress over the pathways in which women and girls entered the justice system. More frequently than not, women were entering the system for sex-related crimes or drug crimes where they were supporting the male but were caught in the process.

- Family Violence: The delegates made arguments that, increasingly, women were finding themselves entering the justice system for domestic violence crimes where they retaliated against an abusive male.

In addition, conference delegates complained about the lack of funding for programs that serve women in general. More specifically, criticisms were made over the lack of programs for incarcerated mothers with children. Throughout the conference, there were repeated concerns that too few resources were being made available to develop gender-specific programs, cognitive curriculums, assessments, and treatments. Many conference delegates did not want to accept the practice of women offenders being forced into interventions designed for men only because the relatively low numbers of women offenders, in comparison to men, did not justify the cost or research and development of gender-specific interventions.

The above listed issues are real and need to be addressed. In fact, the purpose of the What Works: Women and Juvenile Females in Community Corrections Research Conference and the leadership forum was to identify the individuals who could best represent these issues on a national scale. It is one thing to articulate the many issues and needs of women offenders in a public forum. It is quite another to mobilize the support in terms of the individuals, the policies, the politics, and the resources to address the issues.

In my opinion, there is no shortage of bright, capable, and committed professionals wanting to provide services to women and girl offenders. There is however, a void in national leadership. I cannot help but think that if only we could put our politics aside and work together to promote research-validated "What Works" programs for women offenders, that there might be a little less misery today. And if we could sustain these efforts over time, one day we might find larger solutions that would support offender-based services in the community.

In the meantime, ICCA has and will continue to pursue the "What Works" agenda for women offenders. We will continue to work with researchers to identify the assessments, program characteristics, staffing characteristics, evaluations, and responsivity principles that research tells us are necessary for effective programs. ICCA will continue to promote this agenda through its international, national, and regional research conferences. And perhaps, when the time is right, ICCA will renew its efforts to establish a leadership initiative so that it can achieve the goals originally set for itself.

The Book

I have to thank the authors who contributed to this publication. The publication of the papers collected as chapters in this book deserve to be roundly celebrated. This collection of papers will add substantially to the discussions on how we need to change our policies regarding the treatment and sanctioning of women and girls in our justice systems.

Dr. Larry Motiuk and Kelly Blanchette, M. A., have contributed a paper on assessments. Their paper provides an overview of current assessment and classification practices with female offenders. It further discusses how the use of comprehensive assessments may be bound into community reintegration efforts in a way that minimizes decision errors while improving the use of correctional resources and enhancing public safety.

Dr. Beth Glover Reed and Maureen E. Leavitt, MSW, provide a chapter on the concept of "wraparound." The term wraparound has its origins with seriously emotionally disturbed children. The authors make the argument that many of the assumptions behind the concept of wraparound models are congruent with the philosophy of community corrections. Wraparound is particularly compatible with the strengths, responsibilities, and needs of women offenders.

Dr. Stephanie Covington offers a paper on creating gender-specific treatments for substance abusing women. Dr. Covington makes the argument that the vast majority of substance-abusing women in the criminal justice system are nonviolent and could be more effectively and economically treated in the community using gender-based programs.

Dr. Meda Chesney-Lind contributes a paper outlining promising perspectives and effective programs for girls caught in the justice system. She makes the case that while the problems of delinquency for girls are in many ways similar to those faced by boys, girls take on special dimensions as a result of the way gender works in the lives of young women.

Dr. Barbara Bloom writes a paper on evaluation of programs for female offenders in community corrections. Dr. Bloom makes the point that evaluations of programs for women offenders are almost nonexistent. She further makes the argument that rigorous evaluations which measure effectiveness of gender-specific interventions are necessary in order to move towards empirically based documentation of program effectiveness. Her paper examines emerging perspectives regarding evaluation of programs for female offenders in correctional settings.

Andrew Skotnicki delivered and presented a paper exploring ethical issues in the criminal justice system. He argues that it is important for us to understand that there are some things that never change in the correctional milieu. Further, it is his contention that there have been significant errors that have persisted for over one hundred years in getting our taxonomy right, in terms of what ought to change and in what remains the same. He argues that our constant and restless search for what is right will be compromised until we incorporate the concept of good into our methods.

Dr. Paul Gendreau was awarded ICCA's most prestigious award named after the celebrated Dr. Margaret Mead. Dr. Gendreau is perhaps one of the three individuals most responsible for the reemergence of treatment programming for offenders after the debacle of the Martinson "Nothing Works" era.

The work of Paul Gendreau and his associates are the driving force behind the "What Works" movement that is gaining support internationally. We all owe a debt of gratitude to Paul Gendreau for his work and inspiration that has forged a trail that we can follow and build upon.

As part of the Margaret Mead Award ceremony, Dr. Gendreau gave a presentation and wrote a paper titled "Rational Policies for Reforming Offenders." His contribution is contained in this volume.

I trust the following chapters will provide you with valuable information. I want to thank the authors for their valuable contributions and thank the many contributors to the conference including speakers, panel members, workshop presenters, intensive training facilitators, panel members, and of course, the conference planners and host committee.

Peter Kinziger
Executive Director
International Community Corrections Association

Disclaimer

The language and opinions contained in this volume are the personal views of the authors and do not necessarily constitute the policies and teachings of ICCA. ICCA does not assume responsibility for the content of this volume as submitted by the contributors.

In the spirit of academic freedom, ICCA offers the reader the chapters contained herein. It should be noted that in some instances, the opinions expressed are in direct opposition to the opinions and teachings of ICCA and do not contribute desirable policies or practices. ICCA remains dedicated toward promoting the principles of effective interventions empirically derived from evidence-based findings.

Peter Kinziger
Executive Director
International Community Corrections Association

Anne Walker
President
International Community Corrections Association

MODIFIED WRAPAROUND AND WOMEN OFFENDERS IN COMMUNITY CORRECTIONS: STRATEGIES, OPPORTUNITIES AND TENSIONS

1

Beth Glover Reed, Ph.D.
Psychologist
University of Michigan
Ann Arbor, Michigan

Maureen E. Leavitt, MSW
Research Associate
University of Michigan
Ann Arbor, Michigan

You take the wildest beast in the jungle and put [it] in a cage and then take [it] out and put [it] back in the jungle and [it] can't survive.
—Theresa Derry, ex-offender[1]

We cannot train people to swim successfully by tying them hand and foot and placing them on the side of the pool. To learn to swim, they must be in the water.
—Paul Hahn, Department of Criminal Justice, Xavier University[2]

Women offenders[3] have multiple needs and often-unrecognized strengths and supports. This paper describes resources likely to be needed by women in community corrections programs if they are to address the factors that have contributed to their offenses and that are barriers to their ability to survive and be productive without reoffending. We present a number of models for coordinating and integrating services and community supports to develop individualized plans. We emphasize a set of approaches often titled "wraparound," and discuss tensions between some basic wraparound concepts and the requirements of a community corrections setting.

Although efforts to coordinate and integrate services have been implemented for more than thirty years, service systems remain fragmented and thus unable to address the complex needs of women and their families (National Center for Services Integration [NCSI], 1994). Even when significant system-level goals have been accomplished, integration does not necessarily improve the care that individuals get (Talbott, 1995). Improvements in symptoms and quality of life occur when systems coordination results in improved access to high quality services, which must be effective (Ridgely and Jerrell, 1996; Ridgely, et al., 1996). We also have ample evidence that simply linking individuals with parallel services (for example, mental health and substance abuse treatment) is not sufficient to address their needs, unless those services are compatible, coordinated, and well sequenced (Kline, Harris, Bebout, and Drake, 1991). Planning for wraparound is one way of attending to these issues.

After explaining why wraparound is particularly appropriate for women, we contrast and compare its key elements with principles for community corrections. Then, we review the essential elements of a modified wraparound model, including mechanisms for coordinating both within and between client- and systems-levels of services. We use a composite case example to illustrate the process and components of wraparound at both the client/services level and the interagency/systems level. At each of these two levels, we highlight the importance of coordination and call attention to other issues likely to be encountered in implementation. We then discuss some ways to develop and sustain the components for a wraparound approach, with a particular emphasis on teamwork.

We draw from several sets of literature:

- Research on the risk and protective factors (in other words, life circumstances that jeopardize women or that strengthen them and their resilience) and needs of women, and what is known about gender-sensitive services, advocacy, and empowerment for women

2

- A large body of work on case and care management from education, health, and family services

- Some literature on wraparound services

- A growing base of knowledge on interorganizational systems coordination and integration

Similar concepts are appearing in multiple fields, from for-profit corporate systems to communitywide public and private partnerships. Whenever possible, we will cite relevant research, although there is little as yet that investigates these structures and practices within a corrections context. The material available includes practice-based conceptual articles, individual and organizational case studies, program evaluations, and some comparative outcome studies. A number of governmental and foundation-sponsored publications are available that synthesize knowledge and practices about collaborative efforts across different fields. We also have drawn from the program manuals and interviews with individuals from the community corrections program in Washtenaw County, Michigan, which uses a modified wraparound approach.

Due to space limitations, we focus primarily on issues for adult women, although wraparound approaches are likely to be extremely useful for girls as well. Work with adolescents will involve parents or guardians, juvenile or family courts (depending on the location); greater interaction with schools and educational settings; and the coordination of a somewhat different set of services (for example youth programs, runaway shelters, teen support groups, and family interventions). We urge the reader to consider how this information can be adapted for the cultural styles of particular clients, and how to accommodate the resource mix, laws, structures, and histories of particular communities.

Our composite client, whom we will be featuring throughout the paper, fits the profile of an average woman offender in the United States and Canada in all but one of the characteristics—she is white, rather than a woman of color. Women of color (in other words, Aboriginal, African-American, Native American, or Latina) are disproportionately represented in the criminal justice system in both the United States and Canada (Mann, 1995; Richie, 1996; Task Force on Federally Sentenced Women, 1990).

Renae F. Mendel, a twenty-eight-year-old white woman, comes from a so-called "broken" home; her father is deceased, and her mother remarried and divorced before Renae was old enough to remember. As a child, she was sexually abused multiple times, and her current partner is both physically and emotionally abusive. She started using alcohol and other drugs in her early teens and already has participated in several alcohol and other drug treatment programs. She has been arrested for a number of relatively minor, nonviolent offenses. Her education is minimal, and, thus far, she has no secondary school diploma or equivalent. Although she is now living with the father of her two younger children, she bears almost full responsibility for raising her children on minimal resources. Her work history consists solely of entry-level service positions that do not pay enough to support a family (American Correctional Association, 1990).

We will follow Renae through the community corrections/ wraparound continuum to illustrate the stages and key issues at different stages. We will say more later about the characteristics of women offenders, but first we discuss wraparound approaches in general, and how they apply to community corrections.

Wraparound Approaches: An Overview

Models known as "wraparound" arise from the idea of "wrapping necessary resources into an individualized support plan" (Malysiak, 1997, p. 400). The wraparound concept probably appears most frequently in the literature about women and children with special needs, although similar ideas are found in many fields (General Accounting Office [GAO], 1992; Marquart and Konrad, 1996). The wraparound philosophy emerges from constructivist, ecological, and general systems theories (Malysiak, 1997). At the most simplistic level, these theories stress the holistic and fluid nature of systems—that everything is interdependent and interrelated, and that no single perspective is the most objective or correct. The need for wraparound is highest for clients with multiple and complex needs that cannot be addressed by a few sets of services from one or more locations in the community.

In their most "pure" theoretical form, wraparound services engage the family or the individual as decision-making participants, enhance strengths to meet needs in the context of relationships and the community,

4

and emerge out of a collaborative, team-based structure (Malysiak, 1998; R. Malysiak, personal communication, July 24, 1998).

Instead of being expert-determined, the goal is to empower the client to determine her major needs and directions within a strengths-based model (Wilson and Anderson, 1997). Difficulties in functioning are attributed not only to individuals, but also to lack of resources or to systemic problems. New skills are perceived as "best learned in the natural context rather than in artificial service structures in which an expert makes decisions" (Rappaport, as paraphrased in Malysiak, 1997, p. 406).

The emphasis in each case is on working collaboratively with clients in the context of their family, community, and other relationships to arrange a continuum of comprehensive care (Eber and Nelson, 1997; Northey, Primer and Christensen, 1997).[4] Because its emphasis is on addressing multiple and complex goals in a coordinated way, a wraparound approach requires identifying community resources and services. One challenge is to develop procedures and structures that facilitate access, sequencing, and coordination of those resources for individual offenders. Typically, this involves working with line staff who deliver services, and with policymakers and administrators to create and/or modify organizational mechanisms, structures, and policies as needed. Words such as "coordination," "linkages," "collaboration," and "integration" are common in the wraparound-related literature.

The Importance of Wraparound Approaches for Women

Theoretically, a modified wraparound approach to community corrections is likely to benefit male offenders as well as women and girls. Both genders have needs that are more effectively addressed by coordinated resources and services. Services for both men and women can be provided more effectively and at less cost in the community than in institutional settings (Lord, 1994; Singer, Bussey, Song, and Lunghofer, 1995). Another advantage is that "reentry" is facilitated by competencies learned and reinforced in the offenders' natural environments.

Women are good candidates for community-based corrections because they commit far fewer serious or violent offenses than men, and pose less physical threat to the community (Bloom, Chesney-Lind, and Owen, 1994). They also return to prison at a lower rate than men (Chesney-Lind and Laidler, 1997; Immarigeon and Chesney-Lind, 1993). Women are especially likely to need and to benefit from modified wraparound services for at least five other reasons:

(1) A higher percentage of women than men are the primary care-givers of young children. These children have needs of their own; they will require other caregivers if their mothers are incarcerated; and they are at risk for traumatic stress disorders and delinquency (Evens and Stoep, 1997; Johnston, 1995b; Kampfner, 1995). Support for parenting, safe housing, and an adequate family wage are crucial when the welfare of children is at stake.

(2) Women and girls, in general, have been socialized to value rela-tionships and connectedness and to approach life within interpersonal contexts. Approaches to service delivery that are based on ongoing rela-tionships, that make connections among different life areas, and that work within women's existing support systems are especially congruent with women's styles and orientations (*see* Covington, this issue; Finkelstein, Kennedy, Thomas, and Kearns, 1997).

(3) Multiple studies (*see* Appendix A) confirm that women's mental and physical health care needs are different from—and frequently more complicated and severe—than men's. The greater the level of the burden, the more likely a woman will drop out of a service plan and fail to reach her goals. Social support networks and well-coordinated services that address multiple needs are crucial (Brown, Huba, and Melchior, 1995). Although women have many strengths, they also face many barriers to remaining crime-free and are less likely than men to have sufficient sup-port systems to enable them to address their multiple needs and responsibilities (Veysey, De Cou, and Prescott, 1998).

(4) Additionally, women's needs are less likely to be adequately addressed in a criminal justice system designed by and for men (Carter, 1998; Coll, Miller, Fields, and Mathews, 1997; Koons, Burrow, Morash, and Bynum, 1997; Morton, 1998; Muraskin, 1993; Philips and Harm, 1997; Task Force on Federally Sentenced Women, 1990).

(5) Gender also makes a difference in how one is able to make con-nections with women, especially for those with multiple problems (Watkins, Shaner, and Sullivan, 1999).

Wraparound and Community Corrections: Similarities and Differences

In this section, we compare and contrast the underlying philosophies and components of community corrections and wraparound approaches.

Although substantial differences can exist *within* community corrections and *within* approaches called "wraparound," we emphasize the elements that typically distinguish each.

Wraparound and community corrections philosophies and approaches are similar in many ways (*see* Table 1.1). Both are proactive, collaborative models that engage the entire community. Both use problem-solving approaches that strive to include as many participants as possible in the decision-making process. Both arise out of a strengths-based perspective that encourages individual autonomy in the least restrictive context. Both emphasize prevention. Both depend on cooperative, noncompetitive teamwork. Both foster multisystemic linkages (although the proposed linkages may differ). Both strive to coordinate services for a continuum of support, assuming that each component of the system holds a piece of the solution. Each works within a problem-oriented strategy, assuming that solutions can be achieved. Each encourages innovative approaches to old problems.

Despite these similarities, some important differences must be negotiated when wraparound and community corrections are combined. Wraparound models focus on individual clients and their families within a community context, and in their pure form, it is the clients and their families who have final decision-making authority (Malysiak, 1998). Community corrections approaches tend to view the larger community as their "client" and are focused on ensuring public safety. As Chief Probation Officer, Barry J. Nidorf, Los Angeles County Probation Department, characterizes it: "[T]he sanction orientation . . . makes the community, not the criminal, the direct and primary object of the change effort that community corrections traditionally has called 'rehabilitation'"(1996). Individual needs, therefore, must be weighed against the needs of the community as a whole (Barajas, 1996). The tension between these orientations—and their accompanying values, operating principles, and procedures—may be difficult to resolve. On the other hand, if both the community corrections field and the treatment and social services fields can agree on common goals, complete resolution may be unnecessary. In fact (as we shall discuss later), negotiating the tension between these two viewpoints may be useful in promoting client- and system-level changes.

Because of these differences, what we will present in this paper is something of a hybrid version of wraparound. Although most of the components are consistent with wraparound philosophy, the ultimate decision-making authority of the individual/family must be tempered by

Table 1.1. Overview and Comparison of Community Corrections and Wraparound Model Language

Common Components	Community Corrections	Wraparound Services
The client	The *community* as a whole, including offenders, victims, and their families.*	The *individual* in context of family and community.*
Proactive problem-solving	Encourages community to become partners with corrections as coproducers of justice, but decisions *ultimately rest with the community corrections department.*	Engages individual/family in becoming collaborators with service providers. If consensus is not reached, then the *client and family have the final decision-making authority.*
Roots of the problem	Crime and delinquency are not only individual problems, but also symptoms of community disorganization and distress.	Poor social functioning is partly a result of social structures and limited access to resources.
Focus on empowerment	Use least-restrictive alternative ("graduated sanctions") in keeping with the demands of public safety.	Strengths-based perspective, respectful of client's autonomy: "Do not do for the client what she can do for herself."
Reintegration in natural context	When new competencies must be learned, they are best learned in the natural context.	Ecological strengths-enhancement uses strengths of the natural environment, rather than artificially created circumstances supervised by "experts."
Emphasis on prevention	Adequate nutrition and medical care for children; Headstart; after-school programs; parent training; youth programs; Neighborhood Watch; adult education; job training.	Perinatal and postpartum care; affordable housing and child care; job training; substance abuse education and treatment.
Collaborative teamwork	Encourage cooperation among all parties and agencies involved.	Collaborative action and non-hierarchical structure.
Multisystemic linkages	Criminal justice-involved clients, victims, and their families; police officers, court workers, probation and parole officers, institutional personnel; judiciary, prosecutors, members of the bar; governmental officials and funding authorities; general public; educators; interest groups.	Clients and their families; health care; justice system; education/ schools; employers; social welfare; domestic violence; mental health; substance abuse; governmental and regulatory agencies; funding sources; recreation programs; religious institutions.

*Words in italic indicate conceptual differences.

8

consideration for public safety. Our hybrid model also deviates from common community corrections philosophy in that the emphasis on surveillance and compliance to protect the community is balanced by the goals of 1) enhancing and building on individual and environmental strengths and resources and 2) ameliorating individual and environmental factors that have contributed to that criminal activity or that are barriers to remaining crime-free. Both of these depictions, of course, oversimplify the differences, but we believe the potential tensions are not trivial. Thus, in this paper, we will refer to practice that emerges from the intersection of the community corrections and wraparound philosophies as "modified wraparound."

Core Elements of a Modified Wraparound Approach Within Community Corrections

The structures, elements, and procedures for wraparound will differ depending on the size, resources, and history of a community and its justice system. Despite these necessary variations, most who study wraparound-type approaches (for example, Konrad, 1996) distinguish between *services (client-level)* coordination and *systems (interorganizational)* coordination and integration. *Services coordination* occurs at the level of the client and the line staff who interact directly with clients, often using case-management models to create and coordinate services for individual clients. These techniques assist service providers in brokering and coordinating services across agency boundaries.

Typically, if coordination occurs only at the client level, relationships between agencies do not fundamentally change, and case managers and participating service providers have to work hard to ensure that the client's progress is not undermined by conflicting expectations and interorganizational problems. *Systems coordination and/or integration* often requires structural realignments and changes in the manner in which agencies interact with each other—in sharing information, resources, and clients. Without some level of systems coordination, collaboration, or integration case managers repeatedly must renegotiate barriers and services at the client level on a case-by-case basis (Agranoff, 1991). On the other hand, unless efforts to coordinate interorganizational and community resources are driven by client needs and wants, extensive and costly work towards systems-level integration may not improve longer-term outcomes for individuals and families (General Accounting

Office, 1992). Thus, *coordinating mechanisms* are needed not only within each level, but also between levels.

Figure 1.1 depicts the three major elements of a modified wraparound model within community corrections settings. Many steps are required and barriers often are encountered when service providers try to combine resources from multiple locations (Synergos Institute, 1992). Wraparound models require mechanisms for coordinating, planning, and removing or reducing these barriers.

Client/Services Coordination

The bottom oval represents client/services-level coordination, usually through some model of case planning and management. The rectangles beneath the bottom oval are examples of services that, woven together and sequenced, could create a continuum of individualized services. A case manager (or team of service providers) usually is the person (or structural mechanism) responsible for working with the offender-client and coordinating services and resources from individual programs to maintain a continuum of services and support. The mix of available services will vary from community to community and from county to county, as will the names of the programs that provide the services, the sources of funding, and so forth.[5]

Agency/Systems-level Coordination

The top oval in Figure 1.1 represents agency/systems-level coordination and integration. Examples of potential participating organizations are listed in the rectangles above the oval. In most communities, services are fragmented and operated by an only partially coordinated array of public and private agencies (Agranoff, 1991; Konrad, 1996; Kritek, 1996; Woodside and McClam, 1998b). Some agencies provide similar services while other services remain unavailable. Many programs do not have the money to meet the needs of people who have multiple problems and insufficient resources. Services are provided by clinics, hospitals, free-standing private for-profit and nonprofit agencies, and an array of private practitioners (Kirst-Ashman and Hall, 1997; Douglas and Philpot, 1998) and grassroots associations (Smith, 1997). Increasingly, in the United States, these agencies may be linked through behavioral health care networks or consortium organizations developed in response to managed-care initiatives.

FIGURE 1.1. Core Elements of Modified Wraparound (with illustrative systems and services)

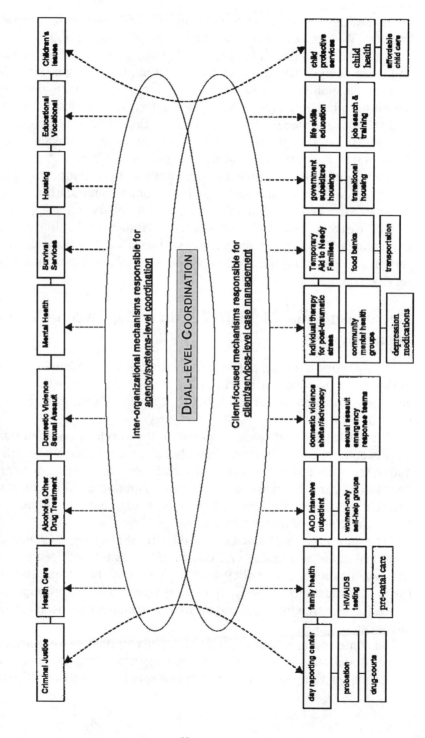

In addition, a whole array of "support" services may be connected to housing, welfare, and social service agencies, and public and private health and mental health facilities (Salamon, 1999). Each service system, and often each organization within a system, has its own goals, funding streams, eligibility requirements, philosophy of service delivery, and operating procedures (Schmolling, Youkeles, Burger, 1993; Challes et al., 1995). Linking services at the client level alone is not sufficient if wraparound is to be optimally effective. Systems-level linkages are also important to facilitate the sharing of services for clients.

Increasing administrative and organizational commitments to collaboration are an important early goal. In some communities, it may be necessary to mobilize community support for collaborative approaches to service delivery, especially for women offenders and other stigmatized populations. This is particularly the case if collaborative team efforts reveal gaps in services requiring additional resources or significant changes in the service systems.

Mechanisms that Mediate Within and Between Client and Agency Levels

Many types of coordinating and mediating mechanisms are possible. In Figure 1.1, we present two interdiscplinary teams, one that is responsible for coordination at each level. We will describe other possible structures later.

The client-focused team responsible for services coordination typically is composed of direct services staff and case managers—both inside and outside the corrections system. Combined case conferences or other coordinating mechanisms facilitate case planning at different stages of the change/treatment process, and may be augmented if situations arise that require special interventions.

The interorganizational team linked to the agency/systems oval is responsible for addressing and coordinating issues between agencies at the organizational and policy levels. The form this takes and the frequency of meetings is likely to vary, depending on how long collaborations have been underway, and on what systems issues need attention at any given time.

In some communities, one team may be responsible for both services and systems coordination, with a single agency taking the lead. In other communities, there may be two or more teams or structures employing a diversity of mechanisms. The structure and composition of the teams are less important, however, than the collaborative process itself.[6]

In our case example, the systems-level coordination occurs primarily within a community corrections advisory committee. This committee is composed of representatives from the community agencies most frequently involved in contributing to wraparound services for women offenders. Agency representatives were selected after a multistage assessment process. Recent additions include a community member who has been a long-term activist on women's issues in the community, and a retired judge who is perceived to be very fair and who has been active in several service clubs and coalitions within the community. The committee is now meeting bimonthly, but it met more frequently while the wraparound process was being developed, and occasionally has extra meetings when urgent situations arise.

Both *horizontal* and *vertical* linkages (communication and joint planning and problem-solving mechanisms) are vital. Horizontally, *within* both levels, service providers and support systems need to find ways to link services and organizations. To do so, they must "broker" differences in philosophy, policies, and procedures between numerous systems, organizations, and the community. Interorganizational conflicts are common in the human services field; conflict becomes even more likely when elements of the criminal justice system are added to the mix (Morrissey, Steadman, Kilburn, and Lindsey, 1984; Douglas and Philpot, 1998).

As depicted by the vertical arrows, cooperation and communication are also necessary *between* levels (in other words, direct service providers and administrators/policymakers). This communication must occur *within* agencies and *between* the coordinating mechanisms at each level. Administrators and policymakers must understand what is working and in what location particular barriers are being encountered. Then, they can work together to fill the most important gaps and address the system-level barriers to impact client outcomes (Moore, 1992; Agranoff, 1991; Woodside and McClam 1998b). All work towards system coordination and integration should be guided by the experiences and needs at the services level.

Modified wraparound—a comprehensive and coordinated continuum of services that can be customized for individual offenders—succeeds only when stakeholders actively assume responsibility for common goals. Teams and other coordinating mechanisms enable representatives from multiple systems to develop goals and work toward them at both the client and the agency/community levels. Successful coordination is a vehicle for empowering offender-clients to take charge of their own lives—with support and, when necessary, with "tough love" from multiple sources.

Life Areas and Useful Linkages Important for Women

Table 1.2 (*see* the following page) lists many of the life areas and needs of women in community corrections with suggested community resources appropriate for each area. Life areas and issues are presented in column one and discussed further in Appendix A, which reviews the literature on the characteristics, strengths, and needs of women in community corrections in the United States and Canada. The second column in Table 1.2 identifies programs and services that may be useful in addressing each life area/need and Appendix B describes more fully the types of community programs and services that can be tapped to construct wraparound services.

In Appendix B, within each category, we discuss factors to consider in designing wraparound approaches for women in community corrections. Appendix C contains a comprehensive list of potential community-based resources. Linkages should include, at a very minimum, culturally sensitive assistance in the following areas: primary health care (including dental, obstetrical, and gynecological services); job training; housing advocacy and support; substance abuse treatment; attention to child welfare issues; mental health services; and advocacy and assistance with domestic violence as well as other physical and sexual abuse issues. Parenting training and support, life skills education and counseling, testing for adult attention deficit disorder, and a range of children's services are also important for many women (Center for Substance Abuse Treatment, 1994b; Finkelstein, 1993). We further illustrate the services women need and the issues they face throughout the composite case study.

Modified Wraparound Processes

In the next sections, we illustrate, in concrete terms, the progress of a client in community corrections using a modified wraparound approach. We begin with an overview of the case management process, including a description of the roles of a case manager and provide specific suggestions for coordination between the criminal justice system, human service programs, and other community resources. Then, using the composite

TABLE 1.2. Life Areas of Women in Community Corrections and Useful Linkages in Wraparound

Needs/Life Areas	Some Useful Linkages
Sexual and physical abuse	Survivor assistance
Alcohol/other drug use	Alcohol/other drug treatment, self help groups
Mental illness	Mental health services
Physical health problems	Primary and urgent health care
Insufficient job skills	Job readiness, education, employment support
Lack of safe, stable housing	Housing advocacy, supported housing
Relationship and efficacy issues	Family services, individual counseling, support groups, women's groups
Complex family/care giving responsibilities	Parenting education and support, child welfare and respite support, children's services
Difficulties in day-to-day living	Emergency services, survival skills (such as, budgeting, self-advocacy)
Disabilities	Attention deficit disorder services, supported living, advocacy
Differences among women	Organizations concerned with sub-groups of women, advocacy groups
Reentry and longer term quality of life issues	Leisure options, faith-based organizations, service and neighborhood organizations

case study, we work through the possible phases of an individualized case plan, highlighting the work of collaborative teams and vertical communication in different phases.

Figure 1.2 depicts the case management process at the client/services level. The middle arrow illustrates the progress of the offender-client through the three phases of the modified wraparound system: assessment, change efforts/treatment, and maintenance/stabilization of progress. A case manager assists the client in formulating objective-based action plans to make the most of change efforts/treatment, maintenance and stabilization of progress, and probation (if applicable).

Combined case conferences (explained below) can occur in any one of the five phases, but are particularly useful in keeping the action plan on track. Combined case conferences mediate movement from stage to stage. With respect to the "augmented case conference," they also create a special stimulus if an offender fails to follow through on her commitments.

Client case management is heavily influenced by the community context. Systems-level inputs range from family members and friends to communitywide resources such as church groups, domestic violence programs, self-help groups, adult education, transitional housing, and mentoring. Although not depicted in the diagram, interaction between the systems and services levels figures prominently in the dynamics of each offender-client's treatment plan. Periodically, we will use examples to illustrate ways of handling system-level goals and problems as we work through the client-level steps and processes.

Case Management

Case management arose out of a need to provide access to and coordinate services for vulnerable or at-risk populations, a majority of whom have complicated, chronic needs. Its origins coincide with the industrialization/urbanization of our society, and the ensuing proliferation and fragmentation of our social service systems. If our social service networks were both comprehensive and integrated, or if individual needs were simple, then it seems safe to assume that case management would be unnecessary (Weil, 1985). But as it is, our so-called "systems" of care are not systems at all in many cases, but autonomous agencies designed with providers, funders, and professionals in mind (Austin, 1993).

Case management practices and models have been around for a long time. Models of case management are being used not only in the criminal justice system, but also in health care, education, adult foster care, employee assistance programs, and the mental health system among others (Leukefeld, 1990). Many types of case management approaches exist (Austin, 1993; Raiff and Shore, 1993; Rapp, 1998) In its simplest form, the primary relationship is between the case manager and a single client (although both participants also interact with other direct service providers) (Weil and Karls, 1985). At its most complicated, case management brings together formal and informal systems that may have different

FIGURE 1.2. Sequence of Modified Wraparound Services at the Client Level

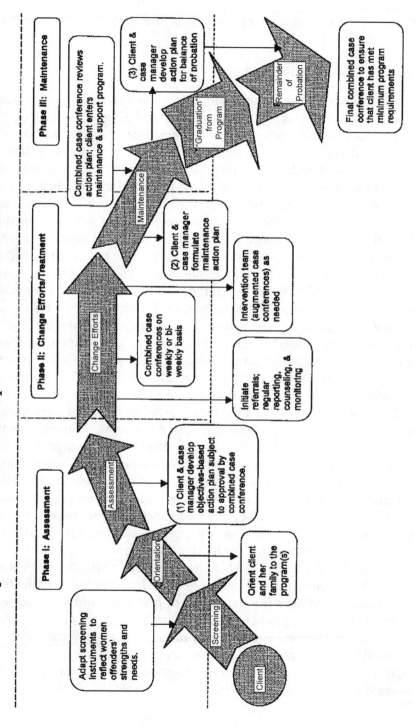

17

goals and that function independently of one another (Woodside and McClam, 1998b).

Roles of a Case Manager

Case managers usually play multiple roles that require knowledge and skills in working directly with clients and in negotiating complex organizational and interorganizational systems. They need skills in assessing individuals, community resources, and organizational, interorganizational, and policy barriers. They must broker services and differences across corrections and community systems and between service sectors in the community. They often advocate for the client's best interests, and act as counselors, teachers/consultants, service providers, and cheerleaders. Some case managers also offer direct services (such as counseling), or assist with monitoring (as in the case of drug testing). They must function well in small group and team sessions, and have a range of group facilitation skills (Rapp, 1998; Rothman, 1991; Raiff and Shore, 1993; Mackelprang and Salsgiver, 1999; Rapp, Kelliher, Fisher, and Hall, 1994). Whatever a case manager's other responsibilities may be, we add another role important for women—providing continuity and support and sometimes "tough love" through a healing and growing process.

As roles and boundaries change, case managers must learn to be flexible (Carey, 1998; Williams and Swartz, 1998). The concept of boundaries (in other words, rules for relationships) between a typical counselor or therapist and client require considerable reconceptualization. Creating and maintaining fluid boundaries and learning how to manage them ethically should be an ongoing focus of staff development and supervision.

The function of case management at the client level is influenced by the availability and integration of services. Depending on the availability of resources and the level of service integration, case managers' responsibilities shift among at least four different roles—brokering, rationing, developing, and matchmaking (or marketing) (Moore, 1992).

As illustrated in Figure 1.3, when there are gaps or duplications in services, a case manager assumes the role of *broker* with the responsibility for coordinating services from a variety of providers into a service continuum. When services are fairly well organized, but there are not enough treatment spots, the case manager may function as a *gatekeeper*, with the responsibility for rationing remaining resources as efficiently and as fairly as possible. In situations where both integration and availability of services are high, the case manager plays a *matchmaker* or marketing role in

FIGURE 1.3. The Service Delivery Matrix*

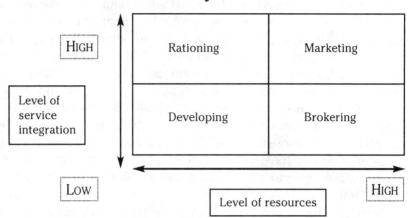

*Adapted from Stephen Moore, "Case Management and the Integration of Services: How Service Delivery Systems Shape Case Management," *Social Work*, Volume 37, Number 5, September 1992, pp. 419-423.

matching the client to the most appropriate bundle of services. And when resources are both inadequate and uncoordinated, case managers must exercise their skills as *developers*, as they attempt to build on and simultaneously organize nearly nonexistent resources.

In the real world, things are never so absolute. But there does seem to be a trend toward the gatekeeping function as services become more integrated and resources grow increasingly scarce. Thus, it is possible for modified wraparound to be implemented in theory, but not in practice. That is, a community may be aware of female offenders' multiple needs, and a continuum of comprehensive services may already be in place. However, the demand may be such that there are simply not enough "slots" available. The focus of case management then shifts from brokering to a form of triage: who is most likely to succeed in these programs, or alternatively, who needs these services most?

Effective Case Management Models

There are many ways to handle case coordination, depending on the size, structure, and resources of the particular community. Models that simply make referrals and broker services are less effective than those that provide active advocacy and some services centrally (Hardcastle,

Wenocur, and Powers 1997; Kline, et al., 1991). Similarly, Schmidt-Posner and Jerrell (1998) found that the most successful case management models both broker services and promote client growth. Johnson and Castengera (1994) recommend working with clients in groups in addition to casework. Clients can work on both intra- and interpersonal issues in group situations while the caseworker uses case management techniques to access resources that are important to assist the client.

Raiff and Shore (1993) and Rapp (1998) found that the best models maintain small caseloads (typically twenty to twenty-five individuals). Effective models are structured in such a way that managers are able to respond quickly; have clear accountability mechanisms (for example, lead casemanagers or clear team responsibilities); have frequent contact with clients; follow individuals from six months to two years; are able to at least consult regularly with an interdisciplinary team; and work "in vivo" (in other words, in the field as "tour guides" rather than as "travel agents") (Hardcastle, et al., 1997).

Case Management Options

With the notable exception of cooperative agreements between substance abuse and the criminal justice fields (for example drug courts and Treatment Alternatives to Street Crime), collaborations between the criminal justice system and the treatment services system are confined to a handful of pioneering programs (Chesney-Lind and Immarigeon, 1995; Greenwood, 1995; Swartz, 1991; Wellisch, Prendergast, and Anglin, 1993).

Probably the easiest model to implement (because it requires the fewest changes) is case management by the criminal justice system. Caseloads could be assigned at specific stages in the system—in other words, pretrial, probation, or jail. A community corrections officer then would be responsible for teaming up with a network of service and treatment providers in the community. This approach might be costly. It also might cause some confusion—among client-offenders at any rate— between the authoritative and therapeutic roles.

Primary responsibility for case management also could be assigned to a treatment agency. The advantage of this is that treatment providers have a better understanding of the service continuum, and of how to tailor programs to the individual client. The disadvantage is that a treatment agency may not appreciate the constraints of the legal system, or it may lack the resources to do effective client-monitoring. If the corrections and treatment agents can learn to collaborate with one another however, the differences in their perspectives may work to their advantage when it comes to motivating noncompliant offenders.

A third alternative is case management by a coordinator extraneous to both the social services and justice systems. This individual or agency could conduct intake interviews and monitor clients' progress through the various treatment, justice, and social systems. An advantage of this model is that the case management coordinator has no vested interest in either system and may be better able to broker differences as a result. The disadvantage to this is that it adds another layer of bureaucracy to an already complicated process.

These simple models are only the basic "building blocks" for any number of creative case management arrangements. Ideally, responsibility for the offender-client would be shared among two or more organizations, with one agent (or agency) taking the lead. It is crucial to be clear about who is ultimately accountable for each client.

The lead agency could be an organization specializing in services for women—women's therapy, women's health care, addiction issues, displaced homemaker reentry, job training for women—with a community-based component for female offenders. Or, it could be primarily a substance abuse treatment facility that provides, in addition to therapy, services that typically are termed "ancillary," such as transportation, employment assistance, childcare, abuse and self-esteem groups, life skills training, and so forth. Or the lead agency might be an "umbrella" organization for many different organizations, one of which serves female offenders. Regardless of structure, however, the lead agency is responsible for combined case conferencing (see below) and for some, if not all, of the client-level case management.

In our composite case study, we assume that the community corrections organization has contracted out case management to a local coordinating/treatment agency, which is also a day reporting center. This arrangement means that although the coordinating/treatment agency falls under the aegis of community corrections, it still maintains a certain autonomy in programming, procedures, and funding sources. Community corrections officers, who pick up offender-client caseloads at pretrial, probation, and parole levels, continue to be responsible for some client-level services, such as weekly drug testing and monitoring. But the "lead agency" responsible for tracking the client through a customized continuum of comprehensive services is treatment-oriented.

Confidentiality

Mechanisms for maintaining confidentiality and protecting offenders' rights are very important. A modified wraparound program requires that information be shared across organizational boundaries, at the same time that methods must be developed to safeguard that information. Release of information forms and interagency agreements are two ways to safeguard a woman's confidentiality.

The client-offender (or, in the case of minors, the parent or guardian) should sign one or more release-of-information forms, preferably right after or as part of the initial screening process. Standard release-of-information forms facilitate communication between community corrections and human service and other community agencies. Without a legal consent form, it is impossible for the corrections supervisor to track the client throughout the change/treatment phase. Corrections personnel will not be able to determine whether the offender-client kept her initial appointment with any of the social service programs. In the United States, substance abuse treatment providers are prohibited, by federal law, from revealing any information that would indicate that an individual has applied for or received any services for alcohol or drug abuse (Brooks, 1994, 1995). Therapists, physicians, and child welfare workers also operate under strict disclosure guidelines, particularly in the case of the duty to warn (when a client has threatened to do harm). Other laws concern nondisclosure about HIV-AIDS. Laws have been instituted to protect the client and encourage her to seek treatment without fear of legal reprisal. Likewise, without a consent form, corrections officers are prohibited from revealing information about past offenses to treatment providers.

In the case of our client, Renae Mendel, a consent form must be signed for the day reporting treatment center, at the very minimum. The day reporting treatment center then would be responsible for obtaining other release-of-information forms on an as-needed basis. A nonviolent repeat offender almost certainly would be jail- or prison-bound in the absence of alternatives to incarceration. Fortunately, Ms. Mendel qualifies for the services at the day reporting treatment center—in this instance, a combination day reporting and substance abuse treatment center—which will assist her in coordinating a continuum of services. [7]

Confidentiality agreements are designed to protect the client's privacy and rights. Each client is entitled to equal opportunity for growth, unconstrained by prejudices or other limiting preconceptions. If community-based providers know an individual's entire legal and treatment history, that knowledge might fortify negative attitudes or promote pessimism about her ability to change. On the other hand, a certain amount of shared information not only is desirable but also necessary to individualize the client's action plan and to avoid duplication of services or gaps in the wraparound continuum. For example, treatment providers may want to know the *intent* of the judge's sentencing requirements: Was the offender-client referred to the day reporting treatment center simply to keep her off the streets, or is this really the best program for her, given her family situation and her transportation and childcare requirements?

Rules about confidentiality vary from organization to organization; it is important to be familiar with the different types of guidelines for particular organizations. Other programs with which the justice system may want to exchange client information include child protective services/foster care, community mental health, attention deficit disorder clinics, alcohol and other drug treatment programs, adult education (in such courses as budgeting, cooking, and parenting), immigration/naturalization services, and domestic violence/sexual assault agencies.

> In its early stages, the community corrections advisory committee worked on creating a mission statement for wraparound services, and on defining a comprehensive continuum of care, including its most important components. Committee members discussed different approaches to case management and developed joint guidelines for case managers of women-offenders to follow, regardless of their agency affiliation. To facilitate exchange of information across agency boundaries, the advisory committee modified an interagency agreement and joint consent form currently used between several community agencies so that it meets appropriate legal requirements (*see* Center for Substance Abuse Treatment, 1997, Appendix B, for a sample Qualified Service Organization Agreement).
>
> Most of the agencies have signed this agreement, thus allowing them to share information about a particular woman if she signs the joint release-of-information form. The agencies experienced considerable conflict while trying to

define common case manager functions, since several of the agencies did not have case managers or were using quite different approaches. Some of these differences have not been resolved, but, generally speaking, the group works amicably, agreeing to disagree as long as their disagreements do not interfere with what is deemed best for a client. Because of the Qualified Service Organization Agreement, Renae can sign one consent form that explains which agencies are coordinating their services, and how her rights and confidentiality will be protected by the interagency procedures.

Automated information systems can be invaluable in enabling organizational partners to work together on behalf of joint clients, but they also pose risks to confidentiality. Safeguards must be implemented so that access is limited to only the information that is needed. Even with such safeguards, some agencies may be unwilling to participate fully in a joint management information system. Those who work with women who are being battered or stalked are likely to be especially reluctant, since they have much experience with how clever batterers and stalkers can be in using seemingly innocuous information to locate and endanger their prey.

At the same time, collaborations have been sabotaged by so-called "confidentiality rules" that in reality have little to do with the legal and ethical limits of confidentiality. Too often, training about confidentiality rules and regulations focuses on what organizations *cannot do*, rather than how collaborators *can* exchange useful information without compromising client rights. Service providers become worried about making a mistake, and to protect themselves, share as little information as possible. When a service provider does not understand the role and function of providers in other systems and does not trust or agree with their approach, information is less likely to be shared.

Information exchange is often difficult, due to competing values and priorities, and may be especially problematic between the justice system and social and health services. Sometimes confidentiality is used as an excuse to avoid collaboration when mistrust is really the issue. For example, in Washtenaw County, Michigan, an adolescent program staffer called to report a runaway and to request police assistance in locating the youth, but would not disclose the runaway's name or any identifying information.

As wraparound services are developed, joint educational sessions on the diverse confidentiality statutes can be valuable, especially if several complex examples can be presented for a multi-agency group to consider.

When participating organizations understand why confidentiality is critical in some situations, they can formulate standards for selected information to be shared in useful ways. Protocols are available for safe information exchange among coordinating organizations, and confidentiality never should be the ultimate reason why wraparound does not work.

Case Management Phase I: Screening, Assessment, and Action Plan

Screening/Determination of Eligibility

Before client-offenders can receive modified wraparound services, they must be screened to determine their eligibility for community placement. Some individuals are automatically disqualified on the basis of their offense or due to mandatory sentencing laws. Screening for the remaining offenders determines appropriate management and treatment needs. Psychological tests and screening instruments designed primarily for the classification of men and male offenders must be adapted to capture the complexities of women's security, programmatic, vocational, and psychological needs (Carter, 1998; Lauren, 1997; Morton, 1998). Computer software (for example, other words, Compas™ from Northpointe Institute for Public Management) and other standard testing measures are available to streamline the process (Lauren, 1997; Pollock, 1998).

> Our composite client, Renae F. Mendel, and two of her three children are currently living with her partner, Marc, age thirty-six, and his parents. Local law enforcement officials have charged Ms. Mendel with larceny over $100 in a building. Ms. Mendel has a history of petty (probably drug-related) thefts and of driving while intoxicated. Although she has once been involved as a claimant in a domestic violence incident, she herself has no previous arrests for a violent offense. Neither she nor society is likely to benefit from her incarceration. If, after the screening and assessment procedure, she is deemed qualified, she may be assigned to the pretrial diversion program in lieu of prosecution. Another possibility is that Ms. Mendel will be sentenced to treatment for alcohol and other drugs as a condition of her probation, following her conviction by the court. In either case, Ms. Mendel's treatment is court-mandated, and must be adhered to based on conditions established by the community corrections system and the courts.

In addition to a quick review of the client's current charges and legal status, the following areas also should be covered: client's criminal history, including peer group/gang affiliations; family situation, including information on dependent children;[8] education; employment; physical and mental health, including childbearing status and medications; alcohol and other drug use; housing needs; and financial problems/poverty. Learning disorders, which can affect one's ability to follow directions or to adhere to a schedule, may cause a client to appear deliberately noncompliant (Goldstein, 1997; Rounds-Bryant, Kristiansen, Fairbank and Hubbard, 1998); therefore, testing for attention deficit hyperactivity disorder (ADHA), undifferentiated attention deficit disorder (ADD), or fetal alcohol effects (FAE) at this point, also may prove helpful. The resulting information, together with what can be obtained through various community corrections providers, police, and legal databases, aids the eligibility specialist in matching the offender-client to services commensurate with public safety (Lauren, 1997). (*See* Figure 1.4 for an abbreviated example of the kinds of information that might be collected in the screening process.)

Client Assessment and Case Planning

Following the screening process, qualified candidates will be referred to a coordinating and monitoring agent/agency for orientation and a more complete assessment. The referral process usually is initiated by a community corrections supervision agent or circuit court probation officer. Orientation is the first link between community corrections and the agency (or agencies) that will be administering modified-wraparound services. Orientation should cover at minimum the basic principles of wraparound, the principles and procedures for confidentiality, the services and expectations of the day reporting treatment center, and the types of agencies that may participate in a wraparound process.

Assessment involves more in-depth evaluation, lasting one or more sessions. Who conducts the assessment will vary depending on the wraparound model being used. The assessment can be conducted by the primary case manager, or various components may be handled by representatives of different agencies specializing in particular life areas. A joint assessment process can introduce various team members to the client, and provide multiple perspectives for treatment planning, although some clients may not be comfortable disclosing parts of their stories to several different people.

Figure 1.4. Screening at Criminal Justice Level (Abbreviated Sample)

Mendel, Renae F.

Personal Information: Respondent's name is Renae Mendel,* age 28, white, unmarried. Three dependents, ages 10 (F), 8 (F), and 5 (M). Maternal grandmother has custody of eldest daughter, 10. Currently in (unsatisfactory) relationship with father of two younger children. Living with partner's parents; use of parents' phone. Unemployed for 9 years. Formerly worked as cashier and in food services. Highest grade completed: 11. Started, but did not complete, GED program.

Medical Conditions: TB negative; allergies.

Psychiatric Conditions: Depression.

Substance Abuse History: Drug(s) of choice: alcohol, cocaine and tobacco. Defendant states daily habit of two 40 oz. beers, and about $20 in crack. Has been using since age 14. Last use was August 22, 1998. Defendant is not currently enrolled in treatment. Denies history of IV drug use.

Criminal History:
Age 16, 2nd degree retail fraud; sentenced to fines/costs/restitution.
Age 19, Larceny in a Building over $100; sentenced to 12 months probation.
Age 21, Driving While Intoxicated; license suspended; sentenced to Impact Weekend Alcohol Awareness Program.
Age 22, Larceny in a Building over $100, 90 days in jail, to do jail-based 30-day substance abuse education and awareness, suspend remainder of sentence.
Age 24, Larceny in a Building over $100; intensive outpatient drug program.

Defendant states no gang associations, not listed with GCATS database.
No assaultive felony convictions or arrests.
Jailed once, never ticketed or written up for fighting.
Violated probation 3 times, revoked on last violation.

Current Charge: Larceny in a Building over $100.

Legal Status: Probation. Defendant qualifies for services under Public Act 511.

Recommendation: Due to her still unresolved substance abuse problems, Ms. Mendel is at risk for repeated and escalating offenses. She is an excellent choice for the highly structured day reporting treatment center, which provides support at the same time that it establishes boundaries.

*This is a composite case history; all of the particulars, including the client's name, are fictional.

Conducting an assessment that is comprehensive enough to inform wraparound planning presents a challenge for corrections personnel. Corrections staff may lack both the time and the training required for in-depth assessments. Moreover, mandated clients are unlikely to volunteer more information than is absolutely necessary for fear that the information will be used against them. Involving personnel from agencies outside the criminal justice system who are perceived to have a helping mission and who can ensure confidentiality may increase the chances of an honest assessment. Even so, it could take more than one or two contacts to develop the requisite trusting relationship. Experiences that are stigmatized or considered shameful (for example, substance abuse, rape, or incest) may be particularly difficult to elicit. These details, which may emerge only over time, are extremely important in customizing women's individual action plans.

An assessment is designed to collect additional information to develop a plan for change. It also can confirm or refute the results of the initial screening. It should identify the offender-client's strengths and personal and environmental barriers to her success. In addition to relevant history and current status in all areas of Table 1.2 (*see* page 15), an assessment should include the following:

- Family history and available support systems

- Complete medical exams, including testing for tuberculosis, hepatitis, retro virus, sexually transmitted diseases, HIV/AIDS, and pregnancy

- Mental health history and current status

- Sexual or physical abuse, both current and past

- Educational background

- Job skills and employment history

- Housing and transportation needs

- Alcohol and other drug use

- Legal status, including outstanding warrants, domestic violence, child custody, adoption, foster care, and divorce

- Recreational/leisure activities

- Current involvement with other social service agencies

Although the information obtained in the assessment is too extensive to be reproduced in its entirety, an abbreviated assessment might look something like the example in Figure 1.5.

Ongoing communication about clients is essential in coordinating the flow of services and in successfully monitoring the offender-client. This should begin during the assessment process. Community corrections officers benefit from reviewing the relevance and effectiveness of their own screening process (Washtenaw County Community Corrections [WCCC], 1998). The offender-client benefits from the sense of continuity that accompanies interagency collaboration. Combined case conferences (which will be covered later in more detail) are one way of maintaining this feedback process.

FIGURE 1.5. Psycho-social Assessment (Abbreviated Sample)

MENDEL, RENAE F.*

Family Background: White female, age 28. Mother of three children: Bonita (10), currently living out-of-state with her maternal grandmother; Julia (8); and David (5 1/2). David has severe asthma, necessitating frequent trips to the emergency room. Client lives with her partner, Marc (36), in the home of his parents, where they are now sharing a single room. Marc is the father of the two younger sibs. Client describes the relationship as unsatisfactory ("He is not a good influence on me and the kids"), but claims she has no other alternatives. Both her parents are still living, but cannot be counted on for support, either emotional or financial. Marc's parents work full-time. Occasionally they will help with the children, but the relationship is, for the most part, acrimonious. (Marc has not paid room and board, as per an earlier agreement, for several months.) Marc is employed as a seasonal landscaper.

Medical/Mental Health History: 3 full-term live births, 2 abortions. First and second births normal; infants slightly underweight. Third pregnancy: pre-term labor at 8 months; "preemie" released from hospital after 30 days. Client reports depression, general lethargy and fatigue. Possible PTSD. She has been on anti-depressants in the past, but none of her prescriptions is current. Client expresses a desire for new medication to increase her energy levels. Has seasonal allergies, but otherwise reports no health problems.

(Continued)

Figure 1.5 (continued)

Sexual/physical abuse: Molested repeatedly from age 9-12 by older male cousin; sexual abuse terminated when cousin graduated from high school. Client does not recognize current relationship as physically abusive: "I'm going through mental cruelty with him, not physical abuse. He knocks me up side the head one moment, and then comes around to give me a kiss, that kinda crazy stuff." Partner has not, to her knowledge, threatened either of the children. Client reports that she herself "gets rough" with the kids "once in a while."

Substance use: Began drinking at age 11, smoking at 15. Uses both marijuana and cocaine, but drug of choice continues to be alcohol. Client acknowledges she "has a problem," but does not self-identify as alcoholic. She has been treated three times for alcoholism: once in a short "scare-tactic" program; a month-long jail-based treatment; and an intensive outpatient program. She quit AA because she "didn't feel comfortable talking in front of a 'mixed' group."

Legal status: No outstanding warrants. Two youngest children in foster care (neglect) 4 years ago, for approximately 8 months. Client and partner were homeless and living in a van when children were removed.

Housing needs: Currently confined to two-bedroom house in rural area belonging to partner's parents; children sleep in the hall. They have restricted access to family phone. Would like own apartment near bus line. Was told by social worker that she does not qualify for Section XIII (government subsidized) housing, but she doesn't know why.

Education/job skills: Dropped out of school halfway through senior year. Completed first 8-week term of adult education. Worked full-time in nursing home kitchen for a year before birth of first daughter; worked part-time as a cashier at Lucky's for 7 months before that. Client has not worked outside the home in 9 years. Motivated to get GED and participate in job training. However, she fears loss of Medicaid (health care benefits for the indigent) upon becoming marginally employed.

Recreational/leisure activities: "No money, no car, no babysitter, no friends, no phone—at least not one I can use, anyway." Feels isolated. Would like to take fitness classes and get back in shape.

Current involvement with other agencies: Youngest child is in special program for the developmentally disabled.

*This is a composite case history; none of the particulars, including the client's name, is true.

Formulating an Objectives-based Action Plan

Following the initial assessment, the case manager or managers, the offender-client, the client's family (if she so desires), and other selected team members will meet together to create an appropriate action plan. (The timing of this appointment depends, of course, on whether the offender-client is entering the program before or after sentencing.) During this session, the client will be encouraged to draw on her strengths, to identify barriers, and to envision her potential in the absence of barriers.

An offender-client's strengths, barriers, resources, and social support systems can be mapped out, visually, using an eco-map (Hartman, 1978, p. 163; Hartman and Laird, 1983, pp. 155-186). This is a valuable tool for both client and case manager. It points out possible gaps in formal and informal support systems and also may highlight hidden resources. Creation of the eco-map may be, in itself, therapeutic, as the client becomes aware of herself in the context of her relationships and the community. This also may be an opportunity to discuss some of the issues that were skipped over in the more cursory assessment procedure.

Client Identification of Strengths and Barriers

In our composite example (*see* Eco-Map, Figure 1.6), it is clear that Renae has few social supports, other than her children, having lost contact with former friends and colleagues during her last out-of-state move. She has one possible source of companionship in Judy, a former colleague at the nursing home cafeteria. Her relationship with Marc's parents is strained, due to their nonpayment of rent. Her relationship with her mother, who lives several hours away and is already supporting her elder daughter, Bonita, on a limited income, is equally tenuous. Her immediate needs are for housing and for a way to support herself and her two younger children independent of her probably abusive partner.

Renae also needs to address the sexual and physical abuse she suffered in her family of origin, as well as problems in her current "unsatisfactory" relationship with Marc. Renae wishes to stop smoking, largely because of her son's allergies and repeated asthma attacks. Although Renae is in less-than-ideal health and reports feeling lethargic, depressed, and unable to

FIGURE 1.6. Ecological Assessment

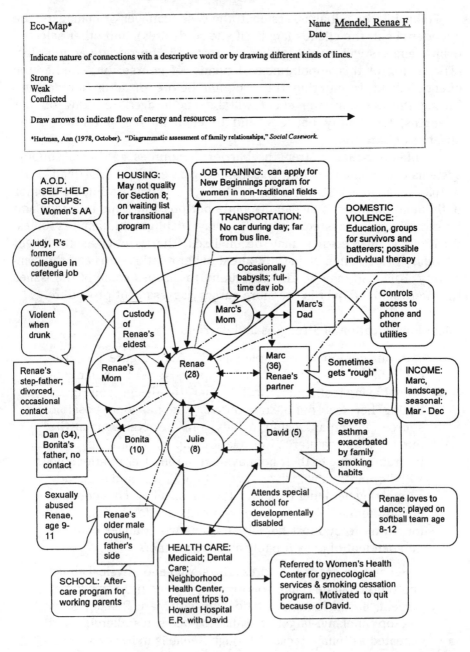

lose weight after her last baby, she enjoyed sports as a young-ster and loves to dance.

Fortunately, her children are old enough to be in school all day; David attends a special school for the developmentally disabled that has an after school childcare program, and Julie can remain after school until 6:00, at the latest. Her children are occupied during the day (except on occasions when one or both of them are ill).

Transportation is a huge problem. Renae has no car—Marc uses the "family" car to go to work—and so, for most of the day, she is stranded at home, without access to a phone or to a bus line. The family lives far enough from the center of town that a taxi is prohibitively expensive. Unless Renae can make arrangements to drop Marc off at work so that she can have use of the car, or unless she can receive special vouchers for transportation, participation in many, if not all, of these programs is impossible.

Initial Change Ideas and Plan

After identifying supports, strengths, problems, and barriers, the offender-client and case manager then identify goals and resources for reaching these goals. Assessing the feasibility of particular options must be a recurring component.

If long-term, low-cost individual therapy is unavailable (which is typically the case in this community), then Renae can be recommended for individual and/or group therapy, sponsored by either a substance abuse treatment or domestic violence program, or both. The availability of all-women Alcoholics Anonymous (AA) and Narcotics Anonymous (NA) groups raises the probability of recognizing and addressing violence-related issues earlier and in a more supportive environment than if she were attending mixed-gender self-help groups. The local assault shelter also has some support groups for child sexual abuse survivors, but participants also must have an individual therapist in order to participate.

Domestic violence programs can provide temporary emergency housing if violence is imminent, but Renae may not qualify, given her unresolved alcohol and drug problems and her unwillingness to recognize the seriousness of Marc's "temper tantrums." Even if she does qualify for government-sponsored low-income housing (doubtful due to her criminal justice record), the waiting list is two to three years long, at the very least. What she needs most is transitional housing that is connected to substance abuse treatment for women with children. Although there is a shortage of transitional housing in the city, she may be able to get into a residential alcohol and drug treatment program that also accepts children. In the meantime, she needs to explore job training options and/or consider completing a secondary school equivalency program. A new program opening up at the local community college offers job training for women considering nontraditional fields. If she qualifies for this program, she may be able to defer enrollment until next fall, while she finishes up the last of her secondary school requirements.

Because her children are in school all day, Renae can participate in day treatment without having to arrange childcare. Renae rejects the idea of a residential treatment program that will not allow her to maintain custody of her children. Renae was also referred to the Women's Health Center's smoking cessation program. (Unfortunately, Marc and his parents also smoke, so until she finds alternate housing, her progress in the program will be difficult.) She also has been encouraged to sign up for programs in nutrition, diet, and exercise at the adult education program, where, due to income, she might be eligible for a scholarship. Until Renae is able to find housing closer to town—or, at least close to the bus line—few of these options are feasible.

Program and Interagency Guidelines and Agreements

After the client has been given an opportunity to outline her expectations of the program, she will be presented with a written set of expectations that the program has for her. These should include a list of rules and the consequences for breaking those rules. Ideally, the consequences will be clear and easy to remember. (Some of this information may have been covered already in an earlier orientation at intake.)

Treatment providers must understand the importance of setting boundaries and holding clients accountable, particularly when dealing with noncompliant offenders. For this reason, it is essential that case managers from both the community corrections and social services systems work together beforehand to establish guidelines for the program. Reporting requirements and responses to rule violations must be confirmed in writing.

Agencies also must agree upon and document procedures for resolving interagency disputes. All participating agencies need to come to an agreement on their separate, but parallel roles, and they must have an understanding on how to work together without stepping on each other's toes.

Committing to a Contract or Schedule

Armed with the information from the eco-map, the assessment profile, and other diagnostic tools, the case manager(s), client, and the client's family are now ready to formulate an objectives-based action plan. This may be in the form of a "contract," ratified by all parties, in which long-term goals, short-term objectives, outcome measures, rules, and consequences are delineated. Or, more simply, it may be in the form of a highly structured schedule, which the offender-client promises to abide by for a specified length of time (*see* Figure 1.7 for a sample schedule). Sanctions could include weekly drug testing, daily check-in at a reporting center, residence in transitional housing, and inpatient residential treatment for alcohol or other drugs. Case managers (and other team members) are responsible for ensuring that the schedule is feasible ("Can the client actually get from Point A to Point B on the bus?"), and that all elements of the plan fit together in a logical and supportive sequence. Ideally, the contract or schedule clearly will specify the frequency and duration of treatment contacts and the consequences for noncompliance. After completion, the action plan is subject to review during a combined case conference, held biweekly, which should include at least one representative from community corrections and one treatment-oriented case manager.

We are assuming, in Renae's case, that she has been fined and sentenced to a year's probation. According to the sample schedule in Figure 1.7, Renae has committed to participate in numerous activities—only some of which—the cognitive treatment group, life skills, self-esteem workshop, and women's issues group—are held at the day reporting treatment center. The job center is located at the local community college, and is accessible by bus. The housing bureau is centrally located, as are the three self-help groups that she has selected, which are held in churches and community centers fairly close to town. Reporting to her probation officer will require, however, at least three transfers on the bus (which is why she cannot make it before 10:00 A.M.); and the women's health clinic is located in the suburbs, where buses do not run.

Initial Case Conference

At a minimum, an initial case conference consists of the client, her case manager, and others most likely to be able to provide support for her change efforts. This conference also may involve a corrections officer, either as a case manager or consultant. It may be more effective, however, to avoid drawing attention to the coercive nature of criminal justice sanctions during the strengths-based planning process. Major goals of the sessions are: 1) to ensure that all members understand what is planned and expected, 2) to identify potential barriers to success and to problem-solve about how to reduce or remove these barriers, and 3) to engender more support for the offender-client's efforts.

Renae's initial case conference is attended by Renae; her partner, Marc; his mother, Georgia Simons; a substance abuse counselor and women's health educator, and Renae's case manager at the day reporting treatment center. Transportation arrangements are the first order of business: Marc's mother agrees to take Renae to the bus stop three mornings a week, after the children have gotten on their respective school buses and before she herself goes to work. She also will loan Renae the car for the morning of her doctor's appointment (not a regular occurrence). The case manager thinks that she can find a volunteer willing to take Renae to her appointments on the remaining two days, if Marc can arrange to pick up both Renae and the children every afternoon, no later than 6:00. Marc, who gets off work at 3:00, agrees to this schedule, provided he has a working vehicle. Marc also says that he is willing to supervise the children in the evening, so that Renae can attend her self-help groups. Ms. Simons gives Renae permission to use their telephone for her Saturday call-in to her

FIGURE 1.7. Client Schedule (Sample)

PA511 DAY REPORTING TREATMENT CENTER

(555) 555-2222 OR (555) 555-3333

Client Name: Mendel, Renae F.Offense:			Week of:		Agent:		Level:
TIME	**MON**	**TUE**	**WED**	**THU**	**FRI**	**SAT**	**SUN**
A M 7:00	Drop off kids	Drop off kids	Drop off kids	Drop off kids	Drop off kids	Family Time	Spirituality
8:00							
9:00	P.O. Report @ 10:00	Self-esteem workshop	Housing Bureau	OB/GYN	Free time		
10:00				Store to fill prescription			
11:00	Cognitive Treatment Group		Life Skills		Women's Issues Group	Job Club	
P M 12:00				Free time			
1:00		Job Center					
2:00							In Home
3:00	Family ed			Family ed	Parenting	In Home Call P.O. at 4:00	
4:00							
5:00	Pick up kids	Pick up kids	Pick up kids	Pick up kids	Pick up kids		
6:00							
7:00	Women for Sobriety	Home	All-women NA Meeting	Home	All-women AA Meeting		
8:00							
9:00							
10:00	Home		Home		Home		
11:00							
Notes:					Signature:		
					Call in number: 555-6666		
Call in times: Monday @10 a.m. & Saturday @ 4 p.m.							

probation officer, and also on those rare occasions when, through no fault of her own, Renae is unable to keep a particular appointment. (Marc agrees to cover any unauthorized charges on the phone bill.)

David's asthma is another important issue, according to Renae. Both Marc and Ms. Simons concur that secondhand smoke is undoubtedly bad for David, but neither commits to stop smoking in the house. ("He can go in the bedroom if he wants.") They are supportive however, of Renae's desire to quit, and will do their best not to smoke in her presence.

After the schedule has been agreed upon by all parties, it will be discussed in a biweekly combined case conference (see below) between Renae's case manager and her probation officer.

Case Management Phase II: Change Effort/Treatment

The change or treatment phase is the process of implementing and monitoring the client-offender's individualized case plan. The case manager must maintain ongoing contact with both offender-clients and service providers. Are services being provided as promised? Is the offender-client complying with the conditions of her contract? Are things, in general, going according to plan?

Collaborative client-level teams or other coordinating mechanisms are crucial in the case of offender-clients, inasmuch as an offender may be under supervision by more than one corrections agent at the same time (for example on probation for one crime and on pretrial release status for another) (Center for Substance Abuse Treatment, 1994a, p. 21). Even if this is not the case, the offender often is engaged in multiple programs sponsored by multiple agencies. The case manager must interact with the staff in other agencies in a manner that encourages cooperation, without threatening the autonomy of the agent or of the organization itself. At both the agency level and the client level, the case manager must be empowered with enough authority to get service delivery back on track. Without follow-up and accountability, the client easily could "fall through the cracks."

Combined Case Conference

A combined case conference is an effective way of monitoring client progress, especially if caseloads are large and several agencies are involved. These conferences can be regularly scheduled and attended by representatives from all of the agencies that work together in a wraparound model. In them, all mutual clients may be reviewed to monitor progress, adjust the change plan if necessary, and identify and work on any glitches or issues impeding a client's success. In some models, combined case conferences happen regularly and review all or most clients. In others, they are convened periodically, and may focus only on selected clients.

If a number of service providers comprise the collaborative client-focused team, then, in the interests of efficiency, one agency usually assumes the leading role. The lead agency or individual conducting the meeting is responsible for:

- Arranging the time and place of the conference

- Obtaining relevant release-of-information forms

- Drafting a tentative agenda

- Informing all participants in advance, of the meeting date and time

- Distributing the agenda

- Introducing all persons to each other if it is a large group

- Ensuring that someone takes minutes, if necessary

- Facilitating the discussion

- Monitoring and following-up on the service plan with involved professionals and resource persons

Team members need to agree on the ground rules for participation: how and what information will be shared (confidentiality issues), and how they will handle decisions when consensus cannot be reached. Once the team has decided on the boundaries and rules for discussion, their strategizing must be objectives-based and concrete: What is the goal or problem? What do we want to accomplish in terms of outcomes? How do we plan to solve the problem, and who will take responsibility for which piece (adapted from R. Malysiak, July 24, 1998, personal communication)?

Establishing Common Ground

As part of a mutually reinforcing team-building process, the treatment case manager must become familiar with the specifics of criminal justice rules and regulations. It helps to be aware of corrections policy restrictions and of the appropriate use of authority in dealing with noncompliant clients. The corrections agent may be constrained by law to make judgments that, on the surface, may appear to those outside the criminal justice system as needlessly punitive. Likewise, the corrections supervisor must learn to view the individual in context to understand the reasons (rather than the excuses) why people sometimes are unable to meet their commitments (N. Riley, Washtenaw County Community Corrections, August 5, 1998, personal communication).

A client may be having trouble keeping her appointments not because she is slacking off, for instance, but because she cannot make the bus connections while accompanied by two small children. Is it possible for existing organizations to fulfill her childcare and/or transportation needs, or will it be necessary to advocate for new services? If the missing links are not forthcoming, team members may need to work with the client in revising her action plan and redefining her long-term goals. In the meantime, program administrators should be working together to develop longer term strategies for addressing resource and coordination problems and gaps in community resources.

Cooperation between the treatment case manager, the corrections agent, and other key service providers is vital to prioritize goals and to ensure the client is not overwhelmed by the sheer number of requirements or by conflicting expectations. In the case of some offenders—those with attention deficit disorder, for example—an inability to stay organized and keep commitments may have been what got them into trouble in the first place (Center for Substance Abuse Treatment, 1994a).

Augmented Case Conference

If things are not going according to plan—say, for example, that the client has missed three intensive outpatient appointments, has had two "dirty" urines, and has been inconsistent in day center reporting—then, the lead agency will call an intervention meeting for the purpose of conferring with the client and reevaluating the service plan. This meeting, variously referred to as an "all-team meeting" or an "augmented case conference," brings together the client and her family, her case manager(s), and, where appropriate, her substance abuse treatment provider and other key participants.

The intent of the meeting is to confront the offender with her behavior in a caring but firm manner and to problem-solve with her and members of her support system. This is an opportunity for the treatment services case manager, the corrections supervisor, and other service providers to put potential interdisciplinary tensions to work. By playing "good-cop/bad-cop" against one another, they may be able to impress upon the offender-client the seriousness of her situation, while simultaneously boosting her determination and instilling hope (P. Carras and S. Thompson, Washtenaw County Community Corrections/Options, Inc., August 7, 1998, personal communication).[9]

According to records maintained by both her probation officer and the day reporting treatment center, Renae has missed seven evening self-help sessions and four "call-ins" to her probation officer in the last two months. In addition, her attendance at the day reporting treatment center has been sporadic—lately she has been missing as many as three days a week. Her case manager has arranged an augmented case conference to which Renae, her probation officer, the substance abuse counselor who runs the day treatment cognitive therapy group, the health educator at the women's health center, and Renae's extended family are invited (via written invitation). Marc attends, but his mother and father do not. The day reporting treatment center case manager, who, as the lead agent, is conducting the conference, reviews the terms of the earlier agreement. Renae's probation officer reads over the days and times of her missed appointments, and explains the legal ramifications of these lapses—the ultimate consequence of which is almost certainly a jail or prison sentence. Renae begins to cry.

Marc reports that his mother has been upset because Renae and the children have not been ready for school on time, making her late for work. Renae reports major problems in getting herself and the children dressed without any assistance, especially on the mornings that they have been up all night trying to deal with David's asthma. After missing the first appointment, she explains, she was embarrassed to keep calling with the same story. She began to feel helpless and depressed. She is extremely worried about what will happen to her and the children if she has to go back to jail. She wishes that she were not so dependent on Marc's mother for her transportation.

Marc states that he has had opportunities for overtime and has been unable to get home on time to stay with the children, so that Renae can take the car to her AA meetings.

He believes that his work performance is suffering because of all the stresses at home caused by Renae's schedule. He feels that he has to prove himself to his manager to compensate. He says that Renae and his mother bicker all the time about the noise the children make, and that Renae is not doing enough around the house.

The case manager suggests that they take a break to think about alternatives. While the substance abuse counselor engages Marc in additional discussion about the stresses he is feeling, Renae's case manager and the health educator take Renae aside to speak privately with her in a separate room. Without Marc present, Renae points out new bruises that Marc inflicted when she tried to talk with him about his commitment to care for the children three nights a week. The case manager and health educator try to impress upon Renae the seriousness of Marc's behavior, work with her to develop a safety plan, and make sure she knows how to contact the domestic violence program.

The case manager suggests that they consider a new short-term emergency housing program, sponsored by the Salvation Army, that is just being introduced in participating apartment buildings around town. Although it is not a permanent solution, with stays restricted to three months or less, it might be enough for Renae and the children to "get on their feet" without having to depend so heavily on Marc and his family for transportation. Provided there are openings, it then would be necessary to make transportation arrangements for the children. David would not be a problem, inasmuch as his bus route covers the whole town, but Julie, unfortunately, might need to change schools. The case manager agrees to explore housing alternatives, including the bus route/school attendance rules.

When the meeting reconvenes, the participants discuss the possibility of alternative housing arrangements to reduce tensions in the living situation. Renae maintains that under the current circumstances, it is too difficult for her to get out at night. The substance abuse counselor suggests that she switch immediately to the intensive outpatient substance abuse program, and pick up the life skills, the parenting, and family education workshops at a later date. Then, she could attend her self-help groups during the day. Until her housing needs can be taken care of, it will be necessary to locate another volunteer/mentor who can provide rides for Renae on Wednesday and Friday as well. Monday morning is still the best time for her appointment with her probation officer; consequently, Renae will be reimbursed for cab fare on that day only. The probation officer impresses on Renae her legal obligation to check in—if only with a phone call—if for some reason she cannot make her appointment in person. He also tells Marc that Renae is likely to be sentenced to jail if she is unable to meet her mandated obligations, which will leave him solely responsible for the children. Marc reluctantly agrees that living separately is probably the best short-term solution.

As is typical of many women involved with the criminal justice system, Renae has very limited and inconsistent social support. Often, a key task within wraparound services is to help to create a new or at least a more positive and consistent support system. Note the teamwork involved as team members investigate the presence of violence by creating an opportunity to speak with Renae alone. Note also the probation officer's role here. While others are working to support Renae and to adjust her schedule to create more options, the probation officer reminds both Renae and Marc of the consequences if they do not make every effort to follow the agreed upon schedule.

Minutes of the meeting, including "next steps" to be taken, are reviewed by all participants. Renae recommits to following through on the new requirements. The case manager makes a note to bring up ongoing transportation and housing issues in the next advisory committee meeting. (We discuss the advisory committee in the Systems-Level Coordination and Problem-Solving section later in the paper.)

Case Management Phase III: Maintenance of Progress/Aftercare

At the end of the treatment phase, the client-offender and her case manager will formulate a plan for maintaining and strengthening progress, outlining behavioral objectives for the period between active work on change goals/treatment and regular community corrections supervision. (Offender-clients who have no conditions of release should be encouraged to join a peer support group immediately, where they can receive support from others who have successfully made the transition back to day-to-day community living.) In addition to specific objectives carried over from her treatment phase, the client can choose additional programming and support services (transitional housing; community-based self-help groups; mentoring programs, for instance) designed to sustain her progress over what, for many, is the most critical period for relapse and recidivism.[10]

Another combined case conference that includes her probation officer, substance abuse therapist, and other community partners will review the plan with the client. After agreeing to the terms of her "contract," she will be formally introduced into the follow-up program. Individuals who have records of alcohol and other drug problems need to be closely monitored during this time period and should have a well-developed relapse prevention plan.

> During the maintenance/aftercare phase, Renae takes advantage of the temporary housing alternative closer to town. Marc continues to live with his parents on weekdays, since this location is closer to his job; he rejoins Renae and the children on weekends. After some difficulty adjusting to new school, Renae and the children develop routines that work better than before. Occasionally their new schedule is disrupted when David's asthma flares up; as a weekday single parent, Renae often has no choice but to take both him and his sister, Julie, to the emergency room.
>
> Renae tries to keep busy to manage her depression and cravings, but finds herself feeling lonely and aimless when the children are not around. She still has difficulty trusting in and making new friends, and has not yet developed a supportive relationship with her AA sponsor. Weekends, when the family is reunited, can be stressful. If Marc is in a good mood, the family manages fairly well together, but often he is explosive, which has an impact on everyone else. Finances continue to be a major source of tension, but Marc and Renae try to find things to do together as a family that they can afford.

Before graduation from the maintenance/aftercare phase, the client and case manager will develop a third and last action plan, which will carry the offender-client through the balance of her probation (if applicable). Team members will hold a final combined case conference to ensure that she has met the minimum program requirements for completion.[11]

Systems-level Coordination and Problem Solving

Models and Conditions for System-level Linkages

Many models for providing modified wraparound are possible, depending on what services are available in which locations, and what linkages and coordination mechanisms are already in place. A number of systems integration experiments for multiple issue populations have been undertaken recently, funded in the United States by such sources as Health and Human Services (HHS), the Health Resources and Services Administration (HRSA), the Robert Wood Johnson Foundation, and the Substance Abuse and Mental Health Administration (SAMHSA). Evaluations of these efforts are beginning to appear in the literature, and should provide useful guidance for modified wraparound in community corrections (Bickman, 1996; Crowson and Boyd, 1993, 1996; General Accounting Office, 1992; Kline et al., 1991; Morrissey, Calloway, Johnsen, and Ullman, 1997; Morrissey et al., 1984; Rog, et al., 1997).

Systems Coordination

Systems coordination typically is undertaken to address goals that cut across service sectors, when organizations need resources for clients that they cannot provide directly, or to address intersystem problems— such as multiple and conflicting expectations of the same client. Most systems coordination models are problem-focused, and use coalitions and other types of interagency exchanges focused on particular populations of need.

Crowson and Boyd (1993; 1996) reviewed the evidence from various sources on efforts to link children's services. They identified many of the administrative problems that are commonly encountered when trying to combine multiple services. These include the sharing of confidential information across different organizations, locating funding sources, developing "trust" between agencies that may not have worked well together in the past, and involving the community in joint efforts. Eventually, a modified wraparound program will need to deal with all these issues, and probably more. It is important to remember that systems coordination is not a static event, but a process (Randolph, et al., 1997). Initial arrangements are likely to evolve substantially over time, and will require sustained work to maintain. Intermediate interorganizational forms are possible that will remain stable for periods of time and then must change to address additional goals or to meet evolving environmental conditions.

From Interaction and Cooperation to Integration: A Continuum

Integrating systems of care and/or improving coordination does not necessarily reduce costs, but should assist a community to use its resources more strategically. The continuum of care has to be designed to meet the needs of the target populations, with useful coordination and sequencing of activities. The number of services is not the most critical ingredient (Bickman, 1996). Careful assessment, selection of services, and planning are important, at both the agency/systems and the client/services levels. Service plans must take into account the consumer's stage of progress and what she can handle at any given time (Lebowitz, Harvey, and Herman, 1993; Minkoff, 1994).

Crowson and Boyd (1993; 1996) found that the terms "coordination," "integration," and "collaboration" are used interchangeably, but often refer to different levels of linkages. Bailey and Koney (1995) use the term "partnership" to refer to a number of these relationships. Kritek (1996) uses the term "coordination" to mean acting together towards a common goal. A manual on collaboration (National Assembly of Voluntary Health and Social Welfare Organizations, 1991) defines collaboration as "a formal sustained commitment to work together for a common mission."

Konrad (1996) synthesizes these definitions, categorizing relationships into a spectrum from the least to the most integrated:

1. No integration–little knowledge or communication across the organizations

2. Information sharing and communicating–the least interdependent with formal and informal information sharing

3. Cooperation–more formalized but still loosely connected, with some shared work, usually with reciprocal referrals or one agency assisting another either at the client or the community level

4. Coordination–still more formalized, with some joint work, follow-up, perhaps some joint staff reviews of cases, and often joint lobbying or working together towards mutual goals in the community

5. Collaboration–more formalized with more shared elements and explicitly common goals. The organizations remain autonomous financially and administratively, however, but may seek some joint funding, provide joint cross-training of staff, and one agency may provide some functions for others who are part of the collaboration.

6. Consolidation/integration–terms used to signify more substantial structural changes, with consolidation usually indicating an umbrella organization with some centralized leadership, administrative, and service functions, although the participating organizations remain structurally separate. These organizations are characterized by high levels of cross-program collaborations and other types of collaboration. Integration is the most comprehensive with authority, activities, and funding blended and pooled. Client eligibility typically is determined only once. In an integrated system, wraparound services may be delivered all at a single site, or in several sites, but with a central intake and single service plan (Konrad, 1996).

At the integrated end of this continuum, participating agencies are likely to have developed a common philosophy about the nature of clients' problems and how to assist them, and have a shared understanding about expected outcomes, mutual roles, and collaboration. Systems integration almost always requires that the participating organizations make internal changes in policies and practices to participate in the shared ideal. Pooled funding is common, often flowing through a designated "lead agency," or through an organization designed to facilitate communitywide collaboration. Integrated treatment teams with multiple competencies are also common. The members of these teams are employed by different agencies (Ridgely and Dixon, 1993; Randolph et al., 1997), but work closely together in assessment and case planning and sometimes in the joint implementation of the plan. (We describe two types of teams in our case example—the case conferencing mechanisms at the client level, and the advisory group at the interorganizational level.)

Systems integration also may lead to or require some agency-level structural changes—such as a shared umbrella organization, jointly-staffed programs, realignment of services, moving services initially provided in separate locations all to one place ("one-stop shopping"), and even mergers. Some integrated service systems have a single authority that is multipurpose and comprehensive in scope. In some cases (especially with pooled funding), eligibility requirements for services are uniform and streamlined and activities are blended across the formerly separate participating organizations. Automated data systems usually are helpful in determining client eligibility, tracking service use and payments, and in linking outcomes to services. A fully coordinated system may have a unified intake and assessment process and shared case management procedures.

Systems Coordination Minimums for Wraparound

Wraparound does not require systems integration; in fact, as we have said earlier, complex systems integration efforts typically have not improved client outcomes unless the changes made were guided by the experience of those providing direct services (General Accounting Office, 1992). Wraparound is greatly facilitated, however, by high levels of cooperation, and there must be mechanisms at the administrative and policy level to address problems that arise there and to pursue agreed-upon mutual goals. At minimum, it is useful for participating organizations to develop cooperative agreements or memoranda of understanding among themselves, or between the community corrections system and other community-based collaborators. Formal contracts also may be appropriate among some organizations, especially if one organization is "buying" services from another, or when two or more organizations are exchanging particular types of activities and resources.

In planning, it is important to recognize that some gaps in community services (for example safe housing, good jobs) must be addressed whether or not they are the focus of the wraparound model. People have a very hard time working on other goals without basic resources for survival. Transportation and childcare responsibilities are also recurring barriers for women with multiple needs, no matter what their other major problems may be. It is extremely useful to have some unallocated money in a wraparound system to address such gaps, and to fill other holes that occur when temporary conflicts among partners interfere with decisions about accountability (Rapp, 1998).

At a minimum, systems coordination requires joint framing of a project's objectives; information gathering as described above; identifying gaps; addressing barriers to coordination; reframing initial tasks based on new information; and communicating regularly with relevant stake-holders. Stakeholders in a modified wraparound model for women in community corrections will include women eligible for wraparound, elected officials, many elements of the criminal justice system, represen-tatives of the agencies and organizations involved, and any other potentially interested parties. Mulroy and Say (1998) found that coordi-nation requires shared values, reasonably compatible service philosophies and a commitment to continuous mutual learning. Group process skills are very important, with lots of joint education and policy development (Casto and Julia, 1994). Hoge and Howenstine (1997) rec-ommend integrative task groups and participatory management models to facilitate horizontal and vertical communication, planning and prob-lem solving. Team building and people performing boundary-spanning roles are also important. Vaill (1991) suggests that leadership often needs to operate within "permanent whitewaters" with less central control as linkages among participants grow.

Before the next meeting of the community corrections advisory committee, the head of the day reporting center and the director of community corrections meet with case managers and review the case conference minutes. They identify some of the major gaps and glitches clients are encountering, and prepare a brief report to take to the advi-sory committee. Inadequate transportation, housing, and childcare are crucial barriers for Renae and several other women in the wraparound system.

At the advisory committee meeting, the two directors ask Renae's case manager to present her case as well as several others in terms general enough to protect client confiden-tiality. Group members then pool their resources in an attempt to find solutions. A local children's agency has been working to develop drop-in childcare co-located with several women's AA meetings, which will make attending these meet-ings easier for women like Renae—if they can find transportation to get there.

Advisory committee members discuss the possibility of acquiring a van to provide specialized transportation, espe-cially in the evening. Legal liability and how to pay for a driver are identified as major concerns. Several agency representa-tives point out that they already provide limited transportation for their clients. A discussion follows on whether agencies can combine already existing resources to assist community corrections clients. For this option, mechanisms would need to be developed to coordinate routes and scheduling across agency boundaries. Several members volunteer to serve on a subcommittee to explore alternative approaches to improving transportation before their next meeting.

Surfacing and Addressing Cross-agency Problems and Conflicts

Criminal justice and community-based helping systems only sometimes work well together. The modified wraparound approach we introduce in this paper undoubtedly will present challenges to all of the participating organizations and their service providers. When everything is working well, organizational differences can enrich the ultimate outcomes, by checking and balancing each other, or by contributing multiple perspectives toward a more complete and unified picture. Sometimes this is not possible, however.

It is extremely important to develop mechanisms to allow conflicts to surface and to address them as they arise, and even to anticipate them. Organizational and interorganizational learning is likely to be greatest while conflicts are being addressed. Many resources are available to assist planners and facilitators to develop such mechanisms (Fisher, 1994; Folger, Poole, Stutman, 1993; Rubin, 1994). Sometimes participants can agree to disagree and to respect each other's positions. In other instances, major conflicts erupt and cannot be contained. Conflicts can arise at both the client and agency levels. Often, case managers and direct services workers can find ways to address client needs despite major differences among them, if they can keep the welfare of clients as their primary goal. Cooperation may be more difficult between organizations.

During the advisory committee discussion, the domestic violence program representative expresses concern that a number of plans focus too much on substance abuse treatment and not enough on battered women's safety. She argues that the pressure the case managers are putting on abusive spouses to provide support for their partner's treatment can increase the risk and severity of violence. In her opinion, a domestic violence advocate should have been invited to meet with women like Renae and her women's group to conduct a safety assessment, provide information, and establish connections with the women. The substance abuse program director is concerned about the number of requirements and personnel that women in community corrections already have to face, and asserts that it will be difficult for Renae to meet her other responsibilities until she has seriously addressed her substance abuse problems. Several people note that it can be hard to reach someone for consultation at the domestic violence program, and a number of women have reported that the intake process at the drug treatment program is very "off-putting." The meeting begins to get tense, with increasingly polarized views about which actions merit the highest priority.

At this point, the retired judge notes that strong safety plans and substance abuse treatment are equally necessary. He asks the group to generate ideas about how both can be carried out within the community corrections context. He reminds members that everyone will need to think creatively about how to address these issues in a setting different from their own. Clients often have strong preferences about how to proceed, which also must be taken into account. He suggests that the group simply generate ideas without critiquing any at first, just to get the creative process going. Group members begin to ask why the domestic violence representative believes that the current plans are insufficient. They also explore ways of incorporating more attention to substance abuse within their orientation process. The substance abuse program director commits herself to developing procedures for an expedited intake process for women in the community corrections program, perhaps with an intake worker stationed at the day reporting center at designated times during the week.

Note, in our example, the importance of having multiple points of view and perspectives openly expressed, and the critical role that the retired judge plays. Because he is perceived as knowledgeable and not in any particular "camp" (in other words, boundary-spanning), he often is able to assist members to step outside of polarized positions to consider alternatives. (We say more about negotiating complex interorganizational relationships in later sections.) Note also that a number of the participating agencies begin to consider making some internal changes to work more effectively with women in community corrections in conjunction with the other agencies. This is a sign that the cooperating agencies are moving towards a more collaborative model. They already have made considerable progress towards a shared view of their joint mission and some jointly agreed-upon procedures. Now they are beginning to recognize deeper conflicts among them, and to consider making some changes.

Integration or coordination may not be necessary when systems are working well. Attention must be paid, however, to the ways that different parts of the system, with competing goals and values, may be working against each other. For example, the Friend of the Court may mandate joint custody of the couple's three children at the same time that the Domestic Violence Association is supporting Renae to separate from her abusive partner. Or, Child Protective Services may demand that Renae demonstrate her ability to care for her two younger children, both financially and emotionally, at the same time that her Welfare-to-Work case manager is insisting that in addition to schooling, Renae also must commit to a low-paying, entry-level job.

Intersystemic conflicts are not only unintentional but often invisible. Clients often feel them, however, and may respond with anger or feelings of inadequacy. Most clients have neither sufficient knowledge of how the interacting systems work to advocate successfully for themselves, nor the clout to leverage change at that level. When workers are unaware of conflicts, clients often are held accountable for meeting contradictory requirements, and may be unfairly labeled as unmotivated or irresponsible. Workers who develop procedures to identify and track patterns of success and failure begin to see commonalities across individual offenders. They then can create mechanisms for sharing this information with administrators and policymakers, to educate them about service-level needs. Negotiating interorganizational boundaries at all these levels takes time, skills, and great commitment. Collaboration becomes more likely when everyone remembers that the ultimate goal is to improve positive outcomes for clients and reduce recidivism.

Usually, more options are possible than are first evident in situations in which only two polarized positions are apparent or a win-lose situation occurs. Developing these options can take time that is not available initially. Perhaps the best that can be done to resolve conflict is to gather as much information as possible, and revisit it later, when time pressures and emotions are less intense. A group reexamination, with explicit learning goals, often can be a productive catalyst to the development of more options the next time. Someone should be designated to ensure that conflicts are reexamined later, however, or the group can develop norms of conflict avoidance that may be counterproductive in the long run.

Vertical Communication

Vertical communication refers to regular information flow between levels of staff, between those who work directly with offender-clients and those responsible for staff supervision and agency management, budgeting, and policymaking. This must occur within each participating organization and between the mechanisms used to coordinate client-level services (in this instance, the case managers and case conferences) and those focused on systems (interorganizational) coordination (in our example, the advisory committee). It often must include the clients themselves as well as program funders and government policymakers.

> After the advisory committee meeting, minutes are distributed to all members of the participating agencies in addition to members of the advisory committee. Each director reports briefly on the advisory committee's key issues at his or her next agency staff meeting and solicits additional information on future strategies and priorities from all staff.

Regular mechanisms are important for reviewing progress and problems and for translating information from the client to the agency level and back again. Vertical communication is evident when the directors or organizational representatives to the systems-coordination mechanism actively solicit information about difficulties that clients are having; keep careful records of policy planning and decisions and widely disseminate them; and encourage face-to-face feedback between intersystem contacts and staff. It is critical that systems-level planning and problem solving are informed by and responsive to client-level realities. Case conference participants are in a position to identify system barriers, such as childcare and transportation, that are impeding access and coordination for particular clients. Case managers and other direct service providers will have the most knowledge about the difficulties and successes clients are experiencing. However, policy, structural, and administrative changes usually require the attention of administrators and/or the approval of boards. Even though clients and direct service providers often have insights into service delivery problems, knowledge from the "street" level of service provision is not always effectively conveyed to those in a position to address those problems.

In addition, practitioners and clients may have only limited access to the "big picture." Often they do not understand administrative and policy constraints getting in the way of potential solutions. Service providers need to understand the sources of administrative and policy barriers and what is being done to address them, so that they can provide feedback about what is and is not working. If vertical communication and planning mechanisms do not occur within participating organizations and across systems, then time-consuming policy, structural, and administrative changes may be made that do not improve the delivery of needed resources and services to the people who benefit from them.

Addressing Longer-term Issues

As Renae nears the end of her probation, she has moved into an apartment in the same school district with a woman she met at an AA meeting. Her roommate has a daughter close in age to one of Renae's children, and the three-bedroom apartment is crowded but workable. She attends a women's AA group regularly two to three times a week. She also participates in a support group at the battered women's program and recently attended a community speak-out on domestic violence. David's asthma attacks occur less regularly now, but are still a serious worry. Renae has started a training program in basic computer skills, and works part-time as a waitress.

Marc sees the children on weekends, but seldom stays overnight due to the lack of privacy in the small apartment. Renae still hopes that she and Marc can work things out, but she has decided she should wait to talk about this with him until she no longer is fighting consistent cravings and periods of depression. She is beginning to understand some of the factors in her life that make the depression so difficult, but knows she has a long way to go in addressing them.

Renae is both excited and anxious about completing the program. She credits herself with the strength to make difficult changes. However, she also wonders whether she can stay sober and out of trouble without the support of her case manager and the other program participants.

Although she has been assured that she can reconnect with the program at any time, she is worried that if she relapses, she will be too embarrassed and ashamed to ask for help. Renae recognizes that she will need to carefully maintain her newly established community network to be successful on her own.

Systems-level planning also can be used to develop longer-term plans to address needs of women in community corrections that are not within the charge of any of the participating agencies. For instance, a long-term need for most women in community corrections is to develop productive ways to spend leisure time and to develop an abiding interest in healthy leisure activities. If possible, some inexpensive options can assist clients with the transition out of community corrections. These include alumni programs, celebrations that involve both current and past clients, and drop-in hours. Often these activities can be planned and implemented by volunteers, or former clients/alumni.

A Working Model

Now that we have described the main elements of modified wraparound, illustrated with a case example, we summarize the key components of one program model in Figure 1.8, Modified Wraparound at Work. In this modified wraparound example, directors of programs who work with community corrections clients (or their designees) meet quarterly. While the program was being developed, however, they met more frequently. Members of the group routinely keep each other apprised of changes and issues within each organization. Jointly they monitor the community and the state for potential resources or events of mutual interest and concern. Every agenda includes a time for presenting issues, successes, and problems identified at the services level. Some of these topics originate in the participating organizations. Others are identified by the wraparound case managers or by case conference participants. When possible, the group develops problem-solving and planning mechanisms to address these issues.

Information about systems coordination activities and problems is conveyed to the line workers in all agencies via minutes and reports so they can understand why things happen as they do. Then, they can make suggestions about how the situation can be improved, without being derailed by circumstances that are not amenable to immediate change.

For instance, if a particular procedure is mandated by law, longer-term efforts can move toward revising the law. In the meantime, participants can identify alternative ways of accomplishing the procedure, can reduce its negative consequences, or at least avoid blaming administrators for things they cannot control. In another example, funders may have set limitations on how agency money can be spent. Motivated individuals may set out to challenge these limitations. Meanwhile, it is helpful to keep everyone informed about the source of the problem, so that collective

FIGURE 1.8. Modified Wraparound at Work

ONE COMMUNITY'S SUCCESS

In a successful attempt to reduce prison and jail commitment rates, the Washtenaw County Community Corrections Department, based in Ann Arbor, Michigan, has instituted a comprehensive continuum of services designed to wrap services not only around the offender, but also the family of the offender (Washtenaw County Community Corrections, 1998, p. 3).

One supervisor from Community Corrections serves as a liaison with treatment providers for women at various phases of the criminal justice process, e.g., pre-trial, probation, and jail. In addition to weekly case conferences in which all active cases are briefly reviewed, augmented case conferences are held as needed. Whenever possible, everyone working with the offender-client is invited; all are asked for feedback about the client's progress and problems whether or not they can attend.

The Community Corrections manager also holds a quarterly meeting with representatives of all of the agencies that have Memoranda of Understanding or contracts with community corrections. At this meeting, agencies update each other about changes and issues since the last meeting and about current community events, such as funding or regulations, that have potential implications for their work together. Particular issues or problems are put on the agenda as needed (e.g., transportation alternatives; how to address a recent incident with a community corrections offender that got front-page negative news coverage). Individual cases are not discussed at this meeting, although case managers report on progress and problems. The purpose of this gathering is to highlight systems issues either communitywide or within a particular agency that the directors need to address.

Included in a continuum of alternative sentencing options, ranging from drug testing to probation residential services, are specialized services for women. These services (among others) are provided primarily through a contract with

Options, Inc., a day treatment and reporting center, whose coordinating and monitoring functions are a critical component of modified wraparound.

As is true of many community corrections programs, Options, Inc., addresses specific risk factors for criminal behavior, as well as the reasons for relapse or recidivism. Core services offered include:

—Intake and assessment
—Individual case management
—Structured daily schedule and long-term action plan
—Employment assistance and advocacy
—Transportation assistance
—Life skills training, such as budgeting, nutrition, parenting

In addition to these core services (which, in most cases are provided on-site), noncore services are available through agreements with other organizations:

—Substance abuse assessment, treatment, and aftercare
—Mental health evaluation and treatment
—Medical evaluations and treatment
—HIV/AIDS education and counseling
—Extended family counseling
—Financial and housing assistance
—Education assistance
—Attention Deficit Disorder coaching
—Mentoring

The required curriculum includes a nine-week cognitive treatment group and choice of any self-help groups (such as, Alanon, Alateen, Narcotics Anonymous) three times per week. Offender-clients also can choose from additional special interest groups. A woman's therapy group focuses on women-specific concerns—first and foremost of which are abuse issues. According to women's group facilitator, Linda Hiller, female offenders often are unwilling or unable to recognize—let alone articulate—their histories of abuse. Ideally, they should have individualized therapy, long enough to carry them through the "re-entry" phase. Group therapy is helpful, but if it does not get at the root causes of addiction and crime, it is not enough. Hiller uses "expressive art" techniques in her groups, to encourage women to attend to and capitalize on their strengths.

efforts can be made to spend the money productively, and to locate or pool money from alternative sources.

The main objective is to identify where problems and barriers are encountered, at both the client and the agency levels. Then, collaborative groups can pool their ingenuity and resources to reduce or eliminate these obstacles, or find ways to go over, around, or through them together.

Periodic systemwide meetings are held for joint planning and problem solving, and the leadership group works hard to plan and facilitate these. Increasingly, e-mail groups and other electronic communications are used for smaller scale planning and information sharing.

Developing and Sustaining a Wraparound System

Now that we have illustrated one model for wraparound services with a case example, we will discuss some steps to follow to develop the wraparound capability within a community corrections program. The first step is to conduct several types of assessments. Such assessments are extremely important in the early planning phases, but also should be updated periodically, to determine whether quality is being maintained or could be improved, and because needs and service system components change over time.

Step I: Conducting Assessments

Guidelines for Assessing the Appropriateness of Services for Women

The following are some guidelines for assessing whether existing services and settings are appropriate for women. These are drawn from multiple sources, although Galbraith's (1998) work demonstrates the usefulness of this perspective with women in the justice system. The basic approach is to assume competency and encourage offender-clients to find hope and meaning in events that have disrupted their lives.

1. *Accessible.* We already have noted many of the barriers that women face when they need to acquire resources and services from multiple settings. These include depression, low self-esteem, and a low sense of efficacy, in addition to difficulties with transportation, complex family responsibilities, fewer financial resources, services delivered in ways that increase shame and trauma, and negative societal attitudes. Transportation, childcare, and affirming social support can help a woman get to the resources she needs, but they also must be available in forms she can use and in an environment that is safe.

2. *Comprehensive.* Ideally, coordinated services for women should provide continuity and comprehensiveness, including involvement of her support systems. Assessment and resources should

include multiple life areas so that unaddressed problems in one do not undermine progress in another.

3. *Supportive.* Gender- and culturally sensitive programming will emphasize support rather than confrontation. Service providers need to demonstrate empathy and instill hope. Although the woman must be held accountable for her actions and "confronted" (presented) with the evidence if she does not follow through, the style should not be confrontational or combative. Most women respond better to supportive approaches, and especially those with abuse histories will be traumatized further if their boundaries are violated with aggressive accusations (*see* Covington in this volume). Aggressive demands also are considered insulting in many cultures.

4. *Individualized.* Services must be geared to where a woman is on the multiple dimensions of need. Recovery and change are *processes*, not an event or simply a set of outcomes (Sullivan and Evans, 1994). Services should be sequenced and paced appropriately.

5. *Strengths-based.* Strengths-based therapies identify and build on strengths, increase self- esteem and efficacy by recharacterizing coping mechanisms as positive attributes rather than as pathological symptoms, deficits, and needs. Services for women should emphasize competency-building, coping, and empowering (Abbott, 1994).

6. *Egalitarian.* Relational approaches assume interactive partnerships with women receiving services. Peer support and expressive group therapies can be used to create atmospheres of mutuality.

7. *Participatory.* Creating an atmosphere in which women can share their stories safely increases trust and promotes engagement. Inviting women to contribute to programming and to direct their own treatment plans reduces the marginalization and silencing that many experience by virtue of their diagnoses and abuse histories. Women become more "visible" the more they participate in services and system planning. They also become active partners in negotiating the fragmented systems that exist within most communities.

8. *Respectful of diversity.* Differences among women must be honored. Age, ethnicity, religious beliefs and practices, sexual orientation, economic class, disability status, and gender, among others, all interact in complex ways that are important to understand and consider in assessment and program design.

9. *Gender-specific.* Treatment should address specific gender issues such as evolving gender roles; the impact of early chaotic relationships on mental and physical health; victimization; stigma; social discrimination; HIV risk; other sexually transmitted diseases; pregnancy; fear of losing custody of children; involvement in sex work; economic survival; and physiological differences in metabolizing substances and in processing experiences (Grella, 1996; 1997). Women's psychosocial development, experiential characteristics, and physiology are sufficiently different from men's to necessitate interventions designed specifically for them (Veysey et al., 1998), especially when they have histories of physical and sexual abuse. Some women also will need help in dealing with role loss and parenting issues (Hagan, Finnegan, Nelson-Zlupko, 1994; Alexander, 1996).

10. *Sensitive to trauma.* Given the high incidence of trauma, programs and services should use relational approaches to assist women in mitigating the effects of isolation and low self-esteem that result from trauma, and to help them revisit and reframe their experiences in empowering ways (Herman, 1992; Covington, this volume).

11. *Contextualized.* Programs must be sensitive to the fact that a woman cannot be successfully treated in isolation from her social support network—relationships with her partner, children, other family members, and friends. The social context and how to work with it may vary considerably in different ethnic and cultural groups. Great care must be exercised to screen for the presence of partner-violence, and this dynamic must be addressed before any conjoint family work is initiated. A goal for many women must be to help develop a positive support system where very little positive support is present.

12. *Prevention-focused within the family.* Children who witness violence within their family of origin or who are victims of violence

are extremely likely to become either recurring victims or per-petrators of violence as adults. The cycle is especially likely to be perpetuated if children experience inadequate nurturing, believe that such violence is normative, and receive no assis-tance in reworking their reactions to these traumas (Gilfus, 1992; Kampfner, 1995). Family-based prevention includes fam-ily-strengthening programs (to build social/interactional skills for parents and children and to promote bonding) and home visitation programs (to promote family functioning and skills) (Johnson et al., 1996; Kumpfer, 1997). Targeting both parents and children is more efficacious than programs focused exclu-sively on the child or the mother (National Institute on Drug Abuse, 1997). Care must be taken to separate surveillance and monitoring functions within a corrections context from family-strengthening approaches that will benefit children.

Types of Assessments

Three types of assessments are important in planning wraparound services. All should be informed by the above criteria, which are espe-cially crucial with regard to the second and third types of assessment.

1. Assessing Population Needs and Strengths

The first type of assessment focuses on the needs and strengths of the target populations, to determine what particular resources and ser-vices are likely to be needed.

- Who are the women eligible for community corrections and wraparound approaches (for example age, ethnicity, family sit-uation, background, history)?

- What are their needs and strengths? Which areas are especially likely to create barriers to remaining crime-free? What strengths can be built upon and nurtured?

- What needs are being satisfactorily addressed? Where are the major gaps in what currently is available for women?

Information can be gathered from women themselves, from the cor-rectional system and court records, and from those who work mostly closely with women offenders. Table 1.2 (page 15) and Appendix A out-line the many life areas that are important to assess. Once this assessment is complete, or while this assessment is being done, it is also important to assess the resources already being used, both within the corrections system and in the community.

2. Assessing Current Resources and Practices Within the Justice System

- What services are available within the criminal justice system generally, and in community corrections in particular?

- In what ways are these services appropriate for women? In what ways are they inappropriate?

- What linkages between community corrections and community-based service organizations are already in place?

- What are the strengths and limitations of these services and of the preexisting linkages between the corrections system and community organizations?

It is not sufficient to simply locate these resources. They also must be structured and delivered in ways compatible with what women benefit from and need. Use these guidelines to inform your assessment. Ask women who have used available services about their experiences.

3. Locating and Assessing Additional Community-based Resources

Once all the information about the potential target population(s) and existing services is compiled, resources and options for wraparound services must be assessed. This assessment should include both the organizations that provide services, and a listing of what coordination and collaborations are currently underway.

- What services and resources are needed?

- How are services now being delivered (as well as what, where, and when)?

- How are different providers perceived?

- What evidence does each provider have about its effectiveness?

- What is their experience with offenders?

- What are the critical gaps in services that women-offender/clients are likely to need?

- What is necessary to fill these gaps?

- What problems are people encountering in their current efforts to collaborate?

- What is the general attitude within the community about women offenders?

[Please refer to Appendices A and C for more comprehensive lists.]

Once these assessments are complete, the planners are ready to consider their various options for constructing a modified wraparound model. Programs can start by adding some options initially and expanding as they develop more experience, although some will engage in a larger system-design process first. Planners will benefit from understanding the options available, however, whatever approach is taken.

Step II: Planning and Getting Started

In addition to the assessments described briefly above, developing modified wraparound is likely to require extensive program planning, creation of a mutually agreed-upon model, and extensive start-up time. This is especially the case when it is necessary to link services provided by diverse agencies across different sectors with different "cultures" and approaches. A participatory process that involves the systems and people who will be affected increases "buy-in," and makes it more likely that the model developed will be compatible with existing practices. Many resources are available to assist planners to consider various options (Bailey and Koney, 1995; Cousins, 1998; Gentry, 1987; Gilcrest, 1998; Joseph and Ogletree, 1996; Mizrahi and Rosenthal, 1992; Sarri and Sarri, 1992; Hardcastle et al, 1997; Minkler, 1997). There are many ways to begin.

It is important to seek input and/or participation from current or former offenders. This not only will ensure that their voices are heard, but also will allow organizational and community participants to develop comfort with and strategies for working collaboratively with women on mutually defined goals.

Planning by a Core Group with Input

One model might invite representatives of selected core organizations to become the initial intersystem planning body. The initial planners, at a minimum, must include representation from the community corrections systems and representation from community-based service organizations. The initial group can expand when additional needs are identified, or when a needs-assessment or plan is ready for broader review. Someone needs to convene at least the initial meeting, where procedures and responsibilities for later meetings and activities can be developed. It usually is helpful to have some information about needs and the current problems and issues available from the start. Alternatively, the group can gather information soon after they begin to work together.

If a corrections system or a particular community organization wishes to undertake a bulk of the planning themselves, one way to create broader input and buy-in is to develop a representative advisory group for a period of time. That group can help define initial goals, give advice about available information and resources, review and interpret needs assessments and plans, and recommend potential structures and participants. The group ought to meet multiple times, with clear agendas, roles, and expectations. Community hearings in which women can tell their stories and the public is asked for input and comment also can be very useful; these are also opportunities for media coverage.

Conferences

Other ways to generate interest and begin planning may be even more useful, depending on time and resources. A communitywide conference focusing on the needs of women in community corrections can be a useful beginning. A variety of persons and organizations can be invited to attend with no initial commitment for ongoing participation. Such a conference can include information sessions to provide a base of knowledge and perspective, and to help to develop a common language and understanding. Knowledgeable speakers, panel discussions of issues and approaches, and presentation of activities going on in other communities can be informative and motivating for those attending.

Influential community members can be asked to speak or participate, and must inform themselves about the issues to do so. Their participation also should increase their commitment to addressing the needs of women in community corrections. Other types of conference sessions might include facilitated groups working to identify resources, gaps, and barriers in the community, or to brainstorm initial ideas about how work towards modified wraparound might proceed in that community. Media representatives can be invited so that the broader community is informed of women's needs within community corrections and of possible ways to address them. Those attending the conference can be asked to complete forms indicating their interest in future work on the issues involved. They also can identify others who should be involved. This will begin to establish a constituency for modified wraparound, will generate many ideas about how to proceed, and will identify people and organizations interested in further participation.

Coalitions

Coalition structures also can be very important. These can be comprised of representatives from many organizations. Planning for modified wraparound could build on already existing coalitions, if their interests overlap with these issues. These could include groups concerned about violence against women, women and substance abuse, children of incarcerated mothers, women and the welfare system, or multi-need populations, such as those with both mental illness and substance abuse problems, the homeless, or those with HIV. Additional members can be added as new issues arise and momentum builds.

Coalition development usually moves through relatively predictable stages (Bailey and Koney, 1995; Bailey and Koney, 1995; Mizrahi and Rosenthal, 1992). It is useful for a coalition to have some sort of leadership structure—a convener or steering committee (Gentry, 1987). A coalition might be short-term and exist primarily during the planning and early implementation stage of a modified wraparound approach, or it might be ongoing. If it continues, periodically it could review the progress and problems of the new program, assist with developing resources and addressing problems, help to locate resources, and serve to broaden coordination and knowledge in the community about the issues.

Step III: Developing Ways to Work Together

Learning about Collaboration from Planning Activities

Collaborative planning processes can be prime opportunities to learn about the issues and problems that must be addressed when developing coordinated or collaborative service models. Group members can experiment with different ways of working together and with different procedures and structures, before beginning the actual provision and delivery of services. Meetings should build in activities that assist the group to identify what is being learned, to clarify emerging issues, and to examine alternative ways to proceed. It will be very important to frame periods of conflict as opportunities for identifying and addressing problems. Exploring the sources of conflict is likely to uncover barriers that will need to be addressed in the eventual model for modified wraparound.

Considering Group Composition

Current or former women offenders can be invited to participate and even to provide leadership in any one of these models. Representatives from key partner agencies should be included. In collaborative ventures, it is very useful to involve "neutral" persons who are not perceived to be members or advocates for particular systems, but are perceived as caring and knowledgeable about the community and the problems being addressed. These individuals often can serve very useful brokering and translating functions across the participating systems (we call them "boundary spanners"). This is most necessary when people are using different languages, stereotyping each other, or becoming polarized about particular points or options. Brokers have to have particular skills as well—skills in communicating, in conceptualizing issues at the systems level, and often in mediating disputes. Brokers may be educators, elected officials, or even representatives of particular constituencies as long as they are trusted and perceived to be knowledgeable and even-handed.

Undertaking Organizational Assessments

In addition to the early needs assessment, it will be useful to conduct more extensive assessments of the organizations most likely to participate in modified wraparound. This will enable the participating programs to learn more about each other, and to identify where their current structures, procedures, and service practices may be more or less compatible. Potential partners should know something about each others' management structures and how decisions are made. In some agencies, the director can make decisions unilaterally. In others, a board or umbrella organization must be consulted, in a multistep process. Some smaller organizations make decisions by consensus among all staff. This knowledge can help potential collaborators to understand and help each other with their internal decision-making procedures.

Similarly, shared knowledge is useful about program design, standards that must be met, major policies of the organization, and guidelines about major agency practices and services. Requirements for staff training and certification, and how and when these occur can be useful in developing joint training programs. They also allow partners to understand the orientations and qualifications of staff in the participating agencies. Finally, it is useful for potential collaborators to share whatever is known about program effectiveness, in order to learn what each organization believes is important, and to begin to gauge each others' organizational competency.

Staff Training

Training may be useful before, during, and after planning begins. These can include cross-training, in which one agency shares key knowledge and practices in its field. Training also can include multi- organizational educational activities, in which people learn and work together. In this way, staff members develop some shared frameworks and common visions, strengthen cross-agency relationships, and exchange a great deal of information. These experiences also can include joint activities, such as participating in simulated case conferences or problem solving, or engaging in interorganizational planning.

Developing Case-management Models

Many manuals and handbooks are available to provide guidance on how to address many of the most common problems, but the content and structure of the wraparound process itself has to be tailored to the goals, values, and resources of particular communities. (See earlier discussion of case management for more detail.) The group will have to identify how and where case management should occur; who will be the case manager; how the participating organizations will communicate; what types of records will be kept; and how information will be shared. Ideal structural and staff components include facilities that are appropriate to the mission and readily accessible. In some communities, this may involve a central location; in others, a series of entry points and case management locations may work.

Addressing Particular Interorganizational Differences and Developing Compatible Procedures

As noted, many potential participants have big differences in approaches and philosophies, which are some of the most difficult barriers to collaboration. Examples include tensions between child protection approaches and advocacy for battered women (Beeman, Hagemeister, and Edleson, 1999); or between approaches to domestic violence and services for alcohol and other drugs (Bennett, 1995; Bennett and Lawson, 1994). These differences and many others will need to be addressed when developing modified wraparound, in addition to the tensions noted earlier between the role and goals of a corrections system and the roles and goals of other community organizations. The following strategies may be useful in identifying differences and creating stronger collaborations.

Conducting Illustrative Case Conferences

A planning group can conduct some illustrative case conferences, with real or composite cases involving contacts with multiple organizations. These require careful planning, so that each agency can conceptualize how they would proceed with this client, what steps they would follow, with what goals. If each agency in turn does this, compatibilities and differences in approach can be identified. It is helpful to practice "in the abstract" before dealing with real clients or during cordial periods of the planning. It also can be useful to study one or more cases in some detail when tensions are high, or when conflicts erupt over how to proceed, as a way to identify underlying issues, and to remind participants that mutual clients—and not "turf"—are the real bottom line. Obviously, it is important to develop clear procedures for ensuring confidentiality.

Developing "Critical Pathways"

One strategy that a collaborative group might undertake is used most often in health care settings to develop approaches to particular health care problems. Often titled *care management*, or *developing critical pathways*, it entails creating the principles, steps, and sometimes models for how different issues and situations will be handled. Usually a group representing different professions and roles within a health care environment will work on this together, involving others to inform them of current practices and to discuss alternatives. The group often begins with defining a "triage" process, in which the urgency of need is identified and different approaches are defined for different levels of need. The group also can outline expected stages and steps for people with varying levels of urgency or paths into the system. The principles and procedures also can take into account the implications of having other problems in addition to the initial target problem or issue. The group diagrams ideal goals and potential pathways to these goals. Decision rules are developed to determine which routes should be pursued under what circumstances. This can help to identify what information is needed at different steps; who should be involved; what policies need to be written or modified; and what roles are useful to make the system work. Participation in developing options and decisions on rules can greatly facilitate the use of resources from multiple locations as well as on the negotiation of interagency differences.

Step IV: Sustaining and Deepening Systems-level Coordination and Collaboration

Unless one agency is able to provide multiple types of services in a one-stop-shopping model, wraparound approaches that benefit individuals usually require at least some coordination of resources from multiple sectors within a community. Even if the planning process and wraparound design are well done, coordination is a process. A wraparound system will evolve over time and will need to adapt to environmental conditions and client needs. All of the mechanisms described in the prior "getting started" section are helpful periodically once basic models and procedures have been implemented, and two additional mechanisms are also important.

Feedback Mechanisms

Ongoing work is greatly facilitated by ongoing information gathering and evaluation, so that partners can examine how they are doing in the context of concrete information. An ongoing advisory or coordinating group or coalition and periodic consultations with even larger representative groups will be especially useful. At a minimum, to maintain systems-level coordination, designated representatives from the key participating agencies should meet, probably no less often than once a month or quarterly when things stabilize. Ideally, the representatives in this team should have influence in their organization, and preferably the ability to make decisions on behalf of the organization. At this meeting, organizational representatives can share any changes or issues from the perspective of their organization. Communication and coordination problems that line staff and case managers are experiencing can be brought to that meeting for problem solving. The group also can tackle a limited number of future goals and plans, consult with each other about issues of mutual concern, and provide support and reinforcement for collaborative activities.

Maintaining, Expanding, and Implementing Commitment and Vision

Collaborative initiatives most often flounder because of "deep structural issues" (Crowson and Boyd, 1993; 1996) within the participating institutions. To sustain initiatives over the long term, organizations need to change fundamentally the ways they think, behave, and use their resources. To some degree, the culture inside all agencies and institutions participating in the initiative must change. Everyone has to be able to envision their organization and themselves within the larger interconnected system. This requires attention at all levels of the participating organizations. It is not sufficient just to target the highest levels or to work only with direct service providers.

Connections to the larger system should be a part of orientation for new staff and ongoing supervision for continuing staff. Strategies must be found to engage supervisors who are critical of within-agency implementation. Periodic meetings of middle managers from participating organizations can be very useful. Having people involved who occupy multiple roles within participating organizations is important so that they do not undermine others' efforts within the modified wraparound models that emerge.

Ultimately, it is useful to develop some shared symbols, incentives, and rewards, so that a new composite culture is created. At the same time, each system brings a particular expertise, resources, and perspective, which must be tapped, honored, and respected. Too much homogeneity and suppression of conflicts will not take advantage of the multiple resources and perspectives that exist in communities. Moreover, work to improve resources for stigmatized populations inevitably will challenge the status quo. It will be very important to ensure the inclusion of the voices and perspectives of those most impacted—in this case, women in community corrections.

Systems-related Gender and Cultural Issues

In all of this, it is crucial to keep the special needs of women in mind if systems integration/coordination/wraparound services are to assist women positively and effectively within the community corrections system. Neither services integration models nor the service-providing organizations themselves have been particularly sensitive to women's roles and needs. Most do not provide gender-specific or gender-sensitive treatment or services, address the particular barriers that women face, or understand the importance of trauma in the lives of women. Gender and trauma are embedded in the structures of society. They require focused and systematic attention if relevant systems are to learn and rearrange themselves so that they cease to offer fragmented services. This fragmentation frequently retraumatizes women, and fails to address their core needs. Cultural and ethnic competencies are also important (Green, 1999; Lum, 1999).

It will be critical to involve some organizations that explicitly advocate for women's needs and for the perspectives of subgroups of women. This is partly because their knowledge and resources will be needed by women within community corrections (for example women's crisis services, domestic violence advocacy, women's health centers, organizations concerned with women's economic well-being, or with women's rights), but also because they have the most experience in how to work with women in empowering ways. Faith-based organizations, community centers, and professional associations that focus on a particular ethnic group are important to include. In many communities, components of the criminal justice system and organizations that address violence against women (rape, incest, battering) or the issues for particular ethnic groups have developed strong working relationships. In others, relationships are more adversarial, and thus, the collaborations required for modified wraparound may be more difficult to initiate and take more effort to sustain. Collaborative efforts must not be avoided, however, or the modified wraparound that develops will be incomplete at best, and at worst, may contribute to women's problems and disempowerment.

Summary and Conclusion

Many women offenders, not only those in community corrections programs, but also those who are currently incarcerated in local/provincial jails and state and federal prisons, would benefit from a modified wraparound approach. Building on a collaborative, team-based model, modified wraparound approaches address the strengths and needs of women and girls within the context of their relationships and their communities. We have called this "modified wraparound" because the goals of wraparound must be tempered by the need to protect the larger community and enforce the law. Linking community services at both the client and the agency level is vital for modified wraparound to be optimally effective. Unlike traditional methods of incarceration, this holistic, coordinated approach to community corrections enables offender-clients to develop and confirm competencies within the environments in which they will be using them.

Coordination and collaboration are processes, developed and sustained by ongoing efforts. When the focus is on women, wraparound requires a different mix of services, and different approaches than are common for men, especially when the women are heavily burdened and stigmatized. Case management is usually a core component in a wraparound approach. Ideal approaches are empowering, addressing the consequences of trauma, and building a woman's healthy relationships. Fostering linkages with other women is important, as are satisfying activities, and some means of adequate financial support.

Adopting modified wraparound will be challenging in that every participating organization is likely to have to modify some of their practices to become a full contributor. It is not necessary for organizations to lose their autonomy or uniqueness, however. In fact, wraparound works because collaborators bring different knowledge and resources to the combined approaches. But wraparound does require that all "players" have a common understanding of their goals and the problems they are striving to address. They must see themselves as participants within a larger system with a common mission, in which each has a particular role to fulfill. They must have mechanisms for mediating differences in philosophy and approach, and for conducting joint planning at both the client- and the interorganizational level. The process takes effort and skills, but is likely to yield many benefits for women offenders and their children.

Appendix A

Life Areas, Strengths, and Needs of Women in Community Corrections

The following review of the literature identifies many of the areas that are important in an assessment of women offenders in general, although there may be some differences in priorities, depending on the characteristics of women offenders and the resources available in particular communities.

Sexual and physical abuse. Women, in general, more often are victimized by family and intimate violence than men (Bachman and Saltzman, 1995; Covington, this volume). Women in the criminal justice system are more likely than men to report histories of physical and sexual abuse, both in childhood and in adulthood. More than 65 to 70 percent of incarcerated women have suffered physical and sexual abuse, not only as children, but also as adults (American Correctional Association, 1990; Coll et al., 1997; Lord, 1994). Reports from community corrections settings suggest that these figures may be even higher among the proportion of female offenders who also abuse drugs (L. Hiller, Options, Inc., August 7, 1998, personal communication, T. Woodhams, Kalamazoo Community Corrections, August 14, 1998, personal communication; *see also* Watterson, 1996, p. 36; and Chesney-Lind and Covington, this volume). Coping strategies range from running away from home as adolescents (a potential status offense), to psychological dissociation, to dependence on drugs, both legal and illegal (Chesney-Lind and Laidler, 1997; Gilfus, 1992). In a study of 1,272 female pretrial detainees in Cook County Jail (Illinois), 33.5 percent met diagnostic criteria for posttraumatic stress disorder because of rape or some other violent assault (Teplin, Abram, and McClelland, 1996). Routine correctional procedures associated with arrest, searches, and confinement are likely to retraumatize women with such histories (Human Rights Watch, 1996; Kendall, 1993).

Substance use. Although the U.S. Bureau of Justice Statistics indicates that drug sales account for only about 20 percent of the charges for which women are arrested and about 12 percent of the crimes for which they end up in prison, most women who are arrested test positive for at least one drug (Greenfeld and Minor-Harper, 1990; Wellisch, Anglin, and Prendergast, 1993). Moreover, many of the income-generating crimes for which women are arrested—shoplifting, forgery, prostitution, and larceny—are indirectly related to their drug addiction (Anglin and Hser,

1987; English, 1993; Hser, Chou, and Anglin, 1990). One in four women in U.S. jails report that they committed their crime for money to buy drugs, compared to about one in six men (Snell, 1992). Of eighty federal offenders interviewed in a Canadian study, only 35 percent of the women claimed to be drug-free, with 35 percent indicating "substantial" to "severe" levels of drug use (Lightfoot and Lambert, 1992). These patterns of multiple drug use are confirmed by a study in the western United States in which female prisoners indicated that they "are more often and more extensively involved in addicting drugs" than male inmates. The difficulty, researchers report, is not in "eliciting admissions of drug use, but in how to categorize the large number of combinations. Polydrug use, often in combination with alcohol, is the rule, not the exception" (Kassebaum and Chandler, 1994, p. 333). In the previously mentioned Cook County Jail study, 60 percent had a current diagnosable substance abuse disorder (Teplin, et al., 1996). Many continue their illicit drug use while in prison (Phillips and Harm, 1997).

Mental illness. Female offenders are inclined to have elevated rates of depression or other mental illness; and are more likely than men to take drugs as a form of self-medication, rather than for recreation or pleasure (American Correctional Association, 1990; Belknap, 1996). Reported rates of mental illness, including anxiety, depression, and suicidal thoughts are higher among women inmates than among men (Barthwell, et al., 1995; Farabee, 1995; Jordan, Schlenger, Fairbank, Caddell, 1996; Teplin et al., 1996). In the Cook County Jail study, 15 percent of women inmates had a current diagnosable severe mental illness (Teplin, et al., 1996). On the average, in the United States, 19 percent of women inmates have received a diagnosis of schizophrenia, bipolar disorder, or major depression (compared to only 9 percent of men), and 34 percent report posttraumatic stress disorder (Gains Center, 1997). One in ten women offenders in the United States received inpatient psychiatric care before admission to prison; and one in eight take medication for emotional or mental health problems while incarcerated (McQuaide and Ehrenreich, 1998). A Quebec study comparing men and women inmates determined that the women received two to four times more medication than their male counterparts (Hattem, 1991, cited in Kendall, 1993). In many cases, women's and girl's mental health difficulties and substance abuse problems can be attributed to their histories of abuse (Acoca, 1998b).

Poor physical health. Approximately 25 percent of women in U.S. jails and prisons are either pregnant or in the perinatal period; more often than not, their prenatal care is inadequate and they run the risk of bearing underweight, drug-exposed infants (Barry, 1989, 1994). In addition to reproductive concerns, women have a higher incidence of physical health problems in general than men, including "asthma, seizure disorders, hypertension, diabetes, hepatitis, heart disorders, gastrointestinal problems, genitourinary disorders" and sexually transmitted diseases (Bershad, 1985, p. 421; *see also* Acoca, 1998a). The incidence of AIDS and AIDS-related problems among women inmates in state prisons, for example, is 3.3 percent, compared with 2.1 percent for men (Snell, 1992). HIV rates among women prisoners in Canada also appear to be higher than among men (Expert Committee on AIDS and Prison, 1993). Lack of health care coverage in the United States, particularly for those who are not Medicaid-eligible, is a barrier for women entering the criminal justice system, who otherwise would have sought medical attention for their children and themselves. Although Canadian women are covered by provincial health insurance plans, the results of a survey of 170 federally imprisoned women indicate that only one-third of the inmates considered prison health care adequate (Shaw, et al., as cited in the Task Force on Federally Sentenced Women, 1990).

Insufficient job skills and lack of safe/stable housing. Ex-offenders have indicated that safe housing and employment are two of the most important factors in preventing further difficulties (Smith, B., 1994). Few women, particularly single parents, earn enough to support their families unaided (Institute for Women's Policy Research, 1996). Without competitive job skills, women are forced to take low-paying, entry-level jobs in the "pink collar" sector, or, providing they qualify, to depend on public welfare. Employment assistance and transitional housing, in which offenders can receive support while they are accommodating to the workforce, enable women to build up their resources—financial and emotional—before venturing out on their own (Axon, 1989; Carp and Schade, 1992; Morash, Haarr, and Rucker, 1994).

Relationship issues. Women, in general, have been socialized to value connectedness, and are more likely than men to view themselves contextually, in relation to their family and friends (Gilligan, 1982; Miller, 1976; Miller and Stiver, 1997; *see also* Covington, this volume). In some cases, families are supportive, but often they are not. A woman's "significant other," for example, may be abusive or serve as a primary source of drugs. Many of women's crimes are relational: they may have been arrested for their roles as drug "mules" (in other words, low-level couriers) or coerced into other illegal acts—for example prostitution, or theft—by drug-dealing partners (Gilfus, 1992; Huling, 1995; Lord, 1994;

Richie, 1996). Even women's patterns of violence reflect their greater embeddedness in relationships: when women commit violent offenses, they are likely to be directed against someone they know—a partner or a child, for instance—than a stranger (Pollack-Bryne, 1990; 1992; Richie, 1996). Children, on the other hand, can be a primary motivator for a woman to succeed in the community, and women's contextual orientation can be a major strength within a wraparound context.

Complex family and caregiving responsibilities. Two-thirds of federally sentenced women in Canada have children; accordingly, child custody and long-distance parenting are mentioned as overriding concerns (Shaw, et al., 1990). In the United States, nearly 80 percent of women in prison are parents of minor children (compared to 59 percent of the men), and are more likely to have been caring for their children before incarceration (Phillips and Harm, 1997), often as single parents (Kessler, 1994). Ninety-one percent of the children of male prisoners are cared for by the children's mothers, but only 33 percent of the women prisoners' children are taken care of by their male partners; the majority are cared for by maternal grandmothers, relatives, or foster parents (Wald, 1995). In some locations, children who are in foster care two or more years must be put up for adoption (Coughenour, 1995). Women offenders who have children "on the outside," more often than not, maintain those connections whenever possible (Coll, et al., 1997); a commitment to her children is a strong incentive for a mother to get out—and stay out—of the criminal justice system. But without the resources to care for her children on release—safe housing, affordable childcare, and an adequate income, for example—being reunited with her children may prove a disincentive and only add to her burdens.

Differences among women. Women also have particular strengths and needs that tend to differ by age, cultural background, ethnic group identification, sexual orientation, religious affiliation, and spiritual background, economic circumstances, and disability status. Language and cultural differences may divide and isolate certain groups of women within the correctional population (Acoca, 1998a). In addition, American Indians, Aboriginal women, and other women of color have to contend with racism within the larger society, and its consequences within their families (Lujan, 1993; Mann, 1995; Task Force on Federally Sentenced Women, 1990). They may have more difficulty finding an appropriate job or housing in many communities. The meaning of social support and of who is considered to be an appropriate helper varies considerably across cultures. Women also have different responsibilities and goals at different stages of the life cycle that are important to consider. Women with same-gender partners may be uncomfortable in many settings in which heterosexuality is assumed (Faith, 1993; Pollack, 1998; Pollack-Bryne, 1990).

Reentry challenges. When they are released, offenders must attempt to reestablish relationships with their children at the same time that they may be juggling dual responsibilities as mothers and breadwinners and coping with society's judgmental attitudes toward women offenders (Wilson and Anderson, 1997). Many women end up in a Catch-22 situation due to lack of job skills and the added burden of a prison record: In the United States, they cannot apply for financial aid until their children are living with them. On the other hand, they cannot afford adequate housing without government assistance (G. T. Smith, 1994), if, in fact, public housing is even available to applicants with a prison record. In states in the United States that enforce the 1996 felony drug law (which denies Title IV-A cash assistance and food stamp benefits to individuals convicted of drug-related felonies), reintegration can be particularly difficult (Phillips and Harm, 1997). Ex-offenders have indicated that safe housing and employment are two of the most important factors in preventing further difficulties (Smith, B., 1994). Unfortunately, job training/education within the prison system seldom prepares women to earn a family wage (Culliver, 1993; Koons et al., 1997; Morash et al., 1994).

Appendix B

Community Resources for Wraparound for Women in Community Corrections

In this appendix, we discuss programs and groups within the community that may be useful in providing resources and services for women in community corrections. They are organized in the categories listed in the second column of Table 1.2 (page 15). In each category, we discuss factors to consider in assessing available resources and designing wraparound approaches for women. Print resources are available that describe the types of programs and services more fully. Community-based funders or those who assist community members to locate appropriate services (for example information and referral centers) also can help planners in community corrections to identify and select local programs (Challes et al., 1995; Douglas and Philpot, 1998; Kirst-Ashman and Hall, 1997; Salamon, 1999; Schmolling, Youkeles, Burger, 1993; Smith, 1997).

Community Resources for Survivors of Family and Sexual Violence. Some communities have programs that work with victims of crime and/or many forms of trauma. These programs may not be focused specifically on women's issues, although they may be helpful for some women. Some agencies that provide general counseling or family and mental health services may have staff who specialize in working with adults who have experienced physical and sexual abuse as children. Expertise in this area should be assessed in all the types of programs that follow, given the high incidence of such abuse among women offenders.

Most rape crisis centers, domestic violence shelters, and other types of programs that work with survivors of violence (including childhood and adult physical and sexual assault) were started by survivors or their advocates and strongly identify with women. Some of these programs employ a sophisticated feminist analysis of the origins of violence against women. Many rely heavily on volunteers to provide crisis services, although most provide extensive training for these volunteers. In some communities, these programs have developed strong ties with other services and with the criminal justice system, working together on issues such as mandatory arrest ordinances for batterers or emergency sexual assault response teams. Some have begun to work closely with alcohol and other drug and mental health programs for women with multiple problems. Staff in programs concerned with violence against women may be good sources of information about which other community agencies and service providers are sensitive to the effects of trauma in women.

Even when working relationships are cordial, however, staff in most organizations concerned with women are very concerned about the tendency to label women with a diagnosis that may further pathologize and stigmatize them. They fear that other service providers and corrections personnel may not recognize the effects of repeated trauma and the shame and blame that many women internalize as a result. They also may be troubled that women are held to different standards than men and blamed for family and relationship problems (Reed, 1990).

Counseling for batterers or sexual abuse offenders is becoming more common and is often linked with court systems. Those who work with survivors may support the presence of these programs in principle, but be very concerned about whether they are effective, especially when programs for women typically have so few resources. (Bennett and Lawson, 1994)

Alcohol/Other Drug Programs. Although some alcohol and other drug programs recognize the needs and issues of women and have responded with appropriate components or approaches for women, for the most part, this is a field that historically has been concerned with the needs and styles of men (Center for Substance Abuse Treatment, 1994b; Nelson-Zlupko, Kauffman, and Dore, 1995; Reed, 1987). Some still use highly confrontational and confessional modes of treatment that do not "fit" the strengths of women, and, in fact, may undermine them. This is especially the case with women who are survivors of violence, who may have fragile boundaries, who may accept anger and violence as "normal," and who have little sense of how to protect themselves. Women with abusive histories can be further traumatized by intrusive treatment techniques; they need counselors who are experienced in balancing work on trauma issues with attention to compulsive or destructive alcohol or other drug use. Knowledge about the requirements of the criminal justice system is crucial to comply with the legal requirements associated with alcohol and drug treatment mandated by the courts. Health care reform in the United States is reducing the intensity and duration of treatment in many communities, which is a factor to consider as well. It is important to locate programs that are sensitive to women's issues, have strong ties to women's organizations in the community, and are experienced in serving substantial numbers of women. Most provinces in Canada and states in the United States have developed some programs that are women-specific and many provide services for children as well (for example, Amethyst Women's Addiction Centre in Ottawa, Ontario, or Prototypes in Southern California).

Mental Health Systems. Mental health services can be provided in many settings, depending on the severity and chronicity of symptoms. Health care reform in the United States is changing the mix of services available for mental health, often in both the private and the public sectors. Although some communities have special services for clients with a dual diagnosis (those with mental health and alcohol and other drug problems), these services are not widespread and may not be particularly gender sensitive. Many mental health providers do not screen well for alcohol and other drug problems or recognize how they interact with psychological and mental health concerns (Reed and Mowbray, 1999).

With the increasing emphasis on managing serious mental illness in most public mental health systems, there may be fewer resources devoted to the treatment of trauma, especially when the symptoms are similar to those of other disorders. Health care professionals often overlook trauma-related disorders and prescribe medication that disguises the symptoms without directly addressing their origin. Some treatment practices may revictimize trauma survivors. Increasingly, brief therapy, which is not likely to be effective with long-term posttraumatic stress, is being promoted to reduce costs. On the other hand, some communities are developing special units and providing extensive training in the combined problems likely among women in community corrections settings.

Health Care. Modified wraparound clients are likely to have a range of health care needs, from emergency services associated with violence or health crises to comprehensive health screening and ongoing health care. Some hospitals and health clinics are heavily involved in developing specialized community services for particular populations, and others might be encouraged to do so. Funders and those who control access to services may be useful partners in health services planning. Some emergency rooms are screening for multiple problems, but often they only are able to deal with the most immediate problem. One task of modified wraparound may be to develop a continuum of health care that works for stigmatized women with multiple problems. Among other things, it is important that all women be screened for sexually transmitted diseases and receive appropriate gynecological examinations and services.

Survival Services: Emergency Shelter, Food, Financial Assistance. Safe and affordable housing is severely limited in many communities, and, in the United States, overt financial assistance is less available with welfare reform, especially for offenders. Most communities have some organizations focused on the homeless or near-homeless, that distribute food and emergency supplies, either from local or governmental sources.

Programs vary considerably in whether and how they address mental health and alcohol and other drug problems, and in how well they work with other service providers in a community. Organizations in the United States that sponsor county extension workers and district home economists in Canada may be able to provide support for coalition building and community education to address basic nutritional and financial needs.

Education/Vocational/Employment Services. Education and employment services are vital for many women who need to become more economically self-sufficient if they are to address unsatisfactory or dangerous living situations. Economic resources and meaningful work are also important in increasing self-esteem and in reducing the risk of economically motivated criminal activity. Every community should have some vocationally related resources—secondary school equivalency exams, vocational testing services, and various training programs. Welfare-to-work initiatives are increasing these options in many communities in the United States. Some women need job readiness preparation as well—assistance in understanding and being able to comply with the very basic requirements for work. These include dress, punctuality, appropriate workplace behavior, and so forth. Community colleges are good resources in this area, as are many workforce training and support programs. Some communities also have developed innovative programs to assist women in becoming self-employed. Adult education programs and community colleges are likely to offer relevant programs. Some of them emphasize educational readiness, while others teach specific skills. Kindergarten through high school programs also may have useful services for multiple-needs children. General Education Diploma (GED) classes sometimes can be offered on-site at no cost to a program.

Transportation. Communities vary widely in the availability of accessible and affordable transportation. In urban areas, public transportation is more likely, although this varies from city to city. For women with children, even good public transportation is expensive and time-consuming, and may be impossible if a child is sick. In rural areas, transportation is usually a major issue, although some communities have developed innovative systems with van pick-ups or may offer service delivery and even group work by telephone. A mutually supported transportation system can be a useful focus for a community collaborative. Some communities have succeeded in changing bus times or in adding bus routes to facilitate client-offender participation in particular services.

Family Services Agencies. These programs have many different names, but most offer an array of services for families and various family members. These programs may or may not be knowledgeable about women's gender issues, alcohol and other drug problems, offender populations, or the consequences of violence. Conjoint family-systems work can endanger a woman's safety when domestic violence is present, for instance. On the other hand, these programs tend to solicit substantial family input, are often very consumer-centered, and may have much experience with certain types of wraparound for special needs children or multiproblem families. Some agencies may be good sources of parenting education and support.

Child Welfare Systems. In some communities, there has been considerable communitywide work on child maltreatment prevention and alternatives to termination of parental rights. This is especially the case for women who are experiencing violence themselves, or who have mental illness or alcohol and other drug problems. In other communities, advocates for women do not view the child welfare system positively. They may experience the attitudes and practices of child welfare staff as punitive and uninformed about the multiple problems many women face. Any wraparound model must ensure the safety of children; this is a prime consideration in addressing the needs of both mothers and children. Unfortunately, many incarcerated women are forced to rely on alternative—and often less desirable—placements for their children if family members are not available to assume custody.

Childcare. Childcare alternatives are critical if women with children are to participate in wraparound services. Some childcare providers in many communities have developed, with the help of child development specialists, innovative models that offer parenting classes and strong linkages with other services. Unfortunately, not all providers are equally good, and women may not be able to afford quality childcare without assistance. Childcare providers may have little experience in addressing the special needs that children of women in community corrections are likely to have. Some communities offer childcare referral services that also provide education and training for childcare workers. These programs can be invaluable allies in developing some childcare providers with the necessary interest and skills. Finding childcare in order to attend 12-step meetings is a particular problem for many women, although childcare co-located with women's self-help group meetings is an option some communities have developed.

Children's Services. Children, especially those who have been involved in multiple living arrangements with multiple caretakers, also may have multiple health, mental health, behavioral, and relationship issues that should be addressed to prevent future problems. Primary health care includes immunizations, regular check-ups, and other health services. Public health departments in the United States and Canada's provincial health care plans provide at least some of the routine health care that children need. Many communities have child guidance clinics or special educational resources that can be mobilized through good coordination mechanisms. Some families may be eligible for early intervention programs now being sponsored by many schools or child-oriented collaboratives.

Self-help Groups. Most communities have an array of 12-step groups for alcohol and other drug problem-related issues (for example, Alcoholics Anonymous or Narcotics Anonymous) and often for other compulsive behaviors as well (for example, gambling or eating disorders). Some of these groups may be women-only or designed for women as alternatives to the 12-step models. Other types of support and self-help groups also may be available, often run by volunteers or supported by professionals. These may focus on particular health problems, survivor issues, parenting, and numerous other topics.

Self-help groups can be invaluable in helping women to broaden their support networks as well as address a range of problem areas. Of course, finding the means and the time to attend meetings regularly is always a challenge. Under modified wraparound, staff can encourage participation by developing a list of such meetings; by attending open meetings (designed for the public); and by enlisting their leadership in dialog about the group's orientation, composition, and basic practices. Clients further along in the wraparound process can assist new clients to get to meetings. Self-help group members who are not corrections clients may be willing to make presentations about the self-help meeting to a group of clients, or may be enlisted as "sponsors." Women should be encouraged to attend meetings several times before deciding they will not be helpful. Groups often differ substantially in their format and composition, and women may want to "shop around" before deciding which ones they will attend regularly.

Organizations Concerned with Subgroups of Women. Organizations that focus on advocacy, education and/or support for members of particular groups are likely to be found in larger communities with diverse populations. These can revolve around ethnic group issues (for example, Black Women's Business Association or Latinas Health Care Association); issues of sexual orientation (some gay rights, or HIV-focused organizations); particular age groups (senior or adolescent centers); or groups whose members face particular challenges (disability rights and services). Linkages with organizations concerned with poverty or welfare rights or with young mothers may be helpful for some women. Group members can encourage wraparound program staff to attend to issues pertaining to their particular subgroup. Groups also may be able to augment the services that a community corrections program is able to provide.

Consumer Advocacy Services. Consumer advocacy services may focus on a diverse array of topics—for example, mental health systems, welfare rights, legal problems, school issues, and others—depending on the location. Some communities have very few structured advocacy services, while others have well-organized advocacy organizations that provide considerable advice and support. Advocacy services may work with individual clients or serve as partners with the corrections system in identifying and addressing pertinent system issues. Often these groups can raise public awareness about problems and generate support for changing them. Some also can provide individual advocacy for clients, and also may challenge some of the practices and policies within modified wraparound. Although the temptation when challenged is to become defensive, the involvement of strong advocacy groups and advocates helps to keep client perspectives "on the table." Encounters can also lead to innovative collaborations that would not have been considered without this pressure.

Organizations that Provide Leisure Options. Learning to "play," have fun, and engage in satisfying and healthy use of leisure time is an important long-term goal for many women who have been involved with the criminal justice system. Many have had difficult childhoods, and have learned to cope and socialize in connection with alcohol or other drugs. Many have no leisure activities that do not expose them to environments that trigger behaviors that got them into trouble with the criminal justice system. They may not know how to interact with their children in pleasurable activities. Thus, developing options for leisure time is an important component of modified wraparound—one that often is overlooked. Community recreation departments as well as businesses that provide recreational activities (for example, bowling alleys and dance clubs) could be useful partners. A number of options are possible, depending on the mix of resources—alcohol-free nights, special leagues or teams, classes to raise skills and confidence. Engaging in one or more of the arts is especially useful for many women—both in terms of satisfaction and also as an aid for surfacing and expressing long-buried memories and feelings. These include poetry reading and writing, journaling, and participating in drama clubs (which can do community presentations to raise awareness), various forms of arts and crafts, and music or dancing. Food preparation and sewing classes can meet women's needs to be creative and to acquire new skills. Creative individuals, working alone or as part of arts or music associations, may be willing to sponsor or provide some activities, sometimes as an integral component of wraparound services.

Faith-based Organizations. Approaches that include spiritual components can be helpful for many women. Churches, synagogues, mosques, and other faith-based organizations can be invaluable resources for a wraparound program. They may provide tangible resources, supportive services, and activities that engage people in working together. In addition, these organizations are a valuable source of volunteers.

Community Service Clubs. Some service clubs, which often focus on specific service projects, might be willing to develop a special relationship with a modified wraparound program for women. This could include helping with fund raising, sponsoring leisure activities, and providing volunteers for home repair or other needed services.

Appendix C

Linkages for Women Offender-Clients in Community Corrections

Original source: P. A. Fazzone, J. K. Holton, and B. G. Reed, Editors. 1997. Substance Abuse Treatment and Domestic Violence. Treatment Improvement Protocol (TIP) Series 25. Rockville, Maryland: Center for Substance Abuse Treatment, Substance Abuse and Mental Health Administration, DHHS Publication No. (SMA) 97-3163.

Health Care

- Screening for Child Abuse and Neglect (SCAN) teams in hospital emergency rooms
- Health administrators
- Veterans health care systems
- Primary care physicians
- Obstetricians/gynecologists
- Pediatricians
- Nurses and nurses assistants
- Midwives
- Nurse practitioners in adult, obstetrician/gynecologist and pediatric settings
- Physician assistants
- Public health workers
- Dentists
- Emergency medical technicians
- Medical social workers
- Home health services
- Forensic examiners
- Plastic and maxillofacial surgeons
- Physical, speech, and occupational therapists
- Health educators
- Wellness groups
- Women, Infants, and Children (WIC) Supplemental Food Program specialists
- Alternative medicine practitioners
- Health care programs (for example, infant mortality reduction programs, HIV/AIDS programs, and tuberculosis programs)

Justice System

It is important to understand the operations of the court system in your jurisdiction and to identify the judges who oversee:
- Drug cases
- Driving Under the Influence (DUI) and Driving While Intoxicated (DWI) infractions
- Child abuse and child neglect cases
- Domestic violence violations
- Custody cases

It is also useful to identify experts in the following offices and programs:
- Probation and parole
- Legal Aid
- District Attorney's office
- Family courts
- Specialty units of attorneys (for example, for child abuse and neglect and family violence)
- Jails and prisons
- Bail bonds people
- Law enforcement (all levels, for example, sheriffs and police)
- Pretrial release agencies
- Public defenders
- Divorce attorneys
- Pro bono attorneys
- Juvenile detention facilities
- Victim assistance programs
- Appropriate section of the local bar

Education/Schools

- School boards
- School administrators
- Teachers
- Teaching assistants
- Guidance counselors
- Special education specialists (emotional and physical problems)
- Early intervention specialists
- School counselors
- School social workers
- School nurses

- General equivalency diploma (GED) specialists
- Head Start and childcare specialists
- Vocational education and training counselors
- School psychologists
- Physical education teachers and coaches
- Prevention specialists
- Parent-teacher organizations (PTOs)
- English as a Second Language (ESL) classes
- Literacy volunteers

Adult Education

- Night schools
- Community colleges
- Senior day care centers
- Community education programs
- Native American centers
- Hispanic-American centers
- Asian-American centers
- African-American centers

Employers

- Employee Assistance Programs (EAPs)
- Human resource administrators
- Foundation administrators
- On-the-job counselors and social workers

Social Welfare

- Foster care (family foster care, relative foster care, and residential foster care, including group homes)
- Social welfare administrators
- Social workers
- Temporary Assistance to Needy Families
- Welfare-to-work programs
- Food stamp programs
- Women, Infant and Child (WIC)
- Child protective services
- Adult protective services
- Head Start

- Income maintenance
- Childcare programs
- Transportation subsidy programs
- Community-based child abuse and neglect prevention services and programs
- Hotlines
- Family support programs
- Community-based family agencies (provide parent education and specialized counseling for children at low or no cost)
- Family preservation programs
- Homeless shelters
- Maternal and child health programs
- Women's programs

Domestic Violence

- Hotlines
- Shelters
- Childcare workers and child advocates
- Programs for children in violent families
- Transitional living (homeless) experts
- Support groups
- Surveillance systems
- Abuse and assault hotlines
- Rape crisis centers
- Victim services
- Clinicians, public and private (for example, therapists)
- Programs for batterers
- Legal advocacy systems
- Visitation centers for children
- Model programs offering specialized services for sexually abused children
- College-based date rape programs
- Survivor support groups
- Forensic nurse examiners

Mental Health

- Clinicians (such as, psychiatrists, social workers, psychologists, and psychiatric nurses)
- Child guidance centers

- Mental hospitals and institutions
- Community-based activity centers for deinstitutionalized persons
- Group homes and halfway houses
- Hotlines and crisis centers
- Hospital inpatient units
- Hospital outpatient services
- Community mental health centers
- Outpatient day services (community mental health day hospitals)

Substance Abuse

- Residential or inpatient detoxification programs, intensive residential programs, and therapeutic community programs and services (private, public, and combined)
- Outpatient drug-free, methadone maintenance, and partial-day programs and services (private, public and combined)
- Self-help groups (for example, Alcoholics Anonymous, Narcotics Anonymous, Cocaine Anonymous, Rational Recovery)
- Al-Anon (support groups for families of substance abusers)
- Prison- or jail-based substance abuse programs
- DUI and DWI programs
- Veterans Affairs substance abuse treatment programs
- Special programs for adolescents, children, and families
- Special treatment programs for pregnant women or women with dependent children
- Halfway houses, recovery homes
- Alcohol and drug prevention programs
- Community-based coalitions for the prevention of substance abuse
- Employee Assistance Programs (government and private)

Other Community Resources

- Government and regulatory agencies
- Funding sources
- Religious institutions (such as, churches and synagogues)
- Community housing programs
- Recreation programs
- Neighborhood Watch associations
- Immigrant services
- Childcare programs

- Transportation programs for persons with developmental and physical disabilities
- Support groups (for example, grandparents as parents)
- Fathers' responsibility projects
- Nutritional centers, food banks
- Senior citizens' agencies
- Travelers Aid

The authors would like to thank Options, Inc. and Washtenaw County Community Corrections for their help in compiling this chapter.

Endnotes

[1] Kathryn Watterson. 1996. *Women in Prison: Inside the Concrete Womb.* Boston, Massachusetts: Northeastern University Press. 329. [Pronoun changed for a more gender-inclusive metaphor.]

[2] Paul Hahn. 1998. *Emerging Criminal Justice: Three Pillars for a Proactive Justice System.* Thousand Oaks, California: SAGE Publications. 131.

[3] Some pretrial defendants may choose to participate in certain components of a wraparound program—drug treatment, for instance—prior to sentencing. Although they are technically not "offenders," for the purposes of our discussion, we will be using the term "offenders," "clients," or "offender-clients" interchangeably.

[4] Wraparound approaches emerge from a human services model of service delivery, as contrasted with medical and public health models. The human services model assumes that "problems in living" experienced by individuals, families, groups of people, or areas of the environment are best addressed by mobilizing available resources in a planning and problem-solving process that can enhance well-being and teach problem-solving skills. In contrast, in a medical model, individuals are diagnosed and treated, usually by a health professional, to restore them to a prior, more healthy state. A public health model identifies those factors that help to resist or create vulnerability to health problems, and develops a range of strategies for strengthening protective factors and reducing risk factors. These strategies are useful at the individual, family, neighborhood, or larger societal levels (Woodside and McClam, 1998a).

[5] A number of publications are available that can assist personnel outside of human services settings to understand the array of services likely to be available in many communities (for example, Douglas and Philpot, 1998; Salamon, 1999; Schmolling, Youkeles, and Burger, 1993; Woodside and McClam, 1998a)

6 According to some interpretations, "case management" and "wraparound" are interchangeable terms. We agree if case management is conceptualized as a continuum, with "microlevel" service planning and delivery at one end and "macrolevel" systems coordination at the other (Austin, 1990), if all levels are addressed, and if coordinating mechanisms are included.

7 Day reporting centers are uniquely positioned to offer individualized and comprehensive case management, according to the needs of the client. Defined as "an intermediate sanction that blends high levels of control with intensive delivery of services" (National Institute of Justice, 1995, as cited in Curtin, 1996), a day reporting center accommodates both ends of the criminal justice system, from presentenced detainees to prison inmates transitioning back into the community. Services are holistic, "taking into account the way women learn, their relationship styles and life circumstances," and are tailored to individual level of need to be as cost-effective as possible (Zaplin, 1998).

8 Often overlooked in the arrest and imprisonment process are the children of women detainees. Children who witness a parent's arrest may be traumatized by and feel responsible for their mother's powerlessness and violation. Detainees seldom have the opportunity to make arrangements for their children, who, in the absence of alternative caregivers, generally become wards of the state. As a rule, the criminal justice system does not keep accurate records of the numbers and needs of offenders' children, let alone provide services so that both mothers and children can accommodate to the enforced, sometimes violent separation that arrest and incarceration entail (Bloom, 1993; Bloom and Steinhart, 1993; Child Welfare League of America [CWLA], 1997; Johnston, 1995a, 1995b; Kampfner, 1995; Smith, G., 1995).

9 Methods that rely on aggressive confrontation, such as might be employed in an intensive probation boot camp or as part of a therapeutic community approach to drug treatment, have been shown to be counterproductive, if not traumatizing, for most women. In this context, "confrontation," simply means that the offender-client is presented with the potential consequences of her choices, both good and bad.

10 Relapse prevention, a strategy that began in the alcoholism field, now is successfully being adapted for offender populations (Gendreau, 1998). Numerous other parallels between treatment for women who abuse alcohol and other drugs and a wraparound approach for women offenders can be found in the literature on women and substance abuse (*see*, for example, Abbott, 1994; Reed, 1987).

11 Information in the foregoing client-level services section draws heavily upon the Center for Substance Abuse Treatment's *Treatment Improvement Protocols*, #12, #17, #21, #23, #25, and #27. See the reference section for details.

12 For example, the *Women for Sobriety* program designed by Jean Kirkpatrick (1986); Stephanie Covington's *A Woman's Way Through the Twelve Steps* (1994); or Charlotte Kasl's *16 Steps to Empowerment* (1992).

References

Abbott, A. A. 1994. A Feminist Approach to Substance Abuse Treatment and Service Delivery. In M. O. Meltzer, ed. *Women's Health and Social Work: Feminist Perspectives.* New York: Haworth Press. pp. 67-83.

Acoca, L. 1998a. Defusing the Time Bomb: Understanding and Meeting the Growing Health Care Needs of Incarcerated Women in America. *Crime & Delinquency.* 441, 49-69.

————. 1998b. Outside/inside: The Violation of American Girls at Home, on the Streets, and in the Juvenile Justice System. *Crime & Delinquency.* 444, 561-589.

Agranoff, R. 1991. Human Services Integration: Past and Present Challenges in Public Administration. *Public Administration Review.* 516, 533-542.

American Civil Liberties Union. 1996. *All Too Familiar: Sexual Abuse of Women in U.S. State Prisons.* New York: American Civil Liberties Union.

American Correctional Association. 1990. *The Female Offender: What Does the Future Hold?* Lanham, Maryland: American Correctional Association.

Anglin, M. D. and Y. Hser. 1987. Addicted Women and Crime. *Criminology.* 252, 359-397.

Austin, C. D. 1990. Case Management: Myths and Realities. *Families in Society: The Journal of Contemporary Human Services.* (formerly *Social Casework*). 398-405.

————. 1993. Case Management: A Systems Perspective. *Families in Society: The Journal of Contemporary Human Services.* (formerly *Social Casework*). 451-458.

Axon, L. 1989. *Model and Exemplary Programs for Female Inmates.* Ottawa, Ontario: Correctional Service of Canada.

Bachman, R. and L. A. Saltzman. 1995. *Violence Against Women: Estimates from the Redesigned Survey.* Washington, D.C.: United States Department of Justice.

Bailey, D. and K. M. Koney. 1995. Community-based Consortia: One Model for Creation and Development. *Journal of Community Practice.* 21, 21-42.

Barajas, E., Jr. 1996. Moving Toward Community Justice. In *Community Justice: Striving for Safe, Secure, and Just Communities.* Louisville, Colorado: LIS, Inc. 1-7.

Barry, E. M. 1989. Pregnant Prisoners. *Harvard Women's Law Journal.* 12. 126-205.

————. 1994. Women in Prison: Programs and Alternatives. *U.S. Senate Committee on the Judiciary Hearing re. S. 1158, Family Unity Demonstration Act, 29 June 1993.* Washington, D.C.: Government Printing Office. CIS Microfiche J103-20. pp. 28-36.

Barthwell, A. G., P. Bokos, J. Bailey, M. Nisenbaum, J. Devereaux, and E. C. Senay. 1995. Interventions/Wilmer: A Continuum of Care for Substance Abusers in the Criminal Justice System. *Journal of Psychoactive Drugs*. 271, 39-47.

Beeman, S. K., A. K. Hagemeister, and J. L. Edelson. 1999, May. Child Protection and Battered Women's Services: From Conflict to Collaboration. *Child Maltreatment.* 4 (2), 116-126.

Belknap, J. 1996. *The Invisible Woman: Gender, Crime, and Justice.* Contemporary Issues in Crime and Justice Series. Belmont, California: Wadsworth Publishing Company.

Bennett, L. 1995. Substance Abuse and the Domestic Assault of Women. *Social Work.* 40, 760- 771.

Bennett, L. and M. Lawson. 1994. Barriers to Cooperation Between Domestic Violence and Substance Abuse Programs. *Families in Society: The Journal of Contemporary Human Services.* 75, 277-286.

Bershad, L. 1985. Discriminatory Treatment of the Female Offender in the Criminal Justice System. *Boston College Law Review.* 26, 389-438.

Bickman, L. 1996. A Continuum of Care: More Is Not Always Better. *American Psychologist.* 51, 689-701.

Bloom, B. 1993. Incarcerated Mothers and Their Children: Maintaining Family Ties. In American Correctional Association. *Female Offenders: Meeting Needs of a Neglected Population.* Lanham, Maryland: American Correctional Association. pp. 61-68.

Bloom, B., M. Chesney-Lind, and B. Owen. 1994. *Women in California Prisons: Hidden Victims of the War on Drugs.* San Francisco, California: Center on Juvenile and Criminal Justice.

Bloom, B.and D. Steinhart. 1993. *Why Punish the Children? A Reappraisal of the Children of Incarcerated Mothers in America.* San Francisco, California: National Council on Crime and Delinquency.

Brooks, M. K. 1994. Ethical and Legal Issues. Center for Substance Abuse Treatment: *Combining Substance Abuse Treatment with Intermediate Sanctions for Adults in the Criminal Justice System,* Tip 12. Rockville, Maryland: Substance Abuse and Mental Health Services Administration. pp. 71-87.

———. 1995. Confidentiality Issues. Center for Substance Abuse Treatment: *Planning for Alcohol and Other Drug Abuse Treatment for Adults in the Criminal Justice System,* TIP 17. Rockville, Maryland: Substance Abuse and Mental Health Services Administration. pp. 73-89.

Brown, V. B., G. J. Huba, and L. A. Melchior. 1995. Level of Burden: Women with More than One Co-occurring Disorder. *Journal of Psychoactive Drugs.* 274, 339-346.

Carey, K. B. 1998. Treatment Boundaries in the Case Management Relationship: A Behavioral Perspective. *Community Mental Health Journal*. 34(30), 313-317.

Carp, S. and L. Schade. 1992. Tailoring Facility Programming to Suit Female Offenders' Needs. *Corrections Today*. 54(6), 152-159.

Carter, S. A. 1998. Designing without Glass Ceilings: An Examination of Trends and Opportunities in Designing Prisons for Women. In J. B. Morton, ed., *Complex Challenges, Collaborative Solutions: Programming for Girls and Women in Corrections*. Lanham, Maryland: American Correctional Association. pp. 61-122.

Casto, R. M. and M. C. Julia.1994. *Inter-professional Care and Collaborative Practice*. Pacific Grove, California: Brooks/Cole.

Center for Substance Abuse Treatment. 1994a. *Combining Substance Abuse Treatment with Intermediate Sanctions for Adults in the Criminal Justice System*, DHHS Publication No. SMA 94-3004. TIP Series 12. Rockville, Maryland: Substance Abuse and Mental Health Services Administration.

————. 1994b. *Practical Approaches in the Treatment of Women Who Abuse Alcohol and Other Drugs*. DHHS Publication No. SMA 94-3006. Rockville, Maryland: Substance Abuse and Mental Health Services Administration.

————. 1995a. *Combining Alcohol and Other Drug Abuse Treatment with Diversion for Juveniles in the Justice System*. DHHS Publication No. SMA 95-3051, TIP Series 21. Rockville, Maryland: Substance Abuse and Mental Health Services Administration.

————. 1995b. *Planning for Alcohol and Other Drug Abuse Treatment for Adults in the Criminal Justice System*. DHHS Publication No. SMA 95-3039, TIP Series 17. Rockville, Maryland: Substance Abuse and Mental Health Services Administration.

————. 1996. *Treatment Drug Courts: Integrating Substance Abuse Treatment with Legal Case Processing*. DHHS Publication No. SMA 97-3163, TIP Series 23. Rockville, Maryland: Substance Abuse and Mental Health Services Administration.

————. 1997. *Substance Abuse Treatment and Domestic Violence*. DHHS Publication No. SMA 97-3163, TIP Series 25. Rockville, Maryland: Substance Abuse and Mental Health Services Administration.

————. 1998. *Comprehensive Case Management for Substance Abuse Treatment.* DHHS Publication No. SMA 99-3222, TIP Series 27. Rockville, Maryland: Substance Abuse and Mental Health Services Administration.

Challes, D., R. Darton, L. Johnson, M. Stone, and K. Traske. 1995. *Case Management and Health Care of Older People*. University of Kent at Canterbury: PSSRU.

Chesney-Lind, M. and R. Immarigeon. 1995. Alternatives to Women's Incarceration. In K. Gabel, and D. Johnston, eds. *Children of Incarcerated Parents*. New York: Lexington Books. pp. 299-309.

Chesney-Lind, M. and K. J. Laidler. 1997. *The Female Offender: Girls, Women, and Crime*. Thousand Oaks, California: SAGE Publications, Inc.

Child Welfare League of America. 1997. *Parents in Prison; Children in Crisis*. Washington, D.C.: CWLA Press.

Coll, C. G., J. B. Miller, J. P. Fields, and B. Mathews. 1997. The Experiences of Women in Prison: Implications for Services and Prevention. *Women and Therapy*. 204, 11-28.

Coughenour, J. C. 1995. Separate and Unequal: Women in the Federal Criminal Justice System. *Federal Sentencing Reporter: Gender and Sentencing*. 83, 142-144.

Cousins, L. H. 1998. Partnerships for Vitalizing Communities and Neighborhoods: Celebrating a "Return!" *Journal of Sociology and Social Welfare*. XXV1, 61-69.

Covington, S. S. 1994. *A Woman's Way Through the Twelve Steps*. Center City, Minnesota: Hazelden Educational Materials.

Crowson, R. L. and W. L. Boyd. 1993. Coordinated Services for Children: Designing Arks for Storm and Seas Unknown. *American Journal of Education*. 101, 140-179.

———. 1996. Structures and Strategies: Toward an Understanding of Alternative Models for Coordinated Children's Services. In J. G. Cibulka and W. J. Kritek, eds. *Coordination among Schools, Families, and Communities*. Albany, New York: State University of New York Press.

Culliver, C. C. 1993. Females Behind Prison Bars. In C. C. Culliver, ed. *Female Criminality: The State of the Art*, Vol. 22. New York: Garland Publishing Co. pp. 397-411.

Curtin, E. L. 1996. Day Reporting Centers. In American Correctional Association, ed. *Correctional Issues: Community Corrections*. Lanham, Maryland: American Correctional Association. pp. 67-85.

Douglas, A. and T. Philpot. 1998. *Caring and Coping: A Guide to Social Services*. London: Routledge.

Eber, L., and C. M. Nelson. 1997. School-based Wraparound Planning: Integrating Services for Students with Emotional and Behavioral Needs. *American Journal of Orthopsychiatry*. 673, 385-395.

English, K. 1993. Self-reported Crime Rates of Women Prisoners. *Journal of Quantitative Criminology*. 94, 357-382.

Evens, C. C. and A.V. Stoep. 1997. Risk Factors for Juvenile Justice System Referral among Children in a Public Mental Health System. *Journal of Mental Health Administration/Journal of Behavioral Health Services & Research.* 244, 443-455.

Expert Committee on AIDS and Prisons. 1993. *HIV/AIDS in Prisons: A Working Paper of the Expert Committee on AIDS and Prisons.* Ottawa, Ontario: Correctional Service Canada.

Faith, K. 1993. *Unruly Women: The Politics of Confinement and Resistance.* Vancouver, British Columbia: Press Gang Publishing.

Farabee, D. 1995. *Substance Use among Female Inmates Entering the Texas Department of Criminal Justice—Institutional Division: 1994.* Austin, Texas: Texas Commission on Alcohol and Drug Abuse.

Finkelstein, N. 1993. Treatment Programming for Alcohol and Drug-dependent Pregnant Women. *International Journal of the Addictions.* 28, 1275-1309.

Finkelstein, N., C. Kennedy, K. Thomas, and M. Kearns. 1997. *Gender-specific Substance Abuse Treatment.* Rockville, Maryland: National Women's Resource Center, Center for Substance Abuse Prevention.

Fisher, R. J. 1994. Generic Principles for Resolving Inter-group Conflict. *Journal of Social Issues.* 501, 47-66.

Folger, J. P., M. S. Poole, and R. K. Stutman. 1993. Changing Conflict Dynamics. In *Working Through Conflict: Strategies for Relationships, Groups and Organizations.* New York: Harper Collins. pp. 229-253.

GAINS Center. 1997. *Women's Program Compendium: A Comprehensive Guide to Services for Women with Co-occurring Disorders in the Justice System.* Delmar, New York: The GAINS Center/Policy Research, Inc.

Galbraith, S. 1998. *And So I Began to Listen to Their Stories . . . Working with Women in the Criminal Justice System.* Delmar, New York: Policy Research Inc.

Gendreau, P. 1998. What Works in Community Corrections: Promising Approaches in Reducing Criminal Behavior. In B. Auerbach and T. C. Castellano, eds. *Successful Community Sanctions and Services for Special Offenders: Proceedings of the 1994 Conference of the International Community Corrections Association.* Lanham, Maryland: American Correctional Association. pp. 59-74.

General Accounting Office. 1992. *Integrating Human Services: Linking At-risk Families with Services More Successful than System Reform Efforts.* GAO/HRD-92-108. Washington, D.C.: U.S. General Accounting Office.

Gentry, M. E. 1987. Coalition Formation and Processes. *Social Work With Groups.* 103, 39-54.

Gilcrest, A. 1998. A More Excellent Way: Developing Coalitions and Consensus through Informal Networking. *Community Development Journal.* 332, 100-108.

Gilfus, M. E. 1992. From Victims to Survivors to Offenders: Women's Routes of Entry and Immersion into Street Crime. *Women and Criminal Justice.* 41, 63-89.

Gilligan, C. 1982. *In a Different Voice: Psychological Theory and Women's Development.* Cambridge, Massachusetts: Harvard University Press.

Goldstein, S. 1997. Attention-Deficit/Hyperactivity Disorder: Implications for the Criminal Justice System. *Law Enforcement Bulletin.* Washington, D.C.: Federal Bureau of Investigation. pp. 11-16.

Green, J. W. 1999. *Cultural Awareness in the Human Services,* 3rd Ed. Boston: Allyn & Bacon.

Greenfeld, L. A. and S. Minor-Harper. 1990. *Women in Prison.* Special Report. Washington, D.C.: Bureau of Justice Statistics.

Greenwood, P. W. 1995. Strategies for Improving Coordination Between Enforcement and Treatment Efforts in Controlling Illegal Drug Use. *The Journal of Drug Issues.* 251, 73-89.

Grella, C. E. 1996. Background and Overview of Mental Health and Substance Abuse Treatment Systems: Meeting the Needs of Women Who Are Pregnant or Parenting. *Journal of Psychoactive Drugs.* 28, 319-343.

————. 1997. Sources for Prenatal Women with Substance Abuse and Mental Health Disorders: The Unmet Need. *Journal of Psychoactive Drugs.* 29, 67-78.

Hagan, T., L. P. Finnegan, and L. Nelson-Zlupko. 1994. Impediments to Comprehensive Treatment Models for Substance-dependent Women: Treatment and Research Questions. *Journal of Psychoactive Drugs.* 262, 163-171.

Hahn, P. 1998. *Emerging Criminal Justice: Three Pillars for a Proactive Justice System.* Thousand Oaks, California: SAGE Publications, Inc.

Hardcastle, D. A., S. Wenocur, and P. R. Powers. 1997. *Community Practice: Theories and Skills for Social Workers.* New York: Oxford University Press.

Hartman, A. 1978. Diagrammatic Assessment of Family Relationships. *Social Casework.* 163.

Hartman, A. and J. Laird. 1983. *Family-centered Social Work Practice.* New York: The Free Press.

Hattem, T. 1991. Vivre Avec Ses Peines: Les Fondements et Les Enjeux De'lusage de Médicaments Psychotropes Saisis À Travers L'expèrience de Femmes Condamnées À L'emprisonnement À Perpétuité. *Criminologie*. 241, 49-61.

Herman, J. 1992. *Trauma and Recovery.* New York: HarperCollins.

Hoge, M. A., and R. A. Howenstine. 1997. Organizational Development Strategies for Integrating Mental Health Services. *Community Mental Health Journal*. 332, 175-187.

Hser, Y. I., C. P. Chou, and M. D. Anglin. 1990. The Criminality of Female Narcotics Addicts: A Causal Modeling Approach. *Journal of Quantitative Criminology*. 62, 207-228.

Huling, T. 1995. Women Drug Couriers. *Criminal Justice*. 94, 15-62.

Immarigeon, R. and M. Chesney-Lind. 1993. Women's Prisons: Overcrowded and Overused. In R. Muraskin and T. Alleman, eds. *It's a Crime: Women and Justice*. Englewood Cliffs, New Jersey: Regents/Prentice Hall. pp. 245-257.

Institute for Women's Policy Research. 1996. *The Status of Women in the States*. Washington, D.C.: Institute for Women's Policy Research

Johnson, A. K. and A. R. Castengera. 1994. A Model for Meeting the Complex Needs of Homeless Persons. *Journal of Community Practice*. 13, 29-47.

Johnson, F., T. Strader, M. Berbaum, D. Bryant, G. Bucholtz, D. Collins, and T. Noe. 1996. Reducing Alcohol and Other Drug Use by Strengthening Community, Family, and Youth Resiliency: an Evaluation of the Creating Lasting Connections Program. *Journal of Adolescent Research*. 11, 12-35.

Johnston, D. 1995a. The Care and Placement of Prisoners' Children. In K. Gabel and D. Johnston, eds. *Children of Incarcerated Parents*. New York: Lexington Books. pp. 103-123.

―――. 1995b. Effects of Parental Incarceration. In K. Gabel and D. Johnston, eds. *Children of Incarcerated Parents*. New York: Lexington Books. pp. 59-88.

Jordan, B. K., W. E. Schlenger, J. A. Fairbank, and J. M. Caddell. 1996. Prevalence of Psychiatric Disorders among Incarcerated Women, II: Convicted felons entering prison. *Archives of General Psychiatry*. 53, 513-519.

Joseph, M. and R. Ogletree. 1996. Community Organizing and Comprehensive Community Initiatives. In Core Issues in Comprehensive Community-building Initiatives. Chicago: Chapin Hall Center for Children at the University of Chicago. pp. 71-79.

Kampfner, C. J. 1995. Post-traumatic Stress Reactions in Children of Imprisoned Mothers. In K. Gabel and D. Johnston, eds. *Children of Incarcerated Parents*. New York: Lexington Books. pp. 89-100.

Kasl, C. D. 1992. *Many Roads, One Journey: Moving Beyond the 12 Steps*. New York: HarperCollins.

Kassebaum, G., and S. M. Chandler. 1994. Polydrug Use and Self Control among Men and Women in Prisons. *Journal of Drug Education*. 244, 333-350.

Kendall, K. 1993. *Literature Review of Therapeutic Services for Women in Prison: Companion Volume I to Program Evaluation of Therapeutic Services at the Prison for Women*. Ottawa, Ontario: Correctional Service of Canada.

Kessler, G. 1994. Women in Prison: Programs and Alternatives. *U.S. Senate Committee on the Judiciary Hearing re. S. 1158, Family Unity Demonstration Act, 29 June 1993*, Washington, D.C.: Government Printing Office. CIS Microfiche J103-20. pp. 48-54.

Kirkpatrick, J. 1986. *Goodbye Hangovers, Hello Life: Self-help for Women*. New York: Atheneum.

Kirst-Ashman, K. K. and G. H. Hull, Jr. 1997. Community Resource Systems. In K. K. Kirst-Ashman, ed. *Generalist Practice with Organizations and Communities*. Chicago: Nelson- Hall, Inc. pp. 219.

Kline, J., M. Harris, R. R. Bebout, and R. E. Drake. 1991. Contrasting Integrated and Linkage Models of Treatment for Homeless, Dually Diagnosed Adults. In K. Minkoff and R. E. Drake, eds. *Dual Diagnosis of Major Mental Illness and Substance Abuse Disorders: New Directions in Mental Health Services*. Vol. 50. pp. 95-106.

Konrad, E. L. 1996. A Multidimensional Framework for Conceptualizing Human Services Integration Initiatives. In K. Marquart, and E. Konrad, eds. *Evaluating Initiatives to Integrate Human Services* Vol. 69. New York: Jossey-Bass Publishers. pp. 5-19.

Koons, B. A., J. D. Burrow, M. Morash, and T. Bynum. 1997. Expert and Offender Perceptions of Program Elements Linked to Successful Outcomes for Incarcerated Women. *Crime and Delinquency*. 434, 512-532.

Kriteck, W. J. 1996. Introduction. J. G. Cibulka, and W. J. Kritek, eds. *Coordination among Schools, Families and Communities: Prospects for Educational Reform*. Albany, New York: State University of New York Press. pp ix-xxv.

Kumpfer, K. L. 1997. What Works in Prevention of Drug Abuse: Individual, School, and Family Approaches. *Center for Substance Abuse Prevention's Secretary's Youth Substance Abuse Initiative: Resource Papers*. Rockville, Maryland: Substance Abuse and Mental Health Services Administration.

Lauren, R. J. 1997. *Positive Approaches to Corrections: Research, Policy, and Practice*. Lanham, Maryland: American Correctional Association.

Lebowitz, L., M. R. Harvey, and J. L. Herman. 1993. A Stage-by-dimension Model of Recovery from Sexual Trauma. *Journal of Interpersonal Violence*. 8, 378-391.

Leukefeld, C. G. 1990. National Health Line: Case Management: A Social Work Tradition. *Health and Social Work*. 15, 175-179.

Lightfoot, L. and L. Lambert. 1992. *Substance Abuse Treatment Needs of Federally Sentenced Women, Technical Report #2*. Ottawa, Ontario: Correctional Service Canada.

Lord, E. A. 1994. Women in Prison: Programs and Alternatives. *U.S. Senate Committee on the Judiciary Hearing re. S. 1158, Family Unity Demonstration Act, 29 June 1993*, Washington, D.C.: Government Printing Office. CIS Microfiche J103-20. pp. 58-66.

Lujan, C. C. 1993. American Indians: Criminal Justice and Stereotyping. American Correctional Association, ed. *Understanding Cultural Diversity*. Lanham, Maryland: American Correctional Association. pp. 56-71.

Lum, D. 1999. *Culturally Competent Practice: A Framework for Growth and Action*. Pacific Grove, California: Brooks/Cole.

Mackelprang, R. W. and R. O. Salsgiver. 1999. *Disability: A Diversity Model Approach in Human Services Practice*. Pacific Grove, California: Brooks/Cole Publishing.

Malysiak, R. 1997. Exploring the Theory and Paradigm Base for Wraparound. *Journal of Child and Family Studies*. 64, 399-408.

———. 1998. Deciphering the Tower of Babel: Examining the Theory Base for Wraparound Fidelity. *Journal of Child and Family Studies*. 71, 11-25.

Mann, C. R. 1995. Women of Color and the Criminal Justice System. In B. R. Price and N. J. Sokoloff, eds. *The Criminal Justice System and Women: Offenders, Victims and Workers*, 2d ed. New York: McGraw-Hill, Inc. pp. 118-135.

Marquart, J. M. and E. L. Konrad. 1996. *Evaluating Initiatives to Integrate Human Services: New Directions for Evaluation*. San Francisco: Jossey-Bass.

McQuaide, S. and J. H. Ehrenreich. 1998. Women in Prison: Approaches to Understanding the Lives of a Forgotten Population. *Affilia*. 132, 233-246.

Miller, J. B. 1976. *Toward a New Psychology of Women*. Boston: Beacon Press.

Miller, J. B. and I. P Stiver. 1997. *The Healing Connection: How Women Form Relationships in Therapy and in Life*. Boston: Beacon Press.

Minkler, M. 1997. *Community Organizing and Community Building for Health*. New Brunswick, New Jersey: Rutgers University Press.

Minkoff, K. 1994. Models for Addiction Treatment in Psychiatric Populations. *Psychiatric Annals*. 24, 412-417.

Mizrahi, T. and B. Rosenthal.1992. Managing Dynamic Tensions in Social Change Coalitions. In T. Mizrahi and T. Morrison, eds. *Community Organization and Social Administrations: Advances, Trends, and Emerging Principles.* New York: The Haworth Press, Inc. pp. 1- 33.

Moore, S. 1992. Case Management and the Integration of Services: How Service Delivery Systems Shape Case Management. *Social Work.* 5, 418-423.

Morash, M., R. N. Haarr, and L. Rucker. 1994. A Comparison of Programming for Women and Men in U.S. Prisons in the 1980s. *Crime and Delinquency.* 402, 197-221.

Morrissey, J. P., M. Calloway, M. C. Johnsen, and M. D. Ullman. 1997. Service System Performance and Integration: A Baseline Profile of the ACCESS Demonstration Sites. *Psychiatric Services.* 483, 374-380.

Morrissey, J. P., H. Steadman, H. Kilburn, and M. Lindsey. 1984. The Effectiveness of Jail Mental Health Programs: An Interorganizational Assessment. *Criminal Justice and Behavior.* 11, 235-256.

Morton, J. B. 1998. Programming for Women Offenders. In J. B. Morton, ed. *Complex Challenges, Collaborative Solutions: Programming for Adult and Juvenile Female Offenders.* Lanham, Maryland: American Correctional Association. pp. 1-17.

Mulroy, E. A. and S. Say. 1998. Motivation and Reward in Nonprofit Interorganizational Collaboration in Low-income Neighborhoods. *Administration in Social Work.* 224, 1-17.

Muraskin, R. 1993. Disparate Treatment in Correctional Facilities. In R. Muraskin and T. Alleman, eds. *It's a Crime: Women and Justice.* Englewood Cliffs, New Jersey: Regents/Prentice Hall. pp. 1-33.

National Assembly of National Voluntary Health and Social Welfare Organizations. 1991. *The Community Collaboration Manual.* Washington, D.C.: National Assembly of National Voluntary Health and Social Welfare Organizations.

National Center for Services Integration. 1994. *Providing Comprehensive Integrated Services for Children and Families: Why Is it So Hard?* NCSI News.

National Institute on Drug Abuse. 1997. *Drug Abuse Prevention: What Works.* Rockville, Maryland: National Institute on Drug Abuse.

National Institute of Justice. 1995. *Issues and Practices: Day Reporting Centers.* Washington, D.C.: National Institute of Justice.

Nelson-Zlupko, L., E. Kauffman, and M. M. Dore. 1995. Gender Differences in Drug Addiction and Treatment: Implications for Social Work Intervention with Substance-abusing Women. *Social Work.* 401, 45-54.

Nidorf, B. J. 1996. Probation and Parole Officers: Police Officers or Social Workers? In American Correctional Association, ed. *Correctional Issues: Community Corrections.* Lanham, Maryland: American Correctional Association. pp. 41-48.

Northey, W. F., Jr., V. Primer, and L. Christensen. 1997. Promoting Justice in the Delivery of Services to Juvenile Delinquents: The Ecosystemic Natural Wrap-around Model. *Child and Adolescent Social Work Journal.* 141, 5-22.

Phillips, S. D. and N. J. Harm. 1997. Women Prisoners: A Contextual Framework. *Women and Therapy.* 204, 1-9.

Pollack-Byrne, J. M. 1992. Women in Prison: Why Are Their Numbers Increasing? In P. J. Benekos and A. V. Merlo, eds. *Corrections: Dilemmas and Directions.* Cincinnati, Ohio: Anderson Publishing Co. pp. 79-95.

Pollack, J. M. 1990. *Women, Prison and Crime.* Contemporary Issues in Crime and Justice Series. Pacific Grove, California: Brooks/Cole Publishing Co.

————. 1998. *Counseling Women in Prison.* Thousand Oaks, California: SAGE Publications.

Raiff, N. R. and B. K. Shore. 1993. *Advanced Case Management.* Thousand Oaks, California: SAGE Publications.

Randolph, F., M. Blasinsky, W. Leginski, L. B. Parker, and H. Goldman. 1997. Creating Integrated Services Systems for Homeless Persons with Mental Illness: The ACCESS Program. *Psychiatric Services.* 48, 369-373.

Rapp, C. A. 1998. The Active Ingredients of Effective Case Management: A Research Synthesis. *Community Mental Health Journal.* 344, 363-380.

Rapp, R. C., C. W. Kelliher, J. H. Fisher, and F. J. Hall. 1994. Strengths-based Model of Case Management: A Role in Addressing Denial in Substance Abuse Treatment. *Journal of Case Management.* 34, 139-144.

Rappaport, J. 1981. In Praise of Paradox: A Social Policy of Empowerment over Prevention. *American Journal of Community Psychology.* 9, 1-25.

Reed, B. G. 1987. Developing Women-sensitive Drug Dependence Treatment Services: Why So Difficult? *Journal of Psychoactive Drugs.* 192, 151-164.

————. 1990. Linkages: Battering, Sexual Assault, Incest, Child Sexual Abuse, Teen Pregnancy, Dropping out of School and the Alcohol and Drug Connection. In P. Roth, ed. *Alcohol and Drugs Are Women's Issues.* Metuchen, New Jersey: Women's Action Alliance and The Scarecrow Press, Inc. pp. 130-149.

Reed, B. G., and C. T. Mowbray. 1999. Mental Illness and Substance Abuse: Implications for Women's Health and Health Care Access. *Journal of the Medical Women's Association.* 542, 71-78.

Richie, B. 1996. *Compelled to Crime: The Gender Entrapment of Battered Black Women*. New York: Routledge.

Ridgely, M. S. and L. Dixon. 1993. *Integrating Mental Health and Substance Abuse Services for Homeless People with Co-occurring Mental and Substance Abuse Disorders.* Rockville, Maryland: Substance Abuse and Mental Health Services Administration.

Ridgely, M. S. and J. M. Jerrell. 1996. Analysis of Three Interventions for Substance Abuse Treatment of Severely Mentally Ill People. *Community Mental Health Journal.* 32, 561- 572.

Ridgely, M. S., J. P. Morrissey, R. I. Paulson, H. H. Goldman, and M. O. Calloway. 1996. Characteristics and Activities of Case Manager in the RWJ Foundation Program on Chronic Mental Illness. *Psychiatric Services.* 47, 737-743.

Rog, D. J., C. S. Holupka, K. L. McCombs-Thornton, M. C. Brito, and R. Hambrick. 1997. Case Management in Practice: Lessons from the Evaluation of the RWJ/HUD Homeless Families Program. *Journal of Prevention and Intervention in the Community.* 152, 67-82.

Rothman, J. 1991. A Model of Case Management: Toward Empirically Based Practice. *Social Work.* 364, 520-522.

Rounds-Bryant, J. L., P. L Kristiansen, J. A. Fairbank, and R. L. Hubbard. 1998. Substance Use, Mental Disorders, Abuse, and Crime: Gender Comparisons among a National Sample of Adolescent Drug Treatment Clients. *Journal of Child & Adolescent Substance Abuse.* 74, 19-34.

Rubin, J. Z. 1994. Models of Conflict Management. *Journal of Social Issues.* 501, 33-45.

Salamon, L. M. 1999. *America's Non-profit Sector: A Primer*, 2d Ed. New York: Foundation Center.

Sarri, R. C. and C. M. Sarri, 1992. Organizational and Community Change Through Participatory Action Research. *Administration in Social Work.* 16(3/4), 99-122.

Schmidt-Posner, J., and J. M. Jerrell. 1998. Qualitative Analysis of Three Case Management Programs. *Community Mental Health Journal.* 344, 381-392.

Schmolling, P. Jr., M. B. Youkeles, and W. R. Burger. 1993. *Human Services in Contemporary American*, 3d Ed. Pacific Grove, California: Brooks/Cole Publishing.

Shaw, M., K. Rodgers, K. Blanchette, J. Hattem, T. Seto, L. Thomas, and L. Tamarack. 1990. *Survey of Federally Sentenced Women: Report to the Task Force on Federally Sentenced Women on the Prison Survey #1991-4*. Ottawa: Ministry of the Solicitor General.

Singer, M. I., J. Bussey, L. Y. Song, and L. Lunghofer. 1995. The Psychosocial Issues of Women Serving Time in Jail. *Social Work.* 401, 103-113.

Smith, B. 1994. Women in Prison: Programs and Alternatives. *U.S. Senate Committee on the Judiciary Hearing re. S. 1158, Family Unity Demonstration Act, 29 June 1993.* Washington, D.C.: Government Printing Office. CIS Microfiche J103-20. pp. 6-15.

Smith, D. H. 1997. Grassroots Associations Are Important: Some Theory and a Review of the Literature. *Nonprofit and Voluntary Sector Quarterly.* 263, 269-306.

Smith, G. T. 1994. Women in Prison: Programs and Alternatives. *U.S. Senate Committee on the Judiciary Hearing re. S. 1158, Family Unity Demonstration Act, 29 June 1993.* Washington, D.C.: Government Printing Office. CIS Microfiche J103-20. pp. 38-42.

————. 1995. Practical Considerations Regarding Termination of Incarcerated Parents' Rights. In K. Gabel and D. Johnston, eds. *Children of Incarcerated Parents.* New York: Lexington Books. pp. 59-88.

Snell, T. L. 1992. *Women in Jail 1989.* Special Report. Washington, D.C.: Bureau of Justice Statistics.

Sullivan, J. M. and K. Evans.1994. Integrated Treatment for the Survivor of Childhood Trauma Who Is Chemically Dependent. *Journal of Psychoactive Drugs.* 264, 347-369.

Swartz, J. 1991. *Implications of the Drug Use Forecasting Data for TASC Programs: Female Arrestees.* Washington, D.C.: Bureau of Justice Assistance.

Synergos Institute. 1992. *Holding Together: Collaborations and Partnership in the Real World.* New York: Synergos Institute.

Talbott, J. A. 1995. Evaluating the Johnson Foundation Program on Chronic Mental Illness: An Interview with Harold Goldman. *Psychiatric Services.* 465, 1.

Task Force on Federally Sentenced Women. 1990. *Creating Choices: The Task Force Report of the Task Force on Federally Sentenced Women.* Ottawa, Ontario: Correctional Service of Canada.

Teplin, L. A., K. M. Abram, and G. M. McClelland. 1996. Prevalence of Psychiatric Disorders among Incarcerated Women, In Pretrial Jail Detainees. *Archives of General Psychiatry.* 53, 505-512.

Vaill, P. B. 1991. *Managing as a Performing Art: New Ideas for a World of Chaotic Change.* San Francisco: Jossey-Bass.

Veysey, B. M., K. De Cou, and L. Prescott, L. 1998. Effective Management of Female Jail Detainees with Histories of Physical and Sexual Abuse. *American Jails.* 12(2), 50.

Wald, P. M. 1995. "What About the Kids?" Parenting Issues in Sentencing. *Federal Sentencing Reporter: Gender and Sentencing.* 83, 137-141.

Washtenaw County Community Corrections. 1998. WCCCAB Day Reporting Center Policies and Procedures. Washtenaw County/City of Ann Arbor Community Corrections.

Watkins, K. E., A. Shaner, and G. Sullivan. 1999, April. The Role of Gender in Engaging the Dually Diagnosed in Treatment. *Community Mental Health Journal.* 35(2), 115-126.

Watterson, K. 1996. *Women in Prison: Inside the Concrete Womb*, rev. ed. Boston: Northeastern University Press.

Weil, M. 1985. Key Components in Providing Efficient and Effective Services. In M. Weil, J. M. Karls, and Associates, eds. *Case Management in Human Service Practice: A Systematic Approach to Mobilizing Resources for Clients.* San Francisco: Jossey-Bass Inc. pp. 29-71.

Weil, M. and J. M. Karls. 1985. Historical Origins and Recent Developments. In M. Weil, J. M. Karls, and Associates, eds. *Case Management in Human Service Practice: A Systematic Approach to Mobilizing Resources for Clients.* San Francisco: Jossey-Bass Inc. pp. 1-28.

Wellisch, J., M. D. Anglin, and M. L. Prendergast. 1993. Numbers and Characteristics of Drug-using Women in the Criminal Justice System: Implications for Treatment. *The Journal of Drug Issues.* 231, 7-30.

Wellisch, J., M. L. Prendergast, and M.D. Anglin. 1993. Criminal Justice and Drug Treatment Systems Linkage: Federal Promotion of Inter-agency Collaboration in the 1970s. *Contemporary Drug Problems.* 204, 611-650.

Williams, J. and M. Schwartz. 1998. Treatment Boundaries in the Case Management Relationship: A Clinical Case and Discussion. *Community Mental Health Journal.* 343, 299-311.

Wilson, M. K. and S. C. Anderson.1997. Empowering Female Offenders: Removing Barriers to Community-based Practice. *Affilia.* 123, 342-358.

Woodside, M. and T. McClam. 1998a. *An Introduction to Human Services: Models of Service Delivery*, 3rd ed. Pacific Grove, California: Brooks/Cole Publishing Co.

———. 1998b. *Generalist Case Management: A Method of Human Service Delivery.* Pacific Grove, California: Brooks/Cole Publishing Co.

Zaplin, R. T. 1998. A Systems Approach to the Design and Implementation of a Day Program for Women Offenders. In J. B. Morton, ed. *Complex Challenges: Collaborative Solutions, Programs for Adult and Juvenile Female Offenders.* Lanham, Maryland: American Correctional Association. pp. 129-140.

Beyond Recidivism: Perspectives on Evaluation of Programs for Female Offenders in Community Corrections

2

Barbara Bloom, Ph.D.
Assistant Professor
Administration of Justice Department
San Jose State University
San Jose, California

Introduction

The increasing numbers of women and girls involved in the adult criminal and juvenile justice systems and the paucity of programs and services that are geared toward their needs has prompted criminal justice professionals to examine their sanctioning and supervision processes in terms of gender. Although there is more extensive data regarding the characteristics of women in prisons and jails and limited data pertaining to girls in juvenile correctional facilities, there is far less information on female offenders in community correctional settings.

The neglect of women and girls in criminal and juvenile justice research has been justified on the grounds that they account for only a small fraction of arrests and commit fewer crimes than males. This justi-fication ignores the fact that women and girls who do enter the justice system, while fewer in number and less violent than their male counter-parts, often have significant program needs. In focusing on the overwhelming number of males in the criminal and juvenile justice sys-tems, programs, policies, and services often fail to develop a diversity of options for dealing with the gender and culturally specific problems of female offenders enmeshed in the system.

Additionally, while research indicates that community-based pro-grams may be successful in dealing with the problems of female delinquents, few programs target the specific needs of girls and young women. There have been few comprehensive research efforts to collect data on the characteristics of adolescent females in order to develop bet-ter program responses for this underserved population.

Furthermore, little is known about the characteristics of programs that serve women and girls or about the criteria or elements that make for effective programs and promote successful client outcomes. This lack of attention makes it critically important to document program characteris-tics that are related to positive outcomes for this population so promising program models can be presented to the criminal justice community.

Many criminal and juvenile justice professionals lack familiarity with criteria for female-specific programs and interventions. Recommendations from academics and program practitioners reflect an understanding of gender differences and needs, but they do not necessarily convey the "how to" elements instrumental to effective program development and evalua-tion (Bloom, 1997; Kempf-Leonard, 1998; Koons, Burrow, Morash, and Bynum, 1997). Thus, it is often difficult to understand how effective female-specific services differ from effective services in general. Rigorous evaluations that measure the effectiveness of gender-specific interven-tions in terms of client outcomes are necessary to move away from impressionistic data and towards empirically based documentation of pro-gram effectiveness.

This paper examines emerging perspectives regarding evaluation of programs for female offenders in correctional settings and addresses the following:

- Review of the literature: effective correctional interventions

- Rationale for gender-specific programming and evaluation

- Theoretical perspectives underlying gender-specific programming and evaluation

- Definition, principles, and criteria for gender-specific programs

- Effective programs and interventions

- Assessment of gender-specificity in programming

- Measurement of effectiveness: evaluation design

- Research methodology

Review of the Literature: Effective Correctional Interventions

The literature regarding gender-specific outcome evaluation is sparse and, for community corrections, almost nonexistent. Most of the meta-analyses that have been conducted over the past several decades have dealt primarily with programs and interventions serving males under criminal justice supervision. Studies often fail to include females, or do not disaggregate samples to examine the results by gender.

Since the early 1980s, researchers have documented evidence supporting the positive impact of correctional interventions (Andrews and Kiessling, 1980; Andrews, Bonta, and Hoge, 1990; Andrews, Zinger et al., 1990; Cullen and Gendreau, 1989; Gendreau and Ross, 1987; Palmer, 1996; Bonta, Pang and Wallace-Capretta, 1995; Andrews, 1994; Gendreau, 1996). This evidence has included individual program evaluations and meta-analyses of program evaluations. Gendreau (1996) developed principles of effective correctional intervention after gathering information from three sources: narrative reviews of the offender treatment literature, meta-analytic reviews of the treatment literature, and individual studies. Gendreau describes these principles as follows:

- Services should be intensive and behavioral in nature.

- Behavioral programs should address the criminogenic needs of high-risk offenders.

- Characteristics of offenders, therapists, and programs should be matched (responsivity).

- Program contingencies and behavioral strategies should be enforced in a firm but fair manner.

- Therapists should relate to offenders in interpersonally sensitive and constructive ways.

- Program structure should promote prosocial activities.

- Relapse prevention strategies should be provided in the community to the extent possible.

- Whenever possible, a high level of advocacy and service brokerage should be attempted whenever community agencies offer appropriate services (pp. 120-125).

Risk and Needs Assessment

Andrews, Bonta, and Hoge (1990) emphasized the importance of assessing offender needs to guide service delivery and to manage offender risk. They distinguished between criminogenic and noncriminogenic needs of offenders. They maintained that not all offender needs are related to their risk to reoffend. Therefore, only criminogenic needs should form the major goals of offender treatment programs. High risk factors include antisocial attitudes, style of thinking and behavior, peer associations, chemical dependency, and self-control issues. It is argued that treatment is more effective with high-risk offenders (Andrews, Bonta et al., 1995; Gendreau, 1996). "[T]o evaluate whether certain offender needs are criminogenic is to assess the predictive validity of these needs. If they do not demonstrate predictive validity, then they are unlikely to be criminogenic" (Bonta et al., 1995, p. 283). It is also argued that more intensive programming should be targeted to higher-risk clients.

While there appears to be some general agreement on the findings of the treatment literature as to what constitutes effective correctional intervention, the question of whether these findings can be generalized to women and girls under correctional supervision is still unanswered. Females represent only a small portion of the total offender population; most studies of program effectiveness involve male populations or coed programs that serve few females. In their review of the literature, Ross and Fabiano (1986) state that researchers generally ignore evaluations of female offender programs. They claim that "the vast majority of the information on the treatment of female offenders is hidden within reports of the treatment of male offenders" (p.3). The few existing evaluations of female offender programs are poorly designed and tend to disregard diversity among women offenders.

Compared to male offenders, female offenders have received little attention in the area of prediction of the risk for reoffending. In fact, there are only a few prediction studies on adult female offenders (Bonta et al., 1995; Coulson, Ilacqua, Nutbrown, Guilekes, and Cudjoe, 1996). For example, in a meta-analysis of the risk prediction literature, Gendreau, Andrews, Goggin, and Chanteloupe (1992) identified nearly 400 studies on the prediction of criminal behavior that produced 1,734 individual correlations between a predictor and outcome. Only 46 of the correlations were based on female offender samples.

The prediction research asserts that criminal behavior can be reliably predicted when the predictions are based on objective empirically based assessment instruments (Andrews and Bonta, 1994; Bonta et al., 1995). The risk scales that are used have been developed and standardized primarily with male offenders. Risk instruments such as the Salient Factor Score (SFS), the Wisconsin Risk-Need Classification instrument, the Level of Service Inventory-Revised (LSI-R), and the Statistical Information on Recidivism scale (SIR) are often applied to female offenders with little validation research (Bonta et al., 1995).

There is a growing body of literature that suggests that current instruments of risk assessment are not necessarily valid for female offender populations. For example, the SIR developed for the Correctional Service of Canada was not effective when used with samples of female and Native offenders (Nuffield, 1989). As with other special populations, certain variables have been found to be predictive of parole success while more traditional traits have not. The few studies that examined prediction of recidivism in female offenders have not consistently replicated similar predictors found for male recidivism (Bonta et al., 1995; Coulson, Ilacqua, Nutbrown, Guliekes, and Cudjoe, 1996). Bonta et al. (1995) found that variables usually predictive of recidivism in male populations (for example, history of juvenile delinquency, weapon-involved offense, and alcohol and drug abuse) did not predict recidivism in female populations. If prediction instruments are to be validated with female offender populations, they should include variables that are reflected in the contemporary research literature on women and crime.

Studies of Promising Programs for Female Offenders

Although there is little evaluation research documenting effective programs for women offenders, there have been a few studies that identify promising practices or strategies. In a recent study of promising correctional programs for women offenders, Koons, Burrow, Morash, and Bynum (1997) identified sixty-seven effective programs for women offenders. Of those, there were specific outcome measures in only twelve programs. Recidivism and/or drug use were outcome measures in only six programs, and none considered which program components were linked to success. Koons et al. noted that program administrators most often attributed positive outcomes to programs that targeted specific or multiple needs and provided continuums of care (p. 526). Additionally, program participants cited program staffing characteristics, the acquisition of skills, involvement in program delivery, and the influence of a social network or peer group as important aspects to successfully addressing their treatment needs (p. 527). Koons et al. note "that a sizable number of promising program models approached the treatment of women offenders using a comprehensive and holistic strategy for meeting their needs" (p. 521).

A study which addressed promising programs for female offenders in the community, *Female Offenders in the Community: An Analysis of Innovative Strategies and Programs*, was conducted for the National Institute of Corrections by Austin, Bloom, and Donahue (1992). This study involved telephone interviews with staff of 100 community-based programs serving women offenders (coed programs were excluded) and site visits to 23 programs. It identified effective strategies for working with women offenders in community correctional settings. Austin et al. found that the most promising community-based programs for women offenders do not employ the medical or clinical model of correctional treatment. Rather than attempting to cure the client of some pathology, effective programs work with clients to broaden their range of responses to various types of behavior and needs, enhancing their coping and decision-making skills. These programs use an "empowerment" model of skill building to develop competencies to enable women to achieve independence.

In addition, effective therapeutic approaches are multidimensional and deal with specific women's issues, including chemical dependency, domestic violence, sexual abuse, pregnancy and parenting, relationships, and gender bias. According to Austin et al., promising community programs "combined supervision and services to address the specialized needs of female offenders in highly structured, safe environments where accountability is stressed" (p. 21).

Additional program aspects included a continuum of care design; clearly stated program expectations, rules and possible sanctions; consistent supervision; ethnically diverse staff including former offenders;

coordination of community resources; and aftercare. Austin et al. found that information on the effectiveness of community programs for women was limited and difficult to compare. The authors found that evaluations had been conducted on only 4 out of the 100 programs that were surveyed. They found that data relating to clients, services delivered, and program outcomes were maintained manually, if at all and, for the most part, without a central database. Additionally, methods for data collection varied widely, impeding comparative analysis across programs (p. 29).

In their study of 165 community-based drug treatment programs for women offenders, Wellisch, Prendergast, and Anglin (1994) concluded that success appears to be positively related to the amount of time spent in treatment with more lengthy programs having greater success rates (Wellisch et al., 1994). Wellisch et al. also found that little is known about the specific needs of chemically dependent women offenders since very few drug abusing women offenders receive treatment in custody or in the community (p. 1). Additionally, many drug treatment programs do not address the multiple problems of women drug offenders, and few have family-focused services or provide accommodations for infants and children. The authors noted that services needed by women are more likely to be found in "women only" programs than in coed programs. The study concluded that it was necessary to improve assessment of client needs to develop better programs to deliver a range of appropriate services. The assessment process also should provide the basis for developing individual treatment plans, establishing a baseline from which progress in treatment can be monitored, and generate data for program evaluation (p. 6).

Rationale for Gender-Specific Programming and Evaluation

The emerging awareness of the differences between the male and female experience, coupled with the increasing rate of female involvement in the criminal justice system, have prompted juvenile and criminal justice professionals to address the gender-specific needs of this population. However, the focus on gender and gender differences is not simply a focus on "women's issues," nor is it simply contrasting women's experiences to those of men. Female offenders tend to have different personal histories and pathways to offending than their male counterparts. More often than not, they have experienced physical and/or sexual abuse as children and adults, sexual assault, domestic violence, adolescent pregnancy, and single parenthood. Many girls and young women first encounter the juvenile justice system because they have run away, often to escape situations involving violence and sexual/physical abuse within the home.

They begin to use alcohol and/or other drugs at an early age, and an increasing number of studies are finding a correlation between chemical dependency and physical and/or sexual abuse. Additionally, criminal justice researchers and practitioners acknowledge that drugs and crime are linked. Drug offenses account for the largest increase in the number of imprisoned women (Bloom, Chesney-Lind and Owen, 1994). While not all women who are incarcerated for drug offenses are chemically dependent, a number of them either are addicted or have experienced drugs as a problem in their lives (Owen and Bloom, 1995; Wellisch et al., 1994). Most female drug offenders also experience a range of health, social, and psychological problems in addition to the addiction itself (Wellisch et al., 1994). Female drug offenders often come from families with histories of alcohol or drug dependency and violence. They are likely to have been victims of physical and/or sexual abuse or rape. Many are single mothers who have limited financial resources and other means of support (Wellisch et al., 1994). Women may present a different profile of addiction than men in that they are more likely to come from abusive backgrounds, and they are more likely to abuse drugs as a form of self-medication. They also appear to be more amenable to treatment.

Criminal justice programs and services have been based on the male experience, often neglecting women's needs. Effective programming for girls and women should be shaped by, and tailored to, their unique situations. Particular program emphasis should be placed on assisting women who are transitioning from a correctional facility to the community. Women transitioning from prison or jail often face different situations than their male counterparts. They must find safe, sober, and affordable housing and employment so they can support themselves and their families. They also face additional challenges such as:

- Regaining custody of and reunifying with children

- Establishing supportive networks

- Avoiding destructive and abusive relationships (past and present)

- Securing and maintaining employment that provides a living wage

- Securing affordable child care

- Maintaining recovery from alcohol and drug dependency

- Adhering to the conditions of probation or parole

Community corrections programs can be designed to address these challenges and the multidimensional problems that women offenders face (for example, substance abuse, trauma related to past physical and/or sexual abuse, negative relationships, fragmented family and community ties), and they also can help women to prepare for a successful transition to their families and communities. Evaluation designs can be tailored to capture the gender-specific characteristics and needs of women offenders and the program elements that address these needs. If reduction in recidivism is going to be included as an outcome, it should be defined clearly.

Theoretical Perspectives Underlying Gender-specific Programming and Evaluation

To develop effective programs for women and girls, it is critical to develop a sound theoretical approach to treatment that is gender-sensitive and which addresses the realities of their lives. The influence of theory on research and evaluation is reflected in the variables studied (Bonta et al., 1995). Theories of criminality are largely based on observations of male offenders. Historically, theorists either have attempted to explain female crime by applying traditional mainstream theories developed to explain male crime and delinquency to women and girls, or to create fundamentally different explanations of female criminality. While social and cultural theories of crime were developed to explain criminality in males, individual and pathological theories were often used to explain female crime (Lombroso and Ferrero, 1895; Pollak, 1950; Thomas, 1923).

Historically, theories of female criminality ranged from biological to psychological and from economic to social. Much of the literature attempts to explain female criminality by focusing on women's (and girls') deviant behavior—that is, behavior that does not conform to traditional female stereotypes. The female "deviant" is deemed to be more deviant than her male counterpart. She experiences greater stigmatization when she transgresses gender standards and in some cases, faces harsher punishment. For example, the criminalization of pregnant, chemically dependent women raises issues related to their suitability for motherhood. The criminal justice system response to women's lawbreaking often has been that of moral reform (Belknap, 1996; Chesney-Lind, 1997; Rafter, 1990).

The profile of female offenders indicates that they are socially and economically marginalized and often victimized by family members and intimates. Pollock (1998) maintains that theories of female criminality typically point to some elements of opportunity, need, or both, in women's entry into crime. She argues that because social structures put more barriers in front of women's criminal opportunities, women offenders' lives may be different from those of law-abiding women. This would explain, for example, the fact that women offenders have histories of sexual and/or physical abuse which appear to be "instigators of delinquency, addiction and criminality" (p. 52). Additionally, while personal relationships (such as marriage and family) generally may serve to prevent lawbreaking by females, the relationships of women offenders with men are often abusive, exploitive and/or the pathway to substance abuse and related criminal activity.

Studies of female offenders highlight the importance of relationships and the fact that criminal involvement often came through relationships with family members, significant others, or friends (Chesney-Lind, 1997; Owen and Bloom, 1995; Owen, 1998; Pollock, 1998). Women offenders who cite drug abuse as self-medication often discuss personal relationships as the cause of their pain (Pollock, 1998). Abusive families and battering relationships are often strong themes in their lives (Chesney-Lind, 1997; Owen and Bloom, 1995). This has significant implications for therapeutic interventions that deal with the impact that these relationships have on women's current and future behavior.

Feminist theories suggest that the focus on gender goes beyond simply adding another variable to the study of female crime. Contemporary feminist research has contributed to our understanding of the female experience in a way that does not simply contrast it to that of men. In general, this research emphasizes the role of patriarchy and sexual exploitation of women and girls, or "women's place" in relation to offending (Chesney-Lind, 1989). Feminist theories also examine female criminality as a reflection of the situations of women's and girls' lives and their attempts to survive (Arnold, 1990; Chesney-Lind, 1997). Many women and girls on the social and economic margins struggle to survive outside of legitimate enterprises, which brings them into contact with the criminal justice system.

Contemporary feminists also assert that the differences between men and women should be viewed as sources of strength, not weakness. These strengths include women's capacity for relatedness and connection. According to Dr. Jean Baker Miller (1976), "women build on and develop in a context of attachment and affiliation with others" (p. 83). Miller calls for a new approach to psychology that acknowledges the different nature of women's development—an approach which affirms that connection, not separation, is the basis of growth for women (Covington, 1998).

Gilligan (1982) explored relational issues in the context of development and moral reasoning. She explained differences in moral reasoning in a manner that did not devalue women's or girls' behavior. According to Gilligan, boys develop their identity in relation to the world, while girls develop their identity in relation to others. In her studies of moral development, she discovered "a different voice" among women that emphasized relationship, commitment, and care.

Covington (1998) proposes a theoretical model for substance abuse treatment that emphasizes affective, cognitive, and behavioral change. She indicates that the affective aspect is particularly important for women and girls because their behavior must be understood in the context of their emotional lives.

Theories that focus on female development and mutual, caring, and empowering relationships can be useful tools for community correctional programs for women and girls. However, while women's focus on relationships can be a self-empowering and growth-producing experience, there are differences among women (for example, race, class, culture, and sexual orientation) that need to be acknowledged in any theoretical or programmatic framework. Additionally, methods of survival and resistance to race, class, and gender oppression need to be articulated in evolving theoretical and programmatic models (Chesney-Lind and Bloom, 1997).

Definition, Principles and Criteria for Gender-specific Programs

To develop effective gender-specific interventions and evaluative tools, a clear definition and statement of guiding principles and criteria are needed. For example, the Office of Juvenile Justice and Delinquency Prevention (OJJDP) defines gender-specific services as those that are designed "to meet the unique needs of female offenders; that value the female perspective; that celebrate and honor the female experience; that respect and take into account female development; that empower girls and young women to reach their full human potential; and work to change established attitudes that prevent or discourage girls and young women from recognizing their potential" (Girls, Inc., 1996, p. 24).

The Oregon Intermediate Sanctions for Female Offenders Policy Group (1995) defines gender-specific programs as those that "take into account real differences between men and women in their learning and relationship styles and life circumstances. They are not those that admit only women and use the same approaches as are applied to men offenders." The Policy Group recommends that women-specific correctional programs include the following (pp. 66-67):

- Facilitation of visitation between women offenders and their children

- Childcare arrangements for women in community-based programs

- Promotion of support systems and relationships that help women to develop healthy connections

- Mentors who exemplify individual strength and growth while also providing caring support

- Residential substance abuse treatment resources for all women whose criminal behavior is related to their chemical dependency

The Valentine Foundation (1990) suggests that:

Females need programs that potentiate relationships of trust and interdependence with other women already present in their lives. Friends, relatives, neighbors, church or special group members can be important providers of insight, strategy, and strength. Girls and women need mentors who reflect a rootedness in realities of their own lives. They need mentors who exemplify survival and growth as resistance and change.

Beth Glover-Reed (1987) defines women-oriented chemical dependency treatment services as those that address women's specific treatment needs; reduce barriers to recovery from drug dependence that are more likely to occur for women; are delivered in a context that is compatible with women's styles and is safe from exploitation; and take into account women's roles, socialization, and societal status. Other definitions include statements about services for women and girls that should affect individual, relational, and community change (Albrecht, 1997; Greene, Peters and Associates, 1997).

A groundbreaking effort was undertaken in Canada by the Task Force on Federally Sentenced Women, which was established to develop a plan that would be responsive to "the unique and special needs of women" (Shaw, 1993, p. 51). The Task Force established a long-term goal of serving female offenders in community-based programs rather than in institutions. The Task Force issued a landmark report (1990) that suggested a need for a holistic approach to the development of programs and facilities for women. The authors argued that women must be seen within their social context with a consideration of gender, race, and class inequalities. "The Task Force emphasized the importance of assessing individual needs and treating those needs as a whole. In essence, the Task Force rejected the male model of corrections, which classified risk, prioritized needs and fit offenders into prestructured programs" (Shaw, 1993, p. 55).

The Task Force report outlined five fundamental principles for effective programming: empowering women, providing meaningful choices in programs and community facilities, treating women with respect and dignity, providing a physically safe and supportive environment, and sharing responsibility among both correctional staff and members of the community (Task Force on Federally Sentenced Women, 1990).

The Ohio Gender-Specific Services Work Group maintains that programs for girls must:

- Allow more opportunity for building trusting relationships

- Provide learning experiences and skill building after these relationships are established

- Provide safety and comfort in same-gender environments

- Help girls understand that they can succeed in life and still maintain personal relationships

- Explore and honor cultural differences (Belknap, Dunn, and Holsinger, 1997, p. 24)

In summary, the following principles could be considered in the development of gender-specific correctional programming and service delivery to women and girls:

- Equality does not mean sameness; in other words, equality of service delivery is not simply about allowing women access to services traditionally reserved for men—equality must be defined in terms of providing opportunities, which are relevant to each gender. Thus, treatment services may appear very different depending on to whom the service is being delivered.

- Gender-specific programs are not simply "female only" programs that were designed for males.

- Females' sense of self is manifested and develops differently in female specific groups as opposed to coed groups.

- The unique needs and issues (for example, physical/sexual/ emotional victimization, trauma, physical and mental health, pregnancy and parenting) of women and girls should be addressed in a safe, trusting, and supportive women-focused environment.

- Whenever possible, women and girls should be treated in the least-restrictive programming environment available. The level of security should depend on both treatment needs and concern for public safety.

- Treatment and services should build on women's and girls' strengths/competencies and promote independence and self-reliance.

- Cultural awareness and sensitivity should be promoted and the cultural resources and strengths in various communities should be used.

Effective Programs and Interventions

Currently, little data exist to help us identify and evaluate appropriate and effective programs for females under criminal justice supervision. In fact, there is a dearth of research that examines the outcomes associated with different types of services, or whether matching women's needs with particular types of interventions or services produce better outcomes. What is missing from the literature is a systematic examination of the theoretical and programmatic implications of our knowledge of criminal justice-involved women and girls. Without such an examination, programs and therapeutic approaches that have been developed for male populations will continue to be adapted to female populations.

Historically, the effectiveness of correctional treatment programs has been measured by their ability to affect recidivism. The research on correctional program effectiveness in terms of reduction in female recidivism has been insufficient. Much of the research on recidivism has focused on male offenders and little empirical evidence exists to suggest what contributes to women's recidivism or successful transition after release from prison. Furthermore, there are problems with the use of recidivism as a measure of program success, in general, which will be discussed in greater detail in the section on "Research Methodology."

Release Planning and Reintegration

O'Brien (in press) identifies factors that contribute to women's successful reintegration on release from prison such as: providing economic and emotional support (involvement in mutually supportive networks), reunifying with children, and participating in substance abuse treatment and recovery. O'Brien suggests the use of "an empowerment framework," which focuses on the notion of *agency*, or the ability to act on one's behalf. This model of empowerment can be enabled by the creation of social support systems for women in transition from prison, jail, or community correctional programs.

In addition, programs that provide women with the education and skills required for jobs that pay a living wage help women reunify with their children and assume their parenting roles, provide or broker substance abuse treatment and recovery services, contribute to women's sense of self-identity, and may increase women's chances of successful reentry.

The Release Study conducted by Shaw et al. (1991) interviewed fifty-seven federally sentenced women on conditional release from prison. They identified several needs of the women surveyed: reunification with children and family-related issues, employment, finances, housing, substance abuse, physical and mental health problems, and problems with criminal justice personnel. Shaw et al. recommended the following:

- More information regarding release planning

- Greater availability of halfway houses and community programs

- Fewer conditions imposed on women released on parole

- Option to decline treatment programs or counseling

- Greater availability of affordable housing, employment, drug treatment, and physical/sexual abuse programs

- Financial advice and support (pp. 24-25)

Criminogenic Needs

Recent research efforts have attempted to link offender treatment needs to a reduction in criminal behavior. There is a mounting body of literature on the "criminogenic needs" (for example, antisocial attitudes and feelings, association with procriminal role models, low self-control, and poor problem-solving skills) of offenders and the efficacy of targeting these needs in terms of tailoring specific treatment approaches (Andrews, Bonta et al., 1990; Andrews and Bonta, 1994). As mentioned previously, various assessment tools have been employed to identify the criminogenic needs of male offenders; however, their relevance to female offenders remains questionable. Does women's offending relate to criminogenic risks and needs, or is it a factor of the complex interconnection of race, class, gender, abuse, trauma, addiction, or a combination? Clearly, more evaluation research is needed to prove or disprove the relevance of criminogenic risks/needs to women offenders. Furthermore, future examination may warrant that the criminogenic risk/needs approach to correctional treatment be questioned in general.

Cognitive-behavioral Approaches

Cognitive-behavioral approaches are gaining popularity with criminal justice professionals in Canada, Europe, and the United States. However, a body of research is not available to support the effectiveness of these types of approaches for female offenders. Most of the evaluations that have been conducted to date have involved male samples.

Ross, Fabiano, and Ewles (1988) reported on an intervention program that is based on cognitive therapy. The program operates under the assumption that offenders have deficits in cognitive skills essential for prosocial adjustment. Training is provided to increase offenders' cognitive abilities with the expectation that this will influence their criminal behavior. Cognitive therapy attempts to undermine underlying "dysfunctional" beliefs and change "criminogenic" thinking processes. A goal of cognitive therapy is to help the individual improve problem-solving capacities and coping mechanisms.

Lombardo and Smith (1996) describe a rational-cognitive therapy program for female offenders. The basis for the Rational Cognitive Therapy (RCT) model, as well as others, is that "individuals control their emotions by how they process life events through their thoughts" (p. 92). Through Rational Cognitive Therapy, clients are taught "to reevaluate life's events rationally, using rational self-analysis. The program emphasizes the preparation of women offenders for their roles as parents and spouses and 'trains' them to deal rationally with the stress and anger of their spouses or other significant adults" (p. 92). It is not known whether Rational Cognitive Therapy was developed specifically for use with women offenders or if it has been validated for use with women in community correctional facilities.

While cognitive approaches may be useful, as with any correctional intervention, a word of caution is offered—one size does not fit all. Program providers must consider the gendered nature of women's and girls' pathways into the criminal justice system in terms of targeting appropriate programmatic responses. A solid theoretical base is necessary to determine the most appropriate program design. Covington (1998) discusses the usefulness of relational theory in developing an approach to programs that are gender-sensitive. She also recommends the addition of two other theories—a holistic theory of addiction and a theory of trauma—as tools for aiding in the design of gender-specific services.

Responsivity

The principle of responsivity is rooted in the notion that there can be strong interactions between the characteristics of individuals and their settings or situations (Gendreau and Ross, 1987). This principle, according to Gendreau (1994), states that treatment should be delivered in a manner that facilitates the learning of new prosocial skills by the offender. The three components of responsivity include: matching the treatment approach with the learning style and personality of the offender; matching the characteristics of the offender with those of the therapist; and matching the skills of the therapist with the type of program (Lauen, 1997, p. 168).

The responsivity principle suggests that behavior—criminal and noncriminal—is influenced by the outcomes of particular acts, which are signaled by the incentives and disincentives of the immediate situation of action. Andrews (1994) describes responsivity in terms of matching the unique styles and features of the "helper" with those of the offender. According to Andrews, styles of communication may be very important in the context of corrections, especially in interaction with a particular type of offender.

The principle of responsivity may have value in terms of programs for female offenders in that it deals with relationships and connections between program staff and clients. As relational theory suggests, behavior change and growth can occur for women through mutually supportive and trusting relationships. Kendall (1998) offers this caution in regards to principles of need, risk, and responsivity:

> While principles such as criminogenic need, risk, and responsivity may point to general patterns, they cannot comprehend the complex relationship between structure and agency, nor account for the variety of influences on program effectiveness.

Feminist Therapy

Feminist therapy has been defined as "framing the experiences of individuals within the broader social environment" and helping people "connect their own experiences and actions and the circumstances that define their lives" (Kendall, 1994b, p. 2). Another definition of feminist therapy is "the focus on understanding gender as both a cause and a consequence of women's experiences in a male-dominated culture" (Okun, 1997, p. 136). Feminist therapy is based on a relationship of equality between the therapist and the client, and it views women's problems as being inseparable from society's oppression of them. Feminist therapy is empowering and discourages treating clients as victims. It emphasizes social, political, and economic action as a major aspect of the therapeutic process (Okun, 1997, p. 136).

Kendall (1994a) expresses concern that feminism is being co-opted by the corrections system. She asks, "How can individual treatment address such issues such as racism, sexism, and violence in the larger society?" Kendall stresses the danger of therapeutic approaches that locate the problem within the individual and claims that in correctional settings, there is still a power imbalance between staff and inmates. As Kendall points out, a psychological therapeutic approach reduces the problems from "the political to the personal" (p. 2). She asserts that even feminist therapy is problematic in that by design, the equitable balance of power that is common to feminist therapy is artificial in a prison setting that is rife with power and authority roles that are endemic to the institution (Kendall, 1994b, p. 3). To a lesser degree, this concern also can be raised in community correctional settings.

The discussion of intervention approaches suggests that no one approach may work with women and girls in community correctional settings. Programs should be designed to be multimodal and sensitive to differences among these populations. Also, program developers should conduct needs assessments with current female offenders (for further discussion *see* Owen and Bloom, 1995) to determine their pathways to crime and the barriers to successful treatment. Additionally, interviews with formerly incarcerated women and girls can help to identify the factors that have aided them to return successfully to their communities. This type of information is not only important to program design but also to program evaluation.

Assessment of Gender-specificity in Programming

Assessment is a critical tool in matching program interventions with an individual's needs. Additionally, assessment instruments can help determine the best use of scarce resources. Often, due to a paucity of programs, women and girls are assigned to programs and services that are available regardless of whether they meet the particular needs of the offender.

How do we measure gender-specificity? What are gender-specific assessment tools and have they been validated? It is important to understand female development and the specific issues which women and girls bring into the treatment setting in terms of assessing gender-specificity in community corrections programs.

Gender-specific programming should provide services designed to intervene comprehensively in a female's life. To accomplish this, some general questions related to appropriate services for women and girls should be asked:

- Does the program acknowledge and affirm commonalities and respect differences among and within groups (for example, race, class, and sexual orientation)?

- Is the program grounded in theory and is it accurately designed around statistical data and developmental research that is verifiable and reliable?

- Does the program acknowledge and value the worth of individuals, regardless of their backgrounds and offense histories?

- Does the staff reflect the client population in terms of race, ethnicity, gender, and sexual orientation?

- Does the program use gender-specific assessment tools and treatment plans and does it match appropriate treatment with the identified needs of the women and girls it serves?

When considering whether a program is gender-specific, practitioners also might want to consider the following questions:

- In co-correctional settings, what is the ratio of women to men? Do men substantially outnumber women?

- If the program is women only, what is the composition of the staff in terms of gender, race/ethnicity, and sexual orientation?

- What are the program's mission, goals, and objectives? Is there mention of the unique needs of women and interventions specific to this population?

- Does the program emphasize a "relational" treatment approach and encourage the development of growth-producing, trusting, and healthy relationships?

- Does the program begin at the point where the woman is in her life and proceed in a manner that is sensitive to the pace and direction that she chooses?

- Does the program use positive female role models and mentors?

- Does the program address trauma related to physical, sexual, and emotional abuse?

- Does the program address chemical dependency as a potential reaction to trauma related to physical, sexual, and emotional abuse?

- Does the program address pregnancy and parenting issues, including family reunification?

- Does the program provide for development of skills that may lead to future employment in both traditional and nontraditional settings?

- Does the program address issues related to transition to the community (for example, safe and affordable housing, after-care, job training and placement, and childcare)?

- Does the program offer components such as: individual change (such as drug treatment); relational change (including dealing with destructive relationships); and community change (such as altering the cultural and structural contexts surrounding women, which may contribute to their problems)?

- Is the program child friendly? Is the environment conducive to enhancing family relationships? Does it offer services to women and their children and caregivers?

- Does the program emphasize the building of support systems (for example, women's resource networks, childcare networks, transportation, racial, ethnic and cultural programs, and advocacy organizations)?

- Does the agency provide staff training in gender-specific and culturally appropriate issues and service delivery?

Measurement of Effectiveness: Evaluation Design

Funders and policymakers increasingly are mandating that programs document their effectiveness. In the aftermath of Martinson's 1974 study of the impact of correctional interventions on recidivism, community corrections programs were thought to be no better or worse than incarceration in terms of changing offender behavior. There is a growing body of research that supports the effectiveness of some community corrections programs and approaches (Andrews, 1994; Gendreau, 1994; Lauen, 1997). However, there is little evidence to support the effectiveness of community corrections programs for women offenders. Despite the increased awareness of female offenders in the criminal justice system, there is very little information about programs that work for women. In most jurisdictions, the lack of uniform data and management information systems (MIS) impedes the design and evaluation of programs for women. Evaluations are needed to better understand what types of interventions are most effective with female offenders. Process and outcome studies could provide more accurate information about the characteristics and needs of women offenders, services provided, agency costs, and outcomes (Austin et al., 1992).

Several studies highlight the importance of designing evaluation research that examines the effects of both treatment components and approaches to the delivery of treatment in programs for female offenders (Austin et al., 1992; Koons et al., 1997). Elements such as a multidimensional approach, individualized treatment plans, opportunities for competency and skill building, and providing a continuum of care, are treatment components that can be included in such an evaluation design. Approaches to the delivery of interventions include program staff/client relationships, peer interactions, and program environment (for example, safe and supportive).

Palmer (1996) suggests that to describe and understand successful programs, researchers systematically should examine combinations of features. The information necessary to reflect an intervention's complexities or potential for success goes beyond simply asking how successful behavioral approaches are. Palmer argues that research should focus on which kinds of behavioral approaches work and for whom? Researchers should determine what combinations of program components significantly contribute to success. These combinations should examine staff-client interactions, program settings, and client differences as well as programmatic approaches (Palmer, 1996, p. 165).

Process and Outcome Evaluations

Process and outcome evaluations are important in terms of making adaptations in program quality and in determining the characteristics of effective interventions. Process evaluations are useful in that they describe attributes of programs and provide feedback to practitioners about the quality and integrity of program components and service delivery. Process evaluations often examine the relationship between the program's mission and its goals and objectives for program activities and services. Process evaluations usually employ qualitative research methods. The Correctional Program Assessment Inventory (CPAI) was created by Gendreau and Andrews (1993) to assess the quality of offender treatment programs. The purpose of the Correctional Program Assessment Inventory is to identify areas that need improvement and suggest constructive remedies to practitioners. It is important to note, however, that the Correctional Program Assessment Inventory is a generic instrument that has been employed primarily to assess corrections programs serving male offenders. Its validity in terms of assessment of female-specific programs has yet to be determined because only a few programs for female offenders have been assessed to date.

Outcome evaluations are valuable because they describe measures of program success or failure. They examine the short and long-term impact of the intervention on program participants. Some examples of short-term outcome measures include program participation, rule violation, escape from program, restitution paid, and arrest for new criminal offense. Examples of long-term outcome measures include reconviction for a new offense, return to custody for a violation of probation or parole, and relapse from alcohol and drug recovery. Some outcome criteria that typically are used in correctional programs include the following items:

- Observed behavior change

- Personality and attitude inventories

- Employment status

- Educational attainment

- Substance abuse recovery

- Probation or parole revocations

- Arrests

- Convictions

- Time to rearrest

- Type of offense

- Seriousness of offense

Ideally, outcome measures used in evaluations should be tied to program mission, goals, and objectives. Outcome measures should go beyond the "traditional" recidivism measures to assess the import of specific program attributes. Short-term and long-term outcome measures for female-specific programs could include:

- Program participation/completion/discharge

- Alcohol/drug recovery

- Trauma recovery

- Attainment of General Equivalency Diploma, a trade, or college degree

- Employment

- Safe and sober housing

- Improved family and significant other relationships

- Effective parenting and regaining custody of children

- Maintenance of physical and mental health

Research Methodology

Methodological concerns plague evaluation research and design. There is no general agreement on the best measure or set of measures to determine program effectiveness. Traditionally, program effectiveness has been measured by a reduction in recidivism. A growing number of researchers assert that the use of recidivism as a measure of program success is problematic (Hudson, 1987; Jones, 1996; Petersilia and Turner, 1993; Kendall, 1998). Hudson (1987) argues that there are problems in using recidivism as an indicator because of the complexities of official criminal statistics. For example, is recidivism determined by actual offenses, arrests, or convictions? In some cases, people reoffend but do not get caught. These offenders would not be reflected in official measures of recidivism and could be included as cases of program success (Kendall, 1998, p. 367). This has significant implications as it is difficult to disentangle the extent to which official measures confound actual criminal behavior with the labeling of criminality in the criminal justice system (Jones, 1996).

There are other concerns regarding the use of recidivism as a predictor of outcome. For example, the length of the follow-up period is an important consideration in terms of the outcome variable. Generally, follow-up periods should not be less than two years, if possible. Another consideration is the level of measurement. For example, the frequency of recidivism, the seriousness of the offense, the timing between first and subsequent offenses should be precisely specified if recidivism is going to be used as an outcome measure. Additionally, the fact that an individual does not recidivate does not fully elucidate other important aspects of the person's life. For example, a formerly incarcerated woman may be having difficulty finding employment, regaining custody of her children, or she may be in an abusive relationship. These factors may tell us more about the quality of a woman's life than recidivism.

In general, there is a lack of evaluation studies using an experimental design (Petersilia and Turner, 1993). Random assignment into an experimental versus a control group has the advantage of avoiding selection bias, which can make an evaluation misleading or irrelevant. While random assignment is important to the scientific integrity of the evaluation, there are ethical issues to consider. For example, offenders are placed in an experimental program randomly; not based on whether an official, such as a judge or probation officer, believes that this placement is appropriate for a particular individual. Additionally, a necessary treatment component or intervention may be withheld from an offender in a control group because of random assignment.

Another limitation of program evaluation is that researchers often do not measure the "black box" of what goes on between offenders' assignment to an experimental or control group and the outcome of the program a year or two later. Often, the measures of program effectiveness include the number of contacts per month with offenders (not the quality of the contacts), or whether an offender was in a particular program (for example, drug treatment) but the nature or quality of the intervention is not measured. As a result, questions remain about program integrity. Can a given program or intervention work if it is implemented appropriately? The lack of clarity related to program goals is another problem for researchers in terms of determining whether the program is successful. For example, is the goal related to community protection or is it specific to the needs of the offender?

Blanchette (1997) concludes there is little or no evidence that institutional programming for female offenders contributes to a reduction in recidivism. To remedy this situation, Blanchette recommends the more intensive use of "actuarial" or statistical measures that employ an experimental design and enhance the determination of statistical association such as meta-analysis, to determine program effectiveness for female offenders (Kendall, 1998, p. 366).

The assumption underlying the emphasis on actuarial measures is that program effectiveness can be determined best by more precise scientific methods. However, Kendall cautions that sole reliance on such methods is misguided. She claims that "actuarial methods tend to pathologize and individualize women's lawbreaking rather than contextualize it" (p. 367). Kendall argues that both qualitative and quantitative approaches should be used in evaluation research as they each measure different aspects of the program. She further states that evaluations must consider the specific context, not only in which programs operate, but also in which offenders and former offenders live (p. 370).

Feminist research methods often give voice to the notion that the less powerful members of society have the potential for a more complete view of social reality than others because of their disadvantaged position. Acknowledging the pervasive influence of gender is the foundation of feminist research. Feminist methodology is aimed at description, analysis, explanation, and interpretation of the female world (Cook and Fonow, 1990). Cook and Fonow (1990) state that central to feminist methods is the use of both qualitative and quantitative methods so that the findings from each may inform and complement each other. There is a range of research methods that can be used by feminists: interviews, participant observation, ethnography, or triangulation (multiple methods).

It is important to note that the environments within which programs operate are important factors for consideration in evaluation research. Program evaluators need to be aware of the unique "culture" of individual programs, in other words, the relationships between staff and offenders, relationships between offenders, and rules and regulations so as to determine how these factors may have an impact on the program. Some community corrections programs focus more on facility security and discipline than on treatment. What effect, if any, does this emphasis have on program efficacy? Also factors such as mandatory versus voluntary participation in treatment programs may affect program effectiveness and therefore should be considered in evaluation design.

Ultimately, the evaluator's frame of reference or theoretical perspective will guide the way in which evaluations are designed. The methods used to evaluate programs will depend on the kind of data that researchers regard as valuable. For example, if a researcher is guided by feminist theory, she or he may conduct face-to-face interviews with women offenders to gain their subjective experience about a program. On the other hand, a researcher who embraces positivist or "scientific" theories of causation will employ sophisticated statistical methods in program evaluation. It is also very likely that this evaluator would use recidivism as the primary outcome measure of program effectiveness. Instead of using one approach or the other, both quantitative and qualitative research methods should be included in program evaluation. This approach provides information on a more comprehensive range of characteristics of programs and participants.

Conclusion

Women and girls who are involved in the criminal justice system present different circumstances and needs than those of their male counterparts. Effective gender-specific programs and interventions may address these issues. Due to the nature of their offenses, which are primarily nonviolent, female offenders are often a lower risk to public safety than male offenders. Thus, this population presents a unique opportunity to implement and expand community corrections alternatives and intermediate sanctions without compromising public safety.

The importance of issues such as racism, sexism, and economic oppression cannot be overlooked in discussions of effective interventions for women offenders. While dealing with individual issues and therapeutic approaches is important, the larger social issues of poverty, and race and gender inequalities have a profound impact on the lives of women and girls involved in the criminal and juvenile justice systems. Successful interventions must relate to the social realities from which women and girls come and to which they will return. They also must be sensitive to cultural differences and expectations, and therapeutic approaches need to reflect this awareness.

As Austin et al. (1992, p. 33) conclude:

> Developing a rational and compassionate justice system which promotes accountability, while acknowledging the underlying causes of women's conflicts with the law, is not an overwhelming task. A range of promising programs throughout the country can serve as examples of integrated, thoughtful, and purposeful designs to provide much needed expansion of the programs for women offenders in the community. This will require the commitment of the criminal justice system to adequately, plan, implement, and support policies and programs to address the multidimensional problems of women offenders.

Given the limitations that have been discussed in this paper, evaluation research can provide policymakers and practitioners with valuable information regarding program design and implementation. This research can help policymakers and practitioners make informed choices about what programs and interventions are most likely to be effective and with whom. Evaluation also can move practitioners beyond developing programs based on impressions, the latest fad, or political expedience. Unfortunately, the lack of evaluation research demonstrating effective program elements for women and girls in community corrections is a barrier to the use and expansion of such programs. This paper offers a call to action for the development of evaluation tools and designs that go beyond recidivism to document "what works" with female offenders in community corrections.

References

Albrecht, L. 1997. *Gender Difference and Girls' Development as a Basis for Program and Service Development for Girls.* Paper presented at the fourth annual conference of RECLAIM, Columbus, Ohio.

Andrews, D. A. 1994. An Overview of Treatment Effectiveness: Research and Clinical Principles. In *What Works: Bridging the Gap Between Research and Practice.* Longmont, Colorado: National Institute of Corrections.

Andrews, D. A., and J. Bonta. 1994. *The Psychology of Criminal Conduct.* Cincinnati, Ohio: Anderson.

————. 1995. *LSI-R: The Level of Service Inventory-Revised.* Toronto, Ontario: Multi-Health Systems, Inc.

Andrews, D. A., J. Bonta, and D. Hoge. 1990. Classification for Effective Rehabilitation: Rediscovering Psychology. *Criminal Justice and Behavior.* 17, 19-52.

Andrews, D. A. and J. Kiessling. 1980. Program Structure and Effective Correctional Practices: A Summary of the CaVIC Research. In R. Ross and P. Gendreau, eds. *Effective Correctional Treatment.* Toronto: Butterworths. pp. 441-463.

Andrews, D. A., I. Zinger, D. Hoge, J. Bonta, P. Gendreau, and F. Cullen. 1990. Does Correctional Treatment Work? Clincally Relevant and Psychologically Informed Meta-analysis. *Criminology.* 28, 369-404.

Arnold, R. 1990. Women of Color: Processes of Victimization and Criminalization of Black Women. *Social Justice.* 173, 153-156.

Austin, J., B. Bloom, and T. Donahue. 1992. *Female Offenders in the Community: An Analysis of Innovative Strategies and Programs.* Washington, D.C.: National Institute of Corrections.

Belknap, J. 1996. *The Invisible Woman: Gender, Crime, and Justice.* Belmont, California: Wadsworth Publishing Company.

Belknap, J, M. Dunn, and K. Holsinger. 1997. *Moving Toward Juvenile Justice and Youth-serving Systems that Address the Distinct Experience of the Adolescent Female.* Cincinnati, Ohio: Gender Specific Services Work Group Report.

Blanchette, K. 1997. Classifying Female Offenders for Correctional Intervention. *Forum on Corrections Research*. 9, 36-41.

Blinn, C., ed. 1997. *Maternal Ties: A Selection of Programs for Female Offenders.* Lanham, Maryland: American Correctional Association.

Bloom, B. 1997. *Defining "Gender-specific": What Does it Mean and Why Is it Important?* Paper presented at the National Institute of Correction's Intermediate Sanctions for Women Offenders National Meeting, Longmont, Colorado.

Bloom, B. and M. Chesney-Lind. 1997. Feminist Criminology: Thinking about Women and Crime. In B. MacLean and D. Milovanovic, eds. *Thinking Critically about Crime*. Vancouver: Collective Press. pp. 45-55.

Bloom, B., M. Chesney-Lind, and B. Owen. 1994. *Women in California Prisons: Hidden Victims of the War on Drugs.* San Francisco, California: Center on Juvenile and Criminal Justice.

Bonta, J., B. Pang, and S. Wallace-Capretta. 1995. Predictors of Recidivism among Incarcerated Female Offenders. *The Prison Journal*. 753: 277-294.

Chesney-Lind, M. 1989. Girls, Crime and Woman's Place: Toward a Feminist Model of Female Delinquency. *Crime and Delinquency*. 35, 5-29.

————. 1997. *The Female Offender: Girls, Women and Crime.* Thousand Oaks, California: Sage.

Chesney-Lind, M. and R. Shelden. 1998. *Girls, Delinquency, and Juvenile Justice,* 2nd ed. Belmont, California: West/Wadsworth.

Cook, J. and M. Fonow. 1990. Knowledge and Women's Interest: Issues of Epistemology and Methodology in Feminist Sociological Research. In J. Nielson, ed. *Feminist Research Methods: Exemplary Readings in the Social Sciences*. Boulder, Colorado: Westview Press, pp. 69-93.

Coulson, G., G. Ilacqua, V. Nutbrown, D. Guilekes, and F. Cudjoe. 1996. Predictive Utility of the LSI for Incarcerated Female Offenders. *Criminal Justice and Behavior*. 23, 95-115.

Covington, S. 1998. The Relational Theory of Women's Psychological Development: Implications for the Criminal Justice System. In R. Zaplin, ed. *Female Crime and Delinquency: Critical Perspectives and Effective Interventions*. Gaithersburg, Maryland: Aspen Publishers. pp.113-131.

Cullen, F. and P. Gendreau. 1989. The Effectiveness of Correctional Rehabilitation: Reconsidering the "Nothing Works" Debate. In L. Goodstein and D. MacKenzie, eds. *The American Prison: Issues in Research and Policy.* New York: Plenum. pp. 23-44.

Gendreau, P. 1994. The Principles of Effective Intervention with Offenders. In A. Harland, ed. *What Works in Community Corrections*. Thousand Oaks, California: Sage.

————. 1996. The Principles of Effective Intervention with Offenders. In A. Harland, ed. *Choosing Correctional Options that Work: Defining the Demand and Evaluating the Supply*. Thousand Oaks, California: Sage. pp. 117-130.

Gendreau, P. and D. A. Andrews. 1993. *The Correctional Program Assessment Inventory, 3rd Ed.* Ottawa, Ontario: University of New Brunswick. Saint John, New Brunswick and Carleton University.

Gendreau, P., D. A. Andrews, C. Goggin, and F. Chanteloupe. 1992. *The Development of Clinical and Policy Guidelines for the Prediction of Criminal Behavior in Criminal Justice Settings*. Ottawa, Ontario: Ministry Secretariat, Solicitor General Canada.

Gendreau, P., C. Goggin, and M. Paparozzi. 1996. Principles of Effective Assessment for Community Corrections. *Federal Probation*. 63, 64-70.

Gendreau, P., T. Little, and C. Goggin, 1996. A Meta-analysis of the Predictors of Adult Offender Recidivism: What Works! *Criminology*. 344, 401-433.

Gendreau, P. and R. Ross. 1987. Revivification of Rehabilitation: Evidence from the 1980s. *Justice Quarterly*. 4, 369-407.

Gilligan, C. 1982. *In a Different Voice*. Cambridge, Massachusetts: Harvard University Press.

Girls, Inc. 1996. *Prevention and Parity: Girls in Juvenile Justice*. Indianapolis, Indiana: Girls, Inc.

Glover-Reed, B. 1987. Developing Women-sensitive Drug Dependence Treatment Services: Why So Difficult? *Journal of Psychoactive Drugs*. 192, 151-164.

Greene, Peters and Associates. 1997. Materials Presented at the Annual Meeting of of the American Society of Criminology, San Diego, California.

Hudson, B. 1987. *Justice Through Punishment*. Houndmills, England: Macmillan Publishing.

Intermediate Sanctions for Female Offenders Policy Group. 1995. *Intermediate Sanctions for Women Offenders*. Oregon Criminal Justice Council and the Oregon Department of Corrections.

Jones, P. 1996. Risk Prediction in Criminal Justice. In A. Harland, ed. *Choosing Correctional Options that Work: Defining the Demand and Evaluating the Supply*. Thousand Oaks, California: Sage. pp. 33-68.

Kempf-Leonard, K. 1998. *Disparity Based on Sex: Is Gender-specific Treatment Warranted?* Paper presented at the Academy of Criminal Justice Sciences Annual Meeting. Albuquerque, New Mexico.

Kendall, K. 1994a. Creating Real Choices: A Program Evaluation of Therapeutic Services at the Prison for Women. *Forum on Corrections Research.* 61, 19-21.

———. 1994b. Therapy Behind Prison Walls: A Contradiction in Terms? *Prison Service Journal.* 96, 2-11.

———. 1998. Evaluation of Programs for Female Offenders. In R. Zaplin, ed. *Female Crime and Delinquency: Critical Perspectives and Effective Interventions.* Gaithersburg, Maryland: Aspen Publishers. pp. 361-379

Koons, B., J. Burrow, M. Morash, and T. Bynum,. 1997. Expert and Offender Perceptions of Program Elements Linked to Successful Outcomes for Incarcerated Women. *Crime and Delinquency.* 434, 512-532.

Lauen, R. 1997. *Positive Approaches to Corrections: Research, Policy, and Practice.* Lanham, Maryland: American Correctional Association.

Lombardo, V. and R. Smith. 1996. Rational Emotive Therapy: A Model Program for Female Offenders. *Corrections Today.* 92-95. October.

Lombroso, C., and W. Ferrero. 1895. *The Female Offender.* London: T. Fisher Unwin.

Martinson, R. 1974. What Works? Questions and Answers about Prison Reform. *Public Interest.* 35, 22-54.

Miller, J. B. 1976. *Toward a New Psychology of Women.* Boston: Beacon Press.

Morton, Joann, ed. 1998. *Complex Challenges Collaborative Solutions: Programming for Adult and Juvenile Female Offenders.* Lanham, Maryland: American Correctional Association.

Nuffield, J. 1989. The "SIR Scale:" Some Reflections on its Applications. *Forum on Corrections Research.* 12, 19-22.

O'Brien, P. In press. *Women in Prison.* New York: State University of New York Press.

Okun, B. 1997. *Effective Helping: Interviewing and Counseling Techniques,* 2d Ed. Pacific Grove, California: Brooks/Cole.

Owen, B. 1998. *In the Mix: Struggle and Survival in a Woman's Prison.* New York: State University of New York Press.

Owen, B. and B. Bloom. 1995. Profiling Women Prisoners: Findings from National Surveys and a California Sample. *The Prison Journal.* 752, 165-185.

Palmer, T. 1996. Programmatic and Nonprogrammatic Aspects of Successful Intervention. In A. Harland, ed. *Choosing Correctional Options that Work: Defining the Demand and Evaluating the Supply.* Thousand Oaks, California: Sage. pp. 131-182.

Petersilia, J. and S. Turner. 1993. Intensive Probation and Parole. In M. Tonry, ed. *Crime and Justice: A Review of Research.* Chicago: University of Chicago Press. pp. 281-335.

Pollak, O. 1950. *The Criminality of Women.* New York: Barnes.

Pollock, J. 1998. *Counseling Women in Prison.* Thousand Oaks, California: Sage.

Rafter, N. H. 1990. *Partial Justice: Women, Prisons and Social Control.* New Brunswick, New Jersey: Transaction Publishers.

Ritchie, B. 1996. *Compelled to Crime: The Gender Entrapment of Battered Black Women.* New York: Routledge.

Ross, R. and E. Fabiano. 1986. *Female Offenders: Correctional Afterthoughts.* Jefferson, North Carolina: McFarland.

Ross, R., E. Fabiano, and C. Ewles. 1988. Reasoning and Rehabilitation. *International Journal of Offender Therapy and Comparative Criminology.* 321 29-35.

Shaw, M. 1993. Reforming Federal Women's Imprisonment. In E. Adelberg and C. Currie, eds. *In Conflict with the Law.* Vancouver, British Columbia: Press Gang Publishers. pp. 50-75.

Shaw, M., K. Rodgers, and T. Hattem. 1991. *The Release Study: Survey of Federally Sentenced Women in the Community.* Ottawa: Ministry of the Solicitor General.

Simourd, L. and D. A. Andrews. 1994. Correlates of Delinquency: A Look at Gender Differences. *Forum on Corrections Research.* 6, 32-35.

Task Force on Federally Sentenced Women. 1990. *Creating Choices.* Ottawa, Ontario: Correctional Service of Canada.

Thomas, W. I. 1923. *The Unadjusted Girl.* Boston: Little, Brown.

Valentine Foundation. 1990. *A Conversation about Girls.* Bryn Mawr, Pennsylvania: Valentine Foundation.

Wellisch, J., M. Prendergast, and D. Anglin. 1994. *Drug-abusing Women Offenders: Results of a National Survey, National Institute of Justice: Research in Brief.* Washington, D.C.: Government Printing Office.

WHAT TO DO ABOUT GIRLS? THINKING ABOUT PROGRAMS FOR YOUNG WOMEN [1]

3

Meda Chesney-Lind, Ph.D.
Professor
Women's Studies Program
University of Hawaii at Manoa
Honolulu, Hawaii

If you're smart and strong enough and keep busy, you can stay out of trouble
—Female ward, Hawaii Youth Correctional Facility[2]

For years people have assumed that all you have to do to make a program designed for boys work for girls is to paint the walls pink and take out the urinals
—Marian Daniels, Female Intervention Team
Baltimore, Maryland, 1996[3]

Girls accounted for one out of four arrests of young people in the United States in 1996 (Federal Bureau of Investigation, 1997). Despite this, young women almost always are forgotten when programs for "delin-quents" are discussed. An exception to this generalization were the 1992 hearings held in conjunction with the reauthorization of the Juvenile Justice and Delinquency Prevention Act, which addressed for the first time the "provision of services to girls within the juvenile justice system" (U.S. House of Representatives, 1992). As a result of these hearings, states were asked to review their services to youths with a specific focus on gender specific services, and they also were given an opportunity to get federal aid to improve on girl's services through Challenge Grants. Twenty-three states embarked on such programs—by far the most popular of the ten possible Challenge Grant activity areas (Girls, Incorporated, 1996).

Such attention is long overdue, and such enthusiasm is much needed and welcome. Not only is little known about girls' delinquency, but for years, programs have endeavored to respond to girls' problems either by ignoring girls completely or assuming that models built around the needs of male adolescents will address girls' needs as well.

Are Girls Getting "Meaner"?: The Shape of Contemporary Female Delinquency

Shortly after the American Association of University Women's study documented the dramatic and widespread drop in the self-esteem of girls during early adolescence (American Association of University Women, 1992), a curious thing happened in the media. There was a dramatic surge of journalistic interest in girls, often girls of color, engaged in nontradi-tional, masculine behavior—notably joining gangs, carrying guns, and fighting with other girls. The fascination with a "new" violent female offender is not really new, however. In the 1970s, a notion emerged that the women's movement had "caused" a surge in women's serious crimes. But this discussion focused largely on an imagined increase in crimes of adult women—usually white women (*see* Chesney-Lind, 1997). The cur-rent discussion, though, has settled on girls' commission of violent crimes, often in youth gangs. Indeed, there has been a veritable siege of these news stories with essentially the same theme—today girls are more violent, they are in gangs, and their behavior does not fit the traditional stereotype of girls' delinquency as simply "minor" and often "sexual" delinquency (*see* Chesney-Lind and Shelden, 1998).

On August 2, 1993, for example, in a feature spread on teen violence, *Newsweek* had a box entitled "Girls will be Girls," which noted that "some girls now carry guns. Others hide razor blades in their mouths" (Leslie et al., 1993: 44). Explaining this trend, the article notes that "The plague of teen violence is an equal-opportunity scourge. Crime by girls is on the rise, or so various jurisdictions report" (Leslie et al. 1993, 44). More recently, the *Boston Globe Magazine* ran a cover story on girls and violence. Against a backdrop of large red letters reading "BAD GIRLS," a text said "girls are moving into the world of violence that once belonged to boys" (Ford, 1998).

A review of girls' arrests for violent crime between 1987 and 1996 initially seems to provide support for the notion that girls have become more violent. Arrests of girls for all Part One Violent Offenses, defined by the FBI as murder, forcible rape, burglary, aggravated assault, larceny theft, auto theft, and arson were up 118.1 percent (Federal Bureau of Investigation, 1997: 219), and arrests of girls for "other assaults" were up 142.6 percent. Girls' arrest rates reflected a similar picture; as an example, girls' arrest rates for violent crimes increased by 99.5 percent (from 20.8 per 100,000 to 41.5 per 100,000) during the period in question. But a closer look at these and other data on girls' violent behavior presents a more complex picture.

First, and most importantly, boys' arrests (and arrest rates) for these offenses have been climbing as well, and they are much higher than girls' (159.9 per 100,000 in 1987 and 184.4 per 100,000 in 1996); as a result, girls' share of serious crimes of violence has changed only slightly during the two time periods and still remains a small portion of the total problem. In 1987, arrests of girls accounted for 11 percent of all arrests of youths for serious crimes of violence; in 1996, the comparable figure was 15 percent (Federal Bureau of Investigation, 1997: 219). Second, serious crimes of violence still constitute only a small proportion of all girls' delinquency, and that figure has remained essentially unchanged. Only 2.0 percent of girls' arrests in 1987 were for serious crimes of violence. By 1996, this figure had climbed to 2.9 percent (13,995 arrests out of a total of 481,164 arrests) compared to 5.6 percent of boys' arrests.

But what about those increases, particularly in "other assaults"? Relabeling of behaviors that once were categorized as status offenses (noncriminal offenses like "runaway" and "person in need of supervision") into violent offenses cannot be ruled out in explanations of arrest rate shifts, nor can changes in police practices with reference to domestic violence. A review of the more than 2,000 cases of girls referred to Maryland's juvenile justice system for "person-to-person" offenses revealed that virtually all of these offenses (97.9 percent) involved "assault." A further examination of these records showed that about half were "family centered" and involved such activities as "a girl hitting her mother and her mother subsequently pressing charges" (Mayer, 1994).

In another example of this pattern of "relabeling," a young woman in Florida tried to run away after an argument with her stepfather. As she was attempting to leave, her mother grabbed her by the hair, and in response to this, she hit her mother. She was arrested and charged with two counts of "battery" (which in that state requires mandatory detention) for this incident (Wright, 1998). Such relabeling, which is also called "bootstrapping," has been particularly pronounced in the official delinquency of African-American girls (Robinson, 1990; Bartollas, 1993), and this practice also facilitates the incarceration of girls in detention facilities and training schools—something that would not be possible if the girl were arrested for noncriminal status offenses.

When exploring the dramatic increases in the arrests of girls for "other assaults" (which, as noted, increased by 142.6 percent between 1987 and 1996), it is also likely that enforcement practices in other arenas have dramatically narrowed the gender gap. Minor or "other" assaults can range from schoolyard tussles to relatively serious, but not life-threatening assaults (Steffensmeier and Steffensmeier, 1980). These authors first noted an increasing tendency to arrest girls for these offenses in the seventies and commented that "evidence suggests that female arrests for 'other assaults' are relatively nonserious in nature and tend to consist of being bystanders or companions to males involved in skirmishes, fights, and so on" (Steffensmeier and Steffensmeier, 1980: 70). Currie adds to this the fact that these "simple assaults without injury" often are "attempted" or "threatened" or "not completed" (Currie, 1998: 40). At a time when official concern about youth violence is almost unparalleled and school principals increasingly are likely to call police onto their campuses, it should come as no surprise that youthful arrests in this area are up.

Detailed comparisons drawn from supplemental homicide reports from unpublished FBI data also hint at the central, rather than peripheral way in which gender colored and differentiated girls' and boys' violence. A study of these FBI data on the characteristics of girls' and boys' homicides between 1984 and 1993, found that girls accounted for "proportionately fewer homicides in 1993 (6 percent) than in 1984 (14 percent)" (Loper and Cornell, 1996: 324).

Their work shows that girls' choice of weapons differed from boys' so that in comparison to boys' homicides, girls who killed were more likely to use a knife than a gun and to murder someone as a result of conflict (rather than in the commission of a crime). Girls also were more likely than boys to murder family members (32 percent) and very young victims (24 percent of their victims were under the age of three compared to 1 percent of the boys' victims) (Loper and Cornell, 1996: 328). When involved in a peer homicide, girls were more likely than boys to have killed "as a result of an interpersonal conflict;" in addition, girls were more likely to kill alone, while boys were more likely to kill with an accomplice (Loper and Cornell, 1996: 328). The authors concluded that "the stereotype of girls becoming gun-toting robbers was not supported. The dramatic increase in gun-related homicides . . . applies to boys but not girls" (Loper and Cornell, 1996: 332).

Finally, a note about self-report data: these always have shown that girls committed more assaults than official statistics reflected (*see* Chesney-Lind and Shelden, 1997). A summary of recent studies on self-reported aggression also reflects that while about a third of girls reported having been in a physical fight in the last year, this was true of over half of the boys (Girls Incorporated, 1996: 13). Girls are far more likely to fight with a parent or sibling (34 percent compared to 9 percent), whereas boys are more likely to fight with friends or strangers. Finally, as Table 3.1 shows, boys are twice to three times more likely to report carrying a weapon in the past month (Girls Incorporated, 1996: 13).

Trends in self-report data of youthful involvement in violent offenses also fail to show the dramatic changes found in official statistics. Specifically, a matched sample of "high-risk" youths (aged thirteen to seventeen) surveyed in the 1977 National Youth Study and the 1989 Denver Youth Survey revealed significant *decreases* in girls' involvement in felony assaults, minor assaults, and hard drugs, and no change in a wide range of other delinquent behaviors—including felony theft, minor theft, and index delinquency (Huizinga, 1997).

Finally, girls' behavior, including violence, needs to be put in its patriarchal context. In her analysis of self-reported violence in girls in Canada, Artz (1998) has done precisely that, and the results were striking. First, she noted that violent girls reported significantly greater rates of victimization and abuse than their nonviolent counterparts, and that girls who were violent reported great fear of sexual assault, especially from their boyfriends. Specifically, one in five violent girls felt they were physically abused at home compared to one in ten violent males and only 6.3 percent of nonviolent girls. Patterns for sexual abuse were even starker; roughly one out of four violent girls had been sexually abused compared to one in ten of nonviolent girls (Artz, 1998: 47). Follow-up interviews

TABLE 3.1. Actual and Potential Involvement in Physical Violence

	FEMALES (%)	MALES (%)	SOURCE
INVOLVED IN:			
Physical fight in the past year	34	51	Adams et al.*
	32	51	Kann et al.**
Four or more physical fights in the past year	9	15	Adams et al.*
FOUGHT WITH:			
Stranger	7	15	Adams et al.*
Friend	24	46	Adams et al.*
Date/romantic partner	8	2	Adams et al.*
Parent/Sibling	34	9	Adams et al.*
Other	4	6	Adams et al.*
Several of the above	24	26	Adams et al.*
CARRIED A WEAPON:			
In the past month	7	17	Adams et al.*
	9	34	Kann et al.**

*Adams et al. (1995: ages 14-17, 1992 data) in Girls, Incorporated 1996.

**Kann et al. (1995: grades 9-12, 1993 data) in Girls, Incorporated 1996.

with a small group of violent girls found that the girls had learned at home that "might makes right" and engaged in "horizontal violence" directed at other powerless girls (often with boys as the audience). Certainly, these findings provide little ammunition for those who would contend that the "new," violent girl is a product of any form of "emancipation."

While the media has focused attention on girls' violent, nontraditional delinquency, most of girls' delinquency is not of that sort at all. Examining the types of offenses for which girls are actually arrested, it is clear that most are arrested for the less serious criminal acts and status offenses (noncriminal offenses for which only youths can be taken into custody like "running away from home"). In 1996, about half of girls' arrests were for either larceny theft (23.7 percent) much of which, particularly for girls, is shoplifting (Shelden and Horvath, 1986) or status offenses (23.4 percent). Boys' arrests were far more dispersed.

Running away from home and prostitution remain the only two arrest categories where more girls than boys are arrested (Federal Bureau of Investigation, 1997: 219), and despite the intention of the Juvenile Justice and Delinquency Prevention Act in 1974, which, among other things, encouraged jurisdictions to divert and deinstitutionalize youths charged with status offenses, arrests for these have been climbing in recent years. Between 1987 and 1996, for example, girls' runaway arrests increased by 20.7 percent, and arrests of girls for curfew violations increased by 155.2 percent.

Status offenses always have played a significant role among the offenses that bring girls into the juvenile justice system. They accounted for about a quarter of all girls' arrests in 1996, but less than 10 percent of boys' arrests—figures that remained relatively stable during the last decade. In 1996, over half (57.5 percent) of those arrested for one status offense—running away from home—were girls (Federal Bureau of Investigation, 1997: 219).

Why are girls more likely to be arrested than boys for running away from home? There are no simple answers to this question. Studies of actual delinquency (not simply arrests) show that girls and boys run away from home in about equal numbers. As an example, Canter (1982) found in a National Youth Survey that there was no evidence of greater female involvement, compared to males, in any category of delinquent behavior. Indeed, in this sample, males were significantly more likely than females to report status offenses.

There is some evidence to suggest that parents and police may be responding differently to the same behavior. Parents may be calling the police when their daughters do not come home, and police may be more likely to arrest a female than a male runaway youth.

Another reason for different responses to running away from home speaks to differences in the reasons that boys and girls have for running away. Girls are, for example, much more likely than boys to be the victims of child sexual abuse with some experts estimating that roughly 70 percent of the victims of child sexual abuse are girls (Finkelhor and Baron, 1986). Not surprisingly, the evidence is also suggesting a link between this problem and girls' delinquency—particularly running away from home.

Studies of girls on the streets or in court populations are showing high rates of both sexual and physical abuse. A study of a runaway shelter in Toronto found, for example, that 73 percent of the female runaways and 38 percent of the males had been sexually abused. This same study found that sexually abused female runaways were more likely than their nonabused counterparts to engage in delinquent or criminal activities such as substance abuse, petty theft, and prostitution. No such pattern was found among the male runaways (McCormack and Janus, 1986).

Detailed studies of youths entering the juvenile justice system in Florida have compared the "constellations of problems" presented by girls and boys entering detention (Dembo, Williams, and Schmeidler, 1993; Dembo et al., 1995). These researchers have found that female youths were more likely than male youths to have abuse histories and contact with the juvenile justice system for status offenses, while male youths had higher rates of involvement with various delinquent offenses. Further research on a larger cohort of youths (N=2,104) who were admitted to an assessment center in Tampa concluded that "girls' problem behavior commonly relates to an abusive and traumatizing home life, whereas boys' law violating behavior reflects their involvement in a delinquent life style" (Dembo et al.,1995: 21).

Putting Girls' Crime in Context

About one girl in twenty will have some contact with the juvenile justice system (Girls Incorporated, 1996). Data on the many and varied problems presented by this group of young women suggest a need to focus on a variety of risk factors related to school and community situations, family circumstances, and individual/peer characteristics (Girls Incorporated, 1996; Chesney-Lind and Shelden, 1998).

Young women residing in poverty-ridden and violent communities face the greatest challenges of growing up optimally. Structural inequity and institutional racism impede girls of marginalized backgrounds from obtaining quality education and employment, accessing resources, and developing positive life choices. Lack of opportunity increases despair and the possibility of engaging in self-destructive, delinquent activities; this is especially true for girls who reside in communities where crime and gang violence are prevalent (Ms. Foundation for Women, 1993). Sometimes, perceived economic necessity leads girls to commit crime. The American Correctional Association (1990) reports that 9 percent of girls broke laws because of economic pressures and an additional 9 percent to pay for drugs.

Academic failure is another salient risk factor related to youth involvement in delinquency. The American Correctional Association (1990) found that 78 percent of female juvenile offenders had neither completed high school nor obtained a GED. A staggering 12 percent had not even gone beyond elementary school. Of the population that did attend school, 29 percent were enrolled in a vocational or technical program.

Another study that focused on the educational backgrounds of incarcerated women in three states revealed that 46 percent of them had been expelled, 28 percent had repeated a grade, and 26 percent had been placed in a special class (Acoca and Austin, 1996). In addition, this population tends to have a disproportionate number of girls with learning disabilities.

Research indicates that girls, in general, are seven times more likely than boys to drop out of school for family reasons, such as needing to care for siblings, elderly relatives, as well as their own children (Fine and Zane, 1989). Girl offenders, in particular, drop out of school because they are pregnant (27 percent) or because they are parents and need to care for their children (20 percent). Many also leave school simply out of boredom and inability to get along with their teachers. Likewise, they feel that their studies are difficult and unrewarding (American Correctional Association, 1990). Clearly, programming geared towards school success needs to be an integral part of services to at-risk girls.

Substance abuse is another prominent characteristic of particularly at-risk girls. The American Correctional Association's study of state training schools for girls in the juvenile justice system (1990) found that 60 percent of this population needs substance abuse treatment at intake and that more than half of these girls are multiply addicted. A vast majority of the girls stated that they used alcohol (59 percent), marijuana (78 percent), and speed (55 percent) regularly (American Correctional Association, 1990: 59-60). Of the girls who are substance-dependent, most first started using between the ages of twelve and fifteen. Girls are more likely than boys to use or abuse substances that can be obtained legally (for example, cough medicine or lighter fluid) or drugs the family makes available, which decreases their likelihood of arrest (Girls, Incorporated, 1996: 12). Additionally, girls tend to use drugs in settings where they are less vulnerable to arrest (Chesney-Lind and Shelden, 1998). Consequently, girls' drug problems can be ignored more easily or overlooked. Although models that delineate the relationship between delinquency and substance abuse largely have involved adolescent males, evidence for females also indicates that substance abuse is highly correlated with disruptive behavior (Girls Incorporated, 1996).

As was mentioned earlier, rates of sexual abuse are disconcertingly high among at-risk girls, but many girls are at risk for victimization. Estimates of the general population of girls at large indicate that a disconcerting 34 percent will suffer some form of abuse before they reach adulthood (Benson 1990). Not surprising, a link between victimization and subsequent delinquent and or self-destructive behavior is evident in court populations.

Girls often respond to abuse by fighting back, "acting out," and running away from home (Girls Incorporated, 1996). Studies show that more than 70 percent of girls on the streets have run away to flee violence in their homes (Chesney-Lind and Shelden, 1998). As a result, runaway girls are at further risk of victimization and often resort to prostitution, petty theft, and drug dealing to survive. The American Correctional Association (1990) reports that more than 80 percent of girls in the system have run away from home, and a staggering 50 percent have run away from home six or more times.

Even girls who are not at-risk for delinquency, per se, are at-risk of not developing optimally. Perhaps the most devastating blow is to a girl's self-esteem. An American Association of University Women study (1992) reported that girls at age nine have higher self-concepts of themselves and their abilities than adolescent girls; thus indicating that girls' self-esteem diminishes drastically during adolescence. These negative self-concepts coincide with girls' disproportionate risk for distorted body images, eating disorders, and chronic dieting. Not surprisingly, girls experience higher levels of stress as a result of internalizing their distress and problems. Two large studies have shown that girls are twice as likely than boys to experience depression (Allgood-Merten, Lewisohn, and Hops, 1990). Interestingly, one of these studies linked girls' depression to dissatisfaction with their physical appearance. Girls also make more suicide attempts than boys (Pipher, 1994; Miller, 1994). In essence, girls are in grave jeopardy of not developing and maintaining psychological resilience.

Shortchanging Girls: Patterns within Youth-Serving Programs

Alder points out that programs often overlook girls since "young men tend to be more noticeable and noticed than young women" (Alder, 1995: 3). When girls go out, they tend to move in smaller groups. There are greater proscriptions against girls "hanging out," and they may be justly fearful of being on the streets at night. Finally, girls have many more domestic expectations than their boy counterparts, and these may keep them confined to their homes. Girls' needs are, in short, easier to ignore (Alder, 1986; 1995). This clearly seems to be the case when the evidence is reviewed on the manner in which traditional youth programming has dealt with girls' needs. As an example, an exhaustive review of delinquency prevention and intervention programs, found a concern about girls almost completely absent. A study of 443 delinquency program evaluations done since 1950 revealed that 34.8 percent of these programs only served males and 42.4 percent primarily served boys. Conversely, a meager 2.3 percent of delinquency programs served only girls, and 5.9 percent served primarily girls (Lipsey, 1992).

Because the majority of delinquency prevention programs are coed, the specific needs of girls are either shortchanged or simply ignored because of the population of boys who outnumber them. Programs that are single-sex within the justice system provide far more options for boys than for girls. In fact, a list of "potentially promising programs" identified by the Office of Juvenile Justice and Delinquency Prevention cites twenty-four programs specifically for boys in contrast to only two programs specifically for girls (Girls Incorporated, 1996). Ironically, one program geared for incarcerated teen fathers has no counterpart for incarcerated teen mothers.

Further, programs for young women in general (and delinquents, in particular) have been of low priority in our society as far as funding is concerned. A review of seventy-five private foundations in 1989 revealed that funding "targeted specifically for girls and women hovered around 3.4 percent" (Valentine Foundation, 1990: 5).

General recreational services appear to be no better; a 1993 study of the San Francisco Chapter of the National Organization for Women found that only 8.7 percent of the programs funded by the major city organization funding children and youth programs "specifically addressed the needs of girls" (Siegal, 1995: 18). Not surprisingly, then, a 1995 study of youth participation in San Francisco afterschool or summer sports programs found only 26 percent of the participants were girls (Siegal, 1995: 20).

Often programs tend to miss the "at risk" years for girls. A comprehensive survey of 112 individual youth-oriented programs (for both delinquent and nondelinquent youths) showed less than 8 percent provided services to girls between the ages of nine and fifteen, the crucial determining years of adolescence, and years when girls' self-esteem plummets (American Association of University Women, 1992). Rather, services and programs tended to serve girls younger than the age of nine and teenagers between fourteen and twenty-one years of age.

Moreover, the few programs available for girls often tend to address single issues—especially teen pregnancy and motherhood, and occasionally problems of substance abuse or gang behavior. This pattern is largely a result of issue-specific funding initiatives, but it means that girls' interconnected and overlapping issues and problems get ignored. Similarly, programs tend to be more intervention oriented than preventive, concentrating more on girls who are already in trouble than on girls who are at risk of getting into trouble (Ms. Foundation for Women, 1993).

Unfortunately, while the data reveals that marginalized youths possess high degrees of overlap in services needed, these needs are increasing just as public funding to meet these needs has been decreasing. Ultimately, at-risk youth's multiple needs point to the necessity of more comprehensive programming than is available within any one given program or system. Some research has suggested the need for interagency, interdisciplinary collaborations to address these needs (Arella, 1993).

Ms. Foundation for Women's study on girls' programs (1993) found that programs typically respond to the outcome or symptom of girls' distress, rather than addressing the underlying, structural problems of inequality and poverty that affect many young women. In addition, few programs addressed the special problems that girls of color experience. Likewise, programs geared specifically to the needs of lesbian and bisexual girls and girls with disabilities are virtually nonexistent. In general, programs do not provide services within a context that acknowledges the realities of sexism, racism, classism, and heterosexism as problematic forces in their lives. Thus, little is offered in the way of giving girls the information and support needed to fathom and combat these mechanisms of multiple marginality (Ms. Foundation for Women, 1993).

Are Gender-specific Programs Necessary?

Despite the mounting evidence that while girls have rather severe problems, youth programs have in the main ignored girls (or assumed that programs crafted to meet boys' needs also will work for girls). Some would contend that the jury is still out on the need for gender-specific programming. Indeed, there appears to be the belief in some critical quarters within the juvenile justice system, that gender-specific programming is unnecessary. In a General Accounting Office study (1995), the results of a national survey of chief probation officers noted that while these juvenile court officials felt that "insufficient facilities and services were available to status offenders," they also believed that "status offenders do not need gender-specific services, except for gynecological services and pre-natal care." They also reported that these same high-level court administrators did not feel that "any significant gender-bias concerns" emerged in the treatment of female and male status offenders.

This perspective on girls' delinquency and a lack of interest in girls' special needs, is reflective of the juvenile justice system's checkered past on the treatment of girls. While the court currently is embracing and valorizing equal treatment as a way to justify contemporary practices and avoid change (particularly when the change might benefit girls), the early history of the court reflects a different, but equally damaging approach to girls' problems.

Specifically, *special* concerns about girls' morality were at the center, rather than at the periphery, of the movement that established the juvenile court (Platt, 1969; Odem, 1995; Kunzel, 1993). As a result, in the earliest years of the court (1899-1920), girls frequently were institutionalized for such offenses as "sexual immorality" or "waywardness," and well into the seventies, contemporary "status offenses" such as runaway often functioned as "buffer charges" for the court's concern about the sexual behavior of girls (*see* Chesney-Lind and Shelden, 1997 for a discussion of these issues).

Correctional reformers, concerned about abuse of the status offense category by juvenile courts (though not necessarily about girls), were instrumental in urging the U.S. Congress to pass the Juvenile Justice and Delinquency Prevention (JJDP) Act of 1974. This legislation required that states receiving federal delinquency prevention moneys begin to divert and deinstitutionalize their status offenders. Despite erratic enforcement of this provision and considerable resistance from juvenile court judges, girls were the clear beneficiaries of the reform. Incarceration of young women in training schools and detention centers across the country fell dramatically in the decades since its passage, in distinct contrast to patterns found early in the century.

National statistics on girls' incarceration reflect the official enthusiasm for the incarceration of girls during the early part of this century. Girls' share of the population of juvenile correctional facilities increased from 1880 (when girls were 19 percent of the population) to 1923 (when girls were 28 percent). By 1950, girls had climbed to 34 percent of the total, and in 1960, they were still 27 percent of those in correctional facilities. By 1980, this pattern appeared to have reversed, and girls were again 19 percent of those in correctional facilities (Calahan, 1986: 130). In 1993, girls comprised 10.3 percent of those held in public detention centers and training schools (Hsieh, 1998).

Despite its success in reducing the number of status offenders, and hence girls, in facilities, the reform effort faced broad resistance from the outset. In 1980, the National Council of Juvenile and Family Court Judges was able to narrow the definition of a status offender in the amended act so that any child who had violated a "valid court order" no longer would be covered under the deinstitutionalization provisions (U.S. Statutes at Large, 1981). This change effectively gutted the 1974 Juvenile Justice and Delinquency Prevention Act by permitting judges to reclassify a status offender who violated a court order as a delinquent. This meant that a young woman who ran away from a court-ordered placement (a halfway house, foster home, and so forth) could be relabeled a delinquent and locked up.

Judges long have engaged in efforts like "violation of a valid court order" or issuing contempt citations to "bootstrap" status offenders into categories that permit their detention. They thereby circumvent the deinstitutionalization component of the act (Costello and Worthington, 1981-1982: 42). These judicial maneuvers clearly disadvantage girls. For example, a Florida study by Bishop and Frazier (1992) reviewed 137,671 cases referred to juvenile justice intake units during 1985-1987. The researchers found only a weak pattern of discrimination against female status offenders compared to the treatment of male status offenders. However, when they examined the impact of contempt citations, the pattern changed markedly. They found that females referred for contempt were more likely than females referred for other criminal-type offenses to be petitioned to court, and substantially more likely to be petitioned to court than males referred for contempt.

Moreover, the girls were far more likely than boys to be sentenced to detention. Specifically, the typical female offender in their study had a probability of incarceration of 4.3 percent, which increased to 29.9 percent if she were held in contempt. Such a pattern was not observed among the males in the study. The authors conclude that "the traditional double standard is still operative." Clearly neither the cultural changes associated with the feminist movement nor the legal changes illustrated in the Juvenile Justice and Delinquency Prevention Act's mandate to deinstitutionalize status offenders have brought about equality under the law for young men and women" (Bishop and Frazier, 1992: 1186).

During the early part of this decade, things seemed to be turning around for girls. Hearings held in 1992 in conjunction with the reauthorization of the Juvenile Justice and Delinquency Prevention Act, addressed for the first time the "provision of services to girls within the juvenile justice system" (U.S. House of Representatives, 1992). At this hearing, the double standard of juvenile justice was discussed, as well as the paucity of services for girls. The chair of the hearing, Representative Matthew Martinez, noted the high number of girls arrested for status offenses, the high percentage of girls in detention as a result of violation of court orders, and the failure of the system to address girls' needs. He ended with the question, "I wonder why, why are there no other alternatives than youth jail for her?" (U.S. House of Representatives, 1992: 2).

As a result of this landmark hearing, the 1992 reauthorization of the act included specific provisions requiring plans from each state receiving federal funds to include "an analysis of gender-specific services for the prevention and treatment of juvenile delinquency, including the types of such services available and the need for such services for females and a plan for providing needed gender-specific services for the prevention and treatment of juvenile delinquency" (Public Law 102-586, November 1992). Additional moneys were set aside as part of the Juvenile Justice and Delinquency Prevention Act's Challenge Grant program for states wishing to develop policies to prohibit gender bias in placement and treatment and to develop programs that assure girls equal access to services. As a consequence, twenty-three states embarked on such programs—by far the most popular of the ten possible Challenge Grant activity areas (Girls Incorporated 1996, 26). Finally, the legislation moved to make the "bootstrapping" of status offenders more difficult (U.S. House of Representatives, 1992: 4983).

Sadly, these changes, while extremely hopeful, were short-lived, and the policy backlash was not long in coming. In more recent years, the U.S. Congress (controlled by the more conservative Republicans in the late nineties) repeatedly has attempted to undertake a major overhaul of the landmark Juvenile Justice and Delinquency Prevention Act, and virtually all of the initiatives they drafted were ominous for girls. The bills introduced in the last session of Congress (1996-1998) sought to refocus national attention on the "violent and repeat juvenile offender" (read boys) while also granting states "flexibility" in implementing the four core mandates of the Juvenile Delinquency Act. Key among the changes proposed was a retreat from the deinstitutionalization of status offenders, though conservative lawmakers also are taking aim at efforts to separate youths from adults in correctional facilities, efforts to reduce minority overrepresentation in juvenile detention and training schools, and efforts to remove juveniles from adult jails (National Criminal Justice Association, 1997: 2-3; Alexander, 1998). The special funds set aside to encourage gender-specific programming also would disappear in all the versions of these bills.

Most ominous for girls were efforts to loosen restrictions on the detention of status offenders. For example, Senate Bill 10—"Violent and Repeat Juvenile Act of 1997"—allowed for the incarceration of runaways if a hearing determines "the behavior of the juvenile constitutes a clear and present danger to the juvenile's physical or emotional well being" or that "secure detention is necessary for guarding the safety of the juvenile" or finally that "the detention is necessary . . . to obtain a suitable placement"(Coalition for Juvenile Justice, 1997 : 2). Both house and senate bills weaken the 1992 initiatives in the area of the detention of youths for violation of a valid court order.

Even more worrisome, all the bills made it easier to hold youths in adult jails. The later provision is most disturbing, since girls not infrequently were held in such situations in the past (as de facto detention centers in rural America). Sadly, abuse is not uncommon in such settings. In Ohio, for example, a fifteen-year-old girl was sexually assaulted by a deputy jailer after having been placed in an adult jail for a minor infraction (Ziedenberg and Schiraldi, 1997: 2; *see* Chesney-Lind, 1988, for other examples). Due to the isolation and abuse in these settings, girls are also at great risk for suicide while being held in adult jails (Chesney-Lind, 1998). While these bills failed to make it out of Congress during its last session (due to intense, last minute pressure mounted by child advocates), the danger to the girls remains since most of the vocal advocates for these changes remain in office as of 2000.

This brief review suggests that whether equity or difference is the legal standard of the day, girls who come into the family court system have found what one scholar in the area has characterized as "partial justice" (Rafter, 1990). Indeed, so problematic is this history that some scholars have concluded the juvenile justice system's long history of paternalism and sexism makes it a problematic site for gender-specific services (for example, Kempf-Leonard, 1998). Certainly, the existence of such "services" should not be used as justification for incarcerating girls, and girl-specific programming never should be an excuse to return to the good old days of girls' institutions where working class girls were trained in the womanly arts.

The debate about the need for gender-specific programming must be lodged within the larger congressional backlash against deinstitutionalization. While the 1992 congressional action emerged from a long overdue recognition that the juvenile justice system has not done well by girls, more recent congressional actions reflect a very different trend. Specifically, at least some key senators agree with Judge David Grossman, who testified before Congress representing the National Council of Juvenile and Family Court Judges. He contended that the deinstitutionalization was a "movement" whose time had passed: "All too often, it left the intended young beneficiaries of its advocacy adrift on the streets, fallen between the cracks" (Alexander, 1998: 46). He advocated, instead, that status offenders be returned to the court's jurisdiction. In essence, he proposes juvenile courts go back to a long tradition of failing to meaningfully address girls' serious problems while actively criminalizing their survival strategies by arresting them and detaining them if they run from abusive homes.

Programming as if Girls Mattered: Getting Past Girls Watching Boys Play Sports

Girls in trouble, particularly those in the juvenile justice system, share many problems with their male counterparts. They are likely to be poor, to have come from disrupted and violent families, and to be having difficulties in school. In addition, however, they confront special problems because of their gender: sexual abuse, sexual assaults, unplanned pregnancies, and adolescent motherhood to name a few.

Programming for girls in the juvenile justice system needs to take into consideration girls' unique situations and their special problems in a gendered society. Traditional delinquency treatment strategies, employed in both preventive and intervention programs, have been shaped largely by commonsense assumptions about what youths—generally boys—need. Sometimes girls will benefit from these assumptions and sometimes not. As Marian Daniel, area director with Baltimore's Female Intervention Team, succinctly put it: "for years people have assumed that all you have to do to make a program designed for boys work for girls is to paint the walls pink and take out the urinals" (Daniel cited in Girls Incorporated, 1996: 34).

Lack of Validated Gender-specific Programs; Programming and the "Forgotten Few"

Readers convinced of the need for gender-specific programs will be disappointed if they expect to find descriptions of many innovative and effective programs for girls that have been rigorously evaluated. Essentially, as Bergsmann (1989) once noted in her national review of programming for female offenders in the juvenile justice system, these girls are the "forgotten few." Many evaluations of particular approaches do not deal with gender issues, and frequently, the evaluated programs do not even serve girls. Further, programs that have been evaluated are often run in training schools—not the best setting to try out a particular strategy (Lipsey, 1992).

Readers also might hope to see a more extensive consideration and evaluation of promising, community-based programs for girls, but these have been few and far between (for an exception *see* Artz and Riecken, 1997). Indeed, in the main, we have descriptions of programs in recent publications, but virtually no solid, empirical research on program effectiveness (*see* Girls Incorporated, 1996).

Challenge Grant Activities

A good snapshot of where we are nationally on girls' issues and girls' programming can come from a brief overview of the activities of the states that successfully applied for Challenge Grant funds from the Office of Juvenile Justice and Delinquency Prevention. This review indicates that most states are in the very early stages of understanding the needs of girls in their systems. As a result, of the states where information is available (N=twenty-one), virtually all (twenty of the twenty-one states) used some of these funds to gather data on the characteristics and needs of the girls in their systems. Slightly over a third (38 percent or eight states) funded a specific new program for girls or expanded an existing program that seemed successful. About a quarter of the states held either a conference and/or undertook special training on girls' needs, and slightly under a quarter formed special committees (such as Florida's Girls Initiative Committee, Ohio's Gender Specific Working Group, or the Hawaii Girls Project). Finally, only two states indicated that their committees were involved in the crafting of specific legislation and/or system policy changes, according to Table 3.2

Gender-specific Risk Factors: A Place to Start

Insights about essential elements of programs for girls can be gleaned from what is known broadly about girls' development and more specifically about girls' delinquency. Careful reviews of the risk factors for boys and girls are sensitive to the fact that young people live in a gendered universe. As an example, the Minnesota Women's Fund contends that the most frequent risk factors for girls and boys differ, and that for girls the list

TABLE 3.2. State Challenge Grant Activities: A National Overview

ACTIVITY*	STATES UNDERTAKING ACTIVITY	
	PERCENTAGE	NUMBER
Profiling girls in system/needs assessment	95%	20/21
New Program Initiative	38%	8/21
Special Conference	28%	6/21
Specialized Training(s)	28%	6/21
Formed Girls' Policy Committee	23%	5/21
Undertook Legislative or Policy Change	10%	2/21

*States can and did undertake more than one activity. Compiled from Chesney-Lind, et. al., 1998.

includes: emotional stress, physical and sexual abuse, negative body image, disordered eating, attempted suicide, and pregnancy. For boys the list includes: alcohol, polydrug use, accidental injury, and delinquency (cited in Adolescent Female Subcommittee, 1994). While clearly not all girls at risk will end up in the juvenile justice system, this gendered examination of youth problems could set a standard for examination of delinquency prevention and intervention programs.

Needs that girls' programs should address specifically include the following: dealing with the physical and sexual violence in their lives (from parents, boyfriends, pimps, and others), confronting the risk of AIDS, dealing with pregnancy and motherhood, handling drug and alcohol dependency, facing family problems, finding employment, getting housing assistance, managing stress, and developing a sense of efficacy and empowerment. Many of these needs are universal and should be part of programs for all youths (Schwartz and Orlando, 1991). However, most of these are particularly important for young women.

Influential girl-serving organizations (like the YWCA, Girls Incorporated, and so forth) are beginning to realize their responsibility for girls who are in the juvenile justice system. This high-level national interest is both necessary and welcome. In addition to advocacy, these organizations have conducted recent reviews of promising programs for girls (*see* Girls Incorporated, 1996; Office of Juvenile Justice and Delinquency Prevention, 1998). A quick review of these inventories indicates that programs that specifically target the housing and employment needs of youths, while also providing them with the specific skills they will need to survive on their own, are emerging. These often include a built-in caseworker/service broker, as well as counseling components. Clearly, many girls will require specialized counseling to recover from the ravages of sexual and physical victimization, but the research cautions that approaches that rely simply on the provision of counseling services are not likely to succeed (*see* Chesney-Lind and Shelden, 1998).

Importance of Culturally Specific Girls Programs

Programs also must be scrutinized to assure that they are culturally specific as well as gender specific, since girls' lives are colored by both their culture and their gender. As increasing numbers of girls of color are drawn into the juvenile justice system (and bootstrapped into correctional settings), while their white counterparts are deinstitutionalized, there is a need for programs to be rooted in specific cultures. Since it is clear that girls of color have different experiences than others of their gender, as well as different experiences with the dominant institutions in the society (Amaro and Agular, 1994; Amaro, 1995; Orenstein, 1994; LaFromboise and Howard-Pitney, 1995; Leadbeater and Way, 1996), programs to divert and deinstitutionalize must be shaped by the unique developmental issues confronting minority girls, as well as building in the specific cultural resources available in ethnic communities.

Programming as if Gender Mattered: A Case Study

A good example of the synergy between understanding, in detail, the dimensions of girls' problems and crafting evaluations of programs with this information in mind comes from the work of Sibylle Artz and her colleague Ted Riecken (1997, 1998). Their review of the outcomes of thirteen individual antiviolence initiatives in Canadian schools (Artz and Riecken, 1997) shows the importance of focusing on gender and the desirability of crafting interventions that are gender specific. Employing pre- and posttests of self-reported violence of both student and parent participants as well as school-based data, the researchers quickly concluded that "one size does not fit all" in violence prevention.

Specifically, the researchers found that "boys are far less likely than girls to have participated in student groups that promote violence prevention" (Artz and Riecken, 1997: 297), and that "boys are less likely than girls to adopt the antiviolence messages of their schools' violence prevention programs" (Artz and Riecken, 1997: 296). Girls, even girls with a history of violence, were more likely to see violence as problematic and to change as a result of intervention (particularly interventions based on skills-based programs and positive reinforcement). General consciousness raising was found to be ineffective with both sexes. Finally, males tended to be reached only when men participated in violence prevention efforts and when fathers (not mothers) condemned bullying (Artz and Riecken, 1997: 298).

Even though girls were being reached by the messages in the generic curriculum, the researchers noted that antiviolence curricula needed to be expanded to include sexual and domestic abuse since virtually none of the existing curricula cover these issues. Other work by these researchers, based on in-depth interviews as well as self-report data, indicated that violent girls were much more likely than nonviolent girls to have histories of abuse and current experiences with abusive boyfriends (Artz, 1998). This same work indicated that girls' violence often tends to be a mimicking of the male violence in girls' lives (they often come from homes with dominating and abusive fathers). According to Artz, girls fight with other girls either to excite boys and get their attention, or they fight to be seen to be as good as boys (Artz, 1998).

Finally, Artz concludes that the prevention of girls' violence means recognizing that "the two kinds of violence against women, male-to-female and female-to-female have their origins in the same belief systems"—a system of sexual inequality that valorizes male violence and has girls growing up "seeing themselves through the eyes of males" (Artz, 1998: 204).

Running Away

Given the large numbers of girls in the system for running away from home, and the well-documented problems with traditional foster care placements for girls, any successful program must address girls' needs for safe housing, and, in some instances, legal emancipation (Schwartz and Orlando, 1991). Economic support for these choices is also clearly desirable (and available in some parts of Canada and Australia, as examples) (Alder, 1986), but sadly unlikely given the current hostility in the United States to young women living independently. Indeed, the current "welfare reform" being pursued in the United States specifically targets young women, particularly those with a history of drug abuse, and seeks to prevent them from obtaining financial support even for their dependent children (Adams, Onek, and Riker, 1998).

Education

At-risk girls have severe educational problems, and significant numbers may have educational disabilities (Girls Incorporated, 1996, Dryfoos, 1990, Hugo and Rutherford, 1992; Belnap, 1997). Thus, programming for female adolescents invariably should address academic difficulties. The educational neglect of young women of color, particularly African-American girls, must be addressed (Orenstein, 1994; Arnold, 1995). Likewise, any program that encourages girls to succeed in the traditionally male-dominated subjects of math and science is likely to bolster self-esteem, school performance, and even career prospects (Sadker and Sadker, 1994).

Dealing with Trauma

Histories of trauma set the stage for substantial problems with depression, self-image, and attempted suicide. One scholar put it this way: "No one will demand and obtain intervention for her because in our country it is more often slashed tires, not slashed wrists, that are noticed" (Wells, 1994: 4). Programming for young women should address, without pathologizing, histories of sexual and physical abuse. Girls' problems with substance abuse, which are substantial (Howell and Davis, 1992), should be informed by understanding that often, for girls, polydrug use is a way of self-medicating.

Peers

Negative peer influence is one of the major contributing factors for engaging in delinquent activity (Girls Incorporated, 1996). Most girls join negative peer groups or even gangs so that they feel like they "belong" and are accepted somewhere. Indeed, almost half (44.8 percent) of the girls in the juvenile justice system reported feeling little or no love or acceptance while growing up (American Correctional Association, 1990). Consequently, girls, particularly delinquent girls, need the positive influence and support of new peers and adult mentors who will encourage them to break or renegotiate bonds with people who have been harmful influences. Thus, ready access to a broad network of adult mentors and peer counselors sensitive to the girl-specific issues and problems should be made available.

Girls seem to prize connectedness and relationships with other people more than boys (Gilligan, 1982). In this respect, a relational approach that emphasizes trust and relationship-building with positive female role models would be highly beneficial. However, trust only can be developed when girls perceive their programs as being "safe" spaces where they do not have to fear experiencing condemnation. This entails creating an atmosphere that allows girls to express their thoughts and emotions freely and appropriately.

Similarly, program staff must be affirmative by acknowledging the worth of each girl despite her attitude or background. Girls' programs also need to create separate time and space for girls, apart from boys, so that issues related to sexism will not be overshadowed by boys' more disruptive behavior. In addition, girls' programs should address the realities of sexism, racism, classism, homophobia, and ableism on girls' lives, and work to change established beliefs that prevent girls from recognizing their potential. Similarly, allowing cultural differences to be understood and validated is essential to empowering girls from marginalized backgrounds.

The Importance of Age

Programs for girls ideally should begin before adolescence, by age nine or ten, and continue through the rest of adolescence; this is consistent with research that suggests that earlier preventive approaches are the most effective (Ms. Foundation for Women, 1993). Likewise, programs, particularly those that are issue-specific, need to provide transition and aftercare services that support young women in maintaining the progress they have made.

Program Setting

Settings for programs are also important; the best research suggests that schools are good, neutral environments within which both school and social service agencies can provide an array of services (Dryfoos, 1990). Private/public collaborations are the most likely to provide the richest array of services to girls without costly redundancy. Impediments to school settings for gender-specific programs, though, exist; notably, there is the notion that all programs should be coeducational. Clearly, this is a difficult issue, but one that must be addressed, since it is clear that coeducational settings, while often beneficial to boys, disadvantage and "shortchange" girls (Sadker and Sadker, 1994).

Recreation

Many troubled and marginalized girls engage in delinquent behavior simply because there is little else to occupy their free time. Clearly, recreational programs should be addressing the issue of boredom as a cause of youthful crime—among girls as well as boys. Unfortunately, all too often, these programs end up being "girls watching boys play sports." Structured recreation that consists of varied activities, including sports, leadership opportunities, programs and projects, arts and crafts, community service, ethnic and culturally oriented activities, dances, and social events, provide a great way for girls to learn new skills, develop responsibility, increase self-esteem and self-confidence, befriend other girls, and most importantly, have fun.

Additionally, time and energy spent on rewarding activities dissuade girls from wanting to engage in delinquent or self-defeating behavior in the first place. Girls already embedded within the juvenile justice system frequently state that had they had opportunities to engage in meaningful, interesting activities, they probably would not have fallen into the system. In the words of one girl at the Hawaii Youth Correctional Facility, having "something to do, like a job or something" could have helped her to be delinquency-free (Chesney-Lind, et al., 1998: 45).

Programs invariably should work to empower girls, and to give them the tools to challenge the pervasive media emphasis on girls' physical appearance (Thorne, 1993; Artz, 1998). We know that self-esteem drops dramatically among adolescent girls. This knowledge underscores the necessity to foster settings and experiences that will allow girls to find, often in peer groups, a bolder, more confident notion of girlhood that is less connected to constructions of "popularity," "beauty," and "sexuality" that are essentially reflections of boys' and men's approval (Durham, 1998). This entails building on girls' innate strengths, skills, and creativity to develop their voices and their abilities to assert themselves. Girls also need the opportunity to aid in the design, implementation, and evaluation of programs that are geared for their benefit. Similarly, programs continually should reevaluate their effectiveness and remain flexible and open to change.

Quality programming for at-risk girls entails a commitment towards positive youth development. To this end, young women, rather than being in need of "fixing," need to be "empowered" through effective preventive and intervention-oriented approaches. This ultimately entails respecting female development processes and celebrating the uniqueness of both girls and women.

Concluding Words: Boys Can't Talk Girl Talk

There is no shortage of work to be done to understand how to better serve the young women who find themselves in the juvenile justice system. What research we do have, both on girls' problems and on girls' experiences with the juvenile justice system, suggests that gender has for a long time played a role in juvenile justice, whether officially recognized or not.

The challenge that confronts us is whether we can take what we know about girls' development, the different ways culture impacts on gender development, and the ways in which girls' problems evolve into female delinquency and craft programmatic responses to these social forces. Clearly, much more research is needed to fully understand all of these topics, and that research should be used to inform both policy and practice.

What scant research we possess suggests that gender-specific programming may allow us to better serve a population that is generally ignored in a criminal justice system that tends to respond to agitated victims and egregious crimes. Lacking a powerful constituency, we have in the past been left with a pattern of "throwaway services for throwaway girls" (Wells, 1994: 4). We can and should do better than this for tomorrow's women.

Admittedly, the jury is still out and will be out for some time regarding the necessity and effectiveness of gender-specific services, but that girls deserve equitable (not equal) treatment and services is undeniable. Perhaps the best case this author has seen for girls' programming is made by a poem written by a young woman in a girls' program in the juvenile justice system in Chicago (*see* page 164); it is also a reminder about the humanity, energy, and talent that girls in our systems can offer the world if we can help develop those undeniable talents and go boldly forward into the world that awaits them.

Boys Can't Talk Girl Talk[5]

Boys can't talk girls talk
because you talk about things
boys shouldn't know
or have no right to know
but maybe they need to know?
or do they?
Boys can't talk girls talk
because women and men are different
but men need to know some things
about women in order to have a
relationship or do they?
Boys can't talk girls talk
because boys would take all of
the attention away from the girls and
would demand it for themselves,
is it their security or our insecurity
no more
what ever it is
boys can't talk girls talk

Endnotes

[1] The author would like to thank Jennifer Koo and Joell Hokulani Yuen for their assistance in preparing this report. She also would also like to express her gratitude to Dr. Maeve McMahon for her help in polishing both her argument and her prose.

[2] Chesney-Lind, Meda, Debbie Kato, Jennifer Koo, Katie Fujiwara-Clark. 1997. p. 45.

[3] Girls Incorporated, 1996, 34.

[4] In a research project funded by the Office of Juvenile Justice and Delinquency Prevention, the author and her colleagues solicited information from each state that received Challenge Grant moneys (Chesney-Lind, Koo, Kato and Clark, 1998). The descriptions we received were reviewed and the activities of each state roughly coded for this report (note that states undertake to do more than one of these activities). All the full descriptions are available in this report.

[5] Anetra, N. 1995. "Girls Talkin . . . Poetry." Chicago: Chicago Girls Project. December 19.

References

Acoca, L. and J. Austin. 1996. *The Crisis: Women in Prison*. Report submitted to the Charles E. Culpepper Foundation (draft). (Available from the National Council on Crime and Delinquency, 685 Market Street, Suite 620, San Francisco, California 94105.

Adams, P. F., C. A. Schoenborn, A. J. Moss, C. W. Warren, and L. Kann. 1995. *Health-Risk Behaviors among our Nation's Youth: United States, 1992*. Vital and Heath Statistics Series 10, No. 192; DHHS Publication. No (PHS) 95-152. Hyattsville, Maryland: National Center for Health Statistics.

Adams, Rukaiyah, David Onek, Alissa Riker. 1998. *Double Jeopardy: An Assessment of the Felony Drug Provision of the Welfare Reform Act*. Washington, D.C.: Justice Policy Institute.

Adolescent Female Subcommittee. 1994. *Needs Assessment and Recommendations for Adolescent Females in Minnesota*. St. Paul: Minnesota Department of Corrections.

Alder, C. 1986. Unemployed Women Have Got it Heaps Worse: Exploring the Implications of Female Youth Unemployment. *Australian and New Zealand Society of Criminology*. 19, 210-224.

————. 1995. Delinquency Prevention with Young Women. Paper presented at the Delinquency Prevention Conference. Terrigal, New South Wales, Australia.

Alexander, B. 1998. Hatch Quarterbacks Sneak Play for Youth Crime Bill. *Youth Today*. October. 46-47.

Allgood-Merten, B., P. Lewisohn, and H. Hops. 1990. Sex Differences and Adolescent Depression. *Journal of Abnormal Psychology*. 99, 55-63.

Amaro, H. 1995. Love, Sex, and Power: Considering Women's Realities in HIV Prevention. *American Psychologist*. 50: 6. 437-447.

Amaro, H. and M. Agular. 1994. Programa Mama: Mom's Project. A Hispanic/Latino Family Approach to Substance Abuse Prevention. Center for Substance Abuse Prevention, Mental Health Services Administration.

American Association for University Women. 1992. *How Schools Are Shortchanging Girls*. Washington, D.C.: AAUW Educational Foundation.

American Correctional Association. 1990. *The Female Offender: What Does the Future Hold?* Lanham, Maryland: American Correctional Association.

Arella, L. 1993. Multiservice Adolescent Programs: Seeking Institutional Partnership Alternatives. *Journal of Youth and Adolescence*. 22, 283-295.

Arnold, R. 1995. The Processes of Victimization and Criminalization of Black Women. In Barbara Raffel Price and Natalie Sokoloff, eds. *The Criminal Justice System and Women*. New York: McGraw Hill. pp. 136-146.

Artz, S. 1998. *Sex, Power, and the Violent School Girl*. Toronto: Trifolium.

Artz, S. and T. Riecken. 1997. What, So What, Then What?: The Gender Gap in School-based Violence and its Implications for Child and Youth Care Practice. *Child and Youth Care Forum*. 26: 4. 291-303.

Bartollas, C. 1993. Little Girls Grown: The Perils of Institutionalization. In Concetta Culliver, ed. *Female Criminality: The State of the Art*. New York: Garland Press.

Belnap, J. M. Dunn and K. Holsinger. 1997. Gender Specific Services Work Group: Report to the Governor. Columbus, Ohio: Office of Criminal Justice Services.

Benson, P. L. 1990. *The Troubled Journey: A Portrait of 6th-12th Grade Youth*. Minneapolis: Search Institute.

Bergsmann, I. R. 1989. The Forgotten Few: Juvenile Female Offenders. *Federal Probation*. March. LIII:1. 73-78.

Bishop, D. and C. Frazier. 1992. Gender Bias in the Juvenile Justice System: Implications of the JJDP Act. *The Journal of Criminal Law and Criminology*. 82: 4. 1162-1186.

Calahan, M. 1986. *Historical Corrections Statistics in the United States, 1850-1984*. Washington, D.C. : Bureau of Justice Statistics.

Canter, R. J. 1982. Sex Differences in Self-report Delinquency. *Criminology*. 20. 373-393.

Chesney-Lind, M. 1997. *The Female Offender: Girls, Women and Crime*. Thousand Oaks, California: Sage Publications.

Chesney-Lind, M., D. Kato, J. Koo, K. Fujiwara-Clark. 1997. *Girls at Risk: An Overview of Female Delinquency in the Fiftieth State*. Honolulu, Hawaii: Social Science Research Institute.

———. 1998. *Girls at Risk: An Overview of Gender-Specific Programming Issues and Initiatives*. Honolulu, Hawaii: Social Science Research Institute.

Chesney-Lind, M. and R. G. Shelden. 1998. *Girls, Delinquency, and Juvenile Justice*. Belmont, California: West/Wadsworth.

Coalition for Juvenile Justice. 1997. Legislative Summary. Internal memo, August 8.

Costello, J. C. and N. L. Worthington. 1981. Incarcerating Status Offenders: Attempts to Circumvent the Juvenile Justice and Delinquency Prevention Act. *Harvard Civil Rights-Civil Liberties Law Review.* 16:41-81.

Currie, E. 1998. *Crime and Punishment in America.* New York: Metropolitan Books.

Dembo, R., S. C. Sue, P. Borden, and D. Manning. 1995. Gender Differences in Service Needs among Youths Entering a Juvenile Assessment Center: A Replication Study. Paper presented at the Annual Meeting of The Society of Social Problems. Washington, D.C. August.

Dembo, R., L. Williams, and J. Schmeidler. 1993. Gender Differences in Mental Health Service Needs among Youths Entering a Juvenile Detention Center. *Journal of Prison and Jail Health.*12:73-101.

Dryfoos, J. 1990. *Adolescents at Risk.* New York: Oxford.

Durham, M. G. 1998. Dilemmas of Desire: Representations of Adolescent Sexuality in Two Teen Magazines. *Youth and Society.* 29: 369-389.

Federal Bureau of Investigation. 1997. *Crime in the United States 1996.* Washington, D.C.: Government Printing Office. 219.

Fine, M. and N. Zane. 1989. Bein' Wrapped Too Tight: When Low-income Women Drop Out of High School. In L. Weis, E. Farrar, and H. G. Petrie, eds. *Dropouts from Schools: Issues, Dilemmas and Solutions.* Albany, New York: State University of New York Press. pp. 23-53.

Finkelhor, D. and L. Baron. 1986. Risk Factors for Child Sexual Abuse. *Journal of Interpersonal Violence.* 1: 43-71.

Ford, R. 1998. The Razor's Edge. *Boston Globe Magazine.* May 24, pp. 13, 22-28.

Gilligan, C. 1982. *In A Different Voice.* Cambridge: Harvard University Press.

Girls Incorporated. 1996. Prevention and Parity: Girls in Juvenile Justice: Indianapolis: Girls Incorporated National Resource Center.

Government Accounting Office. 1995. *Juvenile Justice: Minimal Gender Bias Occurring in Processing Non-Criminal Juveniles.* Washington, D.C.: U.S. General Accounting Office.

Howell, N. and S. P. Davis. 1992. Special Problems of Female Offenders. *Corrections Compendium.* 12:1:1, 5-20.

Hsieh, C. 1998. Personal communication with the author.

Hugo, K. E. and R. B. Rutherford, Jr. 1992. Issues in Identifying Educational Disabilities among Female Juvenile Offenders. *Journal of Correctional Education.* 43: 3. 124-127.

Huizinga, D. 1997. Over-time Changes in Delinquency and Drug-Use: The 1970s to the 1990s. University of Colorado: Research Brief. Boulder, Colorado.

Kann, L., C. W. Warren, W. A. Harris, J. L. Collins, K. A. Douglas, M. E. Collins, B. I. Williams, J. G. Ross, and L. J. Kolbe. 1995. Youth Risk Behavior Surveillance—United States, 1993. March 24. *Morbidity and Mortality Weekly Report 44.* No. SS-1, 2-55.

Kempf-Leonard, K. 1998. Disparity Based on Sex: Is Gender Specific Treatment Warranted? University of Missouri-St. Louis. Unpublished paper.

Kunzel, R. 1993. *Fallen Women and Problem Girls: Unmarried Mothers and the Professionalization of Social Work, 1890-1945.* New Haven: Yale University Press.

LaFromboise, T. D. and B. Howard-Pitney. 1995. Suicidal Behavior in American Indian Female Adolescents. In S. Canetto and D. Lester, eds. *Woman and Suicidal Behavior.* New York: Springer. pp. 157-173.

Leadbeater, B. and N. Way. 1996. *Urban Girls: Resisting Stereotypes, Creating Identities.* New York: New York University Press.

Leslie, C., N. Biddle, D. Rosenberg, and J. Wayne. 1993. Girls Will Be Girls. *Newsweek.* August 2. p. 44.

Lipsey, M. W. 1992. Juvenile Delinquency Treatment: A Meta-analytic Inquiry into the Variability of Effects. In T. A. Cook, H. Cooper, D. S. Cordray, H. Hartmann, L. V. Hedges, R. J. Light, T. A. Louis, and E. Mosleller, eds. *Meta-analysis for Explanation: A Casebook.* New York: Russell Sage. pp. 83-126.

Loper, A. B. and D. G. Cornell. 1996. Homicide by Girls. *Journal of Child and Family Studies.* 5:321-333.

Mayer, J. 1994. Girls in the Maryland Juvenile Justice System: Findings of the Female Population Taskforce. Presentation to the Gender Specific Services Training. Minneapolis, Minnesota.

McCormack, A., M. D. Janus, and A. W. Burgess.1986. Runaway Youths and Sexual Victimization: Gender Differences in an Adolescent Runaway Population. *Child Abuse and Neglect.* 10: 387-395.

Miller, D. 1994. Exploring Gender Differences in Suicidal Behavior among Adolescent Offenders: Findings and Implications. *Journal of Correctional Education.* 45:3, 134-138.

Ms. Foundation for Women, National Girls Initiative. 1993. *Programmed Neglect, Not Seen, Not Heard: Report on Girls Programming in the United States.* New York: Ms. Foundation for Women.

National Criminal Justice Association. 1997. Congressional Roundup. *Justice Bulletin.* 17: 4. April 1-3.

Odem, M. E. 1995. *Delinquent Daughters.* Chapel Hill, North Carolina: University of North Carolina Press.

Office of Juvenile Justice and Delinquency Prevention. 1998. *Guiding Principles for Promising Female Programming: An Inventory of Best Practices.* Green, Peters, and Associates: Nashville, Tennessee.

Orenstein, P. 1994. *School Girls.* New York: Doubleday.

Pipher, M. 1994. *Reviving Ophelia.* New York: Ballantine

Platt, A. M. 1969. *The Childsavers.* Chicago: University of Chicago Press.

Rafter, N. H. 1990. *Partial Justice: Women, Prisons and Social Control.* New Brunswick, New Jersey: Transaction Books.

Robinson, R. 1990. *Violations of Girlhood: A Qualitative Study of Female Delinquents and Children in Need of Services in Massachusetts.* Unpublished Doctoral Dissertation. Brandeis University.

Sadker, M. and D. Sadker. 1994. *Failing at Fairness.* New York: Charles Scribner's Sons.

Schwartz, I. M. and F. Orlando. 1991. *Programming for Young Women in the Juvenile Justice System.* Ann Arbor, Michigan: Center for the Study of Youth Policy, University of Michigan.

Shelden, R. and J. Horvath. 1986. Processing Offenders in a Juvenile Court: A Comparison of Male and Female Offenders. Paper presented at the annual meeting of the Western Society of Criminology, Newport Beach, California.

Siegal, N. 1995. Where the Girls Are. *San Francisco Bay Guardian.* October 4. p. 19-20.

Steffensmeier, D. J. and R. H. Steffensmeier. 1980. Trends in Female Delinquency: An Examination of Arrest, Juvenile Court, Self-Report, and Field Data. *Criminology.* 18:62- 85.

Thorne, B. 1994. *Gender Play: Girls and Boys in School.* New Brunswick, New Jersey: Rutgers University Press.

U.S. Statutes at Large. Ninety-Sixth Congress, 2nd sess. 1981. *Public Law 96-509—December 1981*. Washington, D.C.: U.S. Government Printing Office.

U.S. House of Representatives. 1992. Hearings on the Juvenile Justice and Delinquency Prevention Act of 1974. Hearings Before the Subcommittee on Human Resources of the Committee on Education and Labor. One Hundred and Second Congress, Serial No. 102-125. Washington, D.C.: U.S. Government Printing Office.

Valentine Foundation and Woman's Way. 1990. *A Conversation about Girls* pamphlet. Byrn Mawr, Pennsylvania: Valentine Foundation.

Wells, R. 1994. America's Delinquent Daughters Have Nowhere to Turn for Help. *Corrections Compendium*. 19:11: 4-6.

Whitaker, Agnes, Jim Johnson, David Shaffer. 1990. Uncommon Troubles in Young People. *Archives of General Psychiatry*. 47, 487-496.

Wright, C. Personal communication with the author. July 28, 1998.

Ziedenberg, J., and V. Schiraldi. 1997. *The Risks Juveniles Face When They are Incarcerated with Adults*. Washington, D.C.: Center for Juvenile and Criminal Justice.

HELPING WOMEN RECOVER: CREATING GENDER-SPECIFIC TREATMENT FOR SUBSTANCE-ABUSING WOMEN AND GIRLS IN COMMUNITY CORRECTIONS

4

Stephanie S. Covington, Ph.D., LCSW[1]
Codirector
Institute for Relational Development
La Jolla, California

Some of the most neglected and misunderstood women and girls in North America are those in the criminal justice system. Largely because of the "War on Drugs," the rate of incarceration for women in the United States has tripled since 1980 (Bloom, Chesney-Lind, and Owen, 1994; Collins and Collins, 1996). Between 1986 and 1991, the number of women in state prisons for drug-related offenses increased by 432 percent (Phillips and Harm, 1998). Like their juvenile counterparts, most of these women are nonviolent offenders who could be treated much more effectively and economically in community-based gender-specific programs.

When females are not a security risk, community-based sanctions offer benefits to society, to female offenders themselves, and to their children. One survey compares an $869 average annual cost for probation to $14,363 for jail and $17,794 for prison (Phillips and Harm, 1998). Community corrections disrupts females' lives less than does incarceration and subjects them to less isolation. Further, community corrections potentially disrupts the lives of children far less. Unfortunately, few drug treatment programs exist that address the needs of females, especially those with minor children. This is unfortunate because, when allied with probation, electronic monitoring, community service, and/or work release, community-based substance abuse treatment could be an effective alternative to the spiraling rates of recidivism and reincarceration.

Historically, the differences between women and men have been overlooked, both in substance abuse treatment and in criminal justice policy. A growing body of research in North America indicates that substance abuse treatment programs that address women's and girls' unique needs, such as relationships with their partners, families, and children, and their history of physical and sexual abuse, are more effective (Carten, 1996; Center for Substance Abuse Treatment, 1994; Correctional Service Canada, 1994; Covington, 1998; Finkelstein and Piedade, 1993; Goldberg, 1995). Successful programs can be shaped by what has been learned since the 1970s about substance abuse and about women and girls, in particular. Consequently, this paper addresses:

1. What is known about women and girls who enter our correctional systems

2. What "gender-specific" programs and services and substance abuse treatment are

3. Three theoretical perspectives on addiction, female psychological development, and trauma that provide a foundation for a model of women's treatment

4. The principles of an effective treatment program for women and girls in community corrections

5. The use of twelve-step mutual help programs

Who Are the Women and Girls?

To design a treatment program that matches female offenders' needs, it is important to consider who they are (in other words, the demographics and history of the female population) as well as how various life factors impact on their substance abuse and patterns of offending. A basic principle of clinical work is to know who the client is and what she brings into the treatment setting. "[I]f programming is to be effective, it must . . . take the context of women's lives into account" (Abbott and Kerr, 1995). Therefore, a review of the literature on the lives of women and girls in the criminal justice system is presented.

Reliable and detailed data about females in community corrections programs is not collected annually in the United States or in Canada, although the U.S. national jail census does collect data every five years on women in local jails, and the U.S. Department of Justice's Bureau of Justice Statistics collects annual data on women housed in state and federal prisons. Consequently, most of the following discussion of female offenders is based on data about females who are in jail or prison in the United States and Canada (Austin, Bloom, and Donahue, 1992; Lightfoot and Lambert, 1992). Data about girls is even more difficult to obtain than data about adult women, because girls comprise a small percentage of the juvenile offender population. However, in general, female offenders can be said to differ from their male counterparts in several significant ways.

Nonviolent Property and Status Offenses

First, they are less likely to have committed violent offenses and more likely to have been convicted of crimes involving alcohol, other drugs, or property. Female offenders have been found to play a limited role in drug trafficking as "mules" (Phillips and Harm, 1998). Most of their drug convictions relate to using drugs. Many of their property crimes are economically driven, often motivated by poverty and/or the abuse of alcohol and other drugs. In a study of California inmates, 71.9 percent of women had been convicted on a drug or property charge, versus 49.7 percent of men. Men also commit nearly twice the violent crimes that women do (Bloom, Chesney-Lind, and Owen, 1994). These statistics are consistent with national trends in Australia, Canada, and the United States (Denborough, 1996; Lightfoot and Lambert, 1992; Steffenmeier and Allan, 1998).

Juvenile offenders also reflect this pattern in the type of crime that they commit. Rates for less serious crimes, such as smoking marijuana and shoplifting, are similar for boys and girls. Rates of serious and violent crime are far lower among girls, although there is a perceived shift toward violent crimes (Belknap, 1996; Peters and Peters, 1998). Girls are more likely than boys to be arrested and detained for status offenses— acts that would not be offenses if committed by adults, such as promiscuity, truancy, or running away (Belknap, Dunn, and Holsinger, 1997; Pepi, 1998). Both promiscuity and running away often are connected to physical and sexual abuse in the home.

Of those females in prison for violent crimes, many of them committed their crimes against a spouse, ex-spouse, or boyfriend. They are likely to report having been physically or sexually abused, often by the person they assaulted. Thus, even violent female offenders are not frequently seen as at risk for committing violence against the general public (Browne, 1987; Denborough, 1996; Phillips and Harm, 1998).

Substance Abuse Problems

Substance abuse is a major problem for female offenders. In the United States, "up to 80 percent of the women offenders in some state prison systems now have severe, long-standing substance abuse problems," according to the Center for Substance Abuse Treatment (1997, p. 2). According to Snell (1994), drug violators make up 61 percent of women in U. S. federal prisons (up from 38 percent in 1986), 21 percent of the women in state facilities (up from 9 percent), and 23 percent of those in local jails (up from 9 percent). In Australia, 66 percent of women inmates have severe substance abuse problems (Consedine, 1995). More than 50 percent of U.S. and Canadian offenders (both male and female) self-report that alcohol or other drugs were involved in the crimes that led to their current imprisonment—and this figure is likely to be under the true proportion of substance-related crime (Brennan and Austin, 1997; Weekes et. al, 1997). In a Canadian study (Lightfoot and Lambert, 1992), 25 percent of the women reported that their current incarceration was due to a drug offense, but almost 60 percent said they had used alcohol or other drugs on the day of the offense. Of that 60 percent, 59.6 percent said their substance use had seriously impaired their judgment.

Yet, despite the strong link between substance abuse and crime, only a fraction of inmates receive treatment (Wellisch, Prendergast, and Anglin, 1994). For example, in California, only 3 percent of prisoners have access to any kind of treatment, even voluntary programs such as Alcoholics Anonymous (Bloom, et al., 1994).

To put these statistics into perspective, it is helpful to compare them to statistics on substance abuse of females in the general population. The Substance Abuse and Mental Health Services Administration (1993) reports that 2.1 percent of American females aged twelve and older had engaged in heavy alcohol use in the thirty days preceding the survey; 4.1 percent had used an illicit drug; and 1.2 percent had used a psychotherapeutic drug for a nonmedical purpose. By contrast, the National Center on Addiction and Substance Abuse (1998) found that 54 percent of women offenders in state prisons had used an illicit drug in the month prior to their crimes, and 48 percent were under the influence of either alcohol or another drug when they committed their crimes. Among women offenders in federal prisons, 27 percent had used an illicit drug in the month prior to their crimes, and 20 percent were under the influence when they committed their crimes. Among jail inmates, 54 percent had used an illicit drug in the previous month, and 48 percent were under the influence when they committed their crimes. It appears that substance-abusing females are present in U. S. jails and prisons by six to ten times more than in the general population.

In some states in the United States, these percentages are even higher. The Massachusetts Committee on Criminal Justice estimates that 90 percent of women prisoners have alcohol or drug problems (Center for Substance Abuse Treatment, 1997). In New Jersey, 85 percent of women offenders are in the criminal justice system for drug-related offenses (Gonzalez, 1996). The Bureau of Justice Statistics (1992) found that women are more likely than men to be under the influence of drugs when they commit their offenses.

The severity of female offenders' substance abuse problems varies. In one study of incarcerated women in Canada, 35 percent reported no drug-related problems, 29 percent showed low levels of alcohol or drug problems, and 36 percent were using alcohol or other drugs at moderate to severe levels (Lightfoot, 1997). Several states in the United States screen all offenders in their systems for alcohol and other drug problems. In Delaware, 25.6 percent of incarcerated women meet the screening criteria for long-term residential care, an additional 44.2 percent meet the criteria for short-term residential treatment, and 7 percent meet the criteria for intensive outpatient treatment. Only 9.3 percent of Delaware's women offenders needed no treatment (Peyton, 1994). Similarly, of Illinois women inmates serving time for a class 2, 3, or 4 offense who report any drug dependence, 86 percent meet criteria for residential rehabilitation, 11 percent need intensive outpatient treatment, and an additional 3 percent need standard outpatient treatment (Illinois Criminal Justice State Plan, 1995). "The Illinois Department of Corrections finds that women enter prison at a more advanced and severe stage of drug abuse than men. Addicted women offenders therefore need longer treatment" (Center for Substance Abuse Treatment, 1997, p. 5).

Psychiatric Disorders

Substance abuse is the most common psychiatric disorder among female offenders. A survey of female pretrial jail detainees found that more than 80 percent of the sample met the *Diagnostic and Statistical Manual of Mental Disorders* criteria for one or more lifetime psychiatric disorders (American Psychiatric Association, 1994). "The most common disorders were drug abuse or drug dependence (63.6 percent), alcohol abuse or alcohol dependence (32.3 percent), and PTSD [Posttraumatic Stress Disorder] (33.5 percent)" (Teplin, Abram, and McClelland, 1996, p. 508). Sixty percent of the subjects had exhibited drug or alcohol abuse or dependence within six months of the interview. In addition, 17 percent met the criteria for a major depressive episode. Subjects were mostly nonviolent offenders who had been jailed because they could not pay even the low bail for misdemeanors. This study concluded:

> The American Bar Association recommends that persons with mental disorders who were arrested for misdemeanors be diverted to a mental health facility instead of arrested. With appropriate community programs, nonviolent felons also could be treated outside the jail after pretrial hearings. . . . Unfortunately, community-based programs are rarely available for released jail detainees, who often have complex diagnostic profiles and special treatment needs (Teplin et al., 1996, p. 511).

Because antisocial personality disorder (ASPD) is widely diagnosed among male offenders, treatment for offenders of both sexes often has focused on cognitive-behavioral approaches to treating it. However, antisocial personality disorder is far less prevalent among female offenders than among males. In a Canadian study of opiate injectors, only 27 percent of the women met the full criteria for antisocial personality disorder (Lightfoot, 1997). By contrast, depression, anxiety, and other mood disorders are far more common among substance-abusing females. In one study, major depression co-occurred with alcohol abuse in 19 percent of women (almost four times the rate for men); phobic disorder co-occurred in 31 percent of women (more than twice the rate for men); and panic disorder occurred in 7 percent of women (three-and-a-half times the rate for men). Furthermore, the rate of major depression among the alcoholic women was almost three times the rate in the general female population, and the rate for phobias was almost double. The rate of antisocial personality disorder among alcoholic women was twelve times higher than the rate in the general female population. Still, only 10 percent of the alcoholic women were diagnosed with antisocial personality disorder, far lower than the rates of depression and phobia (Blume, 1990).

The prevalence of dual diagnosis—females with both substance abuse and another psychiatric disorder—has not been well studied. However, in one study of both men and women, 23 percent of those surveyed reported a history of psychiatric disorders, and 30 percent of that group also reported having had a substance abuse problem at some time in their lives (Daly, Moss, and Campbell, 1993).

Dual diagnosis is complex and controversial. Women and girls in early recovery often show symptoms of mood disorders, but these can be temporary conditions associated with withdrawal. Also, it is difficult to know whether a psychiatric disorder existed in a given female before she began to abuse alcohol or other drugs, or whether the psychiatric problem emerged after the onset of substance abuse (Institute of Medicine, 1990). Research suggests that preexisting disorders improve more slowly for the recovering substance abuser and need to be addressed directly in treatment.

Poverty, Lack of Skills, and Ethnicity

Furthermore, most female offenders are poor, undereducated, and unskilled. A survey of female jail inmates in the United States found that "over 60 percent were unemployed when arrested and one-third were not looking for work. Less than one-third of male inmates were similarly unemployed and less than 12 percent were not looking for work" (Collins and Collins, 1996). A Canadian study found that only 52.6 percent of the female offenders had completed secondary school. Most (43.8 percent) of the women in that study reported themselves as unskilled workers; another 10 percent said that their usual occupation was crime or homemaking (Lightfoot and Lambert, 1992). A U.S. study found that of those women who had been employed before incarceration, many were on the lower rungs of the economic ladder, with only 37 percent working at a "legitimate" job. Twenty-two percent were on some kind of public support, 16 percent made money from drug dealing, and 15 percent were involved in prostitution, shoplifting, or other illegal activities (Bloom et al., 1994).

A disproportionate number of female offenders are minorities. Arbour (1996) says Native women are overrepresented in Canadian prisons. Bloom et al. (1994) found that more than half of the women surveyed were African American (35 percent) or Hispanic (16.6 percent), one-third were Caucasian, and the remaining 13 percent were made up of other minorities. (*See* the chapter by Chesney-Lind in this volume.)

Single Motherhood

Motherhood is also common among female offenders. Two-thirds of women incarcerated in the United States have children under the age of eighteen (Bureau of Justice Statistics, 1991). A Canadian survey found that 62 percent of the women were parents, two-thirds of whom had custody of minor children at the time of the crime (Lightfoot and Lambert, 1992). Many of these women felt enormous guilt about being absent from their children's lives and worried about whether they would retain custody of their children when they were released (Bloom and Steinhart, 1993; Watterson, 1996).

Physical and Sexual Abuse

Many women in prison also have a history of physical and sexual abuse. While it is estimated that 30 percent of females in the general Canadian population are sexually assaulted before age eighteen, more than 50 percent of women in Canada's Federal Prison for Women were sexually abused as children, and 75 percent were either physically or sexually abused (Heney and Kristiansen, 1997). Eighty-two percent of the women offenders in another Canadian study reported histories of physical or sexual abuse (Task Force on Federally Sentenced Women, 1990). A U.S. study found that nearly 80 percent of female prisoners had experienced some form of abuse. Twenty-nine percent reported being physically abused as children and 60 percent as adults, usually by their partners. Thirty-one percent experienced sexual abuse as a child and 23 percent as adults; 40 percent reported emotional abuse as a child and 48 percent as an adult (Bloom et al., 1994). Another U.S. study found that 23 percent of female inmates had experienced incest or rape as juveniles; 22 percent had been sexually abused as adults; and 53 percent had been physically abused (Brennan and Austin, 1997).

Research on adolescent girl offenders reveals abuse histories that parallel those of adult women. For example, a study of girls involved in violent street crime in New York City found that almost all came from homes characterized by poverty, domestic violence, and substance abuse. Those who became delinquent as younger adolescents, as opposed to later in their teens, were more likely to have come from neighborhoods with "high concentrations of poverty," to have been sexually or physically abused by a stranger, and to have friends involved in violent crime (Sommers and Baskin, 1994, p. 477). Sexual abuse victims, compared with nonvictims, begin drug use earlier and are more likely to be regular users of illicit drugs (Bodinger-de Uriarte and Austin, 1991).

Girls Most at Risk for Substance Abuse

Researchers once found a gap between rates of alcohol and drug use by girls and boys, but that gap is narrowing. Between 1991 and 1995, the rate of marijuana use within the past month among eighth-grade girls rose slightly faster than the rate for boys, reaching 8.2 percent for girls and 9.8 percent for boys. Twenty-four percent of girls had used alcohol in the past month. Girls' rates for inhalants and stimulants exceeded those of boys, and their rates of tobacco use were the same as boys' (U.S. Department of Health and Human Services, 1995).

Reasons for alcohol and other drug use among juveniles differs in some ways between girls and boys. For example, adolescent girls' use of alcohol correlates more strongly with low self-esteem, stress, depression, and the desire to escape than does alcohol use among boys. While boys are more likely to be introduced to alcohol or marijuana by peers (other males), girls are more likely to be introduced not by peers (other females) but by boys, often in a party or dating situation. Hence, prevention programs that emphasize resisting peer pressure have shown much less effectiveness among girls than among boys (Bodinger-de Uriarte and Austin, 1991).

According to Bodinger-de Uriarte and Austin (1991), girls most at risk for use of alcohol and other drugs:

- Began substance abuse early

- Have parents, especially mothers, who abuse alcohol or other drugs

- Are victims of sexual or physical abuse

- Have weak family and school bonds

- Have a poor self-concept, especially with regard to physical appearance

- Have many opportunities to use drugs

- Have difficulty coping with stress, especially with dating and sexual activity

Adult Profiles

Brennan and Austin (1997) characterize the "typical" female offender in U.S. prisons as:

> probably minority, aged 25 to 29, unmarried, has one to three children, a likely victim of sexual abuse as a child, a victim of physical abuse, has current alcohol and drug abuse problems, multiple arrests, first arrested around age fifteen, a high school dropout, on welfare, has low skills, and has held mainly low-wage jobs (p. 3).

Community correctional settings reflect a similar population. For example, in the 100 community programs surveyed by Austin et al. (1992), most clients were African-American (50 percent) or Caucasian (37 percent) women between twenty-five and thirty years old, unmarried, and with children under age six. Program staff indicated that clients needed alcohol and drug treatment, domestic violence and sexual abuse counseling, employment, education, housing, and legal aid.

The Center for Substance Abuse Treatment (1997, p. 6) observes, "For the high proportion of women [offenders] with substance abuse problems, substance abuse acts as a multiplier for other problem areas, such as family problems, lack of economic self-sufficiency, physical and sexual abuse, and the inability to cope with caring for children." This constellation of high-risk factors associated with relapse needs to be addressed in a comprehensive substance abuse treatment program.

Pathways to Crime

When the profile of girl offenders is compared to the profiles of adult women offenders, both in prison and in community corrections, it becomes clear that they are essentially the same females moving along the system from juvenile detention to jail or community corrections to state prison. Thus, two associations must be considered: the connection between childhood victimization and offending and the connection between substance abuse and offending.

Prefeminist theories about pathways to crime often have claimed to be gender neutral, so separate data was not collected on women or girls or these data were omitted from various analyses. Research in the 1980s and 1990s reveals a pattern by which incest or other childhood victimization often leads girls (and some boys) to run away from home and/or to abuse alcohol or other drugs. Girls on the street then resort to prostitution, selling drugs, and/or engaging in robbery to survive. At any point in this process, a girl may be arrested for running away or using alcohol (status offenses), using other drugs, dealing drugs, or engaging in robbery or prostitution (Arnold, 1990; Belknap and Holsinger, 1998).

Not only are rates of sexual abuse higher among substance abusers than among the general population, but rates of relapse from sobriety are higher among substance abusers with histories of victimization than among the nonvictimized (Belknap and Holsinger, 1998). Female drug users are also more likely than males to report having been depressed before developing a drug problem. Females are less likely than males to use drugs for the "thrill" and more likely to use them to manage emotional pain.

The connection between substance abuse and offending is complex. As already stated, females may commit prostitution and property crimes to support drug habits or to survive economically. People working in corrections often consider the women's substance abuse "just part of the generally deviant lifestyle characteristic of individuals with the propensity to antisocial behavior" (Lightfoot, 1997, p. 10). However, in the Canadian study of opiate injectors discussed earlier, 73 percent of the women lacked the full criteria for antisocial personality disorder. In this case at least, substance abuse appears to have been their pathway to crime, not just a facet of their criminal behavior (Lightfoot, 1997). It would be interesting to know how many of the women with full criteria for antisocial personality disorder were physically or sexually abused as children.

The desire for power also does not seem to be a primary pathway for female offending. The Canadian women studied by Sommers (1995) committed their crimes for reasons that included the desire for acceptance by others, an expression of the pain they had suffered at the hands of others, and in an effort to maintain an adequate standard of living for their families. Relational and economic needs motivated them to commit crimes. These findings stand in stark contrast to theories of male criminality, such as social control theory (which links crime to weak social bonds and low belief in society's rules) and power-control theory (which links crime to power dynamics in the home and workplace) (Belknap, 1996).

Daly (1992) found similar results in a study of U.S. court presentence investigation reports. Based on her research, Daly identified five pathways to female offending: (1) the *street woman*, who was severely abused as a child, lives on the street, and generally ends up in court because she has been supporting her drug habit through selling drugs, engaging in prostitution, and stealing; (2) the *harmed-and-harming woman*, who also was abused as a child, but who responded with anger and "acting out," and who may have become violent through the use of alcohol and/or other drugs; (3) the *battered woman*, who usually reaches court when she has harmed or killed a violent man with whom she is in or has just ended a relationship (unlike the previous two types of women, the battered woman usually does not have a previous criminal record); (4) the *drug-connected woman*, who "uses or sells drugs as a result of her relationships with her male intimate, children, or mother . . . like the battered women, she does not tend to have much of a criminal record" (Belknap, 1996, p. 261); and (5) *other women*, who commit economically motivated crimes, either out of greed or poverty.

In short, the females in the correctional system are mostly young, poor, and undereducated women and girls of color who have complex histories of trauma and substance abuse. Most are nonviolent and are not threats to the community. Survival (of abuse and poverty) and substance abuse are their most common pathways to crime (Chesney-Lind and Bloom, 1997). Their greatest needs are multifaceted treatment for alcohol and other drug abuse and trauma recovery, as well as education in job and parenting skills. They need the opportunity to grow, to learn, and to make changes in their lives.

Gender-Specific Services

Based on this information about who female offenders are, what their pathways to crime are, and how they differ from male offenders, the need for a gender-specific substance abuse treatment program seems clear. But what exactly is a *gender-specific* program?

Legislative and Judicial Declarations

First, the U.S. Congress and courts have mandated equal access to services. The Equal Protection Clause of the Fourteenth Amendment of the U.S. Constitution requires that female offenders have access to the same quality and quantity of services that are provided for males (Collins and Collins, 1996). "Women have a constitutional right to equal protection regarding access and opportunities for education, vocational programs, rehabilitation, treatment, wages, and other privileges" (Brennan and Austin, 1997, p. 13). Litigation called "parity cases" increasingly has exposed the lower quality of services available to females. Gender-specific services should be developed to address this lack of parity.

In 1992, the U.S. Congress reauthorized the Juvenile Justice and Delinquency Prevention Act of 1974. This reauthorization "provided that each state should (1) conduct an analysis of the need for and assessment of existing treatment and services for delinquent girls, (2) develop a plan to provide needed gender-specific services for the prevention and treatment of juvenile delinquency, and (3) provide assurance that youth in the juvenile system are treated fairly regarding their mental, physical, and emotional capacities, as well as on the basis of their gender, race, and family income" (Belknap and Holsinger, 1998). This analysis is still underway in most states.

Differences Between Males and Females

Parity and fairness do not mean copying males' programs and providing them to females. To be effective, such programs must meet the unique needs of females. In a 1997 report to the governor of Ohio on gender-specific services for adolescent girls, Belknap et al. (1997) wrote:

> When examining gender-specific programming, it is important to recognize *equality does not mean "sameness."* Equality is not about providing the same programs, treatment and opportunities for girls and boys. . . . Equality is about providing opportunities that mean the same to each gender. This new definition legitimizes the differences between boys and girls. Programs for boys are more successful when they focus on rules and offer ways to advance within a structured environment, while *programs for girls are more successful when they focus on relationships* with other people and offer ways to master their lives while keeping these relationships intact (p. 23, emphasis added).

All that we know about the differences between males and females needs to be considered in the design of gender-specific programs. For example, males engage in violent and aggressive behavior at five times the rate of females; women are more likely to attribute failure to their own incompetence; and women are more easily influenced by others, especially in contexts they perceive to be supportive (Coll, Miller, Fields, and Mathews, 1998).

At the same time, though, because gender differences have been used historically to justify inferior treatment for women and girls, feminist legal scholars still debate whether acknowledging differences reinforces the tendency toward sexist differences in programming and treatment. We must be sure that gender-specific services do not become sexist services (Belknap and Holsinger, 1998). For example, the argument that female offenders need less funding for services because they are less dangerous to society should be challenged as sexist, just as acknowledging females' need for programs that address psychological trauma should not encourage a stereotype about women's fragility.

Most Promising Practices

It is important to note that gender-specific correctional treatment programs have not been in existence long enough for there to be data on their long-term effectiveness. Descriptions of "most promising" practices given here are based on impressions of early data, as rigorous evaluations still need to be done (Austin et al., 1992).

With this caveat, Austin et al., (1992, p. 31) state, "The most promising approaches to community programs focus on the multidimensional problems of women offenders. These include gender-specific substance abuse treatment; parenting and family preservation; economic survival and life-skills training; sexual abuse and domestic violence counseling; and safe, affordable housing." These conclusions are consistent with the conclusions of the report of the Correctional Service of Canada on substance abuse treatment (Lightfoot and Lambert, 1992) and their international review of model programs for women (Axon, 1989).

Bloom (1997, p. 3) states that the following criteria are necessary for gender-specific services for girls. The criteria are equally relevant for adult women:

> The Office of Juvenile Justice and Delinquency Prevention (OJJDP) defines gender-specific services as those that are designed to meet the unique needs of female offenders; that value the female perspective; that celebrate and honor the female experience; that respect and take into account female development; that empower girls and young women to reach their full human potential; and work to change established attitudes that prevent or discourage girls and young women from recognizing their potential.

Beckman (1994) recommends similar criteria for a gender-specific substance abuse treatment program:

- It is delivered in a setting compatible with females' interactional styles, such as their need for and responsiveness to social relationships

- It takes into account gender roles and female socialization

- It does not allow sexual harassment

- It supports active, interdependent roles for women and girls

- It addresses females' unique treatment issues, such as trauma, parenting skills, coping mechanisms, and self-worth

With regard to the value of community correctional settings, Bloom adds, "Whenever possible, women and girls should be treated in the least restrictive programming environment available. The level of security should depend on both treatment needs and concerns for public safety" (Bloom, 1997, pp. 4–5).

Stressing the importance of relational issues for girls, Belknap et al. (1997) recommend providing "the safety and comfort of same-gender environments," offering learning experiences after trusting relationships have been established, and helping girls to understand "that they can be professionally and emotionally successful in life and still have strong relationships" (Belknap et al., 1997, p. 24).

Issues of women's and girls' lives that gender-specific programs would address include, but are not limited to (Beckman, 1994; Belknap et al., 1997; Bloom, 1997) helping the woman with:

- developing a sense of self and self-esteem

- establishing trust and growth-fostering relationships

- paying attention to physical health

- living with or getting to sobriety

- understanding sexuality

- paying attention to mental health

- becoming more physically fit and engaging in athletics

- learning pregnancy and parenting skills

- learning decision-making skills

- recovering from trauma from physical, emotional, and sexual abuse—treatment and prevention

- being culturally aware and sensitive

- including spirituality in programs

One example of a program designed to be gender specific is a pilot program in Canada's Federal Prison for Women. In that program, a Peer Support Team was created in which inmates with histories of physical or sexual abuse were trained to help other inmates cope with the effects of abuse. Team members were trained in socialization, homophobia, racism, classism, violence against women and children, substance abuse, women's anger, self-injury, suicide intervention, and counseling skills. Interviews with team members and those they counseled revealed that both groups were helped significantly by the peer counseling program (Pollack, 1993).

Treatment Outcomes

Treatment outcomes are also an important element of the definition of gender-specific substance abuse services. Schneider, Kviz, Isola, and Filstead (1995) recommend that abstinence not be the only way to measure the effect treatment has had on females' lives. They propose such additional outcome measures as consumption patterns, fluctuations in abstinence, number of days abstinent, amount of alcohol consumed post-treatment, and improvement in the following areas: physical symptoms, role performance, legal problems, and relationship and family problems.

Available data suggest that simply adding female-only services onto an existing mixed-gender program does not significantly improve female's lives posttreatment (Copeland, Hall, Didcott, and Biggs, 1993). Outcomes of truly gender-specific programs appear more promising. For example, Dahlgren and Willander (1989) compared Swedish women in a gender-specific treatment program to a control group of women in a traditional mixed-gender program. They found that women in the gender-specific program stayed in the program an average of eight months, while those in the traditional program stayed an average of five months. Thirty-five percent of the women in the gender-specific program reported improved relationships with their children, compared with 12 percent of the control group.

Similarly, Stevens and Arbiter (1995) studied a gender-specific therapeutic community for pregnant women, postpartum women, and women with children. They compared women who completed the program with those who dropped out and found that, six months after the end of the program, 64 percent of dropouts indicated alcohol or other drug use, as compared to only 31 percent of those who completed the program. More who completed the program were employed, fewer were receiving government assistance, and fewer had been rearrested.

A report by the National Association of State Alcohol and Drug Abuse Directors details similarly positive results of treatment in thirteen states (Young, 1994). Examples of the data include reduced rates of subsequent arrest (Minnesota Chemical Dependency Division; Texas Commission on Alcohol and Drug Abuse); declines in criminal behavior, arrests, and jail time (Ohio Department of Alcohol and Drug Addiction Services); and reduced rates of criminal activity (California Department of Alcohol and Drug Programs).

Thus, the limited research on treatment outcomes shows a connection between treatment, reduced rates of relapse, and reduced rates of subsequent criminal activity and rearrest. Martin and Scarpitti (1993) found that women who relapse are seven times more likely to be rearrested as those who do not relapse. Therefore, treatment that reduces the likelihood of relapse will significantly affect rates of recidivism.

Systemwide Considerations

It is important to emphasize that a gender-specific program must take into account the entire system of a correctional facility. Glover-Reed observes, "Developing effective services for women cannot just consist of adding some additional components or providing staff training to existing programs. Although these actions are certainly necessary, they are not sufficient. The primary barriers to the provision of more women-oriented services are theoretical, administrative and structural, and also involve policy and funding decisions" (1987, p. 151; *see also* the Glover-Reed chapter in this volume).

History of Treatment for Women and Girls

The theoretical barriers to effective gender-specific services that Glover-Reed refers to become clear in light of the history of substance abuse treatment for women and girls. This historical context highlights what has and has not worked for females in the past.

Alcoholics Anonymous and the Jellinek Curve

In the past, substance abuse by women and girls was largely invisible because of the strong social taboos against women's use of alcohol or other drugs. Men's drinking problems were much discussed in the nineteenth and early twentieth centuries, but there was little talk about women's drinking. In the United States, it was illegal to show a woman drinking in a movie or advertisement until the 1950s. This was not because women did not drink, but because people did not want to see women drinking. Even today, while it is more acceptable for a woman to drink or use recreational drugs, it is still not acceptable for them to be addicted. Families have far more denial about their sisters', mothers', and daughters' substance abuse than about those of the men in the family.

Even after the advent of Alcoholics Anonymous in the 1930s, treatment programs and research focused on male alcoholics and addicts. Alcoholics Anonymous (AA) was highly effective for male alcoholics and became the standard for many kinds of mutual help recovery groups. Women and girls joined programs designed by men for men, and because many females have recovered through AA, it has been difficult to question and discuss the contributions and limitations of AA for females' recovery.

The practical experience of AA became one of two cornerstones on which U.S. treatment programs were based. The second cornerstone was the research analysis of E. M. Jellinek, whose model of how people recover from substance abuse became known as the *Jellinek curve.* In 1945, *The AA Grapevine* mailed 1,600 questionnaires to recovering alcoholics, asking them to describe the process of their addiction and their recovery. Only 158 replies were received—a very poor response rate, even by the standards of statisticians at the time. Although Dr. Jellinek remarked on the data's questionable validity, he agreed to analyze and interpret it for AA. He found that the respondents diverged dramatically into two groups. Ninety-eight respondents described their addiction and recovery in one way, while fifteen described theirs in a very different way (the other 45 questionnaires were improperly filled out and could not be used). The larger group was all male, and the smaller group was female. Because the sample of fifteen women was too small to analyze separately, and because their data "differed so greatly" (Jellinek, 1946, p. 6), Jellinek threw out their responses and based his model on the men's data. No further investigation was made to see whether females indeed followed a distinct pattern of addiction and recovery or needed a distinct model for treatment. The

Jellinek curve has been a cornerstone for treatment programs for fifty years and, like AA, it was based only on the experiences of men.

The Women's Movement

In the 1960s and 1970s, some women began to talk in consciousness-raising groups about previously taboo subjects: incest, rape, violence, and the use of alcohol and other drugs. In 1976, Congress responded to pressure from feminist organizations and alcohol and drug constituency groups with legislation that funded specialized women's treatment for the first time. Meanwhile, the National Council on Alcoholism created a special office on women. The programs launched by these initiatives laid the foundation for an understanding of treatment for women and girls (Galbraith, 1994). These programs demonstrated that females would seek and pursue treatment when it was "holistic" (addressing a broad range of needs, including sexuality, violence, and life-management skills), humanizing, long term, and child friendly—in short, when it was tailored for females. In the succeeding decades, clinicians and researchers have built on these initial findings and developed a solid body of knowledge in best practices for treatment of women and girls.

Juvenile Programs

Despite this growing information on best practices for treating females, male-based programming remains the norm in many settings. Even female-only programs are often merely copies of men's programs, not based on research or clinical experience with women and girls. This problem is especially acute for juveniles. Boys far outnumber girls in the juvenile justice system, so programs are designed with the needs of males in mind, and services for female adolescents simply replicate the male model (Pepi, 1998). In a paper presented to the Australian Institute of Criminology, Tim Keough (1994, p. 3) wrote, "discrimination which affects young women who end up in custody is seen to be part of a broad systemic abuse based on gender. Through such systemic influences the system is seen to repeatedly fail to meet the needs of young women from abusive backgrounds."

Currently, behavior modification is the counseling method of choice in almost 75 percent of juvenile institutions (Siegel and Senna, 1991). This method is often effective in the controlled setting of an institution, where the counselor can manipulate the situation, but usually becomes ineffective when the adolescent returns to the outside world. Further, it fails to address girls' history of physical, sexual, and emotional trauma.

Also, juvenile justice programs often reward girls for compliance and silence, even if that means suppressing their feelings and not voicing issues around abuse (Pepi, 1998). This approach conflicts with research that stresses the importance of girls regaining their "voice," which is often lost in adolescence (Gilligan, 1991).

The Office of Juvenile Justice and Delinquency Prevention concludes, "Girls in juvenile justice need effective programs that do not perpetuate inequities based on gender, race, class, sexual orientation and other personal and cultural factors" (Girls Incorporated, 1996).

Therapeutic Communities

Among adult offender populations, a common model for treatment has been the therapeutic community. Chuck Dederich, an alcoholic and a former Gulf Oil executive, and his wife Betty, who wanted a more challenging and interactive approach to sobriety than AA provided, founded Synanon in 1958. Dederich began hosting meetings with more discussion (cross-talk or responding to someone else's story with feedback), which is discouraged in AA meetings. For economic reasons, recovering alcoholics began living together in what came to be called a "therapeutic community." In that community, heroin addicts also entered recovery without medical intervention (Basic Interface, 1994).

In 1963, Dr. Dan Casriel founded DAYTOP and began to spread therapeutic communities throughout New York and Europe. Dr. Mitch Rosenthal founded Phoenix House in 1967; it continues to have more than a thousand residents in long-term care. The therapeutic-community model has been especially influential in correctional settings, where "modified therapeutic communities" are used frequently.

However, the confrontational approach traditionally used in therapeutic communities has not proven effective with the majority of women, as women require a different basis on which to build community: respect, mutuality, and compassion. An emphasis on assets and strengths, as opposed to tearing down the ego, has proven most effective with them.

A New Model for Treatment

To summarize what has been stated so far, much is now known about who female offenders are, their pathways to crime, and the kinds of gender-specific services they need. Much is also known about the historic barriers to such gender-specific treatment. What is still needed is a treatment program for females that takes all of this information into account.

The author has developed a model for such a gender-specific treatment program in correctional settings based on research into the most promising practices identified in the past twenty years and on her own clinical experience. The program can be used in community correctional settings as well as in jails and prisons. Because many of the issues in the lives of women and girls in the criminal justice system are similar, the model is applicable to both.

Because experience and research have shown that an effective group program for females must deal with the issues specific to their recovery and create a safe and nurturing environment based on mutuality, respect, and compassion, the *Helping Women Recover* program was developed.[2] The program incorporates the guidelines for comprehensive treatment for women established by the Center for Substance Abuse Treatment (1994). It also reflects a theory-in-use model that integrates three theoretical perspectives: the theory of addiction, the theory of women's psychological development, and the theory of trauma. This program reflects the type of substance abuse treatment needed in correctional settings: one that is comprehensive and developmental and that integrates what is known about female recovery, both clinically and theoretically.

Theoretical Integration

It is important to ground a gender-specific substance abuse program in theory—in the knowledge developed in the past twenty years about substance abuse and about women and girls, who often have histories of substance abuse since early adolescence; multiple trauma (including physical and/or sexual abuse, poverty, and racism); and developmental lags because of damaging relationships. The model presented here includes a theory of addiction, a theory of how women and girls grow and develop, and a theory of trauma.

Definitions of Terms

The terms *substance abuse, chemical dependency*, and *addiction* often are used interchangeably, and there has been criticism of their lack of specificity (Lightfoot, 1997). According to the *Diagnostic and Statistical Manual for Mental Disorders* (American Psychiatric Association, 1994), abuse is a recurrent pattern of pathological use that impairs social or occupational functioning. *Dependence* involves, in addition to abuse, increased tolerance or physical withdrawal symptoms. The distinction between physical dependence and psychological dependence is not always clear-cut. Further, most data on women and girls in the criminal justice system does not distinguish between substance abuse and chemical dependence (Lightfoot and Lambert, 1992; Teplin et al., 1996).

The criminal justice systems in both the United States and Canada do distinguish between alcohol and drug abuse/dependence. However, this distinction has to do with legal versus illegal substances, and not with treatment needs. Alcohol is a drug that happens to be legal. Few substance abusers use only one drug.

The model presented here is designed for both substance abusers and the chemically dependent. The theory of addiction used here is helpful regardless of where the female offender falls on the continuum from substance abuse to dependence. Clinical experience suggests that the length and intensity of treatment could vary for substance abusers and the chemically dependent, but that the issues they must work through will be the same. This model is applicable for both women and girls.

The History of Addiction Theory

For generations, societies saw addiction as a moral issue (Sandmaier, 1992). The use of alcohol or other drugs and the behavior of a person while using them were viewed as signs of lapsed morals. Under this moral model, relapse was attributed to a lack of will power or seen as a crime. The Temperance Movement and the United States' "War on Drugs" reflect this model (Parks, 1999).

In the 1950s, mental health professionals proposed an alternative model in which addiction was seen as a sign of an underlying psychological disorder, such as a death wish, a fixation at the oral stage (as described by Freud), or a "sociopathic personality" (Brown, 1995, p. 13). If one could somehow solve the underlying disorder, then the addiction would go away. Any loss of control attributed to drinking or using other drugs was seen as temporary and secondary to the primary problem. It was believed that if a person drank excessively to cope with other difficulties then, if those difficulties were removed, she would go back to drinking in moderation.

During those same years, the chemical dependency field was born. Drawing on the work of AA and the Jellinek curve, practitioners outlined and advocated a model of addiction as a disease, where addiction was not a symptom but a primary condition with its own symptoms. Addiction became seen as a physical disease that carried no moral stigma. It was noted that addiction could not be managed through will power and required a lifestyle regimen for emotional and physical stability. Chemical dependency practitioners also saw that the disease of addiction included not just physical, but also emotional and spiritual dimensions.

In the 1990s, mental health and chemical dependency practitioners began coming together to learn from one another. At the same time, health professionals in many disciplines began to revise their concepts of disease in general. Based on a holistic health model of disease, many now acknowledge that all diseases include physical, psychological, emotional, and spiritual dimensions (Northrup, 1994) rooted in the individual, as well as environmental and sociopolitical aspects.

One way to describe addiction as a disease is to compare it with cancer. Both show large variations from one afflicted individual to another. Both have a physical dimension, one aspect of which is a genetic component. Studies have shown that rats left to themselves prefer water over alcohol, but that they can be trained to seek alcohol. Moreover, their descendants for four generations will seek alcohol *without training*. It is believed that alcohol somehow has changed their genetic material. In the same way, the tendency of addiction to run in families indicates a genetic component, just as a defective gene can cause certain types of cancer to run in families. Researchers also have found that a certain percentage of people actually metabolize alcohol differently from the rest of the population (Anthenelli and Schuckit, 1994).

Both addiction and cancer also have emotional and psychological dimensions. Stress and unhealthy ways of handling stress increase a person's risk of cancer, and, in the same way, they can increase the risk that one will turn to alcohol or other drugs. Alcohol use also is promoted by current social customs: advertisements use sex to sell alcohol, and alcohol is the drug of choice for seduction on college campuses (Kilbourne, 1991).

The sociopolitical aspects of cancer include the huge profits carcinogenic products make for powerful business interests. Similarly, companies that produce and sell alcohol are enormously profitable, even though they are indirectly responsible for more than 23,000 deaths and three-quarters of a million injuries each year (Zawistowski, 1991). Medical doctors prescribe 80 percent of the amphetamines, 60 percent of the psychoactive drugs, and 71 percent of the antidepressants that women take (Galbraith, 1991). Few people question that cancer is a disease, even though as many as 80 percent of doctors link cancer to lifestyle choices (diet and exercise) and such things as pesticides, emissions, and nuclear waste in the environment (Siegel, 1996). Conversely, even though most medical and psychology professionals believe that addiction is a disease/disorder, politically it is still treated chiefly as a crime.

One reason why it is politically difficult to treat addiction as a disease rather than as a crime is that to view it as a disease requires acknowledging that the addict has lost control over an aspect of his or her life. The loss of control conflicts with one of Western culture's deepest beliefs: that the organizing principle of life is the individual's pursuit of power and control over self and others (Brown, 1995).

Professionals may continue to debate the merits of a disease model versus a disorder model, but the holistic disease model is a more helpful way to approach the treatment of females than is a disorder model. The disorder model focuses on social learning theory and a cognitive-behavioral approach to treatment (Parks, 1999). The main limitation of this approach is its focus on only one aspect of a multidimensional problem, ignoring the genetic studies, the affective aspects of both the problem and the solution (Brown, 1985), and the sociocultural and environmental issues. A holistic disease model allows clinicians to treat the addiction as the primary problem (not just as a maladaptive means of coping with problems or as a sequence of learned behaviors), while at the same time addressing dimensions of the disease, such as genetic predisposition, health consequences, shame, isolation, and/or a history of abuse.

Males and females show different patterns in substance abuse. Most family, twin, and adoptive studies have examined the link between substance abuse in fathers and sons, and the research clearly indicates a genetic link in men. However, women have been studied less in this respect. "Researchers often state that they chose male subjects because the effects of hormonal variations in female menstrual cycles could potentially affect the validity of the studies" (Finkelstein, Kennedy, Thomas, and Kearns, 1997, p. 7).

Environmental and psychosocial factors in females' substance abuse have been much more thoroughly studied (Finkelstein et al., 1997). Stigma, or severe social disapproval, is the main psychosocial issue that has been found to distinguish females' substance abuse from males'. While drinking-related behavior often is seen as "macho" in men, it conflicts with society's view of femininity—especially with the roles of wife and mother. Women and girls often internalize this stigma. They may feel guilt and shame, even despair, and fear, as they find themselves unable to control their behavior. Mothers know they may lose their children if they fail in their recovery. Because the stigma is so shameful and potentially threatening to the family unit, females and their families may use denial to protect the status quo. Denial (minimizing the impact of substance use and abuse) by females and denial by their families are two major reasons why women and girls do not seek treatment.

In summary, the treatment model recommended here views chemical dependency as a disease, but from a holistic rather than a traditional (and limited) medical model. It is based on the belief that there are physical, psychological, emotional, spiritual, and even environmental and sociopolitical dimensions to the problem. Persons are not blamed for being addicted, but they are expected to resolve the problem with help from a variety of sources. Both the individual addict and the society that fosters addiction are addressed. This type of model is consistent with the public health model of disease in which the agent, the person, and the environment are all considered important factors. Chemical dependency can be understood best as a public health issue.

The Spiral of Addiction and Recovery

The generic definition of addiction used in this model is as follows: a chronic neglect of self in favor of something or someone else. The process of addiction and recovery can be envisioned as a spiral. The downward spiral of addiction revolves around alcohol or another drug of choice. Addiction pulls the addict into ever-tighter circles, constricting her life until she is completely focused on the drug. The addiction becomes the organizing principle of her life. Using alcohol and other drugs, protecting her supply, hiding her addiction from others, and cultivating her love-hate relationship with her drug come to dominate her world.

When a woman or girl is in this downward spiral, the counselor's task is to break through her denial. She comes to a point of transition, at which she must shift her perceptions in two ways: She must shift from believing, "I am in control" to admitting, "I am not in control" and she must stop believing, "I am not an addict," and admit, "I am an addict" (Brown, 1985, p. 34).

Both shifts in perception can feel humiliating. Our society inflicts far more shame on a female substance abuser than on a male, labeling her a "lush," "slut," "bad mother," and so on. While society may stigmatize a male addict as a bum, it rarely attacks his sexuality or his competence as a parent. It is necessary for a counselor to understand that a woman or girl who enters treatment may come with a heavy burden of shame. She should not be shamed further; rather, she should be offered the hope of recovery.

The upward spiral of recovery revolves around the drug in ever-widening circles, as the addiction loosens its grip and the female's focus moves away from the drug. Her world grows to include healthy relationships, an expanded self-concept, and a richer sexual and spiritual life. The process is not merely turning around and ascending the old downward spiral, but being transformed so that one ascends a different spiral. When women and girls speak of recovery, they speak of a fundamental transformation: "I'm not the same person. I'm different than I was."

Female Psychological Development

The definition given earlier of addiction raises several questions: How does a woman or girl shift from a chronic neglect of self to a healthy care of self? How does a female recover and grow? How can we facilitate and support this process?

Jean Baker Miller posed the question of how women and girls grow and develop in her 1976 book *Toward a New Psychology of Women.* Traditional theories of psychology describe "development" as a climb from childlike dependence to mature *independence*, where the goal is to become a self-sufficient, clearly differentiated, autonomous self. In contrast, Miller said that a female's primary motivation is to build a sense of *connection with others.* According to Miller, a woman or girl develops a sense of self and self-worth when her actions arise out of, and lead back into, connections with others—not one of independence or separation.

Previously, theoreticians had treated women's emphasis on connection as a sign of deficiency. In her book *In a Different Voice: Psychological Theory and Women's Development,* Carol Gilligan (1982) observed:

> The disparity between women's experience and the representation of human development, noted throughout the psychological literature, generally has been seen to signify a problem in women's development. Instead, the failure of women to fit existing models of human growth may point to a problem in the representation, a limitation in the conception of the human condition, an omission of certain truths about life (Gilligan, 1982, pp. 1–2).

Miller's work led a group of researchers and practitioners to create the Stone Center at Wellesley College for the purpose of thinking through the qualities of relationships that foster healthy growth in women (Jordan, 1984, 1985; Jordan and Surrey, 1986; Kaplan, 1984; Surrey, 1985). The basic assumption of the Stone Center model is that "connection" is a basic human need, and that this need is especially strong in women (Jordan, Kaplan, Miller, Stiver, and Surrey, 1991). The model shows that all people need both connection with others and differentiation from others, but that females are more attuned to connection, while males are more attuned to differentiation. Bylington (1997, p. 35) explained this connection as follows:

> Theoretically, girls perceive themselves to be more similar than different to their earliest maternal caretakers, so they do not have to differentiate from their mothers in order to continue to develop their identities. This is in contrast to boys, who must develop an identity that is different from the mother's in order to continue their development. Thus, women's psychological growth and development occur through adding to rather than separating from relationships. Consequently, defining themselves as similar to others through relationships is fundamental to women's identities.

A "connection" in the Stone Center relational model is "an interaction that engenders a sense of being in tune with self and others, of being understood and valued" (Bylington, 1997, p. 35). True connections are mutual, empathic, creative, energy-releasing, and empowering for all participants (Miller, 1986). Such connections are so crucial for women that women's psychological problems can be traced to disconnections or violations within relationships—whether in families, with personal acquaintances, or in society at large.

Mutuality means that each person in a relationship can represent her feelings, thoughts, and perceptions, and can both move with and be moved by the feelings, thoughts, and perceptions of the other person. Each person, as well as the relationship, can change and move forward because there is mutual influence and mutual responsiveness.

Empathy is a complex, highly developed ability to join with another at a cognitive and affective level without losing connection with one's own experience. An empathic person feels personally authentic in the relationship and feels that she can "see" and "know" the other person. A growth-fostering relationship requires mutual empathy, which in turn requires that both parties have the capacity to connect empathically.

Empathy is also one of the five general principles underlying motivational counseling (Miller and Rollnick, 1991) and has been shown to be predictive of success in treating problem drinkers (Abbott and Kerr, 1995).

Mutuality and empathy empower women not with power *over* others but with power *with* others. Women feel more able to share power for constructive, creative ends. A gender-specific treatment program needs to follow such an empowerment model, allowing for mutual, empathic, and empowering relationships, producing five psychological outcomes: (1) increased zest and vitality, (2) empowerment to act, (3) knowledge of self and others, (4) a sense of self-worth, and (5) a desire for more connection (Miller, 1986). These outcomes have been shown to constitute psychological growth for women. Thus, mutuality, empathy, and power with others are essential qualities of a program both to foster growth in women and to help them recover from addiction.

Miller (1990) also described the outcomes of disconnections—nonmutual or abusive relationships—which she termed a "depressive spiral": (1) diminished zest or vitality, (2) disempowerment, (3) lack of clarity or confusion, (4) diminished self-worth, and (5) a turning away from relationships. All relationships involve disconnections, times when people feel their separateness and distance. However, growth-fostering relationships are able to allow disconnections that, with effort on each person's part, can be turned into connections. In nonmutual and/or abusive relationships, disconnections are not turned into true connections. Unfortunately, many women and girls have experienced such relationships and must overcome these effects.

Gilligan's work with adolescent girls reflects a developmental process similar to what Miller found in adult women. Gilligan discovered that, because of their desire for connection, girls aged ten to thirteen tend to give up their senses of self and their own voices to be in relationships with and acceptable to boys (Gilligan, 1982).

Relationships and Substance Abuse

From the perspective of the relational model, some women and girls use alcohol and other drugs to make or keep connections. Finkelstein (1993) suggests that treatment planners for substance-abusing females must take into account past family relationships, current relationships with family, friends, and partners, and relationships developed within the treatment context.

Disconnection and violation characterize the childhood experience of most women and girls in the prison system. According to a recent sampling of women in a Massachusetts prison (Coll and Duff, 1995), 38 percent of the women had lost parents in childhood, 69 percent had been abused as children, and 70 percent had left home before age seventeen. They lacked experience of mutual and empathic relationships. Although Gilligan, Lyons, and Hanmer (1990) report that girls are socialized to be more empathic than boys, female offenders have been exposed repeatedly to nonempathic relationships and so either lack empathy for both themselves and others or are highly empathic toward others but lack empathy for themselves. In order to change, women and girls must experience relationships that do not reenact their histories of loss, neglect, and abuse.

In the same way, disconnection and violation have characterized most of the adult relationships of women in the prison system. Seventy percent of women in the Massachusetts study had been repeatedly abused verbally, physically, and/or sexually as adults (Coll and Duff, 1995). Another study, of drug-abusing pregnant women (Amaro and Hardy-Fanta, 1995, p. 333), found that "[m]en who go to jail, men who do not take care of them or their children, and men who disappoint them fill the lives of these women. Even more striking is the extent to which the women suffered physical abuse from their male partners. . . . Half of the women in this study reported abuse from the men in their lives; occasionally from 'tricks,' although more typically from their partners." Robbery, beatings, and rape by men on the street commonly were reported. Women were often first introduced to drugs by partners, and partners often continued to be their suppliers. Attempts to stop using drugs and failure to supply partners with drugs through prostitution often elicited violence from partners. However, women remained attached to the men despite the neglect and abuse.

Another common form of disconnection women experience is isolation. Females at high risk for drug abuse are frequently socially isolated—single parents, unemployed, or recently separated, divorced, or widowed (Finkelstein, 1993; Finkelstein and Derman, 1991; Wilsnack, Wilsnack, and Klassen, 1986). Psychological isolation also occurs when the people in a woman's world fail to validate and respond to her experience or her attempts at connection. Miller (1990) has described the state of "condemned isolation" in which a female feels isolated in her important relationships and feels that she is the problem; that she is condemned to be isolated. This state of self-blame and isolation is highly correlated with drug use, as drugs become a way of coping with intense feelings and a sense of hopelessness.

Shame is a third aspect of disconnection. Jordan et al. (1991) described the tremendous cultural shaming around females' yearnings for connection, sexuality, and emotionality. Both women and girls are prone to feel personally deficient ("something is wrong with me"), to take responsibility for problematic relationships, and to seek ways to alter themselves. In nonmutual relationships, females often carry the disavowed feelings of pain, anger, or fear of those with whom they are connected. Women and girls in the criminal justice system endure more shame due to stigma from society.

Together, abuse, isolation, and shame can send women into the previously mentioned "depressive spiral": (1) diminished zest or vitality, (2) disempowerment, (3) lack of clarity or increased confusion, (4) diminished self-worth, and (5) a turning away from relationships. This depressive spiral characterizes too well the females in our criminal justice system.

Connections and relationships also are involved in substance abuse in several other ways. First, addiction can be viewed as a type of relationship between the addict and the alcohol or other drugs, "a relationship characterized by obsession, compulsion, nonmutuality, and an imbalance of power. It is a kind of love relationship in which the object of addiction becomes the focus of a woman's life" (Covington and Surrey, 1997, p. 338). Addicted women frequently use relational imagery to describe their drug use, such as "My most passionate affair was with cocaine." At first the drug is her best friend, but as women describe the progress of their addiction, they say things like, "I turned to Valium, but then Valium turned on me." Addiction may be thought of as a contracting of connections until there is only the relationship with the substance. Recovery, then, can be seen as an expansion of connection (Covington and Beckett, 1988).

Females frequently begin to use substances in a vain attempt to feel connected, energized, loved, or loving (Surrey, 1991). Women and girls often turn to alcohol or other drugs in the context of relationships with drug-abusing partners—to feel connected to the partner through the use of drugs. Partners are often their suppliers and often resist their efforts to stop using. Women and girls also use substances to numb the pain of nonmutual, nonempathic, even violent relationships.

Additionally, females may begin to use substances to alter themselves to fit the relationships available. Miller (1990) has described this basic paradox—when a woman cannot move a relationship toward mutuality, she begins to change herself to maintain the relationship. Stiver (1990) has written about children of "dysfunctional" families who frequently turn to substance abuse to alter themselves to adapt to the disconnections within the family, thus giving the illusion of being in relationships when they are not.

Healthy friendships are also challenging for females in the correctional setting. Prison is a difficult place in which to nurture trust. Yet, many women in prison do strive to create whatever level of relationships they can. Some build pseudo-families in which they relate like sisters, mothers, daughters, or lovers (Owen, 1998).

Trauma Theory

Because of the high rate of trauma in the lives of female substance abusers, a gender-specific treatment program for them also must take into account a theory of trauma. Roughly 1.8 million American women are abused each year. "While both male and female children are at risk for abuse, females continue to be at risk for interpersonal violence in their adolescence and adult lives. The risk for males to be abused in their teenage and adult relationships is far less than for females" (Covington and Surrey, 1997, p. 341).

A history of abuse drastically increases the likelihood that a female will abuse alcohol and other drugs. It also increases the likelihood of interaction with the criminal justice system. Alcoholic women are likely to have been abused sexually, physically, and emotionally by more perpetrators, more often, and for longer periods of time than their nonalcoholic counterparts (Covington and Kohen, 1984). Further, trauma is not limited to suffering violence; it includes witnessing violence as well as stigmatization because of race, poverty, incarceration, or sexual orientation. Thus, in treating a substance abuser, counselors must understand that they probably also are treating trauma survivors. Some women and girls who are considered "treatment failures" because they relapsed may be understood better as trauma survivors who returned to alcohol or other drugs to medicate their depression or anxiety, because they know no better ways to comfort themselves. Our increased understanding of trauma offers new treatment possibilities for substance-abusing trauma survivors (Barrett and Trepper, 1991; Lightfoot and Lambert, 1992).

The connection between substance abuse and interpersonal violence is threefold: (1) substance-abusing males are often violent toward women and children; (2) substance-abusing females are particularly vulnerable targets of violence; and (3) childhood abuse and current abuse increase a female's risk of substance abuse (Miller 1991). Consequently, Canadian and United States researchers have agreed that any program for treating substance-abusing females must take into account that most clients will have suffered abuse (Correctional Services of Canada, 1994; Covington, 1998; Heney and Kristiansen, 1997). Staff involved with a substance abuse treatment program need not be experts in trauma recovery, but it is helpful for them to understand the three stages of trauma recovery outlined by Herman (1992): safety, remembrance and mourning, and reconnection.

Safety. In particular, the design of the treatment program described here takes into account the needs of women at the first stage, safety, which is especially appropriate for a criminal justice setting. Safety also is emphasized in the "Substance Abuse Program for Federally Sentenced Women" developed for the Correctional Services of Canada (Abbott and Kerr, 1995). Women and girls must feel safe externally in a facility free of physical and sexual harassment and abuse. A treatment program also can help women feel safe internally by teaching them self-soothing techniques as alternatives to self-medication.

Sadly, for some women and girls, their first experience of feeling safe is in a correctional setting. It is a harsh social reality that some females must be in an institution to feel safe. For other women and girls, their experience in the criminal justice system is traumatizing and triggers memories of earlier instances of abuse. It can be retraumatizing when a sexual abuse survivor has a body search or must shower with male guards nearby or if a battered woman is cursed at by a staff person. (The risk of such retraumatization is just one of the reasons why a community setting is preferable to prison for many offenders.)

Behavior. In addition to understanding the safety needs of abuse survivors, staff members operating a gender-specific treatment program need to understand how a history of abuse affects females' behavior. Survivors of sexual abuse often find that their sexual selves become "shaped in developmentally inappropriate and interpersonally dysfunctional ways" (Finkelhor and Browne, 1988, p. 69). A girl may grow up with misconceptions about morality, aggression, and sexual behavior. She may believe that her only value is her sexuality. "It is not surprising that survivors are more likely to become sex-trade workers" (Heney and Kristiansen, 1998, p. 31). Clearly, these females have an increased risk of entering the criminal justice system. Once in the system, they often are labeled "sexually provocative" and "sexually manipulative" without any acknowledgment of the sexual trauma that may underlie their behavior.

Survivors of abuse also can demonstrate symptoms of posttraumatic stress disorder. Sexually abused children have unusually high rates of posttraumatic stress disorder, especially those abused at a younger age (Wolfe, Gentile, and Wolfe, 1989). Teplin et al. (1996) found that 33.5 percent of pretrial jail detainees in their survey met the criteria for posttraumatic stress disorder, and that this rate did not vary by ethnicity, education, or age. They suggested that this rate was slightly underreported, as some subjects found their experiences of trauma too painful to discuss. Most of the posttraumatic stress disorder cases were victims of rape or other violent assault.

The Diagnostic and Statistical Manual of Mental Disorders (American Psychiatric Association, 1994, pp. 427-429) lists the following symptoms of posttraumatic stress disorder:

- Reexperience of the event through nightmares and flashbacks

- Avoidance of stimuli associated with the event (for example, if a woman were assaulted by a blonde man, she may fear and want to avoid men with blonde hair)

- Estrangement (the inability to be emotionally close to others)

- Numbing of general responsiveness (feeling nothing most of the time)

- Hypervigilance (continually scanning one's environment for danger, whether physical or emotional)

- Exaggerated startle response (a tendency to jump at loud noises or unexpected touch)

Because posttraumatic stress disorder can affect the way a woman or girl relates to staff, peers, and the environment of a correctional setting, it is helpful to ask, "Is this person's behavior linked to posttraumatic stress disorder?" A study of Australian female prisoners "demonstrated that posttraumatic stress disorder and a history of abuse were almost ubiquitous in these women, and that these factors contributed significantly to their criminal histories" (McFarlane and Yehuda, 1996, p. 168).

Understanding posttraumatic stress disorder and a history of abuse is especially important with regard to females diagnosed with borderline personality disorder. This is a diagnosis too often used for women and girls whose behaviors stem from their efforts to survive horribly traumatic experiences (Root, 1992).

Relational Development. Third, a gender-specific treatment program needs to address the ways in which trauma affects a female's relational development:

> Women recovering from childhood molestation, rape, or battering are teaching us about the impact of such trauma on relational development. When early parental relationships are abusive, violating, and dangerous, all future relationships are impacted. The very high rate of substance abuse and addiction among survivors of abuse and violence suggests the likelihood of turning to substance abuse when healthy relationships are unavailable and when faith or trust in the possibility of growth in human connection is impaired. The use of alcohol and other drugs has become a way for women to deal with the emotional pain resulting from earlier abuse by someone close to them, someone they trusted (Covington and Surrey, 1997, p. 342).

Societal Context. Finally, personal violence toward women and girls must be understood in the larger societal context of systemic violence and oppression. This includes racism, classism, heterosexism, and ageism.

Integration of Theoretical Frameworks

Three theoretical perspectives—addiction, women's development, and trauma—have been briefly described thus far. In the past, women and girls often have been expected to seek help for addiction, psychological disorders, and trauma from *separate sources* and to incorporate what they learned from a recovery group, a counselor, and a psychologist into their own lives. This expectation has placed an unnecessary burden on recovering females. A gender-specific treatment program needs to integrate all three approaches for the clients to increase their potential for recovery.

Structure and Content of an Effective Treatment Program

Both structure and content should be considered when designing a gender-specific treatment program for substance-abusing women and girls. Not just the content of the program, but also the context/environment is important. The program needs to have the following qualities:

A Supportive Environment

An environment that supports recovery is characterized by the following:

Safety: The environment is free of physical, emotional, and sexual harassment, and spoken and unspoken rules of conduct provide appropriate boundaries. Although it may be impossible for a staff member to guarantee safety in her agency or institution, it is imperative that the treatment group itself be a safe place.

Connection: Exchanges among the treatment group facilitator and group members need to feel mutual rather than one-way and authoritarian. Females begin to heal when they sense that a group facilitator wants to understand their experiences, is present with them when they recall painful experiences, allows their stories to affect her, and is not overwhelmed by their stories.

Empowerment: The facilitator needs to model how a woman or girl can use power with and for others, rather than either using power over others or being powerless. It is important to set firm, respectful, and empathic limits and to encourage the group members to believe in and exercise their abilities.

Some people question whether a healing environment can be created in a correctional setting. There often can be a clash between the "control" model of corrections and the "change" model of substance abuse treatment. Hence, a correctional setting is rarely therapeutic. However, even within correctional institutions, healing spaces can be found (Boudin, 1998). It is important for the group facilitator to encourage women to struggle with the conditions of the correctional setting and continue to thrive. Recovery can happen in or out of a correctional setting. In fact, for some women, prison offers their only chance of residential treatment.

Psychoeducational Model

Using a psychoeducational model, the facilitator educates women and girls in treatment programs about abuse and violence, about how society socializes women, and so on. In this way, females are enabled to interact both cognitively and emotionally with the content, which is crucial to their learning.

Cognitive models have become popular in criminal justice settings. However, the available research does not support these models for females, whose treatment needs to be based on the premise of the whole person, emphasizing affective, cognitive, and behavioral change. The affective aspect is especially important for women and girls because their substance-abusing behavior must be understood in the context of their emotional lives.

Miller and Stiver (1997, p. 212) believe that:

> This separation of thought and feeling seems clearly linked to a long-standing gender division in Western culture. Thinking has been linked with men and is the valued capacity; feeling has been linked with women and is disparaged. In contrast, we believe that all thoughts are accompanied by emotions and all emotions have thought content. Attempting to focus on one to the neglect of the other diminishes people's ability to understand and act on their experiences.

Instead of dealing with thoughts and feelings as separate entities, Miller and Stiver propose dealing with them as "thought-feelings" or "feeling-thoughts" (p. 27). This is an appropriate concept to incorporate into women's treatment programs.

Three Levels of Intervention

The group process and individual exercises used need to help women and girls on three levels: cognitive, affective, and behavioral.

At the *cognitive* level, education can help to correct their misperceptions and distorted thinking. Women and girls can learn a process of critical thinking for decision making. In the *Helping Women Recover* program (Covington, 1999), for example, females practice the ORID process (Spencer, 1989) of interpreting and responding to an experience. This process includes four stages:

- *Objective:* Obtaining facts through observation

- *Reflective:* Expressing emotional reactions to the event or experience

- *Interpretive:* Assessing the meaning and impact of the event, its significance or usefulness, and its value

- *Decisive:* Identifying actions or decisions in response to the experience

The *affective* level is an especially important component for a female treatment program. The absence of feeling or reduced feeling is common in early sobriety (Brown, 1985), and affect emerges as recovery progresses. Females need to learn to express their feelings appropriately, as well as to contain them in healthy ways through self-soothing techniques. Because females frequently become dependent on drugs to seek relief from painful emotional states, they require an environment during recovery in which to understand their feelings and work through their emotions. Because females often are raised to suppress their feelings and to be compliant, if a treatment program obliges them to act in the same way, it can feel like the original abusive environment in which they learned to keep silent and turn to alcohol or other drugs. Such silence encourages them to avoid dealing with issues that can lead to relapse (Pepi, 1998). As feelings emerge in early recovery, females may feel confused and return to a cognitive focus on their drug of choice unless they have a context in which to learn new ways of handling those feelings.

Goleman's work on emotional intelligence emphasizes the importance of emotional development and its connection to juvenile delinquency and substance abuse. He says that a "craving for calm seems to be an emotional marker of a genetic susceptibility to alcoholism," and that "a second emotional pathway to alcoholism comes from a high level of agitation, impulsivity, and boredom" (Goleman, 1995, p. 254). He further notes a study associating opioid addiction with a lifelong difficulty in handling anger. Such research implies that helping women and girls handle feelings such as anger, agitation, and depression may decrease rates of relapse.

Art therapy is one potential treatment modality for helping females with emotional development. Merriam (1998) describes the benefits of art therapy for trauma survivors in a Canadian prison. It helped the women and girls lower their defenses, decrease anxiety, and gain insight into information that they had denied or dissociated. Art therapy can help to give females a voice when they are unable to verbalize their emotions or experiences.

Finally, a gender-specific treatment program needs a *behavioral* component. Women and girls must make changes in their drinking or drug-using behavior. For addicted females, the goal is abstinence. For the nonaddicted, success may be evaluated by increased levels of functioning in every aspect of their lives.

Asset Model

In a traditional model of treatment, the therapist does a needs assessment and focuses on what is missing or what is "wrong" with the client. The drawback of this model is that the women and girls already are struggling with poor self-perceptions because of the stigmas attached to their substance abuse, their prison records, their parenting histories, and so on. In contrast, an asset model of treatment empowers each woman or girl and increases her sense of self.

Using an asset model, the facilitator helps the treatment group members to see the strengths and skills they already have that will aid their healing. She helps them to look to "the seeds of health and strength" within their symptoms. For example, the facilitator portrays a female's relational difficulties as "efforts to connect," rather than as "failures to separate or to disconnect." The facilitator repeatedly affirms the females' abilities to care, empathize, use their intuition, and build relationships. "As a woman feels more valued, her need for alcohol, tobacco, and other drugs might diminish and her resilience increase" (Finkelstein et al., 1997, p. 6).

The following is an excerpt from a strengths and needs assessment tool developed by Fedele and Miller (1988, pp. 17–18):

The need to state clearly how I feel	The strength to express my feelings in my relationships with others
0 1 2 3 4	0 1 2 3 4
The need to express my anger appropriately	The strength to express my anger appropriately
0 1 2 3 4	0 1 2 3 4
The need to take appropriate action to express myself under stress	The strength to take appropriate action to solve problems
0 1 2 3 4	0 1 2 3 4
The need to address my own substance abuse	The strength to find effective ways of coping with stress
0 1 2 3 4	0 1 2 3 4

The strength to recognize the substance abuse of a loved one

0	1	2	3	4

The need to address the substance abuse of a loved one

0	1	2	3	4

Culture Context

It is important to realize that just as women's lives are different from men's lives, women's lives are not all the same. Although there are common threads in all women's lives because of their gender, it is important to be sensitive to cultural and other differences. For example, there are differences in the lives of African-American women, Hispanic women, and Asian women. There are differences between heterosexual women, bisexual women, lesbian women, and transgendered women. There are differences between older women and younger women. The facilitator must remain aware of and sensitive to the issues of diversity in the group.

Single-gender Groups

Research suggests that although men may benefit from mixed-gender groups, women benefit more from all-female groups (Aries, 1976). In all-male groups, men say little about themselves, their key relationships, or their feelings. In all-female groups, women share a great deal about themselves, their feelings, and their relationships with lovers, friends, and family. In mixed groups, men reveal much more about themselves and their feelings, while women reveal much less (Priyadarsini, 1986).

According to Aries, the amount of sharing differs as much as the content. In all-female groups, women strive to equalize the amount of time each woman talks—they draw one another out, fall silent after long speeches, speak up more after an absence or long silence, and avoid dominating the conversation. However, in mixed groups, women tend to yield the floor to men; women may take up only one-third of the time, even though they make up half of the group. Additionally, men often punish women who fail to yield to them.

Women and girls are much more supportive of one another in all-female groups than in mixed groups. Women and girls often are socialized to compete for male attention when males are around, yet will cooperate with one another when males are not.

Aries found that, over time, women placed in both mixed and single-gender groups expressed a preference for the single-gender groups, while men over time preferred the mixed groups. These preferences make sense, given that mixed groups tended to expand the men's styles of relating while restricting the women's styles.

Aries studied high-functioning young men and women who were conversing about relatively nonthreatening topics. Women and girls who lack secure senses of self and have histories of abuse by males are even less likely to speak up on taboo topics, such as addiction, sexual abuse, and violence, when males are present. Consequently, single-gender groups are essential for females.

Sometimes females say they do not want to be in a female-only group and that they get along better with males. Women and girls who say this usually get along with males by relying on stereotypical female behavior, rather than by expressing their true selves. Also, females are more able to hide parts of themselves in a mixed group. In an all-female group, females tend to challenge one another's pretenses and denial; in a mixed group, females let one another get away with more because they understand the pressure to look good in front of males.

When a female says, "I don't like women" or "I don't like girls," she also is saying, "I don't like myself." Such a female can benefit greatly from learning to trust and respect other females—and her own femaleness—in an environment in which there is no pressure to compete for male attention.

There is some debate among clinicians as to whether female-only groups are preferable for all women. In their review of the literature, McWilliams and Stein (1987) found that single-gender groups were the treatment of choice for certain clinical groups, including sexual abuse survivors and battered wives or lovers. Herman (1992) also emphasized that a trauma survivor who is working on Stage-One recovery—safety—needs to be in a homogeneous recovery group. It is often difficult for females to talk in depth about physical or sexual abuse in front of males until they are ready for Stage-Three recovery—reconnection. Graham and Linehan (1987) found female-only groups to be preferable in dealing with chronic alcoholism. Bernardez (1978 and 1983) pointed out that single-gender groups helped females develop assertiveness, redefine their understanding of feminine behavior, experiment with the balance between their own needs and those of others, and identify positively with other females. On the other hand, Alonso (1987) said that mixed-gender groups offer females more alternatives to hyperfeminine personality traits and better represent the real world in which females live. In assessing Alonso's views, Fedele and Harrington (1990) concluded that single- and mixed-gender groups are appropriate for females at different stages of their lives. When a female is at a stage of needing to consolidate experiences, ideas, feelings, and a sense of self (as in early substance abuse recovery), a single-gender group is preferable. Once her experience has been validated, she has more empathy for herself, and she is more empowered (as in later recovery) and a mixed group may be appropriate for the next stage of her development.

Thus, while mixed groups may have their place in later recovery, it is important that a gender-specific treatment program for early substance abuse recovery use single-gender groups. Treatment group facilitators also must be female.

Four Content Areas

In the context just described, women and girls can deal effectively with the content of a gender-specific treatment program. The Center for Substance Abuse Treatment (1994) has stated the following content issues that are essential to address in a comprehensive treatment program:

1. The process of addiction, especially gender-specific issues related to addiction (including social, physiological, and psychological consequences of addiction, and factors related to the onset of addiction)

2. Low self-esteem

3. Race, ethnicity, and cultural issues

4. Gender discrimination and harassment

5. Disability-related issues, such as transportation and employment, where relevant

6. Relationships with family and significant others

7. Attachments to unhealthy interpersonal relationships

8. Interpersonal violence, including incest, rape, battering, and other abuse

9. Eating disorders

10. Sexuality, including sexual functioning and sexual orientation

11. Parenting

12. Grief related to the loss of alcohol or other drugs, children, family members, or partners

13. Work

14. Appearance and overall health and hygiene

15. Isolation related to a lack of support systems (which may or may not include family members and/or partners) and other resources

16. Life plan development

17. Child care and custody

Rather than seeing these issues as "problems" that a woman and her support system need to "solve," it is more helpful to use the Center for Substance Abuse Treatment list to assess the "level of burden" a woman or girl carries (Brown, Huba, and Melchior, 1995, p. 340). This approach avoids adding to the stigma that females feel because of their problems; it helps counselors understand how to respond when a female does not comply with treatment; and it equips counselors to educate other staff members and family members.

The Center for Substance Abuse Treatment list takes into account physical, psychological, emotional, spiritual, and sociopolitical issues of substance abuse. These seventeen issues may be grouped into four major areas: self, relationships, sexuality, and spirituality. Interviews with women in recovery indicate that these four areas cover the major aspects of life that change during recovery and that are the most common triggers for relapse if not addressed (Covington, 1994). The author's model for a gender-specific program addresses these four areas in four separate modules. The topics covered in each module are sequenced developmentally from least to most sensitive:

Self: In this module, the females discover what the "self" is; learn about the sources of self-esteem; consider the effects of sexism, racism, and stigma on a sense of self; and begin to develop their own senses of themselves. Substance abuse can be understood as a "self-disorder" (a generic definition of addiction is "the chronic neglect of self in favor of something or someone else"). Therefore, one of the first questions women and girls in recovery need to begin to address is, "Who am I?" Females in our culture are taught to identify themselves according to role: mother, professional, wife, partner, or daughter. Those in the criminal justice system also identify themselves—as does society—as offenders, and they become stigmatized. Further, many females also enter the system with poor self-images and a history of trauma and abuse. Creating the kinds of programs that help women and girls to develop a strong sense of themselves, an identification that goes beyond who they are in the criminal justice system, is vital to their reentering society. Recovery is about the expansion and growth of the self. This module enables women and girls to integrate their outer selves (their roles) with their inner selves (their feelings, thoughts, and attitudes).

Relationships: In this module, the women and/or girls explore their roles in their families of origin; discuss myths about motherhood and their relationships with their own mothers; look back on their relationship histories, including possible histories of interpersonal violence; and make decisions about how they can build healthy support systems. Relationship issues are paramount in early recovery. Some females use addictive substances to maintain relationships with drug-using partners, to fill a void in the relationship, or to deal with the pain of being abused. Those in the criminal justice system often have unhealthy, illusory, or unequal relationships with spouses, partners, friends, and family members. For that reason, it is important for programs to model healthy relationships among both staff and participants and to provide a safe place for healing. Being in a community—that is, having a sense of connection with others—is essential for continuous, long-term recovery.

Sexuality: In this module, the females explore the connections between addiction and sexuality, body image, sexual identity, sexual abuse, and the fear of sex when clean and sober. Sexuality is a neglected area in substance abuse treatment, and it is a major cause of relapse (Covington, 1997). Healthy sexuality is essential to a woman's sense of self-worth. Because substance abuse often interrupts the normal process of a girl's or woman's healthy sexual development, she may enter recovery with developmental lags. Many females begin recovery struggling with sexual dysfunction, shame, fear, and/or trauma that need to be addressed so that they do not return to using alcohol or other drugs to manage the pain of these difficulties (Covington, 1997; 2000).

Spirituality: In this module, the women and girls are introduced to the concepts of spirituality, prayer, and meditation, and asked to consider how these can contribute to their recovery. They also create a vision for their immediate future in recovery. Reconnecting to her own definition of spirituality is essential to a female's recovery process. Spirituality deals with transformation, connection, meaning, and wholeness (Covington, 1998a)—all factors in recovery.

Twelve-step Programs and Females

The type of gender-specific treatment program described can be paired effectively with twelve-step programs such as Alcoholics Anonymous (AA). Many people think of twelve-step programs as being only in the United States. However, in 1990, AA had an estimated two million members in more than 80,000 groups around the world. There are also at least 126 other kinds of twelve-step groups, such as Narcotics Anonymous and Cocaine Anonymous, for persons who have other dependencies and for the families of such persons (Alcoholics Anonymous World Services, 1992). The percentages of females in AA groups "range from 10 percent in Mexico to 44 percent in Austria and up to 50 percent in Switzerland" (Makela et al., 1996, p. 170). AA boards in Finland, Mexico, and the United States have held national working groups on women's issues. In fact, there are more women in AA than in professional treatment (Makela et al., 1996).

A 1996 survey by the National Center on Addiction and Substance Abuse (1998) found that 74 percent of prison facilities offer mutual help groups, mostly Alcoholics Anonymous, Narcotics Anonymous, or Rational Recovery. Most local jails also offer groups modeled on AA or NA. The sheer availability and familiarity of these programs makes them a useful adjunct to a gender-specific treatment program.

Mutual help groups such as AA are free, and because of their sheer numbers they are readily available in most urban areas. People are allowed to come and go without signing a contract or having a record kept of their presence. Meetings are consistent in their format, so that a person can drop in on a new group and have confidence that the guidelines that make AA work will be adhered to. Female-only meetings are widely available. In addition, AA provides a bridge back into the community for women leaving jails and prisons. The meetings create a different kind of community from that available in institutions and can expand females' sense of what support is possible. AA also provides a different kind of community from what is available in a community correctional facility. The twelve-step option is especially important in a time when money for substance abuse treatment and psychological services is limited (Covington, 1991).

In recent years, twelve-step programs have been critiqued in various ways. Some feminists have been concerned that the language of the twelve steps seems simplistic, sexist, and reductionist (Bepko, 1991; Berenson, 1991; Kasl, 1992; Rapping, 1996). Certainly AA has limitations. It stresses individual change as the solution and ignores social and political factors that hinder female sobriety, such as the systems of domination in which women live. Also, much of the AA literature is twenty to fifty years old and is overtly sexist. Atheistic, humanistic, and agnostic women may be uncomfortable with AA's references to a "Higher Power," even though AA welcomes a broad range of understandings of the Higher Power, including "Goddess," "Buddha," and a "Deeper Self."

Other mutual-help groups have been formed in recent years to address these limitations. Women for Sobriety groups resemble feminist consciousness-raising groups. Save Our Selves groups follow a format similar to AA's but omit references to a Higher Power in any form.

References to powerlessness in the first of AA's twelve steps also concern many critics. They say that to ask women and girls to admit their powerlessness over alcohol and then over persons, places, and things is to encourage the women and girls to think of themselves as victims who have no control over their lives. However, this critique misses the paradox of powerlessness: by admitting her powerlessness over alcohol, a female accesses areas of her life in which she does have power. For example, by admitting her powerlessness to change someone with whom she has relationship, she is empowered to make decisions about how to relate to that person. Despite the sexist language, women and girls are generally able to interpret the twelve steps in ways that are personally meaningful and useful.

Feminists, in particular, are concerned about the twelve steps' emphasis on powerlessness as liberating. In contrasting the recovery movement with the women's movement, Walters (1990) points out that "one movement encourages individuals to surrender to a spiritual higher power, where the other encourages people to join together to challenge and restructure power arrangements in the larger society" (p. 55).

However, feminist analysis often misses the fact that the masculine "power over" is being relinquished in order to experience the feminine "power with," "power to be able"—that is, a sense of empowerment (Miller, 1982). "The process of recovery from addiction is a process of recovering a different, more feminine, sense of power and will" (Berenson, 1991, p. 74). There is also a confusion between surrender and submission. "When we submit, we give in to a force that's trying to control us. When we surrender, we let go of our need to control" (Covington, 1994, p.48). Recovery encourages surrender and giving up the illusion of control.

French (1985) writes that "life is the highest value for 'feminine' people; whereas control is the highest value for 'masculine' people" (p. 93). As previously noted, Brown (1995) observes that control—the power of the individual over self and others—is the organizing principle of life in Western culture. Moreover, this Western belief in the importance of power and control is one of the foundations of the criminal justice system. Hence, it is not surprising that powerlessness would be an alien and devalued concept in Western culture, especially in criminal justice settings.

If addiction reflects a lack of self-control, then the natural Western goal is to regain control so that one can continue to use alcohol or another drug in a "controlled" manner. If chemical dependency is a learned behavior, then presumably it can be unlearned through behavioral means and the individual returned to a state of self-control. However, if chemical dependency is a disease, irreversible and incurable, then self-control over the disease is not possible. In this case, the individual must learn to acknowledge her lack of control and pursue a process that involves affective, cognitive, and behavioral changes with a goal of abstinence.

At the root of the ongoing controversy over the best treatment for substance abuse are two polar views of AA. Some professionals are strongly in favor of a chemical dependency framework that incorporates twelve-step work, while other members of the mental health field are often skeptical of such a framework. Treatment from a traditional mental health perspective usually focuses on only one approach—behavioral, cognitive, or psychodynamic—whereas an integration of all three is needed to treat this multidimensional disease. In a similar way, when chemical dependency treatment ignores the multiplicity of issues, it too fails to address females' needs fully. AA integrates behavioral, cognitive, psychodynamic, and systems treatment models, as well as addresses spiritual issues. Women and girls require this kind of comprehensive, integrated, developmental model. If addiction is seen as a disease that manifests in many different ways in different women, the need for multiple strategies is clear.

Because females grow and develop in relationships and connections, and because twelve-step programs are free and available in our communities, it makes sense to enable females to have access to them, both while in the criminal justice system and while making the transition back into the community. Twelve-step programs also can be incorporated into community correctional settings, offering an already-existing "continuity of care."

Mutual-help groups cannot be used as substitutes for professional counseling when a female has been raped or battered or is the victim of incest. However, as part of a multifaceted support system, mutual-help groups can be very useful for women and girls in recovery. They provide the kind of safe environment that is needed for trauma recovery and a growth-fostering relational context that serves females' psychological development.

Women's Voices

Substance-abusing women themselves are a valuable resource for educating those of us in the free world. If we are willing to listen, they will tell us who they are, what they need, and what can make a difference in their lives. The following descriptions are excerpts from letters written by women at the Atwood Treatment Program (1994) when the U.S. Federal Prison in Lexington, Kentucky, housed women[3]:

> My name is Mary. I have been incarcerated for about 15 months of a 70 month sentence. My crime is "Conspiracy to Manufacture Methamphetamine." I am a heroin addict, a speed addict, and a drug manufacturer. I've been in and out of my addiction since my early twenties. I am currently forty-seven years old. I have about equal time clean and straight and active addiction.

> My name is Brenda. I am thirty-seven years old and have three children. I was in a very emotional and physically abusive relationship for almost twenty years up until the time I was incarcerated.

> Hello my name is Dorothy. . . . I'm thirty-one years old and have been in and out of jails and institutions since I was thirteen years old. All of my incarcerations have been a direct result from my behavior while using drugs and alcohol.

> My name is Janet, I'm here in prison on a drug charge. I've been in my active addiction since I was seventeen. I'm now thirty-four years old. My idea of a relationship with a man consisted of doing whatever I was told for the last ten years.

Like prostitution, robbery, and a little bit of everything short of murder. Seven of the years he has been locked up and he loved me so I couldn't leave him. When I caught my case and was coming to prison I had nothing to offer him, so he dropped me.

My name is Betty and I am thirty-nine years of age. . . . I am here in prison doing eighteen years and ten months for selling crack cocaine. I have been locked up for three years already. . . . I started drinking when I was thirteen years of age until I came to prison.

Hi, I'm Joyce. I'm from Tennessee. I'm a divorced thirty-four year old woman with a fifteen-month old son. I'm here in Lex doing eight years on a marijuana charge. My mother and little brother are doing time on the same charges. I'm blessed that mama and I are together. We have a better relationship now than ever before.

I am Bonnie. . . . I'm black, age forty, mother of a twenty-three year old daughter, grandmother, and the oldest child of eight. I'm serving five years on a probation violation for a DUI. After doing three years of this five year probation, with two years left, the judge felt that I need to start over with this five years in prison because of my addiction to 'pot.'

My name is Ruth, and I'm forty-four years old. I was very shocked when law enforcement officials confided in my attorney that they believed I was an abused woman. Who me abused? My husband had a short temper, some personality quirks, and yes he had dropped me on floors, knocked me out cold and pushed me down stairs, but gee I never had to go to the hospital. Little did I know that I would discover what constitutes abuse and how this affected me and my children by being in a prison.

My name is Donna. I am a twenty-two year old single female. This is my first time being incarcerated and I am serving a Life plus five year sentence for supposedly knowing that my mate was dealing in crack cocaine.

Other researchers also have begun to listen to women's voices. Galbraith (1998) interviewed formerly incarcerated women who are now living successfully in their own communities to learn about the women and their children, what hurt, what helped, and where we go from here. The following themes emerged from the women's interviews when they discussed what helped them begin to change and recover:

- Relationships with people who cared, listened, and could be trusted

- Relationships with other women who were supportive and role models

- Proper assessment/classification

- Well-trained staff—especially female staff

- Proper medication

- Programs—not just incarceration, but job training, education, substance abuse and mental health treatment, and parenting

- Inmate-centered programs

- Efforts to reduce trauma and revictimization/alternatives to seclusion and restraint

- Financial resources

- Safe environments

Conclusion

In our society, females' primary pathways to crime are substance abuse and attempts to survive poverty and trauma. These crimes are actually social issues. There is no dispute that female offenders have committed crimes. It is crucial, however, that the link between the crimes and each woman's drug addiction, mental illness, and/or economic distress be acknowledged. It is equally important to challenge the belief that incarceration will accomplish what is needed.

Substance-abusing females are often institutionalized, especially if they are poor, when they could be treated more effectively and economically in community-based gender-specific programs. At present, our criminal justice system reflects the invisibility of women in our society; instead, we must apply what we have learned about the lives of women and girls to those who come in contact with the criminal justice system. We must make their lives and needs visible.

Current services not only lack gender specificity; but they often are fragmented, inconsistent, and contradictory. A woman can be in a therapeutic community that regards addiction as a secondary issue, while also attending twelve-step meetings that view addiction as a primary disease and that advocate abstinence and also participating in a cognitive-behavioral program that believes in controlled drug usage. These built-in contradictions can create confusion and lead to relapse. A female is also likely to be in one type of treatment program while incarcerated and then be treated from a different theoretical perspective when in a community continuing-care facility.

One of the most basic principles we must apply with females in the system is to "do no harm." Harm can come because of lack of safety in a facility; retraumatization; the facility's policies and procedures; or ineffective, contradictory, and nongender-specific treatment programs. We must understand the reality of the lives of the females who come into the system in order to develop programs to serve them.

Many women and men who work in criminal justice settings struggle daily with the contradiction that a system based on power and control is antithetical to what helps women to change, grow, and heal. Creating new gender-specific programs or changing an existing program can be a partial solution. Systemic change is essential.

One of the primary goals of the criminal justice system must be to help women and girls reintegrate into society and lead productive lives. What can be done? Interventions can be made on many different levels:

> *Try to change mandatory sentencing laws.* Addicted women and girls need treatment, not prisons. Drugs are a public health problem, not a criminal justice problem. Treatment is both cheaper and more effective than prison at reducing recidivism (Finigan, 1996; Gerstein et al., 1994).

> *Choose an alternative classification principle.* Burke and Adams (1991) recommend that "habilitation" rather than "risk" assessment would be a better principle by which to classify female offenders. While security is an important consideration, equally important is the need to prepare females to function in the community. Alternative sanctions, treatment, and postrelease support all contribute to habilitation.

Females should be classified into the least restrictive setting consistent with safety.

Staff our jails, prisons, and community correctional facilities with more female wardens and correctional officers. Female staff can serve as role models and help to reduce the risk of retraumatization by providing a sense of safety. Only those who can provide that sense of safety have the right to work with females.

Give supplementary training to correctional officers. Training academies often teach information and skills that apply only to men's facilities. Officers in women's facilities need to understand the realities of women's lives and the value of mutually empathic relationships, not just the rules and structure that may be effective with men, and how disconnection, addiction, and trauma affect women.

Teach women and girls to value life, especially their own. It is hard for females to do so in a misogynist society where the message is that their lives are trivial.

Help women keep contact with their children. Currently, women's facilities are often set at great distances from cities where women's children live, so that visitation is difficult. It is often their connections with their children that keep women alive and motivate them to change. It is equally essential that children's need for connection with their mothers is supported and facilitated. Maintaining these relationships is a way to help prevent recidivism by the mothers and to help the children avoid the cycle of alcohol/drug abuse and incarceration.

Become aware of our own attitudes about women and girls. We need to commit to changing our personal social systems, moving away from power and control and toward mutually empowering relationships. We need to create an environment for change and healing in our own lives.

We have the knowledge, based on sound research and experience, to design a system that frees female offenders from the cycle of substance abuse and recidivism. The rate of female incarceration need not continue to rise exponentially if we are willing to act.

The ultimate challenge as we move into the twenty-first century is to acknowledge the deep connections between the personal and the political in the lives of women and girls in the criminal justice system. If we truly want to be of service, then it is time to move beyond the culture of punishment and retribution that characterizes the system and create a culture of community and healing. It is time for transformation.

End Notes

[1] This paper is based in part on material from Stephanie Covington's *Helping Women Recover: A Program for Treating Substance Abuse*. 1999. San Francisco: Jossey-Bass. In this paper, the terms *female offender* and *female offending* will refer to females of all ages. *Delinquent* will describe only persons under eighteen years old. *Women offenders* will refer to persons over eighteen.

[2] Covington, S. 1999. *Helping Women Recover: A Program for Treating Substance Abuse*. San Francisco: Jossey-Bass. This publication is a special edition of the *Helping Women Recover* program. It is tailored especially for use in the criminal justice system. It is a complete program that includes both a facilitator's guide and a participant's journal.

[3] Women no longer are incarcerated in this prison. They currently are in various federal prisons across the country.

References

Abbott, B. and D. Kerr. 1995. *Substance Abuse Program for Federally Sentenced Women*. Ottawa, Ontario, Canada: Correctional Services of Canada.

Alcoholics Anonymous World Services. 1964. *The Grapevine*. New York: Alcoholics Anonymous.

———. 1992. *Analysis of the 1990 A.A. Membership Survey*. New York: Alcoholics Anonymous World Services.

Alexander, M. 1996. Women with Co-occurring Addictive and Mental Disorders: An Emerging Profile of Vulnerability. *Journal of Orthopsychiatry*. 66(1). January.

Alonso, A. 1987. Discussion of Women's Groups Led by Women. *International Journal of Group Psychotherapy*. 37:2. 155–162.

Amaro, H. and C. Hardy-Fanta. 1995, October/December. Gender Relations in Addiction and Recovery. *Journal of Psychiatric Drugs*. 27:4, 325–337.

American Psychiatric Association. 1994. *Diagnostic and Statistical Manual of Mental Disorders*, 4th ed. Washington, D.C.: American Psychiatric Association.

Amity, Inc. 1994. *Basic Interface*. Volume 1. Tucson, Arizona: Amity, Inc.

Anthenelli, R. and M. Schuckit. 1994. Genetic Influences in Addiction. In N. S. Miller, ed. *Principles of Addiction Medicine*. Chevy Chase, Maryland: American Society of Addiction Medicine. pp. 1–14.

Aries, E. 1976. Interaction Patterns and Themes of Males, Females, and Mixed Groups. *Small Group Behavior.* 7:1 , 7–18.

Arbour, L. 1996. *Commission of Inquiry into Certain Events at the Prison for Women in Kingston*. Ottawa, Ontario, Canada: Canada Communication Group.

Arnold, R. 1990. Women of Color: Processes of Victimization and Criminalization of Black Women. *Social Justice*. 17:3, 153–166.

Atwood Treatment Program. 1994. Personal correspondence from inmates. Lexington, Kentucky: Federal Prison for Women. June.

Austin, J., B. Bloom, and T. Donahue. 1992 . *Female Offenders in the Community: An Analysis of Innovative Strategies and Programs*. Washington, D.C.: National Institute of Corrections.

Axon, L. 1989. *Model and Exemplary Programs for Female Inmates: An International Review*. Ottawa, Ontario, Canada: Ministry of the Solicitor General.

Barrett, M. and T. Trepper. 1991. Treating Women Drug Abusers Who Were Victims of Childhood Sexual Abuse. In C. Bepko, ed. *Feminism and Addiction*. New York: Haworth Press. pp. 127–146.

Basic Interface. 1994. *Origins: Restorative Paradigms*. Tucson, Arizona: Amity, Inc.

Beckman, L. 1994 . Treatment Needs of Women with Alcohol Problems. *Alcohol, Health and Research World*. 18:3, 206–211.

Belknap, J. 1996. *The Invisible Woman: Gender, Crime, and Justice*. Cincinnati, Ohio: Wadsworth.

Belknap, J., M. Dunn, and K. Holsinger. 1997. *Moving Toward Juvenile Justice and Youth-serving Systems that Address the Distinct Experience of the Adolescent Female*. A Report to the Governor. Columbus, Ohio: Office of Criminal Justice Services.

Belknap, J. and K. Holsinger. 1998. An Overview of Delinquent Girls: How Theory and Practice Have Failed and the Need for Innovative Changes. In R. Zaplin, ed. *Female Crime and Delinquency: Critical Perspectives and Effective Interventions.* Gaithersburg, Maryland: Aspen Publishers.

Bepko, Claudia, ed. 1991. *Feminism and Addiction.* New York: Haworth Press.

Berenson, D. 1991. Powerlessness—Liberation or Enslaving? Responding to the Feminist Critique of the Twelve Steps. In C. Bepko, ed. *Feminism and Addiction.* New York: Haworth Press. pp. 67-80.

Bernardez, T. 1978. Women's Groups: A Feminist Perspective on the Treatment of Women. In H. H. Grayson and C. Loew, eds. *Changing Approaches to the Psychotherapies.* New York: Spectrum.

————. 1983 . Women's Groups. In M. Rosenbaum, ed. *Handbook of Short-term Therapy Groups.* New York: McGraw-Hill.

Bloom, B., M. Chesney-Lind, and B. Owen. 1994. *Women in California Prisons: Hidden Victims of the War on Drugs.* San Francisco, California: Center on Juvenile and Criminal Justice.

Bloom, B., and D. Steinhart. 1993. *Why Punish the Children? A Reappraisal of Incarcerated Mothers in America.* San Francisco, California: National Council on Crime and Delinquency.

Blume, S. 1990. Alcohol and Drug Problems in Women: Old Attitudes, New Knowledge. In H. B. Mikman and L. I. Sederer, eds. *Treatment Choices for Alcoholism and Substance Abuse.* New York: Lexington.

————. 1997. *Defining 'Gender Specific': What Does it Mean and Why is it Important?* Paper presented at National Institute of Corrections Intermediate Sanctions for Women Offenders National Project Meeting. Longmont, Colorado. September.

Bodinger-de Uriarte, C. and G. Austin. 1991. Substance Abuse among Adolescent Females. *Prevention Research Update.* Portland, Oregon: Northwest Regional Education Laboratory.

Boudin, K. 1998. Lessons from a Mother's Program in Prison. In J. Harden and M. Hill, eds. *Breaking the Rules: Women in Prison and Feminist Therapy.* New York: Haworth Publishers. pp. 103-125.

Brennan, T. and J. Austin. 1997. *Women in Jail: Classification Issues.* Washington, D.C.: National Institute of Corrections. March.

Brown, S. 1985. *Treating the Alcoholic: A Developmental Model.* New York: John Wiley and sons.

————. 1995. *Treating Alcoholics*. San Francisco, California: Jossey-Bass.

Brown, V., G. Huba, and L. Melchior. 1995. Level of Burden: Women with More than One Co-occurring Disorder. *Journal of Psychiatric Drugs*. 27:4, pp. 339–345.

Browne, A. 1987. *When Battered Women Kill*. New York: Free Press.

Bureau of Justice Statistics. 1991, March. *Women in Prison*. Special Report, Executive Summary. Washington, D.C.: U.S. Department of Justice.

————. 1992 . *Women in Jail in 1989*. Washington, D.C.: U.S. Department of Justice.

————. 1997. Bulletin: *Prison and Jail Inmates at Midyear 1996*. Washington, D.C.: U.S. Department of Justice. January.

Burke, P. and L. Adams. 1991. *Classification of Women Offenders in State Correctional Facilities: A Handbook for Practitioners*. Washington, D.C.: National Institute of Corrections.

Bylington, D. 1997. Applying Relational Theory to Addiction Treatment. In S.L.A. Straussner and E. Zelvin, eds. *Gender and Addictions: Men and Women in Treatment*. Northvale, New Jersey: Jason Aronson. pp. 33–45.

Carten, A. F. 1996. Mothers in Recovery: Rebuilding Families in the Aftermath of Addiction. *Social Work*. 41. pp. 214–223.

Center for Substance Abuse Treatment. 1994. *Practical Approaches in the Treatment of Women Who Abuse Alcohol and Other Drugs*. Rockville, Maryland: Department of Health and Human Services, Public Health Service.

————. 1997 . *Substance Abuse Treatment for Incarcerated Women Offenders: Guide to Promising Practices*. Rockville, Maryland: Department of Health and Human Services, Public Health Service.

Chesney-Lind, M. 1992. *Rethinking Women's Imprisonment: A Critical Examination of Trends in Female Incarceration*. Unpublished manuscript.

Chesney-Lind, M and B. Bloom. 1997. Feminist Criminology: Thinking about Women and Crime. In B. MacLean and D. Milovanovic, eds. *Thinking Critically about Crime*. Vancouver: Collective Press. pp. 54-65.

Collins, W. and A. Collins. 1996. *Women in Jail: Legal Issues*. Washington, D.C.: National Institute of Corrections. December.

Consedine, J. 1995 . *Restorative Justice: Healing the Effects of Crime*. Christchurch, New Zeland: Ploughshares Publications.

Copeland, J., W. Hall, P. Didcott, and V. Biggs. 1993. A Comparison of a Specialist Women's Alcohol and Other Drug Treatment Service with Two Traditional Mixed-sex Services: Client Characteristics and Treatment Outcome. *Drug and Alcohol Dependence.* 32:1, 81–92.

Correctional Service Canada. 1994. *Correctional Program Strategy for Federally Sentenced Women.* Ottawa, Ontario, Canada: Correctional Service Canada.

Covington, S. 1991. Sororities of Helping and Healing: Women and Mutual Help Groups. In P. Roth, ed. *Alcohol and Drugs are Women's Issues.* New York: Scarecrow Press. pp. 85- 92.

————. 1994. *A Woman's Way Through the Twelve Steps.* Center City, Minnesota: Hazelden.

————. 1997. Women, Addiction, and Sexuality. In L.A. Straussner and E. Zelvin, eds. *Gender Issues in Addiction: Men and Women in Treatment.* Northvale, New Jersey: Jason Aronson.

————. 1998. The Relational Theory of Women's Psychological Development: Implications for the Criminal Justice System. In R. Zaplin, ed. *Female Crime and Delinquency: Critical Perspectives and Effective Interventions.* Gaithersburg, Maryland: Aspen Publishers.

————. 1998a. Women in Prison: Approaches in the Treatment of Our Most Invisible Population. *Women in Therapy.* 21:1, 141–155.

————. 1999. *Helping Women Recover: A Program for Treating Substance Abuse Addiction.* San Francisco, California: Jossey-Bass.

————. 2000. *Awakening Your Sexuality: A Guide for Recovering Women.* Center City, Minnesota: Hazelden.

Covington, S., and L. Beckett. 1988. *Leaving the Enchanted Forest: The Path from Relationship Addiction to Intimacy.* San Francisco, California: Harper San Francisco.

Covington, S. and J. Kohen. 1984. Women, Alcohol and Sexuality. *Advances in Alcohol and Substance Abuse.* 4:1, 41–56.

Covington, S. and J. Surrey. 1997. The Relational Model of Women's Psychological Development: Implications for Substance Abuse. In S. Wilsnack and R. Wilsnack, eds. *Gender and Alcohol: Individual and Social Perspectives.* New Brunswick, New Jersey: Rutgers University Press. pp. 335–351

Dahlgren, L. and A. Willander. 1989. Are Special Treatment Facilities for Female Alcoholics Needed? A Controlled 2-year Follow-up Study from a Specialized Female Unit EWA Versus a Mixed Male/Female Treatment Facility. *Alcoholism: Clinical and Experimental Research.* 13:4, 499–504.

Daly, D., H. Moss, and F. Campbell. 1993. *Dual Disorders: Counseling Clients with Chemical Dependency and Mental Illness.* Center City, Minnesota: Hazelden.

Daly, K. 1992. Women's Pathways to Felony Court: Feminist Theories of Lawbreaking and Problems of Representation. *Review of Law and Women's Studies.* 2. pp. 11–52.

Denborough, D., ed. 1996. *Beyond the Prison: Gathering Dreams of Freedom.* Adelaide, South Australia: Dulwich Center Publications.

Ensminger, M., C. Brown, and S. Kellan, 1982. Sex Differences in Antecedents of Substance Abuse among Adolescents. *Journal of Social Issue.* 38:2, 25–42.

Fedele, N. and E. Harrington. 1990. *Women's Groups: How Connections Heal.* Work in Progress No. 47. Wellesley, Massachusetts: Stone Center.

Fedele, N. and J. Miller. 1988 . *Putting Theory into Practice: Creating Mental Health Programs for Women.* Work in Progress No. 32. Wellesley, Massachusetts: Stone Center.

Finigan, M. 1996. *Societal Outcomes and Cost Savings of Drug and Alcohol Treatment in the State of Oregon.* Prepared for the Office of Alcohol and Drug Abuse Programs, Oregon Department of Human Resources.

Finkelhor, D. and A. Browne. 1988. Assessing the Long-term Impact of Child Sexual Abuse: A Review and Conceptualization. In G. Hotaling, D. Finkelhor, J. Kirkpatrick, and M. Straus, eds. *Family Abuse and its Consequences.* Newbury Park, California: Sage. pp. 270-284.

Finkelstein, N. 1993, July. The Relational Model. In D. Kronstadt, P. F. Green, and C. Marcus, eds. *Pregnancy and Exposure to Alcohol and Other Drug Use.* Washington, D.C.: U.S. Department of Health and Human Services, Center for Substance Abuse Prevention. pp. 126-163.

Finkelstein, N. and L. Derman. 1991. Single-parent Women: What a Mother Can Do. In P. Roth, ed. *Alcohol and Drugs Are Women's Issues.* New York: Scarecrow Press. pp. 78-84.

Finkelstein, N., C. Kennedy, K. Thomas, and M. Kearns. 1997. *Gender-specific Substance Abuse Treatment.* Washington, D.C.: Center for Substance Abuse Prevention, draft. March.

Finkelstein, N. and E. Piedade. 1993. The Relational Model and the Treatment of Addicted Women. *The Counselor.* pp. 8–12. May/June.

French, M. 1985. *Beyond Power: On Women, Men, and Morals.* New York: Ballantine Books.

Galbraith, S. 1991. Women and Legal Drugs. In P. Roth, ed. *Alcohol and Drugs Are Women's Issues.* New York: The Scarecrow Press, Inc. pp. 150-154.

———. 1994. *Best Practices: Models of Care for Pregnant Alcoholic and Drug Dependent Women and their Children.* New York: Legal Action Center.

———. 1998. *And So I Began to Listen to Their Stories. . . : Working With Women in The Criminal Justice System.* Delmar, New York: Policy Research Inc.

Garcia Coll, C., and K. Duff. 1995. Reframing the Needs of Women in Prison: A Relational and Diversity Perspective. *Final Report, Women in Prison Pilot Project.* Wellesley, Massachusetts: Stone Center.

Garcia Coll, C., J. Miller, J. Fields, and B. Mathews. 1998. The Experiences of Women in Prison: Implications for Services and Prevention. In J. Harden and M. Hill, eds. *Breaking the Rules: Women in Prison and Feminist Therapy.* New York: Haworth.

Gerstein, D., R. Johnson, H. Harwood, D. Foutain, N. Suter, and K. Molloy. 1994. Evaluating Recovery Services: The California Drug and Alcohol Treatment Assessment. Unpublished report.

Gilligan, C. 1982. *In a Different Voice: Psychological Theory and Women's Development.* Cambridge, Massachusetts: Harvard University Press.

———. 1991. Women's Psychological Development: Implications for Psychocounseling. In C. Gilligan, A. Rogers, and D. Tolman, eds. *Women, Girls, and Psychocounseling: Reframing Resistance.* New York: Haworth.

Gilligan, C., N. P. Lyons, and T. J. Hanmer, eds. 1990. *Making Connections.* Cambridge, Massachusetts: Harvard University Press.

Girls Incorporated. 1996. *Prevention and Parity: Creating Solutions for Girls in Juvenile Justice.* Indianapolis, Indiana: Girls Inc. Summer.

Glover-Reed, B. 1987. Developing Women-sensitive Drug Dependence Treatment Services: Why So Difficult? *Journal of Psychoactive Drugs.* 19:2 , 151–164. April/June.

Goldberg, M. 1995. Substance-abusing Women: False Stereotypes and Real Needs. *Social Work.* 40. pp. 789–798.

Goleman, D. 1995. *Emotional Intelligence.* New York: Bantam.

Gonzalez, F. 1996. *Profile of the Female Offender: a Statistical Analysis.* Trenton, New Jersey: New Jersey Department of Corrections, Bureau of Community and Correctional Services. January.

Graham, B., and N. Linehan. 1987. Group Treatment for the Homeless and Chronic Alcoholic Woman. In C. Brody, ed. *Women's Therapy Groups: Paradigms of Feminist Treatment.* New York: Springer. pp. 177-197.

Heney, J. and C. Kristiansen. 1997. An Analysis of the Impact of Prison on Women Survivors of Childhood Sexual Abuse. *Women and Therapy.* 20:4, 29–44.

Herman, J. 1992. *Trauma and Recovery.* New York: HarperCollins..

Illinois Criminal Justice State Plan Working Group. 1995. *Managing Substance Abuse in Corrections: A Comprehensive Plan for Treatment of Illinois Inmates.* Springfield, Illinois: Illinois Criminal Justice State Plan Working Group. January.

Institute of Medicine. 1990. Populations Defined by Functional Characteristics. In *Broadening the Base of Treatment for Alcohol Problems.* Washington, D.C.: National Academy of Sciences. pp. 385–386 .

Jellinek, E. 1946. Phases in the Drinking History of Alcoholics: Analysis of a Survey Conducted by the Official Organ of Alcoholics Anonymous. *Quarterly Journal of Studies on Alcohol.* pp. 1–10. June.

Jordan, J. 1984. *Empathy and Self Boundaries.* Work in Progress No. 16. Wellesley, Massachusetts: Stone Center.

———. 1985. *The Meaning of Mutuality.* Work in Progress No. 23. Wellesley, Massachusetts: Stone Center.

Jordan, J. and J. Surrey. 1986. The Self-in-relation: Empathy and the Mother-Daughter Relationship. In T. Bernay and D. Cantor, eds. *The Psychology of Today's Woman: New Psychoanalytic Visions.* New York: Analytic.

Jordan, J. V., A. G. Kaplan, J. B. Miller, I. P. Stiver, and J. Surrey. 1991. *Women's Growth in Connection: Writings from the Stone Center.* New York: Guilford.

Kaplan, A. 1984. *Female or Male Psychotherapists for Women: New Formulations.* Work in Progress No. 83-02. Wellesley, Massachusetts: Stone Center.

Kasl, C. 1992. *Many Roads, One Journey.* New York: Harper Collins.

Keough, T. 1994. *The Psychology of Adolescent Female Offenders: Programs and Their Response to the Challenge.* Paper presented to the Australian Institute of Criminology Conference, Terrigal., New South Wales, Australia.

Kilbourne, J. 1991. The Spirit of the Czar: Selling Addictions to Women. In P. Roth, ed. *Alcohol and Drugs Are Women's Issues,* Vol. 1. New York: Scarecrow Press. pp. 10–22.

LeBlanc, A. N. 1996. A Woman Behind Bars Is Not a Dangerous Man. *The New York Times Magazine,* pp. 35–40. June 2.

Lightfoot, L. 1999. Treating Substance Abuse and Dependence in Offenders: A Review of Methods and Outcomes. In E. Latessa, ed. *Strategic Solutions: The International Community Corrections Association Examines Substance Abuse.* Lanham, Maryland: American Correctional Association.

Lightfoot, L. and L. Lambert. 1992. *Substance Abuse Treatment Needs of Federally Sentenced Women.* Technical Report #2. Kingston, Ontario, Canada: Correctional Services of Canada.

Makela, K., I. Arminen, K. Bloomfield, I. Eisenbach-Stangl, K. Bergmark, N. Kurube, N. Mariolini, H. Olafsdottir, J. Peterson, M. Phillips, J. Rehm, R. Room, P. Rosenqvist, H. Rosovsky, S. Kerstin, G. Swiatkiewicz, B. Woronowicz, and A. Zielinski. 1996. *Alcoholics Anonymous: A Study in Eight Societies.* Madison, Wisconsin: University of Wisconsin Press.

Martin, S. and F. Scarpitti. 1993. An Intensive Case Management Approach for Paroled IV Drug Users. *Journal of Drug Issues.* 23:1 , 43–59.

McFarlane, A. and R. Yehuda. 1996. Resilience, Vulnerability, and the Course of Posttraumatic Reactions. In B. A. van der Kolk, A. C. McFarlane, and L. Weisaeth, eds. *Traumatic Stress: The Effects of Overwhelming Experience on Mind, Body, and Society.* New York: Guilford. pp. 155-181.

McWilliams, N. and J. Stein. 1987. Women's Groups Led by Women: The Management of Devaluing Transferences. *International Journal of Group Psychotherapy.* 37:2 , 139-162.

Merriam, B. 1998. To Find a Voice: Art Therapy in a Women's Prison. *Women and Therapy.* 21:1, 157–171.

Miller, D. 1991. Are We Keeping up with Oprah: A Treatment and Training Model for Addictions and Interpersonal Violence. In C. Bepko, ed. *Feminism and Addiction.* New York: Haworth. pp. 103-126.

Miller, J. B. 1976. *Toward a New Psychology of Women.* Boston: Beacon Press.

————. 1982. *Women and Power.* Work in Progress No. 82-01. Wellesley, Massachusetts: Stone Center.

————. 1986. *What Do We Mean by Relationships?* Work in Progress No. 22 . Wellesley, Massachusetts: Stone Center.

————. 1990. *Connections, Disconnections, and Violations.* Work in Progress No. 33. Wellesley, Massachusetts: Stone Center.

Miller, J. B. and I. P. Stiver. 1997. *The Healing Connection: How Women Form Relationships in Therapy and in Life.* Boston: Beacon.

Miller, W. and N. Rollnick. 1991. *Motivational Interviewing: Preparing People to Change Addictive Behaviors.* New York: Guilford.

National Center on Addiction and Substance Abuse. 1998. *Behind Bars: Substance Abuse and America's Prison Population.* New York: Columbia University. January.

Northrup, C. 1994. *Women's Bodies, Women's Wisdom.* New York: Bantam.

Owen, B. 1998. *In the Mix: Struggle and Survival in a Women's Prison.* New York: State University of New York Press.

Parks, G. and G. A. Marlatt. 1999. Keeping "What Works" Working: Cognitive-behavioral Relapse Prevention Therapy with Substance-abusing Offenders. In E. Latessa, ed. *Strategic Solutions: The International Community Corrections Association Examines Substance Abuse.* Lanham, Maryland: American Correctional Association.

Pepi, C. 1998. Children Without Childhoods: A Feminist Intervention Strategy Utilizing Systems Theory and Restorative Justice in Treating Female Adolescent Offenders. In J. Harden and M. Hill, eds. *Breaking the Rules: Women in Prison and Feminist Therapy.* New York: Haworth.

Peters, S. R. and S. D. Peters. 1998. Violent Adolescent Females. *Corrections Today,* June, pp. 28-29.

Peyton, E. 1994, March. A Coordinated Approach to Managing the Drug Involved Offender: the Second Report of the Treatment Access Committee, a Permanent Committee of the Delaware Sentencing Accountability Commission. Unpublished report from the Delaware Sentencing Accountability Commission.

Phillips, S. and N. Harm. 1998. Women Prisoners: A Contextual Framework. In J. Harden and M. Hill, eds. *Breaking the Rules: Women in Prison and Feminist Therapy.* New York: Haworth. pp. 1-9.

Pollack, S. 1993. *Opening the Window on a Very Dark Day: A Program Evaluation of the Peer Support Team at the Kingston Prison for Women.* Unpublished master's thesis, Carlelton University, Ottawa, Ontario, Canada.

Priyadarsini, S. 1986. Gender Role Dynamics in an Alcohol Therapy Group. In D. Strug, S. Prizyadarsini, and M. Hyman, eds. *Alcohol Interventions: Historical and Sociocultural Approaches.* New York: Haworth. pp. 179-196.

Rapping, E. 1996. *The Culture of Recovery.* Boston: Beacon Press.

Root, M. 1992. Reconstructing the Impact of Trauma on Personality. In L. S. Brown and M. Ballou, eds. *Personality and Psychopathology: Feminist Reappraisals.* New York: Guilford. pp. 229-265.

Sandmaier, M. 1992. *The Invisible Alcoholics: Women and Alcohol,* 2nd ed. Blue Ridge Summit, Pennsylvania: TAB Books.

Schneider, K., F. Kviz, M. Isola, and W. Filstead. 1995. Evaluating Multiple Outcomes and Gender Differences in Alcoholism Treatment. *Addictive Behaviors.* 20:1 , 1–21.

Siegel, B. 1996. Personal communication with Stephanie Covington.

Siegel, L. and J. Senna. 1991. *Juvenile Delinquency, Theory, Practice, and Law,* 4th ed. St. Paul, Minnesota: West.

Snell, T. 1994. *Women in Prison: Survey of State Prison Inmates,* 1991. Washington, D.C.: U.S. Department of Justice, Bureau of Justice Statistics.

Sommers, E. 1995. *Voices from Within: Women Who Have Broken the Law.* Toronto, Ontario, Canada: University of Toronto Press.

Sommers, I. and D. Baskin. 1994. Factors Related to Female Adolescent Initiation into Violent Crime. *Youth and Society.* 24:4. 468–489.

Spencer, L. 1989. *Winning through Participating.* Dubuque, Iowa: Kendall Hunt.

Steffenmeier, D. and E. Allen. 1998. The Nature of Female Offending: Patterns and Explanation. In R. Zaplin, ed. *Female Crime and Delinquency: Critical Perspectives and Effective Interventions.* Gaithersburg, Maryland: Aspen.

Stevens, S. and N. Arbiter. 1995. A Therapeutic Community for Substance-abusing Pregnant Women and Women with Children: Process and Outcome. *Journal of Psychoactive Drugs.* 27:1, 49–56.

Stiver, I. P. 1990. *Dysfunctional Families and Wounded Relationships.* Work in Progress No. 38. Wellesley, Massachusetts: Stone Center.

Substance Abuse and Mental Health Services Administration. 1993. *National Household Survey on Drug Abuse: Population Estimates, 1992.* Rockville, Maryland: Substance Abuse and Mental Health Services Administration.

Surrey, J. 1985. *Self-in-relation: A Theory of Women's Development.* Work in Progress No. 13 . Wellesley, Massachusetts: Stone Center.

———. 1991. *Women and Addiction: a Relational Perspective.* Colloquium presented. Wellesley, Massachusetts: Stone Center.

Task Force on Federally Sentenced Women. 1990. *Creating Choices: Report of the Task Force on Federally Sentenced Women.* Ottawa, Ontario, Canada: Correctional Services of Canada.

Teplin, L., K. Abram, and G. McClelland. 1996. Prevalence of Psychiatric Disorders among Incarcerated Women. *Archives of General Psychiatry*. 53. pp. 505–512. June.

U.S. Department of Health and Human Services. *Monitoring the Future Survey.* 1995. Washington, D.C.: U.S. Department of Health and Human Services.

Walters, M. 1990. The Co-dependent Cinderella Who Loves Too Much... Fights Back. *The Family Therapy Networker.* 53-57. July-August.

Watterson, K. 1996. *Women in Prison: Inside the Concrete Womb*, rev. ed. Boston: Northeastern University Press.

Weekes, J. R., A. E. Moser, and C. M. Langevin. 1999. Assessing Substance-abusing Offenders for Treatment. In E. Latessa, ed. *Strategic Solutions: The International Community Corrections Association Examines Substance Abuse*. Lanham, Maryland: American Correctional Association.

Wellisch, J., M. Prendergast, and M. D. Anglin. 1994. *Drug-abusing Offenders: Results of a National Survey*. National Institute of Justice. Research in Brief. Washington, D.C.: U.S. Department of Justice. October.

Wilsnack, S., R. Wilsnack, and A. Klassen. 1986. Epidemiological Research on Women Drinking, 1978-1984. In National Institute on Alcohol Abuse and Alcoholism. *Women and Alcohol: Health-related Issues.* NIAAA Research Monograph No. 16, DHHS Publication No. ADM 86-1139 . Washington, D.C.: U.S. Government Printing Office. pp. 1-68.

Wolfe, V., C. Gentile, and D. Wolfe. 1989. The Impact of Sexual Abuse on Children: A PTSD Formulation. *Behavior Therapy*. 20: 215–228.

Young, N. 1994. *Invest in Treatment for Alcohol and Other Drug Problems: It Pays.* Washington, D.C.: National Association of State Alcohol and Drug Abuse Directors.

Zawistowski, T. A. 1991. Criminal Addiction/Illegal Disease. *The Counselor.* 8-11. March-April.

ASSESSING WOMEN OFFENDERS: WHAT WORKS*

5

Laurence L. Motiuk, Ph.D.

Kelley Blanchette, M.A.

Research Branch
Correctional Service of Canada
Ottawa, Canada

For several decades, researchers in community corrections have been highlighting conceptual and methodological advances in offender risk assessment technology, distinguishing between "statistical" and "clinical" prediction, and between "static" and "dynamic" factors. Early researchers focused on false positives—that is, incorrect containment or intensive supervision of criminal offenders who subsequently succeeded. The focus has shifted, however, with improvements in the accuracy of various risk scales, to false negatives—that is, premature release or minimal

---

*The opinions expressed in this paper are those of the authors and do not necessarily represent the official views of the Correctional Service of Canada.

supervision of offenders who subsequently failed. More recent research on false negatives has been fueled by public concerns for community safety and new legislation enacted to allay those concerns.

Jurisdictions may vary in their tolerance of false negatives, particularly with specific types of offenders or specific types of failure. Because society has such a low tolerance, decision makers have become overly concerned about failures, and this excessive concern may be impeding community reintegration efforts. Although there has been a recent increase in research on women offenders, there is still a noticeable absence of development in gender specific classification. Instead, assessment instruments developed for male offenders are often "borrowed," which may be contributing to over estimates of risk for female offenders.

By improving systematic offender risk and needs assessment strategies and standards of practice, correctional decision errors can be reduced. Such a strategy should help to identify candidates for early release and provide them with appropriate levels of supervision/intervention while in the community. This paper provides an overview of current assessment and classification practices with women offenders. Further, it illustrates how risk and need assessments may be bound into community reintegration efforts in a way that effectively minimizes decision errors, improves the use of correctional resources, and enhances public safety.

Resolving uncertainty about correctional decisions, after all due consideration of relevant static (criminal history) and dynamic (case need) factors, is the cornerstone of any effective risk management program. What works from here? In practice, the analysis of offender risk and need should serve to structure much of correctional decision making with respect to custody/security designations, temporary and conditional release, supervision requirements, and program placement (Motiuk, 1997). It is not surprising, therefore, to find that attempts to design, develop, and implement objective procedures for classifying criminal offenders have proliferated throughout North America (Andrews, Bonta, and Hoge, 1990).

Most of the objective female offender classification instruments being used today were originally developed on male offenders during the late 1970s and validated on females in the late 1980s and early 1990s. Examples include: the Level of Supervision Inventory or LSI (Andrews, 1982; Coulson, 1993; Coulson, Nutbrown, Guilekas, Cudjoe, and Ilacqua, 1996); the Wisconsin Risk-Needs (Baird, 1981; Bonta, Parkinson, and Barkwell, 1994); the Salient Factor Score or SFS (Hoffman, 1982); the Statistical

Information on Recidivism Scale or SIR (Nuffield, 1982; Bonta, Pang, and Wallace-Capretta, 1995), and the Custody Rating Scale or CRS (Porporino, Luciani, Motiuk, Johnston, and Mainwaring, 1989; Luciani, Motiuk, and Nafekh, 1996; Blanchette, 1997a). A paucity of research effort has gone into the development and validation of classification instruments specifically for women offenders. Notwithstanding that, acceptance of these instruments into everyday correctional practice remains uneven.

Although objective classification instruments can yield significant gains both in understanding and predicting criminal behavior, the fact remains that the amount of variance left unexplained continues to outweigh that which can be explained for a variety of important correctional outcomes (for example, temporary absence and parole). While this may be cause for some disillusionment with classification tools per se, it suggests that women offender evaluations will have to move beyond the limitations of any one tool and view classification as an integrated process incorporating a variety of methodologies (Motiuk, 1993).

To meet the correctional challenges of the late nineties, offender intake assessment processes coupled with a program of systematic community-based reassessment have made significant gains in the management of women offender populations. To this end, the Correctional Service of Canada implemented an Offender Intake Assessment (OIA) process in 1994.[1] Among the most important characteristics, which guided the design and development of this new assessment model were predictive validity, reflecting reality; flexibility, emphasizing professional discretion; consumer satisfaction; and being both qualitative and quantitative.

A comprehensive assessment at the admission stage is critical to gauge accurately the risk and needs of women offenders during the later phases of the sentence, when decisions as to reintegration potential are taken. At the same time, it is noteworthy that a successful model of community intervention assessment coexists for conditionally released women offenders in the community. This work provides a continuum of female offender assessment from admission to the end of the sentence. As a result, institution and community-based assessment processes are combined into one integrated system.

First, we describe, in some detail, an approach currently being used to assess criminal risk and identify needs of women offenders at the time of admission. Then, we go on to explain a community reassessment process.

The Offender Intake Assessment (OIA) Process

Previous research regarding the predictive value of female offender risk and needs assessments has led to three major conclusions: criminal history variables are strongly related to postrelease outcome (Hoffman, 1982; Blanchette, 1996); a consistent relationship exists between the type and number of needs that women offenders present and the likelihood of their reoffending (Simourd and Andrews, 1994; Blanchette, 1997b); and most importantly, combined assessment of both the level of risk and level of needs significantly can improve our ability to differentiate cases according to likelihood of reoffending (Coulson et al. 1996; Blanchette, 1997c).

Risk principle considerations address the assessment of risk, the prediction of recidivism, and the matching of levels of treatment service to the risk level of the offender (Andrews, Bonta, and Hoge, 1990). While there is considerable empirical evidence to support the "risk principle," it cannot be fully operationalized until a framework is put into place for establishing program priorities, implementing programs, and allocating resources to best meet the needs of women offenders (Motiuk, 1991). The Correctional Service of Canada saw the necessity for a comprehensive and integrated process to assess women offenders at intake.

The Offender Intake Assessment (OIA) process represents the latest generation of risk and need assessment technology (Motiuk, 1993; 1998). It integrates information gathered from a variety of sources (police, court, probation, family, employers) using many techniques (self-report, face-to-face-interviews, case-file reviews).

Beginning at the time of sentence, parole officers coordinate the collection of all relevant information about women offenders from sources within and outside the criminal justice system. This case-based information forms the basis for all future decisions and recommendations that parole officers must provide throughout the course of managing the offender's sentence. In addition to being the central figure in the OIA process, our parole officers play a major role in correctional planning; institutional supervision; preparing cases for decision (parole board and release); and community supervision.

Upon receiving a federal sentence (two years or more), each woman offender is interviewed by a parole officer. Whether the recently sentenced offender is at a local jail, remand or detention facility, the parole officer begins the OIA process by orienting the offender to the federal correctional system. First, and foremost, parole officers start with identifying any critical concerns (for example suicide, security, or health). Then, the parole officer collects each woman offender's court, police, probation, forensic, and jail records. Shortly thereafter, this information is transferred along with the offender to a federal institution for women offenders.

After a woman offender has been transferred, a parole officer located in the community where the offender was sentenced begins a postsentence community investigation. The postsentence community assessment report contains collateral sources of information. Knowledge of the offender is gained in areas such as the nature of the relationship with significant others (for example, family and employers), the personal impact of future contacts with the offender during incarceration or at time of release, and the degree of support that others are prepared to offer to the offender on her return to the community. Moreover, collateral perceptions of the offender's needs are obtained in relation to employment, marital/family relations, substance abuse, and so forth.

Upon arrival at the institution, women offenders undergo an admission interview and orientation session. During this period, each woman offender receives an initial assessment that screens for immediate physical health, security (personal and others safety), mental health, and suicide concerns. In fact, nine separate suicide potential indicators (for example, previous suicide attempts, signs of depression, a plan to commit suicide) are systematically administered to each new arrival. At this initial stage of the assessment process, should any concerns arise, a psychological referral is made, followed by an appropriate intervention, if it is required.

Loucks and Zamble (1994) have noted that almost half of their sample (n=100) of the Canadian federal female offender population had a history of attempted suicide. This was true for less than 15 percent of their male counterparts. A 1998 review of OIA suicide potential indicators yielded the same percentage for males but double that rate among female offenders. This finding is especially noteworthy considering that a history of attempted suicide was found to be a potent predictor of violent recidivism in a sample of federally sentenced women (Blanchette and Motiuk, 1995).

Specifically, the authors used a sample of eighty-one federal women offenders who were available for a postrelease follow-up of at least one year. Of those, seventeen (21 percent) reoffended violently within the follow-up period: eight robbery, seven assault, one utter threats, and one manslaughter. Overall, the explained variance in violent recidivism was 45 percent. Having a history of attempted suicide was the most highly predictive variable, explaining 20 percent of the variance in recidivism.

Accordingly, other researchers found much higher rates of previous self-injury among female recidivists than nonrecidivists (Bonta, Pang, and Wallace-Capretta, 1995). Although past self-injury or suicide attempts reflect static risk factors, it is feasible that early assessment and prevention might help to mitigate recidivism for female federal offenders.

After having passed through an initial assessment, women offenders then proceed to the two core components of the OIA process: 1) Criminal Risk Assessment and 2) Case Needs Identification and Analysis. A closer look at some of the information being gathered and analyzed in these components will illustrate the progress we believe is being achieved towards improving female offender assessment technology.

Assessing Static Factors

At intake, a rating of criminal risk for every woman offender is based on the following: the criminal history record, the offense severity record, whether detention criteria are met, and any other risk factors as detailed in a criminal profile report. The criminal profile report provides details of the crime(s) for which the offender is currently sentenced, and is provided for all newly admitted federal offenders: both male and female.

The Criminal History Record. By systematically reviewing the offender's file, which includes police reports, court transcripts, and criminal records, a criminal history record is completed on both the previous offense(s) and the current offense(s). Information is gathered on previous offense(s), the number and type of convictions, youth court dispositions, adult court sanctions, and crime-free periods. This information reflects the nature and extent to which an offender has been involved with the criminal justice system.

The Offense Severity Record. Similarly, a systematic review of the offender's file is used to complete an offense severity record covering both previous and current offense(s). This offense severity record consists of a historical index of offense severity and an index of the severity of the offense for which the offender is currently serving a sentence. As for current offense(s), the type of conviction(s), sentence length, the number and types of victim(s), the degree of force used on victim(s), and the degree of physical and psychological harm to victim(s) are all taken into account. This information reflects the nature and degree to which an offender has inflicted harm on society in general, and victims in particular. The determination of whether the current offense resulted in death or serious harm to the victim(s) is recorded. Information is also gathered on prior psychological or psychiatric assessments, prior treatment or intervention, and current treatment or intervention for criminal offending. Finally, all this case-based information reflects the nature and extent of criminal behavior, the amount of harm inflicted on victims and previous involvement in assessment, treatment, or intervention in relation to criminal offending.

Criminal Risk Level. An overall rating of criminal risk is the compilation of professional judgments derived from the results of the criminal history record and the offense severity record. In addition, a review of detention criteria for the current offense(s) is provided. This reflects the nature of the offense(s) and the degree of harm to victim(s). One should keep in mind that the establishment of criminal risk level might also incorporate a great deal of other assessment information as well. For example, additional information might be obtained from specialized assessments (for example, violent offenders) and input from case conferences.

Gender Differences—Static Factors at Intake

Table 5.1 shows a distribution of selected Criminal Risk Assessment indicators for all completed OIAs since implementation by gender. What can we say about the criminal history background of the female (n=453) and male (n=11,890) federal admission population? The table clearly illustrates considerable previous involvement with the criminal justice system. In fact, roughly two-out-of-three female and eight-out-of-ten male admissions were repeat offenders. Also noteworthy is the finding that female admissions are significantly less likely than male admissions to have had previous involvement with the criminal justice system. This type of information allows the Correctional Service of Canada to profile its woman offender population on the basis of criminal history background that incorporates exposure and response to previous criminal sanctioning.

Assessing Dynamic Factors

The Case Needs Identification and Analysis protocol collapsed the twelve currently defined need areas of the Community Risk/Needs Management Scale (CRNMS; Motiuk and Porporino, 1989) into seven need dimensions. These include employment, marital/family, associates/social interaction, substance abuse, community functioning, personal/ emotional orientation, and attitude. A list of about 200 indicators (*see* Appendices) and rating guidelines are provided for each of the seven

TABLE 5.1. Selected Criminal History Background Indicators of Male and Female Offenders

	MALE OFFENDERS (11,890)		FEMALE OFFENDERS (453)	
PREVIOUS YOUTH COURT ***	4,840	41%	104	23%
Community Supervision ***	3,458	30%	62	14%
Open Custody ***	2,525	22%	51	11%
Secure Custody ***	2,729	23%	49	11%
PREVIOUS ADULT COURT ***	9,827	82%	299	65%
Community Supervision ***	8,052	67%	243	53%
Provincial Terms ***	8,077	67%	223	49%
Federal Terms ***	3,194	27%	44	10%
PREVIOUS:				
Segregation (disciplinary) ***	2,765	24%	68	15%
Escape/Unlawfully at Large ***	2,677	22%	59	13%
Failure on Conditional Release ***	4,058	34%	85	19%
<6 Mo. Since last incarceration ***	2,742	23%	54	12%

Note: *$p<.05$; ***$p<.001$

need dimensions. In rating each need area during assessment, the woman offender's entire background is considered. This includes personal characteristics, interpersonal influences, situational determinants, and environmental conditions (Motiuk, 1991).

Case Need Levels. An overall rating of needs consists of the compilation of professional judgments derived from the results of an initial assessment (medical, mental health, suicide risk) and the observations or impressions (in other words, degree or severity of need) on each of the seven need areas.

Gender Differences—Dynamic Factors at Intake

The Offender Intake Assessment process gathers information on each offender's need domain ratings. Based on available data (*see* Table 5.2), we see that there is considerable variation across the different need areas between female (n=469) and male (n=12,265) offenders.

TABLE 5.2. Percentage Distribution of Case Need Levels (at time of admission)

NEED LEVEL: DOMAIN	MALE OFFENDERS (12,265)	%	FEMALE OFFENDERS (469)	%
AN ASSET:				
Employment ***	934	7.6	27	5.8
Marital/Family	1,231	10.0	32	6.8
Associates ***	996	8.1	46	9.8
Substance Abuse ***	—	—	—	—
Community Functioning ***	1,028	8.4	28	6.0
Personal/Emotional ***	—	—	—	—
Attitude ***	1,127	9.2	76	16.2
NO DIFFICULTY:				
Employment	2,736	22.3	66	14.1
Marital/Family	4,339	35.4	94	20.0
Associates	3,005	24.5	89	19.0
Substance Abuse	3,632	29.6	207	44.1
Community Functioning	4,651	37.9	134	28.6
Personal/Emotional	1,303	10.6	56	11.9
Attitude	3,985	32.5	285	60.6
SOME DIFFICULTY:				
Employment	5,156	42.0	275	58.6
Marital/Family	3,867	31.5	230	49.0
Associates	4,719	38.5	257	54.8
Substance Abuse	2,688	21.9	79	16.8
Community Functioning	5,012	40.9	280	59.7
Personal/Emotional	3,597	29.3	246	52.5
Attitude	3,303	26.9	76	16.2
CONSIDERABLE DIFFICULTY:				
Employment	3,439	28.0	101	21.5
Marital/Family	2,828	23.1	113	24.1
Associates	3,545	28.9	77	16.4
Substance Abuse	5,945	48.5	183	39.0
Community Functioning	1,574	12.8	27	5.8
Personal/Emotional	7,365	60.1	167	35.6
Attitude	3,850	31.4	33	7.0

Note: ***p<.001

At time of admission, women offenders were more likely to have had difficulties in the area of associates/significant others. However, male offenders were more likely to have been experiencing problems in substance abuse and attitude. There appear to be no statistically meaningful differences between female and male offenders with respect to difficulties in employment, community functioning, or personal/emotional orientation. That is, overall, female and male offenders were equally as likely to have been experiencing difficulties in these three areas.

Appendices A to G present the distribution of Case Need Domain indicators for all completed Offender Intake Assessments since implementation by gender. What can we say about the case needs of the female and male federal admission population? Clearly, at the indicator level, a number of gender-specific issues emerge for female offenders relative to their male counterparts.

As a group, female offenders (at time of admission) are more likely than male offenders to be underemployed or unemployed and have experienced relational (marital, maternal, sibling, and other relative) difficulties. They also tend to have more family members involved in crime, have been victims of spousal abuse, be single, have parenting responsibilities, and be easily influenced by others. Women offenders' drug use is more likely to interfere with their health, and there is a greater likelihood of dietary problems among them. Financially, female offenders are more likely than male offenders to have relied on social assistance and lack credit. Also, relative to their male counterparts, female offenders are more likely to be unaware of consequences, take more risks, worry unreasonably, and have problems asserting themselves. Further, female offenders are more likely than male offenders to have been diagnosed as mentally disordered, to have been prescribed medication, and to have been hospitalized in the past.

Clearly, the Offender Intake Assessment process yields a comprehensive and accessible base of information about the female offender population. Equipped with this information, service providers are able to employ the available range of correctional interventions more effectively. In other words, one can measure a woman offender's performance in relation to objectively defined risk and need indicators, which in turn serves as a basis for evaluating the effects of programming and other interventions.

Validity

One way of looking at the validity of the Offender Intake Assessment process is by examining the relationships between its various components—Criminal Risk Assessment and other related risk measures derived from the Custody Rating Scale (CRS). The CRS involves a systematic review of a woman offender's official criminal and institutional record to complete two subscales—Institutional Adjustment and Security Risk. The CRS is an initial security level placement scoring system.

In Table 5.3, we present the statistical relationships between Criminal History Record (any, previous—youth court, previous adult court) and Criminal Risk Level drawn from the Offender Intake Assessment process. Custody Rating subscale scores (Institutional Adjustment and Security Risk) were significant and in the expected direction. Similarly, Offense Severity Record converged on these other measures of offender risk.

Another important way to explore the validity of the Offender Intake Assessment process for women offenders is by means of the relationships between individual need level ratings and the number of indicators endorsed in each of the seven need domains (*see* Table 5.4). For example, the overall level of need for each domain should be positively correlated with the number of indicators (hits) checked off. Overall need domain levels are listed along the top of Table 5.4, and the number of indicators endorsed within the domains are listed along the left side of the table.

The Pearson correlation coefficients in the shaded diagonal of 5.4 represent the extent to which these relationships are consistent and in the

TABLE 5.3. **Relationships Between Offender Intake Assessment Criminal Risk Assessment Components and Other Risk Measures (438 women offenders)**

	Risk Level r	Institutional Adjustment Score r	Security Risk Score r
Criminal History Record (any)	.42***	.50***	.23***
Previous—Youth Court	.31***	.44***	.36***
Previous—Adult Court	.37***	.38***	.11*
Offense Severity Record	.60***	.43***	.50***

Note: ***p<.001; *p<.05

TABLE 5.4. Relationships Between Offender Intake Assessment Case Need Level Ratings and Domain Indicators (469 female offenders)

NEED LEVEL INDICATORS	EMPLOYMENT	MARITAL/ FAMILY	ASSOCIATES	SUBSTANCE ABUSE	COMMUNITY FUNCTIONING	PERSONAL/ EMOTIONAL	ATTITUDE
Employment M=8.9 SD=4.9	.40	.20	.35	.41	.25	.25	.20
Marital/Family M=7.4 SD=4.4	.24	.52	.22	.44	.19	.34	.13
Associates M=3.6 SD=2.3	.30	.32	.56	.47	.28	.37	.19
Substance Abuse M=9.1 SD=9.4	.26	.34	.37	.85	.13	.38	.16
Community Functioning M=4.9 SD=2.6	.31	.27	.29	.31	.41	.26	.12
Personal/ Emotional M=10.0 SD=7.0	.23	.34	.26	.39	.23	.59	.37
Attitude M=2.4 SD=3.4	.27	.18	.27	.36	.21	.41	.54
Total M=46.3 SD=24.9	.37	.44	.43	.71	.29	.53	.33

Note: M=Mean (or average) number of indicators endorsed; SD=Standard Deviation; all r's $p < .001$

expected direction. Specifically, it would be expected that, as more indicators are endorsed (suggesting more problems), the overall need level would be higher. Outside the diagonal is the extent to which the need areas being assessed are interdependent. As we can see, all of the relationships are significant for women offenders. Of special note, there is considerable interdependence among the various need domain indicators and level ratings, particularly in the area of substance abuse.

To date, explorations of the predictive validity of the Offender Intake Assessment process for women offenders in relation to recidivism are hampered by extraordinary low base rates (less than 5 percent) of outcome criterion. A recent study tracked 219 women offenders who had undergone Offender Intake Assessment and had been released and followed-up (at least six months) for any returns to federal custody. Of the eight (or 3.6 percent) cases returned, none were re-admitted on a new warrant of committal, one woman offender had her conditional release revoked with a new offense and the remainder (seven of eight) returned for technical violations. While fortunate from a correctional point of view, conducting correlation analyses becomes problematic. It may be that the increased attention on relevant risk and need variables at intake coupled with prescriptive intervention and appropriate supervision influenced the postrelease outcome of these women offenders. Perhaps extended follow-ups may boost base rates leading to a different conclusion.

Other Inputs to the Intake Assessment Process

Added to the intake assessment process are psychological evaluations, behavioral observations by line staff, and supplementary assessments (for example education, substance abuse). All of the aforementioned case-based information is then brought together at a case conference that is attended by a multidisciplinary case management team. It is recognized that any consensus reached by the case management team about the offender's risk and needs should result in significant improvements in the predictive validity of intake assessments.

The end product of our intake assessment process is a summary report about the offender. This report contains for each woman offender a bottom-line or overall risk/needs level ranging from low-risk, low-need to high-risk, high-need; a statement on each of the seven need areas ranging from "factor seen as an asset to community adjustment" to "considerable need for improvement"; a prioritization of needs; an estimate of motivation; a custody rating designation ranging from minimum-, medium- to maximum-security; a complete social history; and a security level placement decision. It is expected that this comprehensive and integrated assessment package serves as the basis to formulate a correctional plan for each woman offender.

Institution and Community-based Assessment Linkages

The results of Offender Intake Assessment are used by parole officers as the basis on which to develop a correctional plan for each woman offender. Basically, the correctional plan is designed to address the dynamic factors that have been identified as contributing to criminal behavior. Like Offender Intake Assessment, the correctional plan is fully automated on the Correctional Service of Canada's Offender Management System. It has three sections: 1) overview, 2) need analysis, and 3) needs and program objectives. For example, the later section could identify a need domain (such as personal/emotional orientation), that has a principal component (such as cognition), and recommends a particular program (such as cognitive skills training).

Each woman offender's programming needs are prioritized so that interventions can be delivered in a logical fashion. The correctional plan is reviewed regularly and revised as dynamic factors needs are met or progress is made in reducing the level of risk. Moreover, a correctional plan also ensures that there is continuity in programming between institutions and the community.

While the Offender Intake Assessment process was developed principally for assessing offender risk and needs upon admission to federal custody, the scope of our community risk/needs assessment and reassessment process has been streamlined. In keeping the individual ratings for both "criminal risk" and "case need" levels as well as for each need area, alignment of the community version of risk/need assessment process with the intake version was straightforward. This situation makes possible a systematic assessment and reassessment process, which spans admission to the end of the sentence. Presently, full automation of this new community reassessment process is complete.

Dynamic Risk Assessment

A systematic assessment and reassessment approach can assist in identifying appropriate treatment targets by cataloging those changes during treatment that are associated with changes in the likelihood of prison maladjustment or postrelease recidivism (Bonta, Andrews, and Motiuk, 1993). This test-retest methodology also can play a critical role in measuring changes that can have a significant impact on the design and development of effective correctional programs.

We consider need areas to be dynamic factors and a subset of an overall offender risk. More importantly, case need dimensions are designed to be able to reflect change. Whereas the Community Risk/Needs Management Scale had emphasized the evaluation of offender risk and needs with respect to recidivism, it gave relatively little consideration to the interaction between risk/needs and the level of intervention. Our approach to community reassessment should lend itself well to the application of the "risk principle" for levels of service. Basically, it should improve our ability to identify appropriate targets of rehabilitative effort. Andrews et al. (1990) described this aspect of case classification for effective rehabilitation as the "need principle." In practice, the "need principle" essentially puts the focus on offender characteristics (for example, substance abuse) that, when changed, are associated with changes in the chances of recidivism.

Re-engineering Assessment Procedures

Development of any new assessment tool should purposefully follow and expand on the classification procedures currently in place. The intention is to capitalize on existing information-gathering practices, retain essential outputs, and build on risk assessment training to date. The Correctional Service of Canada's Community Risk/Needs Management Scale is nearly ten years old and much has been learned through its application. As such, it now has undergone a revision, as most offender risk/need instruments should when, after a period of time, they begin to loose their predictive potency or relevancy. Some of the major reasons for a classification tool's decline in effectiveness include shifts in the offender population profile (such as age, racial, or cultural composition) and changes in legislation or policy. Perhaps an even more compelling reason for retooling assessment procedures is the drift towards over classification that appears to be inherent in most correctional systems (Bonta and Motiuk, 1992).

The Community Reassessment Process

In compliance with the standards for conditional release supervision (Correctional Service of Canada, 1988), parole officers are required to use a systematic approach to assess the needs of male and female offenders, their risk of reoffending, and any other factors which might affect successful reintegration to the community. In keeping with this standard, the "Community Intervention Scale" (formerly called the Community Risk/

Needs Management Scale, *see* Appendix H) is used to capture case-specific information on "static factors" (criminal history) and a critical set of "dynamic factors" (case needs) for classification while on conditional release (Motiuk and Porporino, 1989).

Static Factors. To assess static factors for risk of reoffending systematically and consistently, parole officers conduct an extensive review of each woman offender's official criminal record so that her criminal history background can be established in an objective, reliable, and accurate way. Parole officers pay particular attention to the number, variety, and pattern of criminal convictions as well as breaches of trust.

Dynamic Factors. The domain areas selected for the dynamic factors component of the Community Intervention Scale (formerly called the Community Risk/Needs Management Scale) are typical of those included in most offender need assessment instruments used in other jurisdictions. A total of twelve dynamic factors are covered as follows: academic/vocational skills, employment pattern, financial management, marital/ family relationship, companions/significant others, living arrangements, behavioral/ emotional stability, alcohol usage, drug usage, mental ability, health, and attitude. Although each dynamic factor is rated according to specified guidelines, an overall rating of "Dynamic Factors" is simply the compilation of parole officer judgments into three level groupings; low, medium, and high.

While the Community Intervention Scale clearly was intended to be used as a means of focusing supervision resources (in other words, frequency of contact) and monitoring changes in the offender's behavior, attitudes, and circumstance while under supervision, it essentially puts into practice a simple scheme that allows parole officers to classify offenders.

The appropriate frequency of contact for parole supervision is determined by linking the two types of assessments, static and dynamic, in a matrix format. In constructing a Community Intervention Scale that would attend to the community supervision needs of certain special categories of offenders (in other words, mentally disordered), additional special categories are included. A special needs category of "other" is reserved for those who did not meet the aforementioned criteria but are viewed by parole officers as meriting an override rating. For instance, a "low risk" offender who is assessed by the Community Intervention Scale as "low need" normally would be required only minimal frequency of contact with her parole officer. However, if the parole officer notes mitigating circumstances in the "other" category, he or she may override the matrix decision of "minimal" contact to increase the frequency of contact with the offender.

In field testing the early Community Intervention Scale (the CRNMS), it was found that parole officers could easily differentiate offenders by the nature and level of intervention required. Moreover, these offender intervention assessments consistently were related to outcome on conditional release (Motiuk and Porporino, 1989). It was also found that by simply combining parole officer assessments of static factors with global ratings of dynamic factors, almost half of the offenders assessed as high-risk, high-needs were suspended within six months of their initial assessment. On the other hand, substantially fewer offenders assessed as low-risk, low-need were suspended (5 percent) while on conditional release.

Of particular interest, this low-risk, low-need group was the largest category among the risk/need level groupings that were identified, representing about one-third of the total sample of cases that were assessed. Therefore, reducing the frequency of supervision for these lower-risk cases had important implications for the reallocation and refocusing of community resources (Andrews et al., 1990). It is important, however, to consider that the field test results are based on a sample of 453 *male* offenders. Prospective testing with female samples will increase confidence in generalizing these results to women.

Presently, parole officers across Canada administer and re-administer the Community Intervention Scale to federal women offenders under community supervision. It provides an efficient system for recording static and dynamic factors, the level of dynamic factors, the level of intervention, required frequency of contact, and related background information on each offender (in other words, release status, and warrant expiration). More importantly, the Community Intervention Scale assists community staff in managing offender risk and needs. For example, the process of suspension of conditional release, which may lead to a revocation, is one possible measure, which can be used to assure that the level of intervention is acceptable.

Gender Differences—Dynamic Factors in the Community

To examine gender differences in dynamic factors across the phases of conditional release, we collapsed the female (n = 292) and male (n = 7,125) caseload snapshots into three groups: 0 to 6 months, 6 to 12 months, and 12 months or over (*see* Table 5.5). We found some interesting patterns. Generally, female and male offenders who have been in the

TABLE 5.5. Percentage Distribution of Identified Dynamic Factors by Phase of Release (Female and Male Offenders)

FACTOR		0-6 MONTHS	6-12 MONTHS	MORE THAN 12 MONTHS	P
Academic/vocational	Female (%)	79.4	71.4	51.5	***
	Male (%)	59.7	57.0	40.8	***
Employment	Female (%)	77.3	76.8	64.6	***
	Male (%)	70.0	67.6	55.2	***
Financial management	Female (%)	75.3	69.6	60.8	ns
	Male (%)	62.2	61.1	53.3	***
Marital/family relations	Female (%)	60.8	64.3	55.4	ns
	Male (%)	50.0	47.0	38.2	***
Companions	Female (%)	70.1	46.4	39.5	***
	Male (%)	58.9	53.0	37.3	***
Accommodation	Female (%)	20.6	25.0	30.0	ns
	Male (%)	16.6	17.6	22.2	***
Behavioral/emotional	Female (%)	83.5	82.1	63.1	***
	Male (%)	71.2	68.1	47.2	***
Alcohol use	Female (%)	23.7	17.9	10.8	*
	Male (%)	35.8	27.8	17.2	***
Drug use	Female (%)	29.9	26.8	16.2	*
	Male (%)	38.8	31.1	18.3	***
Mental ability	Female (%)	3.1	7.1	5.4	ns
	Male (%)	8.2	9.0	6.0	***
Health	Female (%)	20.6	26.8	43.3	**
	Male (%)	20.7	22.6	30.9	***
Attitude	Female (%)	11.3	5.4	10.1	ns
	Male (%)	17.2	7.8	14.5	**

Note: ns= not statistically significant; *p<.05; **p<.01; ***p<.0

community twelve months or longer have much less need on all dimensions than more recently released offenders. However, women offenders appear to continue experiencing difficulties in employment, financial management, marital/family relations, and accommodation at later phases of conditional release. Also noteworthy, women offenders under supervision for longer periods are more likely to be experiencing more health-related problems. This situation may be due to an aging female offender population under community supervision.

Targeting Reintegration Potential

Current assessment strategies and standards of practice should help to identify those women offenders at admission who have a good potential for successful community reintegration (Motiuk and Serin, 1998). For example, women offenders with high reintegration potential at the time of admission might be defined as low-risk offenders or moderate-risk offenders who are manageable in the community with prescriptive intervention and appropriate supervision. Women offenders with medium reintegration potential at the time of admission might be reevaluated as offenders having high reintegration potential on successful program completion at the time of release eligibility.

The reintegration potential profiles explored in the body of this report are based on objective classification information derived from the Correctional Service of Canada's Offender Management System (OMS). Note that the profiles for women offenders reflect available Offender Intake Assessment information. A review of the Offender Management System indicates that variations exist in the number of classification instruments completed (those admitted prior to implementation may be missing information). Future analyses will be more complete. It is expected that judicious attention and improved efficiency will increase safe reintegration.

Reintegration potential criteria encompass Offender Intake Assessment results and time served to earliest release (parole) eligibility. A recent review of the Correctional Service of Canada's female inmate population yielded a distribution of Custody Rating Scale (CRS) designations of 50 (25.5 percent) minimum-security, 131 (66.8 percent) medium-security, and 15 (7.7 percent) maximum-security. The Offender Intake Assessment need rating distribution was 40 low (20.4 percent), 82 medium (41.8 percent) and 74 (37.8 percent) high. The Offender Intake Assessment risk-rating distribution was 52 low (26.5 percent), 89 medium (45.4 percent), and 55 high (28.1

percent). By taking various combinations of CRS minimum-rated, OIA-need low/medium-rated and OIA-risk low/medium-rated cases, high-reintegration potential designations were recorded. In a similar fashion, other combinations yielded medium- or low-reintegration potential. As these independent evaluations converge, there is an incremental gain in predictive accuracy, which minimizes decision errors.

Using this reintegration potential approach, 53.1 percent of the female offender population in Canadian institutions were assessed to be high-reintegration potential, 26.0 percent medium, and 20.9 percent low. Such a strategy could be used to target women offenders viewed as high-reintegration potential for less intensive services and expedite their safe and controlled release at the earliest possible moment in the sentence.

Conclusion

One can use applied research to build a credible and efficient assessment system for women offenders. Clearly, a systematic assessment and reassessment approach can provide correctional agencies with important information about women offenders under supervision. This dynamic assessment method serves to instruct caseworkers about those with whom they are dealing, what they are like, and what kinds of problems they faced before they arrived on probation, in prison, or in parole caseloads. While targeting key offender need areas (such as employment) for service delivery while in the community has considerable merit, the kinds of intervention strategies one envisages to respond to women offenders' needs continues to be the real challenge. There remains an urgent need for research to help guide us in delivering workable programs to women offenders.

Appendix A.

A Breakdown of Employment Indicators as Assessed by the Offender Intake Assessment Process: Male and Female Offenders

Employment Indicators	Male Offenders (12,072)	Female Offenders (462)
Has less than grade 8 ***	24.8%	17.1%
Has less than grade 10 ***	54.7%	42.2%
Has no high school diploma ***	78.6%	67.0%
Finds learning difficult ***	30.6%	18.2%
Has learning disabilities **	19.2%	7.2%
Has physical problems which interfere with learning ***	5.4%	2.0%
Has memory problems **	21.3%	16.0%
Has concentration problems ***	31.0%	23.7%
Has problems with reading ***	29.9%	10.0%
Has problems writing ***	35.0%	11.1%
Has problems with numeracy ***	41.5%	18.9%
Has difficulty comprehending instructions *	12.6%	9.4%
Lacks a skill area/trade/profession	57.3%	59.7%
Dissatisfied with skill area/trade/profession *	41.5%	48.0%
Has physical problems that interfere with work	14.7%	12.4%
Unemployed at time of arrest ***	65.1%	76.6%
Unemployed 90% or more ***	31.3%	44.7%
Unemployed 50% or more **	58.6%	65.5%
Has an unstable job history ***	68.3%	60.5%
Often shows up late for work ***	8.8%	2.7%
Has poor attendance record ***	10.4%	3.4%
No employment history ***	10.3%	19.9%
Has difficulty meeting workload requirements ***	11.0%	3.3%
Lacks initiative ***	26.6%	5.7%
Has quit a job without another ***	43.5%	33.1%
Has been laid off from work ***	57.5%	24.9%
Has been fired from a job ***	26.7%	13.2%
Salary has been insufficient	40.4%	38.0%
Lacks employment benefits *	56.6%	51.0%
Jobs lack security ***	58.4%	48.1%
Has difficulty with coworkers **	5.1%	1.8%
Has difficulty with supervisors ***	11.5%	4.7%
Prior vocational assessment(s)	10.9%	13.1%
Has participated in employment programs *	24.8%	26.9%
Completed an occupational development program ***	12.1%	20.7%

Note 1: * p< .05; ** p<.01; *** p < .001   Note 2: Indicator numbers may vary slightly.

Appendix B.

A Breakdown of Marital/Family Indicators as Assessed by the Offender Intake Assessment Process: Male and Female Offenders

MARITAL/FAMILY	MALE OFFENDERS (11,979)	FEMALE OFFENDERS (459)
Childhood lacked family ties	25.6%	23.3%
Mother absent during childhood *	18.5%	22.7%
Maternal relations negative as a child ***	22.2%	29.4%
Father absent during childhood	37.1%	39.1%
Paternal relations negative as a child	40.8%	38.1%
Parents relationship dysfunctional during childhood	47.1%	50.0%
Spousal abuse during childhood	29.9%	29.6%
Sibling relations negative during childhood ***	11.9%	17.4%
Other relative(s) negative during childhood ***	10.7%	20.1%
Family members involved in crime *	36.1%	41.3%
Currently single *	59.2%	63.8%
Has been married/common law in the past *	76.8%	81.4%
Dissatisfied with current relationship	12.6%	12.5%
Money problems affect relationship(s) past/present *	28.1%	32.2%
Sexual problems affect relationship(s) past/present	11.6%	13.6%
Communication problems affects the relationship(s) *	38.2%	43.2%
Has been a victim of spousal abuse ***	11.8%	53.1%
Has been a perpetrator of spousal abuse ***	25.6%	13.7%
Has no parenting responsibilities ***	47.2%	35.4%
Unable to handle parenting responsibilities ***	14.7%	20.1%
Unable to control the child's behavior appropriately	7.1%	7.9%
Perceives self as unable to control the child's behavior	3.8%	5.4%
Supervises child improperly	9.6%	9.2%
Does not participate in activities with the child *	10.0%	7.1%
Lacks an understanding of child development	11.9%	10.0%
Family is unable to get along as a unit **	25.0%	18.4%
Has been arrested for child abuse	3.3%	2.6%
Has been arrested for incest ***	4.2%	0.4%
Prior marital/family assessment(s) ***	5.3%	11.6%
Has participated in marital/family therapy	6.5%	12.4%
Has completed a marital/family program **	1.9%	3.8%

Note 1: * p< .05; ** p<.01; *** p < .001   Note 2: Indicator numbers may vary slightly.

Appendix C.

A Breakdown of Associates/Social Interaction Indicators as Assessed by the Offender Intake Assessment Process: Male and Female Offenders

ASSOCIATES/SOCIAL INTERACTION	MALE OFFENDERS (11,946)	FEMALE OFFENDERS (458)
Socially Isolated ***	20.9%	28.8%
Associates with substance abusers ***	66.8%	58.6%
Many criminal acquaintances **	61.5%	54.3%
Mostly criminal friends ***	38.9%	28.2%
Has been affiliated with a gang ***	11.6%	6.0%
Resides in a criminogenic area	25.8%	26.3%
Unattached to any community groups ***	59.1%	49.2%
Relations are described as predatory	18.5%	9.6%
Often victimized in social relations ***	16.9%	35.0%
Easily influenced by others **	44.4%	51.9%
Has difficulty communicating with others	23.5%	25.4%

Note 1: * p< .05; ** p<.01; *** p < .001   Note 2: Indicator numbers may vary slightly.

Appendix D.

A Breakdown of Substance Abuse Indicators as Assessed by the Offender Intake Assessment Process: Male and Female Offenders

SUBSTANCE ABUSE	MALE OFFENDERS (11,894)	FEMALE OFFENDERS (459)
Abuses alcohol ***	58.8%	41.8%
Began drinking at an early age ***	45.6%	32.9%
Drinks on a regular basis ***	41.9%	24.9%
Has a history of drinking binges ***	43.7%	32.7%
Has combined the use of alcohol and drugs ***	43.7%	32.8%
Drinks to excess during leisure time ***	43.9%	29.9%
Drinks to excess in social situations ***	46.5%	31.9%
Drinks to relieve stress ***	39.6%	32.5%
Drinking interferes with employment ***	24.7%	17.5%
Drinking interferes with marital / family relations *	36.1%	29.5%
Drinking interferes with social relations *	28.8%	23.8%
Drinking has resulted in law violations ***	47.2%	31.6%
Drinking interferes with health	16.7%	17.3%
Abuses drugs ***	63.8%	51.4%
Began using drugs at an early age ***	44.0%	32.9%
Used drugs on a regular basis ***	44.9%	34.7%
Has gone on drug-taking sprees	40.2%	38.1%
Has combined the use of different drugs	36.9%	33.3%
Uses drugs during leisure time ***	53.3%	40.8%
Uses drugs in social situations ***	52.6%	40.8%
Uses drugs to relieve stress	43.0%	41.7%
Drug use interferes with employment	26.3%	25.7%
Drug use interferes with marital / family relations	34.5%	35.3%
Drug use interferes with social relations	29.5%	30.3%
Drug use has resulted in law violations	46.9%	41.1%
Drug use interferes with health ***	19.8%	28.9%
Prior substance abuse assessments ***	37.5%	27.2%
Has participated in substance abuse treatment *	40.3%	35.6%
Has completed substance abuse treatment	29.6%	27.0%

Note 1: * p< .05; ** p<.01; *** p < .001   Note 2: Indicator numbers may vary slightly.

Appendix E.

A Breakdown of Community Functioning Indicators as Assessed by the Offender Intake Assessment Process: Male and Female Offenders

COMMUNITY FUNCTIONING	MALE OFFENDERS (11,853)	FEMALE OFFENDERS (451)
Has unstable accommodation	36.4%	35.7%
Residence is poorly maintained	7.7%	7.6%
Has poor self-presentation **	8.3%	4.2%
Has poor hygiene	3.9%	2.2%
Has physical problems	25.7%	25.6%
Has dental problems *	14.8%	10.5%
Has dietary problems *	7.2%	10.2%
Difficulty meeting bill payments	45.4%	41.8%
Has outstanding debts **	40.1%	33.2%
Has no bank account	47.1%	47.7%
Has no credit *	62.0%	67.7%
Has no collateral	62.4%	66.1%
Has problems writing ***	22.1%	8.6%
Unable to express self verbally	7.4%	6.3%
Has no hobbies ***	26.5%	15.4%
Does not participate in organized activities ***	52.3%	28.9%
Unaware of social services *	3.4%	5.1%
Has used social assistance ***	70.5%	80.3%
Prior assessment for community functioning	6.7%	6.3%
Has participated in a community skills program	7.6%	10.0%
Has completed a community skills program	6.3%	7.1%

Note 1: * $p < .05$; ** $p < .01$; *** $p < .001$ Note 2: Indicator numbers may vary slightly.

Appendix F.

A Breakdown of Personal/Emotional Orientation Indicators as Assessed by the Offender Intake Assessment Process: Male and Female Offenders

PERSONAL/EMOTIONAL ORIENTATION	MALE OFFENDERS (11,885)	FEMALE OFFENDERS (454)
Feels especially self-important ***	17.1%	8.8%
Physical prowess problematic ***	10.4%	3.3%
Family ties are problematic	44.7%	43.2%
Ethnicity is problematic	5.1%	3.8%
Religion is problematic	1.6%	1.6%
Gang member ***	7.3%	2.4%
Unable to recognize problem areas ***	49.3%	35.5%
Has difficulties solving interpersonal problems ***	69.6%	45.9%
Unable to generate choices	58.7%	55.9%
Unaware of consequences *	46.7%	54.1%
Goal setting is unrealistic ***	26.7%	13.1%
Has disregard for others ***	57.3%	13.9%
Socially unaware ***	27.4%	12.0%
Impulsive ***	66.9%	56.4%
Incapable of understanding the feelings of others ***	36.3%	9.8%
Narrow and rigid thinking ***	38.8%	12.7%
Aggressive ***	45.0%	23.4%
Assertion problem ***	38.7%	52.1%
Copes with stress poorly ***	64.2%	53.3%
Poor conflict resolution ***	67.5%	50.5%
Manages time poorly ***	44.3%	14.9%
Gambling is problematic **	5.7%	2.4%
Has low frustration tolerance ***	44.2%	28.8%
Hostile ***	25.1%	16.2%
Worries unreasonably *	19.5%	23.5%
Takes risks inappropriately *	56.5%	61.5%
Thrill-seeking **	29.0%	22.3%
Non-reflective ***	50.7%	26.5%
Not conscientious ***	37.7%	9.8%
Manipulative ***	43.5%	24.8%
Has difficulty performing sexually	6.6%	6.3%
Sexual identity problem ***	4.5%	1.4%

Note 1: * p< .05; ** p<.01; *** p < .001   Note 2: Indicator numbers may vary slightly.

(CONTINUED)

Appendix F. (continued)

PERSONAL/EMOTIONAL ORIENTATION	MALE OFFENDERS (11,885)	FEMALE OFFENDERS (454)
Inappropriate sexual preference(s) ***	16.1%	1.6%
Sexual attitudes are problematic ***	22.0%	5.8%
Low mental functioning	3.5%	2.7%
Diagnosed as disordered in the past ***	9.3%	14.8%
Diagnosed as disordered currently ***	6.0%	11.8%
Prior personal / emotional assessments	28.8%	32.0%
Prescribed medication in the past ***	20.9%	43.2%
Prescribed medication currently ***	9.0%	30.2%
Past hospitalization ***	15.5%	26.2%
Current hospitalization	1.8%	1.5%
Received outpatient services in the past ***	15.8%	26.1%
Received outpatient services prior to admission ***	4.8%	12.4%
Past program participation *	19.9%	24.4%
Current program participation ***	5.9%	19.6%

Note 1: * p< .05; ** p<.01; *** p < .001   Note 2: Indicator numbers may vary slightly.

Appendix G.

A Breakdown of Attitude Indicators as Assessed by the Offender Intake Assessment Process: Male and Female Offenders

ATTITUDE	MALE OFFENDERS (11,861)	FEMALE OFFENDERS (451)
Negative towards the law ***	43.9%	17.1%
Negative towards the police ***	34.4%	16.7%
Negative towards the courts ***	32.4%	19.8%
Negative towards corrections ***	20.0%	12.7%
Negative towards community supervision ***	24.6%	9.7%
Negative towards rehabilitation ***	16.5%	6.5%
Employment has no value ***	17.8%	8.3%
Marital / family relations have no value ***	9.9%	3.8%
Interpersonal relations have no value ***	10.8%	5.5%
Values substance abuse ***	43.8%	17.2%
Basic life skills have no value ***	12.7%	5.5%
Personal / emotional stability has no value ***	10.6%	4.9%
Elderly have no value	1.7%	1.3%
Women / men roles are unequal	17.1%	15.1%
Ethnically intolerant **	4.3%	1.4%
Intolerant of other religions	0.8%	1.1%
Intolerant of disabled persons	0.6%	0.0%
Disrespectful of personal belongings ***	36.1%	8.4%
Disrespectful of public property ***	25.5%	8.5%
Disrespectful of commercial property ***	34.7%	9.4%
Supportive of domestic violence ***	16.3%	2.7%
Supportive of instrumental violence ***	37.1%	12.6%
Lacks direction ***	60.7%	36.9%
Nonconforming ***	53.4%	28.6%

Note 1: * p< .05; ** p<.01; *** p < .001   Note 2: Indicator numbers may vary slightly.

Appendix H.
The Community Risk/Needs Management Scale

Case Need Areas			
Academic/Vocational Skills:	No current difficulties	Level of skills causing minor interference	Level of skills causing serious interference
Employment Pattern: Stable pattern of employment	No current difficulties	Employment situation causing minor adjustment problems	Employment situation causing serious adjustment problems
Financial Management: Pattern of effective management	No current difficulties	Situational or minor difficulties	Severe difficulties
Marital/Family Relationship: Pattern of stable and supportive relationships	No current difficulties	Occasional instability in relationships	Very unstable pattern of relationships
Companions/Significant Others: Pattern of noncriminal and/or positive associations	No current difficulties	Some criminal and/or negative associations	Mostly criminal and/or negative associations
Accommodation: Pattern of satisfactory accommodation	No current difficulties	Occasional changes in residence, or temporarily situated	Frequent changes in residence, or no permanent address
Behavioral/Emotional Stability:	No current difficulties	Behavioral/emotional problems that indicate some need for assistance	Severe behavioral/emotional problems that indicate significant need for assistance
Alcohol Usage:	No current difficulties	Some alcohol usage causing moderate adjustment problems	Frequent or uncontrolled usage, causing serious adjustment problems
Drug Usage:	No current difficulties	Some drug usage causing moderate interference	Frequent or uncontrolled usage, causing serious adjustment problems

(CONTINUED)

Appendix H. (continued)

CASE NEED AREAS			
Mental Ability:	No current difficulties	Deficiencies limit but do not prohibit independent functioning	Deficiencies severely limit independent functioning
Health:	No current difficulties	Physical handicap or illness that interferes with functioning	Serious physical handicap or illness that severely interferes with functioning
Attitude: Actively involved and responding consistently well to assistance	No current difficulties	Recognizes problem areas but not receptive to assistance	Unable to recognize problem areas and not receptive to assistance
Special Needs:	Sex Offender	Mentally Disordered	Other
Case Needs Rating:	Low	Medium	High
Criminal History Risk Rating:	Low	Medium/High	

Endnotes

[1] The OIA process is used for both male and female Canadian federal offenders.

References

Andrews, D. A. 1982. *The Level of Supervision Inventory (LSI): The First Follow-up.* Toronto: Ministry of Correctional Services Ontario.

Andrews, D. A., J. Bonta, and R. Hoge. 1990. Classification for Effective Rehabilitation: Rediscovering Psychology. *Criminal Justice and Behavior.* 17, 19-52.

Baird, S. C. 1981. Probation and Parole Classification: The Wisconsin Model. *Corrections Today.* 43, 36-41.

Blanchette, K. 1996. The Relationships Between Criminal History, Mental Disorder, and Recidivism Among Federally Sentenced Female Offenders. Masters Dissertation. Ottawa: Carleton University.

————. 1997a. *Risk and Need Among Federally Sentenced Female Offenders: A Comparison of Minimum-, Medium-, and Maximum-Security Inmates.* Report R-58. Ottawa: Research Branch, Correctional Service of Canada.

————. 1997b. Comparing Violent and Non-violent Female Offenders on Risk and Need. *Forum on Corrections Research.* 9 2, 14-18.

————. 1997c. Classifying Female Offenders for Correctional Interventions. *Forum on Corrections Research.* 9 1, 36-41.

Blanchette, K., and L L. Motiuk. 1995. *Female Offender Risk Assessment: The Case Management Strategies Approach.* Poster session presented at the Annual Convention of the Canadian Psychological Association, Charlottetown, Prince Edward Island.

Bonta, J., D. A. Andrews, and L L. Motiuk. 1993. Dynamic Risk Assessment and Effective Treatment. A paper presented at the 45th Annual Meeting of the American Society of Criminology, Phoenix, Arizona.

Bonta, J., and L. L. Motiuk. 1992. Inmate Classification. *Journal of Criminal Justice.* 20, 343- 353.

Bonta, J., B. Pang, and S. Wallace-Capretta. 1995. Predictors of Recidivism Among Incarcerated Female Offenders. *The Prison Journal.* 75, 277-293.

Bonta, J., R. Parkinson, and L. Barkwell. 1994, November. Revising the Wisconsin Classification System. Paper presented at the Annual Meeting of the American Society of Criminology, Miami, Florida.

Correctional Service of Canada. 1988. *Case Management Manual.* Ottawa: Correctional Service of Canada.

Coulson, G. 1993. Using the Level of Supervision Inventory in Placing Female Offenders in Rehabilitation Programs or Halfway Houses. *IARCA Journal.* 5, 12-13.

Coulson, G., V. Nutbrown, D. Giulekas, F. Cudjoe, and G. Ilacqua. 1996. Predictive Validity of the LSI for Incarcerated Female Offenders. *Criminal Justice and Behavior.* 23:3, 427-439.

Hoffman, P. 1982. Females, Recidivism, and Salient Factor Score. *Criminal Justice and Behavior.* 9, 121-125.

Loucks, A. and E. Zamble. 1994. Some Comparisons of Female and Male Serious Offenders. *Forum on Corrections Research.* 6: 1, 22-25.

Luciani, F., L. L. Motiuk, and M. Nafekh. 1996. *An Operational Review of the Custody Rating Scale: Reliability, Validity and Practical Utility.* Report # R-47. Ottawa: Research Branch, Correctional Service of Canada.

McLean, H. 1995. Psychological Assessment of Women Offenders. In T. Leis, L.L. Motiuk, and. J. Ogloff, eds. *Forensic Psychology: Policy and Practice in Corrections.* Ottawa: Correctional Service of Canada.

Motiuk, L. L. 1991. The Antecedents and Consequences of Prison Adjustment: A Systematic Assessment and Reassessment Approach. Doctoral Dissertation. Ottawa: Carleton University.

————. 1993. Where Are We in Our Ability to Assess Risk? *Forum on Corrections Research.* 5, 14-18.

————. 1997. What Works in Corrections? A Blueprint for Action. In R. Ville, U. Zvekic, and J. Klaus, eds. *Promoting Probation Internationally.* United Nations Interregional Crime and Justice Research Institute.

————. 1998. Classification for Correctional Programming: The Offender Intake Assessment OIA Process. *Forum on Corrections Research.* 9: 1, 18-22.

Motiuk, L. L. and F. J. Porporino. 1989. *Field Test of the Community Risk/Needs Management Scale: A Study of Offenders on Caseload.* R-01. Ottawa: Correctional Service of Canada.

Motiuk, L. L. and R. Serin. 1998. Situating Risk in a Reintegration Potential Framework. *Forum on Corrections Research.* 10: 1, 19-22.

Nuffield, J. 1982. *Parole Decision-making in Canada: Research Towards Decision Guidelines.* Ottawa: Communications Division.

Porporino, F., F. Luciani, L. L. Motiuk, M. Johnston, and B. Manwaring. 1989. *Pilot Implementation of the Custody Rating Scale. R-02.* Ottawa: Correctional Service of Canada.

Simourd, L. and D. A. Andrews. 1994. Correlates of Delinquency: A Look at Gender Differences. *Forum on Corrections Research.* 6: 1, 26-31.

THE TRUE AND ONLY DISCOURSE—SECULAR REASON AND PRISON REFORM[1]

6

Andrew Skotnicki
Associate Professor
St. Patrick's Seminary
Menlo Park, California

This essay shall make two claims, one theoretical and the other practical. The theoretical contention is that contemporary movements to reform the criminal justice system are flawed at the source. They no longer reflect or speak to the moral experience of the people in our society. More specifically, the problem lies with the secular, scientific framework of the social sciences. The framework emerged over a century ago both as the means through which information is channeled into the criminological discussion and as the mode of discourse for the discussion itself. Penal professionals, academics, and others involved in overseeing and amending the system invariably speak this language. They trust the validity of terms such as "evidence-based practice," "outcome-based management," and "inmate management units" to present objective, value-free data from which enlightened decisions can be made. Furthermore, they have accepted its claim to have transcended the need to ponder fundamental questions about the moral life. I do not say this to disparage the need for reform. Nor do I say it because the people concerned about new approaches in the field of corrections are deficient in intellect, compassion, or the courage of their convictions. I say it because the very way criminal justice is spoken about in our contemporary context limits the ability to understand the nature of the problem and therefore fails to provide a clear procedure for its amelioration.

The second claim of this paper is that the initial step in seeking how to punish the criminal offender is procedural. The language of criminal justice must be broadened to include a substantive discussion on the meaning of basic moral questions: what is a good life and how does one live it? This alteration in the method of forming criminal policy would entail that we first think about change, not in terms of institutional structures or sentencing policy, but with regard to the manner or format in which those decisions are made. Without such a procedural and, if you will, moral shift, a more effective solution to the problem of crime will continue to evade us.

The paper will first seek to outline briefly how the social-scientific paradigm emerged at the end of the nineteenth century. It will then discuss the limitations of the model, especially its ethical assumptions. The final section will present an expanded justification for the assertion that prison reform must begin with a moral conversation and will suggest a possible model for such a procedure.

The Prison as a Moral Institution

It has become a rather stable part of contemporary conversation and a growing feature of the national ethos to decry the cold efficiency of large institutions. Radio talk shows and the op-ed pages of daily newspapers are filled with diatribes against the over-administered society, the top heavy government bureaucracy, and the sanitized efficiency of corporate life. While the frustration is based on legitimate grievances, one fact is ignored in this populist climate: anything that is true must be institutionalized.

Institutions are repositories of shared meaning. They embody the truths that we as a people hold dear. They evaluate performance in terms of those truths and they build in sanctions to protect the integrity of those meanings. To threaten the principles that underlie social truth, and the corporate bodies whose duty it is to organize our life in conformity to those truths, is to call the world into question.

The sociologist, Emile Durkheim, spent his life pondering the tension between personal freedom and the absolute need to provide order and discipline in our common life. He was convinced that a moral impulse of self-sacrifice on behalf of others in society was the only way to harmonize the tension between freedom and obedience. He believed, therefore, that punishment of the thoughtless and cruel citizen was essential. It was done not only to remind the offender that life in society entailed basic rights and duties, but, more importantly, as a collective statement of assent to the moral truths that bind citizens one to another and thus are held sacred.[2]

The penal system is constructed on moral ground. It is an arm of society, expressing its rightful claim that certain behavioral and moral parameters have been established by communal consent and are normative for all. The duty and the challenge of criminal justice is to be ever aware of the moral agreements that underlie the common life. Those entrusted to oversee the correction of the disobedient and rebellious must order their institutions not only in conformity to law but also to the shifting social mores that provide its basis and support.

The prison system as we know it today was organized in this country in the early decades of the nineteenth century. The moral consensus at that time was dominated by an evangelical religious consciousness. In those years, virtually any enlightened person (in this case meaning one in tune with the reformist impulse) spoke an evangelical, Christian language and was convinced that the creation of penitentiaries was a divinely inspired work.[3] The spiritual and, by extension, behavioral conversion of the confined was the purpose of corrections and provided its meaning and motivation. This end was given metaphorical expression in elegant architectural structures often called "moral hospitals." They were to shine like beacons to those far and near, a constant reminder of the call to inner renewal in light of the imminent return of Christ "to judge the quick and the dead."[4]

A half-century later, the penitentiaries had fallen into disgrace. The cost of maintaining separate cells proved to be prohibitive for state officials and the tax-paying public that elected them. The rigorous demand of silence and the ban on inmate fraternization led several autocratic administrators to severely abuse inmates who violated the code of conduct. But, most importantly, the penitentiaries failed because the value and meaning of the evangelical religious philosophy was no longer in harmony with the moral self-understanding of the American people. The old meanings were called into question as the wider public came under the influence of Romanticism and the general current of optimism that ran through the century.[5] Moreover, the mood of the times dramatically shifted as the intellectual community, and those under their tutelage, embraced the ideas of Darwin and Comte.[6] It was at this time that the social sciences began to emerge as the privileged way of analyzing public policy in terms of the collection of statistical data. These developments, coupled with the social destabilization and the resulting rise in crime rates following the Civil War, had withered the enthusiasm for the penitentiary philosophy. To use Theodore Parker's oft-quoted epigram, the "dangerous classes" still existed, but reformers—adopting the name of Progressives—insisted on a new way to instill the values of society into the lives of the recalcitrant.

The leaders of the movement, in tune with the sprit of the age, called for a new type of penal order based on the use of scientific data and incorporating innovations that were being tested in other countries.[7] The result was the historic gathering in 1870 of the first National Prison Congress in Cincinnati. The meeting galvanized support for a dramatic shift in penal policy—one focused on the development of a fully rational approach to corrections.[8] Rational, scientific analysis, it was maintained, was universally valid and yielded a foundation for discussion and evaluation of the criminal justice process that was incontrovertible. The meeting led to the establishment of the reformatory as the hope of the nation in solving the problem of crime.

Treatment and incapacitation became standard terms in penal discourse. The reformers had captured the moral consensus of their own time, a perspective that no longer viewed society as a spiritual wasteland in dire need of conversion. This was the era of unparalleled optimism, of industrial and economic expansion, of big business and international adventurism. Delinquent individuals had fallen out of step with society's victorious march and scientific analysis had provided the unmistakable explanation for their rebelliousness. Theirs was not a freely willed rejection of the grace of God that stood in need of conversion. Rather, they were helpless tools in the hands of either of the two great artisans of human behavior: heredity and environment. Through a rigorous apparatus of scientific testing, the source and extent of an offender's antisocial tendencies could be detected and appropriate treatment provided by a growing coterie of technical instructors and medical personnel. Those resistant to or genetically incapable of benefiting from treatment would be rendered helpless through incapacitation.[9]

The growth of the scientific paradigm and its quantitative conceptual apparatus—so easily joined to a market-oriented understanding of society—led to more than a change in prison architecture and programs. It featured the belief that morality was contained within the canons of dispassionate rational analysis. In seeking to distance themselves from the failure of the penitentiary, the reformers of the day assumed that the errors of the past could be overcome by replacing the imprecise, sentimental, and "superstitious" language of religion, and its moral constraints, with the value-free language of the social sciences. Zebulon Brockway, one of the architects of the new penology, stated that reforming the criminal was "a purely scientific process, the modification of character by the wise use of rational means and methods."[10]

This belief did not reside only with the intellectual elite. The religious community, clergy, and laity, assented in great numbers to the claim that belief was a purely private matter and that ethics was contained, as Kant had stated, within the limits of reason alone. Robert Walker, a prison chaplain at the Concord Reformatory in Massachusetts, was typical of his generation in placing religion at the service of the truths of science and the market:

> One who is familiar with the kind of young men who are sent to prison to-day knows that a large majority of them are incapable, through lack of education, through defective mind, through weak inheritance and through unwholesome environment, of fulfilling their financial obligations. They have fallen behind in the race, and resort to foul means in order to share in the prosperity that results from honest labor, thrift, and obedience to moral and civic duty.[11]

Thus did the language of scientific analysis assume almost complete control over how crime was to be understood and remedied. More importantly, it became the language under whose dispassionate, rational gaze, public questions about the moral life were to be understood.

The True and Only Discourse

Many of the particular insights of the nineteenth century reformers have come and gone. The heyday of the reformatories lasted about as long as the penitentiaries. In the decades that followed, there were numerous developments in criminal justice: probation and parole, the anthropological criminology of Lombroso and the resulting eugenics movement (sterilization of the genetically "defective"), sociological criminology and the focus on status and labeling theory. There have been radical criminologists who argue that society is the real criminal and hosts of theorists and practitioners who have raised treatment and its psychological and medical aspects to the forefront of institutional practice. In recent years, there has also been a widespread call for "just deserts" and the use of strict sentencing guidelines to reinstate a focus on punishment and correct the errors of judicial discretion. At the same time, there has been a rebirth in the belief in rehabilitation as well as a focus on both diversion and community corrections.

What these various innovations have in common is they have maintained the belief that rational, analytical methods grounded in quantitative analysis reveal unbiased and vital insights into the data that needs to be interpreted for the creation of an effective correctional system. Inevitably, if there is a study relating to this field, it is done in the input, output, control group format.[12] Departments of sociology thrive on formulaic production of scientific studies to bolster existing or potential programs. Not only are there possible procedural flaws of many sorts with this methodology,[13] the near absolute reliance of policymakers and public officials on such studies virtually assures that there will be sufficient evidence to support the contention of any interested party. Criminology has become a war between the experts. But what is different now, as opposed to a century ago, is the experts no longer express the moral beliefs of the society. Now, they mostly argue among themselves.

The greatest problem with the current methodology, and, by extension, the entire organization of contemporary corrections, is not that those who sanction the studies or those who produce them are somehow disingenuous or faulty in their research. The problem is that the model ignores the truths that Durkheim made clear: the correctional system can only have meaning and coherence when it expresses the moral beliefs people hold most dear. That is its primary justification. Failing in that aspect, it becomes the very type of unfeeling bureaucracy that contemporary Americans find so distasteful.

The rational, analytical paradigm is thought to assume what we need to know about morality. And what we are assumed to know is that people are self-interested, that ethical and rational behavior largely refer to the same thing, and that what can be quantitatively proved under the input, output, control group format of social scientific analysis reveals reliable facts concerning human motivation and behavior. These beliefs are held in sacred space and thought to be as certain as the bricks in a cellblock. Simply put, this professional consensus no longer reflects the increasingly complex moral beliefs of the society in which we live.

A transformation has been taking place in the American ethos ever since the sweeping social and moral upheavals of the 1960s. The breakdown of the traditional moral consensus has severely impaired the process of social integration. The authority of church, family, and schools has been dramatically weakened. Public confidence in the law, the courts, and the police has been diminished. Watergate tarnished the moral confidence in government. And in 1971, with the prison revolt at Attica, the public turned its eye, largely in horror, to the penal system. Public figures as well as ordinary citizens began to attack the "crime of punishment." Their disillusionment was fed by continual exposure of the routine violence and racism of prison life, illumining what seemed to be the utter futility of the criminal justice system.[14]

In the wake of these changes, the nation has witnessed a tidal wave of new cultural and religious expressions. Since 1965, twenty million immigrants have entered the United States through Mexico and its Pacific ports of entry alone. Moral conflicts of an unprecedented nature and with a bewildering virulence and tenacity have driven the nation to the brink of despair. One author wisely termed these "culture wars," as various religious and social ideologies struggle to define the meaning of America.[15]

People are cynical about criminal justice. Of this we are all aware. Some believe that it is too lenient, others too exacting. To some, it is a disgrace to a civilized society, while others view it is the last hope of the republic against hordes of sociopaths. Everyone has an opinion, a moral opinion—this much, at least, is revealed in the national confessional of talk shows. But the babel of angry and frustrated voices cannot simply be ascribed to the nihilism of the age or to contemporary disdain for large institutions. It is also, this author believes, an unmistakable reminder that a new moral consensus is required on the meaning and shape of the correctional process. It is an equally unmistakable repudiation of the assumption that foundational moral questions can be avoided or neatly assumed within the methods and language of social scientific analysis. As Malcolm Davies recently stated:

> The complexities of the human interface with good and evil, deviance and conformity were never duplicated by the simpleminded, pain avoiding pleasure-seekers of utilitarian philosophy, nor by its offspring "Economic Man," nor by the

medically inspired psychiatrists and their offers for cure, nor by the politically oriented conflict theorists, nor by the social determinists. They offer a view of mankind that does not exist. They are like "maps which should be banned."[16]

The language that "spoke" to the age of progress and the theorists of decades past is no longer capable of providing meaning in the present age. There will be no prison reform until this disparity is addressed.

Moral Consensus in a Pluralist Age

The second contention of this paper is that the correctional system must establish a procedure whereby fundamental moral questions can be restated in a way that captures the social and moral vision of contemporary Americans—inside and outside of the criminal justice system. This challenge is all the more troubling because America is no longer a largely homogeneous society. What was once a Protestant empire has fragmented into a bewildering mosaic of religions and cultural expressions.

The separation of church and state was thought the ideal way to minimize tiresome and endless ideological conflicts. It assumed that one could leave one's deepest moral and religious motivations at home, or in the church or synagogue of one's choice. This author suggests that this claim can no longer prevail if a genuine hope exists to reform the penal system. Ideological conflicts are precisely what need to be investigated. Within their intense passion are contained visions of the good life, how it is to be lived, and how failure to live it is confronted and remedied. Furthermore, the hope of the criminal justice system, not to mention the hope of society, is that these disputes are not hopelessly condemned to rancor and division.

Aside from their obvious contentiousness, virtually all moral conflicts reveal that their proponents maintain an ethical naturalism: that there are wrong behaviors and that there are proper modes of conduct befitting not only citizens but human beings in general. Each of these conceptions of the good is as clear and consistent to its proponents as the latest scientific study is to an avowed rationalist, or as an emotional, public display of religious fervor is to an evangelical Christian.

We often fear such politically volatile debates because they rarely end in dialogue. Competing parties become rancorous. The moral combat seems interminable. I am suggesting that there are procedures available to allow for a practical synthesis of worldviews. They are based on the assumption that while difference of opinion over the good is radical, it is not primordial, that each conception of the good life rests on a common foundation. As Michael Perry suggests, when we talk about the good, we are, in the end, all looking at the same thing.[17] True, we will come at the issues from widely divergent points of view. The sociology of knowledge reveals as much. But like the blind people trying to discern the elephant, we are all, despite our varieties of opinion, talking about the same thing.

For all the cynicism accorded to late-medieval Jesuits and the development of casuistry (the relationship between normative ethical beliefs and lived human experience with an eye to developing exceptions), the method understands that diversity of moral opinion need not render one helpless. Nor must diversity condemn us to a unilateral subscription to one particular point of view.

It is noteworthy to reflect for a moment on the origin of the verb "to pontificate." It was not based on the fact that the one at the top of the hierarchy arbitrarily rendered unilateral judgments in patriarchal fashion. It emerged, much like the thinking regarding casuistry, from the belief that debates that seem endless have at their core a common view of the good. The community sought a mediator, a wise person who was mutually agreed upon who embodied qualities and virtues that each side recognized, much as we point to civil heroes whose character reveals something transcending parochial concerns. The arbitrator rendered a practical judgment (pontificated), having listened carefully to the presentations from each side.[18] Here there was at least no illusion that one size fits all when it comes to envisioning the morality of social affairs. And while it is true that not everyone went home happy, there was also the legitimate opportunity to air one's deepest opinions in the presence of a respected and respectful audience. A new moral consensus was achieved, more satisfying than what had existed previously.

Some contemporary thinkers have begun to approach moral questions in a similar manner. In his recent work on abortion and euthanasia, Ronald Dworkin rightly assumes that despite social philosophies emanating from widely dissimilar beliefs, both sides of the debate on abortion know that life is sacred. Each, he suggests, is beginning from a view of the good, an understanding of the meaning of a life well lived and from a noble ethical foundation. While the disagreements are profound, each side, like those touching the elephant, is talking about the same thing.[19] In other words, the possibility exists for a harmonization of worldviews.

There are many ideas out there about the good life, how it looks, how it is attained and preserved, and what to do with those who fail in the

attempt to live it. Public institutions are alienating and ultimately mean-
ingless if they fail to express in their philosophy and programs at least a
rough congruence with what matters most to the average person. Secular
reason was once the true and only discourse. It is no longer, and those
responsible for shaping criminal justice can ignore this fact only to their
peril and that of those committed to their care.

Endnotes

1 The title is used with conscious reference to Christopher Lasch's *The True and
Only Heaven* (New York: Norton, 1991). Lasch argued that the modern notion of
progress has been stripped of its metaphysical and religious foundations and now is
viewed as the endless expansion of information and economic production.

2 The most mature statement of Durkheim's thought can be found in *The
Elementary Forms of Religious Life*, trans. Karen E. Fields (New York: The Free Press,
1995), Book II, ch. 7. For his thought on criminal justice, *see* "Two Laws of Penal
Evolution," in Steven Lukes and Andrew Scull, eds. *Durkheim and the Law* (Oxford:
Martin Robertson,1983), 65-95.

3 The word "evangelical" has undergone subtle shifts in meaning throughout
American religious history. In the early nineteenth century, it referred to, among other
things, the need to create institutions that would lead to the conversion of sinners
before the second coming of Christ. *See*, e.g., Charles C. Cole, *The Social Ideas of the
Northern Evangelicals* (New York: Octagon Books, 1977); Whitney R. Cross, *The
Burned-Over District* (New York: Octagon Books, 1981). *See also*, James Davison
Hunter, *Evangelicalism* (Chicago: University of Chicago Press, 1987).

4 *See* W. D. Lewis, *From Newgate to Dannemora* (Ithaca: New York University
Press, 1965); David Rothman, *The Discovery of the Asylum* (Boston: Little, Brown and
Company, 1971), ch. 4.

5 *See* Ann Douglas, *The Feminization of American Culture* (New York: Knopf, 1977).

6 Auguste Comte was a French philosopher who has been called the "father of
sociology." His philosophy, Positivism, held that the evolution of knowledge had its
primitive foundations in religion but had reached its zenith with the development of
science. Only that which could be proven by the precise methods of scientific analysis could be considered to be true.

7 Among the innovations were those of Walter Crofton in Ireland: graded prisons (essentially the maximum, medium, minimum classification of today), and "ticket
of leave" (parole). They were also influenced by the ideas of Alexander Maconochie
in Australia, who created a system of rewards for good behavior. *See* Blake McKelvey,

American Prisons: A History of Good Intentions (Montclair, New Jersey: Patterson Smith, 1977), ch. 4

8 One of the notable reformers responsible for the congress was Enoch C. Wines, secretary of the Prison Association of New York. The Association presented a detailed report on the Congress. *See*, Prison Association of New York, *Annual Report* (Albany, 1871).

9 *See* David Rothman, *Conscience and Convenience* (Boston: Little, Brown and Company, 1980); Andrew von Hirsch, *Past or Future Crimes* (New Brunswick, New Jersey: Rutgers University Press, 1985). A firsthand account of the reformatory philosophy can be found in the autobiography of the most notable warden of the Progressive period. *See* Zebulon R. Brockway, *Fifty Years of Prison Service* (New York: New York Charities Publication Committee, 1912).

10 Brockway, op.cit., 308.

11 Board of Prison Commissioners of Massachusetts (Boston, 1911), 52.

12 Ray Pawson, "Evaluation Methodology: Back to Basics" in *Evaluating the Effectiveness of Community Penalties* (Aldershot: Avebury, 1997), 152-56.

13 *See*, e.g., H. Chen and P. Rossi, "The Theory-Driven Approach to Validity," *Evaluation and Program Planning* 10 (1983), 95-103; R. Martinson, "What Works?— Questions and Answers About Prison Reform," *Public Interest* 35 (1974), 22-45.

14 *See*, e.g., Karl Menninger, *The Crime of Punishment* (New York: Penguin Books, 1968); Charles Silberman, *Criminal Violence Criminal Justice* (New York: Vintage Books, 1978); Tom Wicker, *A Time to Die* (New York: Quadrangle, 1975).

15 James Davison Hunter, *Culture Wars* (New York: Basic Books, 1991).

16 Malcolm Davies, *Punishing Criminals* (Westport: Greenwood Press, 1993), 7-8.

17 Michael Perry, *Morality, Politics and the Law* (New York: Oxford University Press, 1988).

18 *See*, Stephen Toulmin, "Equity and Principles," *Osgoode Hall Law Journal*, 20 (1982), 1-17.

19 Ronald Dworkin, *Life's Dominion* (New York: Knopf, 1993), 68-84.

Assisting Female Offenders: Art or Science?—Chairperson's Commentary

7

Maeve McMahon, Ph.D.
Department of Law
Carleton University
Ontario, Canada

Introduction

> Crime must be answered in a convincing way; but imprisonment can accomplish this purpose only by generating new injustices. . . . There *is* no frictionless medium in which retributive pain can be unproblematically delivered. Imprisonment is not just a neutral system of moral accounting; it is a violent ritualization of power, and, as such, it produces effects that undermine and overwhelm its capacity to represent justice (Cayley, 1998, p. 347).

In the summer of 1998, the International Community Corrections Association asked me to chair their conference on "What Works: Women and Juvenile Females in Community Corrections" (Arlington, Virginia,

September 27-30). They also asked me to edit this volume of papers from the conference, and to write a paper on female offenders[1] in the context of the conference content.

In considering the ICCA requests, I was somewhat hesitant. This hesitation arose given that most of my criminological research has involved minimal attention to gender issues (McMahon, 1988, 1990, 1992, 1995, 1996, 1998, 2000). My hesitancy was fueled by the fact that the only gender-related research I had done previously was on the topic of women working in corrections, and particularly in prisons for men, and their experiences of discrimination and harassment by their male colleagues (McMahon, 1999). In short, I had never written on the topic of female offenders and questioned whether I had the expertise to carry out the proposed tasks.

At the same time, I was attracted by the ICCA requests. For, although I had not written in the area, my interest in female offenders is long-standing. This interest was intensified pursuant to the scandal about "certain events" at Canada's Prison for Women in 1994, and by the aftermath of the scandal. As this scandal involved issues which arise later in this paper, some information about it may be instructive for the reader.

In April 1994, following disturbances at the Prison For Women,[2] management decided to call in the IERT (Institutional Emergency Response Team) from a neighboring institution for male offenders. The IERT was asked to deal with eight women seen as the main culprits in the disturbances.

By the time the IERT came into the Prison for Women, each of the women was asleep in individual cells in the segregation area. Despite the fact that the trouble was over, and no immediate threat to the institution's security was being posed by the women, the IERT swung into action. In doing so, they followed the procedures that they used in dealing with men. Each of the women was confronted in her cell by the eight male IERT members and their male coordinator, as well as by a female staff member of the prison. In accordance with standard procedures, the men's dress and equipment were designed to be "intimidating." As Louise Arbour, commissioner to the later inquiry into the events, noted:

> The dress consists of a black combat suit and associated protective gear—shin pads, safety boots, gas mask with an eye shield, and a protective helmet. The weapons carried by IERT members include batons, mace cans, and at least one plastic shield per team (Arbour, 1996, p. 67).

The IERT carried out their task in accordance with the policies of the Correctional Service of Canada. Their standard procedure for stripping and removing prisoners was as follows. The team:

> marches into the area in formation (as it is part of the intim-
> idation technique) and approaches the cell of the inmate
> who is to be extracted. The plastic shield is banged against
> the cell, producing a loud and frightening noise. The inmate
> is told to lie face down on the floor and warned that if the
> order is not obeyed, mace will be used. If the inmate com-
> plies, the cell door is opened and members of the team enter
> the cell and assume an "on guard" stance with batons and
> mace around the inmate. Restraint equipment—usually
> handcuffs and leg irons—is applied to the inmate. The
> inmate's clothing is cut off, and the inmate's body is visually
> inspected. . . . If the cell is to be stripped, the inmate is taken
> from the cell and made to walk backwards. . . . The only IERT
> member who speaks during this procedure is the team
> leader, who issues any necessary instructions. Other IERT
> members do not speak, and do not answer questions from
> the inmates (Arbour, 1996, pp. 67-68).

These demeaning and dehumanizing procedures inflicted on the women prisoners were captured on video as the IERT—as part of its pro-fessional approach—records its activities. The purpose of the video is (ironically) to protect members from allegations by inmates, and for use as a training tool. The video provides a series of chilling images. Commissioner Louise Arbour describes the opening scenes as follows:

> Prior to the video being turned on, the IERT marched into the
> Segregation Unit in standard formation, approached Joey
> Twins' cell and banged on the bars of her cell with the shield.
> She immediately did as she was ordered, and when the video
> begins she is lying face down in her cell surrounded by IERT
> members who are holding her down. An officer now identi-
> fied as a female staff member of the Prison for Women staff
> cuts off Ms. Twins' clothing . . . while IERT members hold her
> down. . . . Ms. Twins' hands are cuffed behind her back and
> her legs are shackled. She is marched backwards out of her
> cell naked, and led to the corner of the range. There she is

held against the wall with the clear plastic shield, with her back against the wall. Some IERT members stand around her. . . . The corner where Ms. Twins is standing is visible to anyone on the unit or standing in the doorway separating the disassociation side from the protective custody side of the Segregation Unit. Those who attended in those areas over the course of the evening included members of the prison's correctional staff, the institutional physician, Dr. Mary Pearson, the Case Management Coordinator, Marjo Callaghan . . . Correctional Supervisor Warnell . . . and the maintenance men.

While she is still being held in the corner, a paper gown is brought to Ms. Twins and tied around her neck. The effect is something like that of a bib. The paper gown neither covers her, nor provides warmth.

Upon her return to the cell, an IERT member begins the extremely lengthy process of attempting to apply a body belt in substitution for her handcuffs, during which procedure her gown comes off. A body belt is a form of restraint equipment which, as its name implies, consists of a locked chain around the inmate's waist to which are attached locked cuffs attaching the wrists to the locked belt, more or less at the side of the body.

Finally, this lengthy procedure is completed and she is left lying on the floor of her cell in restraints—body belt and leg irons—with a small paper gown.

Throughout this procedure, she is evidently distressed (p. 71).

When sections of this video were publicly broadcast (about nine months after the strip-searches and with the women's consent), my reaction, similarly to that of much of the Canadian public, was one of shock and horror. Each woman, alone in her cell, is swarmed by men in riot gear. Each woman's clothes are removed by force or under duress, and in the presence of these masked, armed, silent, anonymous, men. Few words are spoken by the supervisor. Each woman is given a paper gown—inadequate to cover them with any modesty—and is subsequently subjected to other degrading procedures.

For me, these events at the Prison for Women were not only horrifying, but also puzzling. For, in many respects, Canada from the late 1980s has also been a world leader in attempting to reform women's imprisonment. The report *Creating Choices* (Task Force on Federally Sentenced Women, 1990) embodied proposals for the closure of the Prison for Women and its replacement with more progressively oriented institutions. Implementation of these proposals was in progress at the time of the strip searches. The juxtaposition of progressive discourses and repressive practices was stark. As a result of this contradiction, I followed with interest the work of the ensuing Commission of Inquiry, its recommendations and attempts at their implementation, as well as research accounts about recent policy shifts with respect to federally sentenced women in Canada (*see* especially the work of Kelly Hannah Moffat itemized in the references). I also began to reflect more systematically on the situation of female offenders when called on by the Commission as a "resource person" in their examination of cross-gender staffing in prisons for women.[3]

The invitation of the International Community Corrections Association for me to chair, edit, and write provided a welcome springboard from which to pursue this fledgling interest in female offenders, and their situations more generally. As one who believes that the vast majority of prisoners could be better worked with beyond prison walls, the ICCA effort to focus on community corrections was likewise welcome. However, I want to remind the reader of my novice status concerning this topic. What follows is as much a matter of my own education as it is an effort to educate the reader.

An Outline of This Paper

A striking comment made at the conference by several participants was that "Women [offenders] exist in the shadow of men." This statement certainly resonates in the United States where women have been sentenced to lengthy prison terms simply because they have cohabited with men who have been active in the illicit drug trade. More generally, women offenders have existed in the shadow of men in that the relatively small numbers have been associated with a lack of policymakers' attention to their situations and needs. Women have been, and are, frequently incarcerated in prisons for men.[4] Programming has been inadequate. Typically, activities available to women in prison (notably laundry and sewing) have tended firstly, to serve the needs of the institution more than those of women, and secondly, to keep women offenders engaged in traditionally female occupations. For those women imprisoned in prisons for men, where broader programming should be available, security concerns often are cited as a rationale for preventing their access to other programs and activities.

Just as the theme that "women exist in the shadow of men" surfaced repeatedly at the conference, so did the assertion that—especially with respect to formulating criminal justice policy—"one size does not fit all." In identifying what might "fit" for female offenders, it is useful to consider the situation with respect to punishment generally, both currently and historically. In this paper, therefore, this author first provides an historical overview of correctional policy, particularly since the 1960s. She then goes on to focus on female offenders, and to discuss contributions at the conference by presenters and participants under the following headings: points of consensus; and dilemmas, contradictions, and dissension involved in attempts to assist female offenders (with dissension mainly focusing on the actuarial discourse of "risk/needs assessment" as applied to female offenders).

Following this, she identifies some challenges facing those who wish to humanistically and holistically assist female offenders despite the constraints of an increasingly bureaucratic and technocratic justice system. This paper concludes with reflections on the limits and potential of different approaches to assisting female offenders and asks whether related efforts should be viewed as primarily involving art or science.

Although her perspective is, by reason of experience and education, primarily western and Anglo-American based, she hopes that the discussion also might be useful to those from other cultures, not least in stimulating them to challenge the boundaries of dominant approaches, and to offer other visionary and progressive alternatives.

An Historical Overview of Penal Policies and Ideologies[5]

> [I]t is indeed time to look again at the institution of prison. It was created in quite a different age, as an alternative to transportation to the colonies or to Australia or to replace physical punishment. An institution devised for the needs of the eighteenth and nineteenth centuries and carried on throughout the twentieth with only minor changes needs to be reviewed for the twenty-first century (Stern, 1998, p. xxi).

As we enter the new millennium, the picture which prevails of imprisonment around the world is depressing. The conditions to which prisoners are subject in many places almost defy belief. For example, in Russia as of 1998, nearly 100,000 prisoners, or 10 percent of all prisoners, were suffering from active tuberculosis. Owing to Russia's economic crisis, it was impossible for the authorities to provide them with the necessary drugs (Penal Reform International, 1998). Meanwhile, those who were ill further suffered, as did the prison population more generally, from the lack of adequate accommodation, food, and heating.

The size of prison populations is also depressing. While there are huge variations in the size of prison population in different jurisdictions,[6] and while many complex factors explain the size of prison population in any given jurisdiction,[7] during the last decades of the twentieth century, there has been a strong perception among prison critics that the predominant tendency is that of a growth in prison populations internationally. In conjunction with this, societal attitudes toward crime appear to have become increasingly punitive. As expressed by David Cayley (1998, p. 41) in the course of his discussion of the "U-turn" in crime policy since the mid-1970s:

> [D]espite the huge variation in prison numbers between say, Norway and the United States, the changes that have taken place seem to have certain common features. Everywhere emphasis has shifted from rehabilitation to retribution, from the culpability of society to the culpability of the offender, and from reasoned policy to symbolic gesture.

With the use of imprisonment growing internationally, with deplorable conditions being not uncommon, and with the public mood becoming more harsh, Vivien Stern's call for a reasoned examination of the possibility of progressive alternatives to imprisonment is compelling.

How do we understand the growing use of imprisonment at the end of the twentieth century? Obviously, this basic question cannot fully be answered here. But, at least from a Western perspective, some important developments since the 1960s assist in explaining the recent evolution of logic with respect to penal policies. Understanding these recent developments, in turn, is illuminated by a brief consideration of the longer history of imprisonment and rehabilitation.

The Rise of Rehabilitation

Given the current emphasis of reformers on the need and moral imperative to establish more alternatives to imprisonment, it is easy to forget that the prison itself as a form of punishment was initially established as an alternative. In the wake of the French Revolution, previously used penalties were seen as unjust and less than civilized. Specifically, the inception of the prison marked several shifts in penal policy. Where punishment often had been carried out in the public sphere (for example, in the market square), it later would be administered in a more private and hidden way—behind prison walls. Where punishment often had been directed at the body (as with whipping, flogging, using of stocks and pillories, and providing transportation), it later would be more directed at the soul of the individual (Foucault, 1977).

The birth of the prison as a form of punishment[8] was closely paralleled by that of social science as a form of inquiry into the human condition. The nineteenth century saw the emergence of psychology, psychiatry, sociobiology, and sociology. The emergence of criminology late in the century drew from these approaches and particularly from their positivist orientation: early criminologists (similarly to their mainstream successors up to the present day) had as their scientific objective the identification of the individual and social characteristics of offenders, and thereby of the factors underlying criminal behavior. In conducting this task, the prison—by virtue of its spatial, legal, and administrative segregation of prisoners from wider society—provided the "institutional surface" whereby the concerns of the new discipline of criminology could be explored (Garland, 1985, p. 80). As criminological historian David Garland has elaborated (p. 82), early criminological knowledge became synonymous with that of knowledge of prisoners:

> The prison provided a kind of new experimental laboratory, a controlled enclosure in which the new knowledge could develop. It provided the possibility for the long-term observation of criminals who could be examined, measured, photographed and catalogued in an organised manner. It produced statistical data on conviction rates, recidivism patterns, and criminal careers, which were invaluable criminological materials unavailable elsewhere. It even allowed a degree of experimentation in so far as various regimes of labour, diet, discipline and so on could be compared with one

another to assess the effects of each upon the prison population and the causes of crime.

From the outset, positivist inquiries in the prison setting were not solely scientific endeavors. They fused with utilitarian and reformist efforts to discover the causes of, and thereby suitable treatment for, criminal behavior. The social scientific genesis of criminology paralleled and reinforced the emergent policy-reform discourse of rehabilitation. As the rehabilitative ethos gathered support among social scientists and correctional reformers, the orientation of punishment changed: the earlier emphasis on the offense, and on legal and classical principles of justice, was moderated by growing attention to the offender and the utility of strategies of classification, differentiation, and individualization in the provision of treatment (Cullen and Gilbert, 1982). Over time, penal practices increasingly incorporated rehabilitative strategies. The political, legal, and administrative groundwork was laid for the development of treatment-oriented programs such as probation, parole, and halfway houses.

Within the public realm, utilitarian, reformist, and scientific interests overlapped with issues of costs, humaneness, and effectiveness. Penal officials sought assurance that vocational, educational, and other therapeutic programs not only were having their intended effect, but were doing so in a cost-efficient manner. Reformers sought support for their humanitarian objectives and their claims about rehabilitation as a penal strategy. And social scientists sought to advance their knowledge of the causes of criminal behavior through examination of the results of treatment, especially with respect to recidivism.

Of course, the pace of the development of rehabilitation, and of the development of criminological knowledge, varied greatly from jurisdiction to jurisdiction. Nonetheless, while it is true that criticism of the prison has been "endemic to its history" (Ignatieff, 1978, p. 19), it is also true that the popularity of rehabilitation as an associated strategy grew to the point that the period following the second World War, and especially the 1960s, saw "its fullest and widest support" (Young, 1983, p. 98). Until the late 1960s, rehabilitation "remained unchallenged as the dominant correctional ideology" (Cullen and Gilbert, 1982, p. 82).[9]

Martinson and a Watershed in Penal Reform

Where the 1960s represented the culmination of the gradual rise in the belief in the rehabilitative ideal, the 1970s represented a watershed in penal reform. Perspectives at the end of the decade contrasted sharply with those at the outset. Within this watershed, Robert Martinson's article published in 1974, and titled "What Works? Questions and Answers About Penal Reform" was a major precipitating factor. In brief, Martinson's article provided a meta-analysis of more than 200 studies, which had assessed correctional and treatment programs. In conducting such assessments, and in evaluating whether programs "worked," the phenomenon of recidivism—or of the tendency of an offender to relapse into crime—had come to be regarded as crucial by criminologists and correctional authorities alike (Garland, 1985b, pp. 61-62; Mannheim, 1960; Ohlin, 1956; Third International Congress of Criminology, 1955). Having conducted an extensive review of existing studies, Martinson's baldly stated and gloomy conclusion was that: *"with few and isolated exceptions, the rehabilitative efforts that have been reported so far have had no appreciable effect on recidivism"* (p. 25. Emphasis in original).

At first glance, from today's perspective, this might be seen as a damning indictment of rehabilitation. But it is important to note that Martinson's conclusion was not novel. Some earlier researchers had come to a similar conclusion. For example, in 1961, Leon Radzinowicz commented on how there appeared to be little difference between the effectiveness of programs in the prison setting and nonincarcerative dispositions. In his words, "the similarity of success and failure rates, as measured by the after-conduct of offenders, irrespective of whether they were put on probation, fined [or] sentenced to short-term imprisonment, or to longer corrective detention, is indeed striking" (1961, p. 169).

If at one level Martinson's findings were nothing new, why were they so energetically received and rapidly translated into the buzz phrase "Nothing works!"? What seems to be of most significance here is not so much the actual findings as the way in which Martinson interpreted their significance. Where earlier researchers had used such findings to reinforce their commitment to rehabilitation, and to call for better ways of accomplishing it,[10] Martinson used his findings as a basis for questioning the very notion of rehabilitation itself. Having first followed his predecessors in querying whether the lack of effectiveness of programs might only be reflecting the need for "a more full-hearted commitment to the strategy of treatment," Martinson (1974, 1979) went on to state:

> It may be, on the other hand, that there is a more radical flaw in our present strategies—that education at its best, cannot overcome, or even appreciably reduce, the powerful tendency for offenders to continue in criminal behavior. Our

present treatment programs are based on a theory of crime as a "disease"—that is to say as something foreign and abnormal in the individual which can presumably be cured. This theory may well be flawed.

Meanwhile, developments in the public culture and academic spheres contributed to Martinson's assertions being taken seriously elsewhere. The social and political events of the 1960s and early 1970s had already generated much scepticism about the state's potential in "doing good" through criminal justice and other institutions. As Cullen and Gilbert have expressed it in the context of the United States of America, the "turmoil" of the 1960s and the emergence of the civil rights movement "marked the beginning of a period in which the legitimacy of state authority was subjected to continued and widespread debate among liberal forces . . . optimism about the possibilities for genuine reform within the confines of existing institutional arrangements would be replaced by a deep sense of pessimism" (1982, pp. 104-105).

In the correctional context, prison disturbances contributed to the waning credibility of correctional practices. Iconic among these were those at Attica, New York in 1971[11] where dozens of people died. As Cullen and Gilbert have explained with reference to Attica and the United States (1982, 108):

> Traditionally, reformers had championed the infusion of the rehabilitative ideal into the criminal justice system and the expansion of discretionary powers that would allow for the individualized treatment of offenders. While the difficulties surrounding correctional programs were not ignored in the past, many liberals nevertheless held tenaciously to the belief that the state could ultimately be induced to exercise these powers in a benevolent manner. But the bloody suppression of the uprising at Attica compelled even the most adamant supporters of enforced therapy to re-examine this assumption. In focusing attention on the plight of society's captives, Attica revealed how badly the liberals' faith in the state had been misplaced. It was now clear that the state used its discretion not to better inmates but to brutalize them, not to effect individualized treatment but to incarcerate only the poor and non-white.

Reflecting this climate of cynicism, liberals began to refer to the "crime of treatment" (American Friends Service Committee, 1971, p. 83). Rehabilitation was described as a myth that fostered the victimization of prisoners themselves. Earlier themes of doing "more good" were overtaken by those of doing "less harm."

Calls for doing less harm also resonated with similar thinking in the social sciences. Throughout the 1960s, phenomenological, ethnomethodological, and symbolic interactionist approaches to the study of deviance and control—by highlighting the socially constructed nature of deviance—had been providing a challenge to positivist approaches in criminology. Labeling and related perspectives also called attention to how the actions of criminal justice institutions and agencies could be read as "amplifying deviant behavior" (Vold, 1979, p. 264; SEE ALSO Cicourel, 1968; Lemert, 1951, 1967, 1971; Skolnick, 1966; Bittner, 1967; Sudnow, 1965; Emerson, 1969; and Scheff, 1966). Sociologists in the 1960s and early 1970s drew on critiques of psychiatry in pointing to the coercive and repressive aspects of rehabilitation programs, and thereby to their punitive elements. In short, many social scientists now ascribed pathology to the correctional system itself, rather than to those being processed by it (for example, Goffman, 1961; Greenberg, 1970, 1972; Kittrie, 1971; Frankel, 1972; Conrad, 1973; Mitford, 1973; Rosenhan, 1973; and Gaylin, 1974).

A major legacy of Martinson's work and ensuing debates has been the accelerated use of community corrections in many Western countries. One of the ironies here is that community programs initially were established under the ethos of rehabilitation.[12] It might have been expected, therefore, that critiques of rehabilitation would yield the curtailment, rather than the expansion, of community corrections. However, the studies reviewed by Martinson also included some community corrections programs, notably probation and parole. And here, in contrast to his otherwise pessimistic conclusions, Martinson identified "one encouraging set of findings." Observing that such programs have cost advantages, and that offenders in them did not do any worse than those in institutional contexts, Martinson concluded that "the implication is clear: *if we can't do more for (and to) offenders, at least we can safely do less*" (1974, p. 48, emphasis in original). In short, Martinson's findings echoed the notion of "doing less harm" that was prevalent in other reformist sectors. His work supported calls for "deinstitutionalization," and reinforced the impetus toward the development and expansion of community programs (including, for example, probation, parole, halfway houses, community service orders, and victim-offender reconciliation programs).[13]

The notion that "nothing works" increasingly would be challenged—especially in the 1990s—both concerning efforts at rehabilitating offenders and at reforming criminal justice systems (for example, Cullen and Gilbert, 1982; McMahon, 1990, 1992; Stern, 1998; Cayley, 1988; Currie, 1998; Andrews et al, 1990, 1990a; Harland, 1996). However, the 1980s were in many ways a political and theoretical void in terms of corrections. If "nothing works" then for what might one advocate? Logically, the best course of action often seemed to be to attempt nothing innovative at all. If you persisted in being reform-minded, the best strategy seemed to be to concentrate on the legal protection of offenders. Meanwhile, where critical criminologists often had previously advocated for reform, they became more likely to confine themselves to analysis and critique. And where policymakers had sought visionary solutions, they became more likely to confine themselves to the management of existing problems.

Sadly, this cynicism about the prospects for penal reform was paralleled by an increasingly punitive public culture in many jurisdictions subsequent to the 1970s. While one can point to the relative stability, and even decline, of crime rates (Currie, 1998), and while one can debate long and hard about the extent and sources of this punitiveness, it seems futile to dispute the fact that public culture expressions of concern about crime, and calls for punishment, had become far more prevalent by the 1990s than they were three decades previously. The American "War on Drugs" is one manifestation of this public culture preoccupation and has played a major part in the growth of the prison population in the United States of America.

In summary, the penal climate at the turn of the millennium is an exceedingly punitive one. Imprisonment rates generally seem to be rising, and in some countries (for example, the United States of America and Russia) at a pace that almost defies belief. Faith in the potential of rehabilitation has been seriously undermined since the 1970s, and the voices of those few who argue that treatment programs and penal reform can work tend to be drowned out in the public culture by media, and political and other sources advocating tougher measures against crime. In turn, this get-tough approach is associated with hardening attitudes more generally towards those in the poorer, and vulnerable, sections of society. Welfare states and social services were radically diminished in many countries during the closing decades of the twentieth century.

Within the criminal justice system itself, discretionary, humanistic, and rehabilitative approaches have been supplanted by those emphasizing just deserts, retribution, determinacy, and proportionality. As previous clinically oriented approaches give way to actuarial ones, the ultimate penalties, despite the rhetoric, often appear very far from any notion of proportionality of justice. A notorious case in point here is the "three-strikes-and-you're-out" legislation in California and elsewhere in the United States of America. Under such legislation, life imprisonment hypothetically can be imposed on anyone convicted of a third felony. As of 1995, more people in California had been sentenced under the legislation "for simple marijuana possession than for murder, rape and kidnapping combined, and more for drug possession generally than for *all* violent offenses" (Currie, 1998, p. 49). Thus, while the discourse promoting the legislation emphasized its use on dangerous and violent offenders, it has been as likely in practice to be directed at petty and minor offenders.

At a general level, it seems reasonable to contend that the dominant trend internationally is a punitive one. But caution must be exercised in making sweeping generalizations.[14] For example, it generally can be said that the prison population in the United States of America is at least four times higher proportionately than that in Canada. David Cayley (1998, p. 351), in his discussion of the use of conditional sentences in Canada, provides a stunning example of the differing approaches to sentencing in the two countries:

> [I]n May of 1997, Mr. Justice Forestall of the Ontario Court's General Division . . . handed down a noncustodial sentence in the case of [a] St. Catherine's man whose drunken driving had killed two people. The offender was ordered to do 240 hours of community service over 18 months, surrender his driver's licence for four years, undergo counselling, and spend 75 hours over the next two years making presentations to students on the consequences of drinking and driving. On the same day in Winston-Salem, North Carolina, a man facing similar charges was given two life sentences after a jury rejected the prosecutor's argument that he should be executed.

From these cases, one easily might infer that Canada is far more lenient than the United States of America. However, as David Cayley himself points out, this is not so when one examines the subgroup of young offenders. Indeed, where young offenders are concerned, it has been argued that the custodial rate in Canada is twice that in the United States of America, and is also higher than that in other Western societies.

Similar caution must be exercised in making statements about female offenders and responses to them. Having briefly addressed the broader context of penal policies and politics, we now can turn to their situation. In doing so, this author's objective, rather than providing a summary of research, is to provide some reflections stimulated, as explained earlier, by her position as chair of the 1998 Conference of the International Community Corrections Association—"What Works: Women and Juvenile Females in Community Corrections." These reflections draw both from the other papers in this volume, and from the discussions which they stimulated at the conference itself. The aim is to provide the reader with some insights into beliefs and concerns about female offenders and the penal system raised at the conference.

A Focus on Female Offenders

> [T]he study of female criminality and its control, as well as the issue of gender in more general theories, faces constant problems of marginalization, incorporation, and tokenism (Downes and Rock, 1998, p. 309).

In deciding to host a research conference on female offenders and community corrections, the International Community Corrections Association was innovative in a variety of ways. It was innovative firstly in putting the focus on female offenders—a topic which has been relatively neglected not only within the field of criminology generally, but also within the subfield of gender issues in criminology. Attention to gender issues in criminology increased enormously during the last decades of the twentieth century. But, where women are concerned, there has been a far stronger focus on their experiences as *victims* of crime than as *perpetrators* of it.[15] This focus makes sense given that women are far more likely to be victims than offenders, and given that the vast majority of the offending population is male. It also makes sense given the multiple forms of victimization experienced by female offenders themselves.

However, there are also what might be described as ideological factors at work, which have inhibited a focus on female offenders, and particularly from feminist perspectives. As Downes and Rock (1998, p. 320) observe:

[Some researchers] more feminist than criminological, would deflect attention away from the criminal woman. Feminist politics or grand theories urge the ending of what has just begun. Just as an earlier generation did not wish to endanger the politics of race by looking too closely at the links between blacks and crime (other than in the context of the unjust criminalization of blacks and the racism of the criminal justice system), so some feminists have argued that no good purpose can be served by exploring the criminality of women. . . . A feminist criminology, it has been argued, is prone to "correctionalism" and collusion with patriarchy, [and] being used as an instrument *against* women.

Focusing on female offenders *does* raise difficult dilemmas. But avoiding them is hardly the best path to their resolution. This is so especially in light of the preoccupation of public culture with violence by women (*see* Chesney-Lind, this volume), which in turn produces a thoroughly misleading stereotype about female criminality more generally. Therefore, it seems incumbent on us to counter public misperceptions with a clearer picture.

The International Community Corrections Association was also innovative in bringing together speakers from diverse backgrounds and disciplinary perspectives. In particular, by bringing together speakers from psychological and sociological points of view, the stage was set for an opportunity to confront both the actions of female offenders and reactions to them. While the interdisciplinary dialog that ensued was not always an easy one, nor by any means comprehensive,[16] the papers presented and the discussions which followed, represented some important steps towards addressing issues about female offenders from more holistic perspectives. Certainly, as a sociologist, this author learned much from the psychological insights offered, and particularly those presented by Stephanie Covington. While statements frequently are made in more sociologically oriented literature in criminology about the high percentages of female offenders who have experienced physical and sexual abuse, and who themselves engage in substance abuse and other forms of self-harm, it is rare to see such a thorough documentation of these problems, and in the specific context of female psychological development.

As a critical criminologist, this researcher also appreciated Stephanie Covington's and other contributors' emphasis on the similarities between those women who happen to be in conflict with the law and women more generally. Many girls and women have had experiences of physical and sexual abuse, but it is those of us who are additionally disadvantaged because of poverty and racism who are most vulnerable to becoming enmeshed in the criminal justice system. As Covington concisely states, their crimes "are actually social issues." Taking this statement as seriously as it should be has enormous implications for how one views both the problems of female offenders and potential responses to them.

With respect to the latter, the International Community Corrections Association conference was further innovative in directing attention to the importance of using community-based programs for female offenders (*see* especially Glover-Reed and Leavitt, this volume). Yet, just as there has been a dearth of feminist research on female offenders, and just as social-psychological perspectives on the topic have been lacking, so have community corrections more generally been an under-researched topic. In any given country, there tends to be far more literature available about prisons than about community alternatives. Moreover, and as already noted, such literature as does exist tends to be overwhelmingly focused on programs for males.[17] Once again, then, dialog at the conference was often impeded by a lack of basic information, as well as by the absence of a history of well-formulated thought on females and community correctional programs.

As chair of the conference, this author sometimes felt that she was witnessing a schizophrenic moment with respect to discussions of female offenders. One reason for this was the diversity of discourses and perspectives brought to the topic by participants—including psychological, sociological, managerial, journalistic, practitioner, and reformist. Another reason for this feeling was that this conference was taking place at a specific time for both feminism and female offenders. The past few decades have seen a tremendous growth in knowledge about, and sensitivity to, gender issues. But they also have seen various forms of "backlash" against feminism (Faludi, 1991; Bashevkin, 1998). With respect to criminal justice, a growing awareness of the need for programing, including community programing, specific to women has been evident.

Yet, and as discussed by Meda Chesney-Lind in the particular case of the United States of America, the 1990s also saw a fascination with a "new" violent offender and specifically with "girls, often girls of color, carrying guns, and fighting with other girls." The question of whether violence by females is increasing remains unresolved. But at the conference, there was less preoccupation with this than with the impression that we are witnessing a transition: those working for and with females in criminal justice are dissatisfied with females continuing, despite all of the rhetoric, to be an afterthought with respect to policy, and are looking for a new, more resolute, and more specifically woman-centered focus in the development of programs, and especially community-based ones. The observations which Pat Carlen and other feminist scholars have been making for decades still ring true, and even more strongly than previously has been the case (Carlen, 1990, p.2, emphasis added).

> In view . . . of the vast feminist literature on the need for women to circumvent the demands of traditional gender controls and develop as persons in their own right, in view, too, of our increasing knowledge of the particular needs of women law-breakers and ex-prisoners, *there has been an astonishing dearth of supportive and rehabilitative programmes fashioned specifically for female offenders.* (O'Dwyer et al, 1987)

Having identified this preliminary but vital point of consensus—that the dearth of programming specific to women is even more unacceptable now than previously—let us go on to consider other points of agreement evident at the conference.

Points of Consensus about Female Offenders and Corrections

The Profile of Female Offenders

One of the clear points of consensus at the conference concerned the profile of female offenders, and especially those imprisoned. Here, Vivien Stern's (1998, p. 137-8) observations about female imprisonment around the world are familiar in light of materials presented at the conference:

> [T]he most remarkable fact about women in prison is how few of them there are. All over the world women make up a tiny proportion of those locked up. The proportions are truly startling. On average only one out of every twenty prisoners is a woman. Women constitute roughly 50 per cent of the population of any country, yet provide only 5 per cent of its prisoners. This is not specific to any one country or region, but is reflected all over the world. In Spain, the proportion of

women is 10 per cent, in the United States over 6 per cent, in France 4 per cent, in Russia 3 per cent, and it Morocco it is 2 per cent. But nowhere in the world do women make up more than one in ten of the whole prison population.

Not only is there a general consensus that women make up a small proportion of overall prison populations, but there is also a consensus about the kinds of women likely to end up in prison. Vivien Stern in her global profile again concisely states what has been reiterated in this volume:

Who are the women in prison? The answer to this too is similar in every country. Women in prison are overwhelmingly poor. Many have themselves been victims of abuse, sexual or physical, sometimes from early childhood.

While the size of the female prison population is small compared to that of men, concerns were expressed at the conference about the rapid rate at which the imprisonment of women seems to be increasing. The most dramatic and well-documented case of this is in the United States of America where, as Elliott Currie (1998, p. 14) observes:

[I]n 1970 there were slightly more than 5,600 women in state and federal prisons across the United States. By 1996 there were nearly 75,000—a thirteenfold increase. For most of the period after World War II, the female incarceration rate hovered at around 8 per 100,000; it did not reach double digits until 1977. Today it is 51 per 100,000. Women's incarceration rates in Texas, Oklahoma, and the District of Columbia now surpass the overall rates for both sexes that prevailed nationally in the late 1960s and early 1970s. At current rates of increase, there will be more women in America's prisons in the year 2010 than there were inmates of both sexes in 1970.

Of note is that this increase proportionately outstrips that of men. As reported by Stern (1998, p. 153), where the U.S. male prison population tripled between 1980 and the mid 1990s, the female prison population grew sixfold during that period. Signs of growth in women's imprisonment are similarly evident in England and Wales. Where there were 1,800 women prisoners in 1987 (Carlen, 1990, p. 74), by June 1997 there were 2,624 women prisoners. Where between 1992 and 1995 alone there was a

29 percent increase in the imprisonment of men, the corresponding increase with respect to women was 57 percent (Stern, 1998, p. 153). Data from other countries is less readily available. But there are the indications that dramatic increases in the incarceration of women also are taking place. For example, in Chile between the early 1980s and the mid 1990s, the rate at which women were imprisoned rose by 100 percent (Cooper, 1998).

A further point that clearly emerged at the conference is that while poverty and social disadvantage, as well as histories of abuse, render women vulnerable to coming into conflict with the law, this situation is exacerbated for members of some ethnic minority groups. In the United States of America, the staggering rates of imprisonment of women of color gives much rise for concern. As Chesney-Lind and Bloom have observed (1997, p. 51):

> [W]omen of color are disproportionately incarcerated in the United States. . . . African-American women are incarcerated at a rate of seven times that of white women (143 versus 20 per 100,000), and women of color represent more than 60 percent of the adult women in state and federal prisons nationwide (American Correctional Association, 1992). Women of color are also disproportionately represented on the death rows of this country relative to their proportion in the general population.

In the Canadian context, similar trends are evident,[18] with the situation of aboriginal women being particularly bad. Although aboriginal people constitute less than 5 percent of the Canadian population, all estimates suggest that the rate at which aboriginal women are imprisoned greatly exceeds their proportion in the population. According to Faith (1993, p. 138), for example, almost 25 percent of federally sentenced women in Canada are Native.[19]

The Limits of Our Information

Ironically, while the conference saw a strong consensus about the basic profile of women in prison—and particularly about their vulnerable status—there was also a strong consensus that we know embarrassingly little about them from a research perspective. In the first place, many basic facts and figures about women and corrections remain unclear. For example, Canadian participants at the conference could not readily agree on how many women there actually are in Canadian prisons. When it came to documenting the situation of women in community corrections, the picture was even more murky. For, and as noted by Covington (this volume) "[r]eliable and detailed data about females in community corrections programs is not collected annually in the United States or in Canada. . . ." No doubt, diligent digging would produce data on women in specific community programs, for example in the Canadian context on women in the federal parole system, or in individual provincial parole systems. But this vital task remains to be done, and it, in turn, is only part of the picture which needs to be compiled. Completing a community corrections profile of females in community corrections in the Canadian context also would require gathering data on probation systems, as well as on fine option, bail supervision, and miscellaneous other programs in Canada's ten provinces, the Northwest Territories, and Nunavut.

This dismal lack of information with respect to basic statistical data on the involvement of women in community correctional programs extends to matters of substance, about what is actually going on within those programs. Fragments of information exist, and there are descriptive studies of individual programs. But when it comes to assessing the outcome of community programs, the picture is obscure. Barbara Bloom's (this volume) opening statement in her paper is apt: "The literature regarding gender-specific outcome evaluation is sparse and, for community corrections, almost nonexistent." As Meda Chesney-Lind (this volume) observes, a similar situation applies with respect to consideration and evaluation of community-based programs for girls where there is "virtually no solid, empirical research on program effectiveness."

Shared Perspectives on Female Offenders

While the conference was startlingly short on what might be described as "hard" data about women and community correctional programs, there was, nonetheless, a wealth of knowledge and insights shared by speakers, discussants, and participants. Moreover, people's diverse experiences (for example, as researchers, managers, policymakers, legal decision makers, reformers, and front-line workers), and ensuing reflections seemed for this chair, to coalesce into what might be described as a set of shared principles. In a brief summary such as this, oversimplification is inevitable. Nonetheless, the principles articulated can be described as follows:

- Women offenders should be defined primarily as *women*, rather than as *offenders* (with the same applying for girls). As Stephanie Covington expressed it: "our lens should be that of women's lives."

- Correctional programs for women should be gender-sensitive, but not biologically reductionistic.

- The importance of relatedness and connectedness for women's mental and personal health needs to be recognized. This, in turn, suggests that top priority should be given to the use of community correctional programs, and that the use of imprisonment should be radically reduced. Imprisonment, by definition, fosters alienation and isolation from society. Community programs carry the potential for positively strengthening bonds between individual women and multiple resources in the community.

- The fact that the vast majority of female offenders have been victimized in various ways should not be allowed to inhibit recognition of the resourcefulness of female offenders, their strengths, and their capacities for survival.

- There should be a holistic definition of the situation of female offenders, and a holistic approach in the delivery of community services. In turn, this means that it is not only women's *behavior* but their *feelings* that should be addressed. A holistic approach involves giving attention to women's individual and social situations, including issues of housing, employment, education, recreation, and so on.

There was further a consensus that, as people working in and around the system:

- We need to improve our ability to articulate our positions and standpoints, both in communicating among ourselves and with others.

- We need to create more opportunities for discussion between, and build more alliances among, researchers, policymakers, reformers, practitioners, and females subject to the criminal justice system.

- We need to create public awareness about the expense, waste, and dangers of incarcerating women and girls.

- We need to become more political, and to communicate our views more effectively in the public culture—including to the media and politicians.

Dilemmas, Contradictions, and Dissension

Discursive Dilemmas and Contradictions

> [A] competent feminist probation officer might know, on the one hand, that her client will gain advantage if it can be demonstrated that she is a good housewife and mother. On the other hand, by privileging that woman's housewifely and mothering performances she will also be colluding in, and promoting, the stereotype of the criminal woman who is NOT a wife and mother, and thereby possibly disadvantaging single, divorced, childless and lesbian female offenders. That such dilemmas exist should not be surprising (Carlen, 1990, p. 109).

Discussion at the conference was replete with dilemmas, ironies, and contradictions. This, in turn, gave rise to numerous important questions. Each of these could be discussed at length. However, space limitations preclude this, and the purpose, once again, is to attempt to provide the reader with the tenor of the discussion.

One predicament that arose is that many people at the conference seemed to feel that they intuitively know what is "good" for female offenders. For example, statements to the effect of "I feel in my gut that we should . . ." were not uncommon. At the same time, participants seemed to feel a compulsion to have their ideas in some sense "proved," and typically in the language of evaluation. It was as if participants hoped that a magic wand of social science might be waved over a plethora of woman-centered and community-based programs, and the blessing to be given was that of solid proof that these programs "work" (specifically in the form of reducing recidivism). Some of the researchers who presented papers also adhered to this kind of thinking. For example, one of the researchers stated and questioned: "We instinctively know what works. But how do we prove it?"

In effect, there was an expectation that social scientific research would provide a mantle of credibility to community-based and holistic programs for women, and ultimately by providing incontrovertible evidence that such programs reduce, and carry the potential to eliminate, reoffending. In practice, however, and given the paucity of relevant studies, and the lack of such evidence, related discussions periodically ended up in a vacuum. Yet, the vacuum was never acutely felt because the values, which most participants (including this author) shared—of care, compassion, and empowerment—served to carry the discussion along, despite various theoretical, political, and research impasses met along the way.

Nevertheless, the line of thinking that "we know intuitively what is good and what should be done, and we want social science research to prove the benefits with respect to recidivism" raises some fundamental issues. This author has no wish to throw sociological cold water on admirable reformist visions, but much of the history of the past few centuries of correctional reform, at least in North America, can be read as a series of well-intentioned movements followed by unintended, and often negative, consequences. As David Rothman (1980) has expressed it, the "conscience" of reformers becomes the "convenience" of administrators. Michel Foucault (1977) has even more trenchantly critiqued modern, and supposedly progressive, reform in the penal sphere. For him, knowledge and power are reflections of one another, and social scientific knowledge in general is synonymous with the sinister, complex, and subtle exercise of social control. In turn, Stanley Cohen (1985) has used a Foucauldian analysis in deconstructing the use of community corrections generally, and in revealing their dark side—particularly with respect to their potential of yielding "wider, stronger, and different nets of social control" exerted on offenders who most likely would never have gone to prison in the first place.

While this author takes issue with aspects of Foucault's and Cohen's perspectives (McMahon, 1987, 1990, 1992, 1996), they are also critically important in directing attention to, and stimulating reflection on, the ideological frameworks within which we are currently operating. Some of the immediate questions arising, and which were more or less explicitly alluded to at the conference include: What is the notion of "good" to which we adhere in discussing female offenders and community corrections? Are there intuitive views of what is good being expressed in discussions which are at odds with those adhered to in much of the research literatures, and particularly in those which are positivist in orientation? How do we reconcile the feminist ethic of caring, empathy, and empowerment articulated in discussions and in some of the papers with the mainstream criminological emphasis on "What Works?" and the use of recidivism rates as a primary indicator? While Barbara Bloom (this volume) raises some questions about research preoccupations with recidivism, this is an issue which perhaps needs to be confronted more directly and extensively. It is pertinent that journalist and commentator Sasha Nyary was puzzled by the research emphasis on meta-analysis involving as many studies as possible, and by the key focus on recidivism. Who, she questioned, is asking for this? How often do the media, politicians, and the public focus on such studies anyway? In short, the research discourse and its preoccupations often seemed far removed from public culture, and even those of people actively involved in corrections.

In advancing discussion about ethics and morality in relation to female offenders and corrections, the words of Andrew Skotnicki[20] are pertinent. In discussing correctional reform during the past few centuries, he contends that our reliance on social scientific discourse constitutes a barrier to our considering more pluralist conceptions of "the good." In his words:

> [T]he meaning and justification for the criminal justice enterprise has been continually appraised in terms of a set of theoretical propositions grounded in the methodologies of the social sciences. These methodologies have been accorded a "de jure" status in channelling information into the debate over the direction of criminal justice, and in setting the linguistic parameters for the debate itself. It is my contention that the weight created by the burden of crime and its cure is simply too strong for such a foundation to bear. Fundamental questions of meaning currently rest, without significant opposition, on a "thin" conception of the "good." . . . our constant and relentless search for the right form will be seriously compromised, along with all other correctional innovations, until we incorporate a more pluralist conception of the good into our reformist methodologies (1998, pp. 1-2).

It seems to this author that the humanitarian and feminist discourses articulated at the conference represent one strategy for a broadened conception of the "good" as called for by Skotnicki. Within these discourses perhaps the most notable feature is a relentless focus on the person as, first and foremost, a human being.[21] Where problems began to arise was in the juxtaposition of this arguably broader and deeper perspective with conventional criminological perspectives on indicators such as recidivism rates and using the latter as barometers of what is desirable. In short, the journey down a more pluralistic and humanistic route seemed to reach an impasse when the junction with positivism was encountered.

A basic question requiring further attention then is: what are the content and contours of the discourses currently being applied to female offenders—and especially in their feminist, humanitarian, and social scientific forms? How do these discourses complement, contradict, and circumvent one another? What are their points of incompatibility, and how might we deal with these?

Dilemmas and Contradictions of Holistic Approaches in Repressive Contexts

Other dilemmas that arose at the conference could give rise to similarly extended discussions. But, for the sake of brevity, they are expressed in bullet form.

- Many participants were aware that there is now a general tendency whereby governments have been withdrawing support for public and welfare services, and, at the same time, extending and expanding the repressive arm of the state. While it is admirable to advocate for increased programs and service provision for female offenders, such advocacy needs to be done firmly within a context of broader social, economic, and political realities. This is particularly the case in the United States of America with its appallingly high rate of imprisoning women. If one considers, for example, the situation in New York State, where there has been a mandatory minimum of ten years for a minor drug offense (Cayley, 1998, p. 27), the question needs to be raised: should one's primary attention be directed to focusing attention on the fundamental injustice,[22] futility, and costs of this rather than on the provision of more programs within the prison system itself? In conjunction with this, should not there be greater protest about the decline of services and the need for more programs within the community?

- A related dilemma is embodied in the question: how compatible is a holistic approach and its therapeutic component with the ultimately coercive and repressive orientation of corrections? Stephanie Covington (this volume) expresses this concern, shared by some of the other speakers and participants, as follows:

> Many women and girls who work in the criminal justice settings struggle daily with the contradiction that a system based on power and control is antithetical to what helps women to change, grow, and heal. Creating new gender-specific programs or changing an existing program can only be a partial solution. Systemic change is essential.

Discussant Joanne Belknap similarly raised concern by asking: what could be the "nightmare" of gender-specific programs in corrections? Such fears have also been raised by Kathleen Kendall on the basis of her research into the contradiction of therapy behind prison walls. She states (1994): "I am concerned that the language of feminism is being stripped of its subversive potential by corrections in order to facilitate the correctional agenda." These concerns need to be articulated more thoroughly, and confronted in more depth, than has been the case in this volume.[23]

- Another related dilemma, which received even less attention at the conference than the previous ones can be expressed in the question: Would a more holistic approach simply make the female correctional system more subtle and effective in exerting control over those who are already among the most vulnerable women in our societies?[24] Few of the participants paid much attention to earlier literature embodying critiques of previous forms of the rehabilitation approach. Again, while this author is more than sympathetic to the reformist endeavor, it also is incumbent on us to be mindful of historical pitfalls— including the potential linking of therapeutically oriented programs with lengthened and indeterminate sentences. The ethics of coerced treatment also need to be considered. Arguably, resolving these issues may again point feminist researchers in reductionist and abolitionist directions: women offenders' problems are, for the most part, social problems and thereby best addressed, insofar as is possible, outside of the criminal justice system (Carlen, 1990).

Dissension about Definitions of "Success" and the "Client"

Where points of dissension are concerned, this author has alluded to some of them. For example, many presenters, commentators, and participants were uncomfortable with the notion of reduced recidivism as the primary sign of "success." Overall, the importance of recidivism rates appeared to be simultaneously rejected and maintained. More direct confrontation of this issue, and more systematic explorations of alternative theoretical and methodological frameworks should be considered as priorities.

Another point of dissension revolved around the question: who is the "client" when it comes to female corrections? For most participants, it is individual female offenders. But for others, and notably those oriented in more positivist and managerial directions, it was the public that seemed to be the client. At first glance, one's definition of the client appears to be a relatively simple matter. It is also one often resolved at that level through making assumptions. But the consequences of these assumptions are enormous. Defining the public as the primary client of corrections can lend itself to the development of increasingly punitive penal policies. This is reflected in North America where political preoccupation (often in the absence of adequate or accurate information) with perceptions of public concern about crime is used as a rationale for intensified policing and toughening of sentencing. It would be an interesting and important research project to examine how definitions of the client are interwoven with contemporary penal policy both generally, and in the specific case of female offenders.

Dissension about, and Discomfort with, Actuarial Approaches

The most important point of dissension, this author thinks, was many people's dissatisfaction with the actuarial approach in corrections. In this volume, the actuarial approach is most clearly evident in the article by Motiuk and Blanchette. The immediate focus of participants' concern about actuarial justice was on the current use of, and emphasis on, concepts of "risk" and "criminogenic needs." It is particularly important to address this issue given the Correctional Service of Canada's emphasis on actuarial approaches both in research and in practice,[25] as well as Canada's international influence in this respect. Indeed, as Larry Motiuk stated in his presentation, he had just returned from a European conference on corrections, and Europeans consider Canada as the "foremost leader" with respect to matters of "risk" in corrections.

While issues of risk and actuarial justice are extremely important, they are also, at least in this author's experience, not always easily articulated. She frequently asks: "What is wrong with risk, and, by extension, with actuarial justice?" This question can be difficult to answer. For, although many feminists interested in criminal justice have expressed discomfort with the notion of risk, the content of their discomfort has not been expressed in any great detail. As Kelly Hannah Moffat (1999, p. 75) notes, "feminists have not yet analysed the concept of risk as it applies to women's penal regimes; nor have they provided a detailed critique of existing techniques for measuring risk, except to suggest that these measures do not adequately reflect the context of women's experiences and behaviours." As in the feminist literature more generally in criminology, conference participants' concern about risk and related concepts as currently used were stated more implicitly than explicitly. Therefore, this author will attempt to bring some of these concerns more clearly into focus.

The first problem that many participants seemed to have with notions of risk/criminogenic need and actuarial justice is that this frame of thinking permeates the correctional system more generally and thereby primarily is focused on men. The themes "one size does not fit all" and "equality does not mean sameness" were repeated frequently in making this basic observation.

This author agrees that the uniform application of analytical frameworks across genders can be problematic. But it is also important to question—as indeed some participants did—whether it is appropriate or helpful to apply the actuarial approach to male offenders either. Indeed, one might argue that the feminist approaches promoted in this volume also have much to offer in improving correctional approaches to men. Extended discussion of this, unfortunately, is beyond the present scope.

The emphasis on "risk" in actuarial discussions of female offenders seems strange for several reasons. It is strange firstly because the notion of risk is—albeit more or less explicitly—in turn allied both with notions of dangerousness and likelihood of reoffending. Yet, women are far less likely to engage in violently dangerous behavior than men. Further, the data presented by actuarial proponents suggest very low recidivism rates on the part of federally sentenced women in Canada. Specifically, in the recidivism study of 219 released women discussed by Motiuk and Blanchette, only 1 had her conditional release violated in connection with a new offense. This represents an offense-related recidivism rate of less than 1 percent! While seven other women were returned to custody owing to "technical violations"[26] and while the follow-up period of six months was relatively short, the image of 218 of 219 released women not being convicted of new offenses is difficult to reconcile with the emphasis on risk. As Motiuk himself observed in his presentation: ". . . we're enjoying very low recidivism [by female offenders]."[27] Further, he and Blanchette noted in a preface to their paper: " . . . assessment instruments for male offenders often are 'borrowed,' which may be contributing to over estimates of risk for female offenders." Having said this, however, they then proceed to present their research using these virtually gender-neutral instruments.

Another problem with the actuarial approach in corrections is that it is often, at least in this author's experience, difficult to understand what is actually being said. The terms "criminogenic" and "risks" as used in the literature are cases in point. Therefore, it was a bit of a relief to hear Motiuk state, in the context of the European conference he had just attended, that the concept of criminogenic needs is "hard for foreigners to understand." In essence (and see Bloom, this volume, for elaboration), the logic is that certain of an offender's needs are considered to be risk factors with respect to recidivism. In the words of Motiuk and Blanchette: "We consider need areas to be dynamic factors and a subset of an overall offender risk." In turn, the correctional system's business is to focus on those representing high risks and to concentrate its efforts in that direction (Andrews et al, 1995; Gendreau, 1996; Bonta et al, 1995). Meanwhile, those considered lower-risk could be used as a "target . . . for less intensive services [expediting] their safe and controlled release at the earliest possible moment in the sentence."

While this approach is logical at one level, it carries some disturbing implications. The first is that if women are recognized as low risk (and especially compared to the higher risk believed to be posed by men), following the actuarial approach would suggest that they be a low priority for receipt of services. In short, the traditional neglect of women within corrections seems to be reinforced by the actuarial approach.

Also disturbing is the view of female offenders, which emerges in the actuarial literature. As Bloom questions: "Does women's offending relate to criminogenic risks and needs, or is it a factor of the complex interconnection of race, class, gender, trauma, or both?" This author would add to this that we also need to consider the actions of criminal justice agents and agencies. Women's actions are only part of the picture. Also important are decision-making by police, prosecutors, and others in determining who actually ends up in corrections.

A further question is: what precisely are the "criminogenic needs" with respect to female offenders? While Motiuk and Blanchette discuss many of the problems also discussed by other authors in this volume, this author has difficulty providing specific answers based on their paper, or on the actuarial literature more generally.[28] Rather, the concept of "needs" seems to merge with that of "risks" and, in the process, the focus gets shifted away from the feminist emphasis on the offender as a person, and toward a focus on their potential criminal behavior. As reaffirmed by Kelly Hannah Moffat (1999, p. 83), within the Correctional Service of Canada there is "an interesting slippage" between needs and risks to the point that, in some cases, "these two categories are indistinguishable."

One example of this merging and shifting is Motiuk and Blanchette's unusually unequivocal statement that: ". . . a history of attempted suicide was found to be a potent predictor of violent recidivism in a sample of federally sentenced women (Blanchette and Motiuk, 1995)." When this author first read this statement, she had a mental image of the governor of the women's prison in Lithuania[29] reading Motiuk and Blanchette's article and finding that this was one of the most clearly understandable statements in the article. She then had the image of the governor using the statement to direct his staff to put any female prisoners who had ever attempted suicide into the most secure section of the prison, and to make sure that they stayed there until their full sentences had been served, with no possibility of early release. Of course, no such interpretation is intended by Motiuk and Blanchette, but arguably their analysis easily *lends itself* to such an interpretation.

A woman who has been, or is, suicidal is a woman with problems and in need of assistance. But putting this scenario into an actuarial and purportedly recidivism-predicting framework diminishes the focus on her problem and shifts it into an image of her as a "high risk" candidate, not only for recidivism, but for violent recidivism. With this focus, surely the orientation of the correctional system moves towards delaying and constraining her access to the community.

A further problem with the observations that "a history of attempted suicide was found to be a potent predictor of violent recidivism" and in Motiuk and Blanchette's attendant observations that between one-third and half of the federal female offender population have a history of attempted suicide, is that they are difficult to reconcile with these authors' own observations elsewhere about the low recidivism rate of female offenders. Again, while not intended, the sequential observations that up to half of female offenders have attempted suicide, and attempting suicide is a potent predictor of violent recidivism among female offenders, logically can lead in the direction of linking federally sentenced women/ violent/reoffending. While not wishing to dispute that some federally released women do go on to reoffend, and occasionally violently, it is the *generality* of the image which is disturbing, and arguably misleading.

Meanwhile, the data cited by Motiuk and Blanchette in presenting their case about the link between attempted suicide and recidivism are sketchy. No information is presented about the basis on which the eighty-one federal female offenders studied were selected. Further, the information that seventeen of these reoffended, that eight of these were for robbery,[30] that over half of the variance in the "violent recidivism" remained unexplained, and that 20 percent of the 45 percent that was explained was attributed to "[h]aving a history of attempted suicide" seems to me to greatly dilute the authors' claim. If the authors are interpreting the data correctly, the "most highly predictive variable" of attempted suicide explained less than 5 percent of the recidivism by 21 percent of the women studied. Meanwhile, no information is provided about the remaining 79 percent of the sample who did not violently reoffend (or reoffend at all?) and their histories of attempted suicide. This fragmentary picture seems a long way from the image of a "potent predictor."

Also of concern is Motiuk and Blanchette's linking of their observations about attempted suicide and violent recidivism to those on the significance of self-mutilation by women prisoners when they state: "Accordingly, other researchers found much higher rates of previous self-injury among female recidivists than non-recidivists." Again, rather than positing self-mutilation as an indicator of a woman's need for help, the focus is on its being a potential predictor of reoffending.

Another problem with the actuarial literature produced by Canadian correctional researchers is its frequently authoritative tone. In part, this tone derives from the authors' emphasis on the scientific nature of their approach. As Motiuk and Blanchette state, the Offender Intake Assessment process consists of "the latest generation of risks and needs assessment technology" and one which uses "objective assessment tools." The purportedly scientific nature of the approach was more clearly highlighted by their colleague Paul Gendreau in a talk preceding the conference where he elaborated on the virtues of the "actuarial" approach, in contrast to the more old-fashioned, and implicitly unscientific, "clinical" approach. Thus, he emphasized that under the actuarial approach, there is a "statistical association between prediction and outcome," and that "predictors are measured by standardized, reliable, objective measures." By contrast, the clinical approach relies more heavily on people and professionals and "the rules for collecting and interpreting information are subject to considerable personal discretion." In Gendreau's account, in terms of delivering "superior performance," the actuarial approach "is three to four times better" than the clinical one. Following his vision, the argument is that computerized forms with relevant items being checked off by technocrats is far superior than, for example, having a social-scientifically trained intake officer sitting down with an offender to discuss how they might best proceed through the morass of correctional institutions and programs.

Taken to its logical extreme, one can envision a future where even the need for correctionally employed technocrats is eliminated. Why should not the offenders themselves sit in front of a computer and check off relevant items, perhaps attached to a lie detector, which imposes mini electric shocks as necessary to minimize the potential for errors in replying?[31]

One can imagine the appeal of this highly assertive tone to correctional policymakers and politicians. Consider, for example, the title of an article by Don Andrews (1996) which confidently states: "Criminal Recidivism is Predictable and Can Be Influenced." What are in practice very complex phenomena get transmuted into appealingly simple statements, and sometimes even into slogans.

In fairness, the complexities of understanding and predicting recidivism are not completely ignored in the literature. For example, Motiuk and Blanchette stated in their presentation (italics added): "Although objective classification instruments can yield significant gains both in understanding and predicting criminal behaviour, *the fact remains that the amount of variance left unexplained continues to outweigh that which can be explained for a variety of correctional outcomes* (for example, temporary absence, parole)." However, once mentioned, this crucial point is left to the side and they proceed as if their data and approach were all encompassing. Although they mention the need for a "variety of technologies," no elaboration is provided.

While the tone of the actuarial literature in corrections is often authoritative and confident, actually making sense of it can be very difficult. Some of these difficulties already have been discussed. They, in turn, frequently are added to by the obscurity of the language used. Consider, for example, the statement by Motiuk and Blanchette:

> While the OIA process was developed principally for assessing offender risks and needs upon admission to federal custody, the scope of our risks/needs assessment and assessment process

has been streamlined. In keeping with individual ratings for both "criminal risk" and "case need" levels as well as for each need area, alignment of the community version of risk/need assessment process was straightforward. This situation makes possible a systematic assessment and re-assessment process which spans admission to the end of sentence. Presently, full automation of this new community re-assessment is complete.

If this author understands Motiuk and Blanchette correctly, they are saying: "Our assessment process was initially designed for offenders entering federal prisons. It is now also used during offenders' transition to the community. The data are computerized."

Understanding the literature is further complicated in that many of its claims are highly contestable. For example, it is frequently claimed that the system is "objective." The first point one can make here is that the correctional system *per se* is in no way objective. Those offenders who end up in corrections do so as a result of a long series of decision-making by individuals where subjectivity comes into play at every step of the way—including decisions by members of the public (for example, by victims about whether to report), and by the police (for example, about whether to lay charges, and what charges to lay), as well as by prosecutors, defense lawyers, judges, and juries. Therefore, what is being studied by correctional researchers is not any objective picture of offenders, but rather a relatively small subgroup of offenders, predominantly from vulnerable groups in any given society, who have been successfully focused on, and processed by, other components of the justice system.

The claim that these newer assessment "tools" are objective is further questionable in that they currently continue to rely on the mainstay of traditional clinical approaches, namely professional judgment. As Motiuk and Blanchette stated in their presentation (italics added):

> An overall rating of criminal risk is the compilation of *professional judgments* from the results of the criminal history record and offense severity record. In addition, a review of detention criteria for the current offense(s) reflects the nature of the offense(s) and the degree of harm to the victim(s) is taken into account. One should keep in mind that the establishment of criminal risk might also incorporate a great deal of other assessment information as well.

Given the acknowledgment that professional judgments are still key in actuarial decision making as currently engaged in, issues arise of a disjuncture between discourse and practice. Although the actuarial discourse emphasizes notions of being scientific and objective, actual practices within the complex world of corrections may have much in common with traditionally established ones. As Moffatt (p. 75) notes: "[i]n practice, the assessment and management of women prisoners' risk is quite subjective and fluid." Moreover while the research publications of the Correctional Service of Canada give the impression that various classification instruments determine where an offender is sent, Moffat (p. 78) documents that in the real world of corrections, other factors come into play including perceptions of "escape risk" and "*notoriety*-likely to evoke a negative public image . . ." (Emphasis in original). Indeed officials of the Correctional Service of Canada have acknowledged their own departures from actuarial practice. In the words of one report quoted by Hannah-Moffat (p. 81; Federally Sentenced Women Programme, 1994, p. 11, emphasis added):

> [Practical uses of risk technologies are not] depersonalised or concerned primarily about independent, abstract statistical categories and populations. . . . when actuarial tools are used, correctional officials frequently use "overrides" to adjust risk assessment scores to what *they feel* is most appropriate. The use of overrides means that exceptions can be made to the initial classification instrument *when warranted,* both to increase and decrease the security classification.

More generally, the very notion of objectivity raises deep epistemological issues which are, unfortunately, beyond the present scope. In a nutshell, this author's own position is that no analytical framework is ever objective, and rather represents a partial, and to some extent ideological, view of the matter at hand (Mannheim, 1936). Rather than claiming objectivity, it is perhaps more fruitful, and truthful, to be reflexive about the frameworks we use, including the interests that they represent, and those that they undermine (Smith, 1999; Weber, 1949). Informed and transparent subjectivity is arguably preferable to detached and highly questionable objectivity.

Overall, while the assessment tools discussed by Motiuk and Blanchette, and by their colleagues, might be useful in matching individual offenders to correctional programs, it is arguably a dangerous enterprise to link their use to overconfident claims about their ability to reduce recidivism. This is especially so given the inevitability of some recidivism occurring, and current media and public culture preoccupations—in the Canadian case, particularly with respect to ex-prisoners (usually males) who reoffend—on the actuarial approach with its emphasis on "risk,"[32] which can easily be used in moving in a very repressive direction. At an extreme, this repressive direction could lead to the totalitarian conclusion: every prisoner—male or female—is potentially a recidivist and, therefore, the only way to prevent recidivism is to prevent the release of all prisoners. The abolition of parole in many places in the United States of America, and the thinking behind "three-strikes-and-you're-out" legislation, as well as calls for increased use of capital punishment are contemporary steps in the direction of this dire logic.[33]

Challenges to Be Faced in Assisting Female Offenders

[W]e have to change our belief system.
(Dave Worth,[34] quoted in Cayley, 1998, p. 362)

Perhaps the greatest challenge to be faced by those who wish to assist female offenders is to be constantly vigilant in being aware of the broader context. At any given moment, a practitioner may be preoccupied with helping an ex-prisoner to regain custody of her children, or to recover from relapse into an addiction; a researcher may be preoccupied with tracking down an elusive piece of data; a policymaker may be preoccupied with how to respond to a minister's request for a "quick fix" speech in response to the latest crisis; and a prison correctional officer may be preoccupied with evaluating the mood of those under her or his charge. But unless we bear in mind that crime "usually begins in circumstances of poverty, joblessness, family breakdown, sexual violence, drug addiction, and neighbourhood abandonment" (Cayley, 1998, p. 357), we are vulnerable to having our work usurped and carried off in directions not of our own choosing. A particular danger is that women-centered and holistic approaches might be accepted and used only insofar as they are amenable to the actuarial approach which is ascendant in corrections.

Here, Canada represents an important case in point. For, despite having produced a resolutely woman-centered and holistic blueprint, which emphatically rejected an emphasis on risk (Task Force on Federally Sentenced Women, 1990), and having established five new women's prisons, recent developments suggest that the vision has been only partially implemented, and that a preoccupation with purported risks continues to be predominant. In short, the subsuming of needs to risks proceeds apace. As Kelly Hannah Moffat observes (1999, p. 73):

. . . the implementation of this model has been marred by exclusion, and by redefinitions of the meaning of woman-centred corrections and of the experiences and realities of the female offender (as outlined in *Creating Choices* and by feminist researchers and advocates). Some of the most significant of these changes include the definition, assessment and management of women's risk and need in the new regional prisons.

Hannah-Moffat goes on to elaborate on how multiple discourses of need are present in correctional settings—including therapeutic, administrative, feminist, and actuarial vocabularies. Moreover, with the actuarial slippage between needs and risks, the fact that women are often defined as high need, according to Moffat, has made little difference in how they are actually treated. She elaborates (p. 88):

The emergent needs-talk which informs women's correctional management does not rely on feminist interpretations of women's needs or their claims to entitlement; rather, it depends on correctional interpretations of women's needs as potential or modified risk factors that are central to the efficient management of incarcerated women. The Correctional Service of Canada's adoption of the premise that federally sentenced women are generally "high need" and not "high risk," their claims that these prisoners do not require the same level and type of security measures as are required for male offenders (Task Force on Federally Sentenced Women, 1990) and the subsequent development of a unique security management model to address these qualities illustrates an organizational commitment to serving women's needs as they define them. Thus far, this tactic has co-opted and distorted the feminist critique of correctional risk assessment and risk management practices. The fact that women are now constructed as "high need" as opposed to "high risk" makes little substantive difference in their correctional management. Increasingly, needs are being treated in the same manner as risks in terms of defining carceral responses to women.

Keeping the broader picture in mind requires paying attention to what Stephanie Covington referred to in her presentation as our "mental maps." As she noted, every field or discipline carries its own assumptions, and, especially as we work for a long period in one area, these often can go unexamined. In turn, individuals tend to look at issues through a particular "lens" and that chosen in any given instance has a profound effect on how related problems are defined. Historically, criminal justice issues have tended to be seen through the lens of men's eyes.[35] Whether one chooses to emphasize the "criminal," "cognitive therapy," or "addiction," said Covington, will likewise lead one down certain routes and simultaneously away from others. Her own chosen lens—and one shared by many conference participants—of women's lives leads clearly in a holistic direction in assisting female offenders. In short, one challenge is to be aware of the contours of our own "maps"—including both their strengths and limitations.

But being reflexive about our own approaches is only one part of the challenge. We also need to be aware of the contours of the "maps," which are actually at work within the system. In particular, we need to be reflexive about the contours of the actuarial map and its emphasis on risk. The reflections offered in this paper are a very modest step in this direction. What is needed is more empirical research on how these relatively new instruments are actually being used, and how they differentially impact on people in corrections on the basis of gender, ethnicity, class, and so forth.[36]

Another challenge facing us, and especially as researchers on female offenders, is to keep the complexity of related issues front and center stage. There seemed to be a feeling at the conference that researchers should be able to deliver clear and unequivocal guidelines about how to proceed. For example, Richard Billack, President of the ICCA, stated: "we want the research community to give us *tools*" (emphasis added). The actuarial approach, by sidestepping or ignoring issues of the broader workings of the criminal justice system, appears most able to deliver in response to this request. But, as has been argued, this is done at the expense of considering the strong tendency of the criminal justice system to focus on those who are already vulnerable. Aiming simply to provide tools arguably turns researchers into technocrats and turns them away from considering the nuances of given situations.

Perhaps the job of the academic researcher primarily is to bring the contours of dominant "maps" more clearly into focus so that in turn we all can better address the various principles, perspectives, and moral issues that are involved in definitions of, and responses to, crime. This is not to say that academic researchers cannot suggest plans of action. For, as the papers in this volume evidence, they certainly can. What is different is that the plans of action offered are far clearer in articulating their presuppositions, the context of the actions required, and their potential consequences. In short, there are no magical tools, and the task of the social scientific community is to articulate the complexity of social problems and suggest potential directions in responding to them.

In conclusion, it seems that points of dissension and debate at the conference ultimately circulated around competing views about "ways of knowing" or "ways of seeing" female offenders and their behavior, and how to proceed in responding to them. In turn, these ways of knowing seemed to divide into those who emphasized an intuitive, woman-centered and holistic approach as against those who emphasized a scientific and highly rational approach. The underlying debate then, might be described as art versus science.

How might this debate be advanced? Here the words of Leonid Ponomarev are useful, as he reflects on the strengths and limitations of science and art as two ways of knowing:

> It has long been known that science is only one of the methods of studying the world around us. Another—complementary—method is realized in art. The joint existence of art and science is in itself a good illustration of the complementarity principle. You can devote yourself completely to science or live exclusively in your art. Both points of view are equally valid, but, taken separately, are incomplete. The backbone of science is logic and experiment. The basis of art is intuition and insight. But the art of ballet requires mathematical accuracy and, as Pushkin wrote, "Inspiration in geometry is just as necessary as in poetry." They complement rather than contradict each other. True science is akin to art, in the same way as real art always includes elements of science. They reflect different, complementary aspects of human experience and give us a complete idea of the world only when taken together. . . . We cannot assess the degree of damage we undergo from a one-sided perception of life.

In attempts to assist female offenders, our efforts can be aided by intuitive insights coupled with scientific rigor. But to proceed only through one route or the other is to increase the danger of the penal system further oppressing women and girls who are already among those who are most vulnerable in our societies.

Endnotes

1 For their comments on an earlier draft of this paper I thank: Angelika Schafft (Norway), Kelly Hannah Moffatt, Mary Jane Mossman, Don Evans, and Dawn Moore (Canada), Kathleen Kendall (England), and Russ Immarigeon, Stephanie Covington, Barbara Bloom, and Meda Chesney-Lind (USA). The Toronto workshop on female offenders and "risk" organized by Kelly Hannah Moffatt and Margaret Shaw in May 1999 was helpful in the course of revisions to this paper. Thanks also to Hannah Ranger for her superb research assistance.

2 The Prison for Women is in Kingston, Ontario. It is occupied by women serving federal sentences of two years and more. The federal system is administered by the Correctional Service of Canada. Until the early 1990s, the Prison for Women was the only federal prison for women. Since then, four new regional prisons and an aboriginal "healing lodge" for women have opened. The context of this reform is discussed later in this paper. Female prisoners on remand and those serving sentences of less than two years in Canada are held in provincially run prisons.

The disturbances at the Prison for Women in April of 1994 included a "brief but violent physical confrontation" between some prisoners and staff, and various forms of "acting out" by inmates (Arbour, 1996).

3 This author presented her initial reflections on the strip searches and their significance at a criminology conference in Tallinn, Estonia in the summer of 1996 (McMahon, 1996a). In brief, she analysed the strip searches, and particularly their use of "Standard Operating Procedures" as part of a broader trend toward the "McDonaldization" of corrections and criminal justice (cf. Ritzer, 1996).

4 In Canada, this also has been true for women on remand, and for those serving provincial sentences of less than two years. There has been minimal research attention to this sector of the female prison population. More attention has been directed to federally sentenced women serving two years or longer.

5 Some of the material in this section is drawn from my book *The Persistent Prison? Rethinking Decarceration and Penal Reform* (1992).

6 Rates vary from more than 600 prisoners per 100,000 population in the United States of America and Russia to lows of less than 70 in the Scandinavian countries, as well as in the Netherlands, India, Japan, and the Republic of Ireland (Stern, 1998, pp. 31-2).

7 For an informative investigation of why, during the decades following the second World War, imprisonment in Britain increased while that in the Netherlands decreased, *see* Downes (1988).

8 Prisons did exist prior to the nineteenth century, but primarily were used for those awaiting trial, and for persons who had been fined and had not yet paid. Imprisonment *as* punishment evolved about two centuries ago.

[9] While the ideology of rehabilitation was gathering strength until the late 1960s, the rate at which it was implemented in practice varied enormously across jurisdictions.

[10] Those for whom the repeated finding of continued recidivism in face of a wide variety of treatment programs did not result in a diminished commitment to rehabilitation, but rather in calls for more of the same, included theoretical criminologist George Vold. Rather than questioning the principles of such programs, he highlighted the recursive relationship between theory, research, and practice. In his words (1958, p. 302): "more adequate theory on which to base a more adequate treatment program may only be expected with more fruitful research into, and a more complete understanding of, crime causation."

[11] Disturbances at Kingston Penitentiary in Ontario in 1971 served to raise similar issues in the Canadian context. For a discussion of prison struggles in Europe during the early 1970s, *see* van Swaaningen (1997).

[12] Community corrections were initially established as a mechanism to facilitate "reintegration into the community" rather than as "alternatives to prison" (*see* McMahon, 1992, for elaboration of this in the Canadian context).

[13] In addition to contributing to the demise of the rehabilitative ideal and the rise of community corrections, Martinson's work and reactions to it also fueled the rise of more legalistic approaches in corrections, especially with respect to sentencing where a shift took place towards more fixed and determinate sentencing. Martinson's work also generated reverberations within the field of criminology itself as not only mainstream, but also critical criminologists, adopted the logic that "nothing works." For a discussion of negative perspectives that prevailed by the mid 1980s about the possibility of reforming either offenders or the criminal justice system itself, *see* McMahon, 1992.

[14] For example, many former Soviet Republics, following the fall of communism, are taking steps to reform their penal systems in progressive directions, and in a manner more sensitive to human rights. The use of capital punishment is being reduced, penal codes are being rewritten, and alternatives to imprisonment are being established. For some of the newly independent countries, a major impetus, apart from their commitment to democracy and human rights, is their desire to bring their criminal justice systems more into line with west European norms, and so enhance their prospects of joining the European Union. Yet, even in these countries, just as official policy is ameliorating in some respects, the public mood is becoming much tougher. For discussion of related issues in the Baltic countries, *see* McMahon (1995). For information on criminal justice developments in countries of the former Soviet Union more generally *see* publications by HEUNI (The European Institute for Crime Prevention and Control, affiliated with the United Nations, Helsinki, Finland).

[15] For an example, *see* Walklate (1995). For an exception *see* Sommers (1995).

[16] As in the literature on women and crime more generally, the emphasis tended to be on the status of women, including female offenders, as victims. Another factor which inhibited the conference from being comprehensive was the omission of female offenders themselves as a distinct group of participants. While individuals such as Kim Pate from the Canadian Association of Elizabeth Fry Societies spoke eloquently on the basis of her advocacy work with female offenders, it is this author's belief that the conference would have been immeasurably enriched by the inclusion of some of those with whom participants were working.

[17] For an exception, *see* Carlen (1990).

[18] Except with respect to capital punishment which Canada abolished in the early 1970s.

[19] For poignant autobiographical and biographical accounts of one Canadian aboriginal woman's, and one African-American woman's, experiences with the criminal justice system *see* Wiebe and Johnson (1998) and Dash (1997).

[20] The conference on female offenders ran parallel to one on the "Community Corrections Act" also organized by the ICCA. Professor Skotnicki, of St. Patrick's Seminary, Menlo Park, California, presented a keynote address to participants at both conferences on September 28, 1998. His presentation was titled "Continuity and Change in the Pursuit of Criminal Justice."

[21] This emphasis on persons as human beings has, this author believes, much in common with the work of abolitionist criminologists, and especially the work of Nils Christie (1977, 1982, 1994).

[22] David Cayley (1998, p. 27) quotes federal court judge and former deputy mayor of New York Robert Sweet on the discomfort he has felt when applying such mandatory minimums for drugs. They are, says Sweet, "debasing the rule of law."

[23] For historical analysis of how various woman-centered discourses have played out in practice within the Canadian prison system for women *see* Hannah-Moffat (1997). With respect to contemporary developments in the federal imprisonment of women in Canada, Kelly Hannah Moffatt has also provided informative analysis of the woman-centered report Creating Choices, and discussed problems in its implementation (1995, 1999).

[24] This question was also raised and discussed with respect to women as victims, and in the context of aboriginal sentencing circles in Canada and the broader idea of restorative justice. Some participants were enthusiastic about the idea of restorative justice, especially given its compatibility with a feminist emphasis on the need for healing, and in a supportive community environment. But others cautioned about how such approaches, particularly in cases of sexual assault by men, can reinforce gender power imbalances, which already exist in the community both through lenient sentencing and neglect of the female victim's needs. For excellent discussion

of both the positive and negative potential of restorative justice, including reflections on gender issues, *see* Cayley (1998, Chapter 2).

[25] Articles in the Correctional Service of Canada's journal *Forum on Corrections Research* contain numerous examples of the actuarial approach.

[26] This is one pitfall which advocates of multiple programming for women in community corrections need to be mindful of: the more that these programs are made available through conditions of parole, the greater the probability of women violating and being returned to prison. For example, if attendance at a drug treatment center is made a condition of parole, failure to attend could be cause for revoking parole. The challenge is to have the necessary programming available without increasing the coercion to which female offenders are subjected.

[27] According to Correctional Service of Canada officials at the conference, the general recidivism rate of federally sentenced women is about 5-7 percent.

[28] 'Criminogenic needs' with respect to the correctional population generally are said to include antisocial attitudes and feelings, association with procriminal role models, low self-control, and poor problem-solving skills.

[29] This author spent 1993-94 in Lithuania and since then has had some involvement in correctional reform in that country.

[30] The remaining nine women who reoffended had the following offenses: seven assault, one utter threats, and one manslaughter. No information is provided about the nature of the violence involved in these crimes, nor with respect to the eight women convicted of robbery.

[31] Companies vending electronic monitoring devices in the United States of America already promote products which permit prison staff to inflict electronic shocks on prisoners from a distance. Discussing the issue of privatization and corrections is beyond the present scope. But the rise of actuarial justice is in many ways interlinked with the growing tendency for private corporations to engage in "control as enterprise" (*see* McMahon, 1996).

[32] Corrections is not alone in recently promulgating the discourse of "risk." Notions of loss, harm, danger, uncertainty, and hazard have come to permeate daily life, and with an attendant emphasis on the need for security and protection. New homes come with burglar alarms, new cars with airbags, and condoms with warnings about AIDS. Whole communities increasingly try to protect themselves—from the establishment of "WalkSafe" and antiharassment programs on university campuses to "walled communities" in North America, which employ their own private security police forces. In short, the growing emphasis on "risk" within corrections is but one facet of the emergence of the "risk society."

The "risk society" is one where "governance is directed at the provision of security" (Ericson and Haggerty, 1997, p. 85). As Ericson (1994) has observed, technocratic and future-oriented discourses are used, and a three-fold logic is evident:

> First, there is a negative logic. Threats and dangers, and fears about them, are dealt with by the construction of "suitable enemies" (Christie, 1986) and attendant negative labelling, denial, avoidance and exclusion. Solidarity is based in a commonality of fear . . . .

> Second, there is a logic of controlling the irrational by rational means. Fear becomes a basis for rational action. People turn to experts to rationalize fears and make probability choices. . . .

> Third, there is a logic of insurance. The concept of risk is a neologism of insurance. In modernity the institution of insurance is central to the rationalization of risk.

Space limitations preclude more detailed discussions of the "risk society," but *see* Feeley and Simon (1994), O'Malley (1992), and Simon (1987).

[33] For reflections on totalitarian tendencies in contemporary criminal justice, and particularly in the United States of America, *see* Nils Christie's *Crime Control as Industry: Towards Gulags Western Style (1994)*.

[34] Dave Worth has been active in establishing victim-offender mediation programs in Canada.

[35] This author was struck at the conference by how male-associated imagery often was used by participants in discussing issues. For example, the actuarial approach relies heavily on developing "tools" and "instruments." For Motiuk and Blanchette, attempted suicide is a "potent" predictor of female recidivism. And for Richard Billack, ICCA President, the work of Paul Gendreau is a "proactive arsenal" with which one could challenge misguided public culture images of crime and criminals.

[36] Kelly Hannah Moffat already has done much important work in this area. She and Margaret Shaw currently are undertaking a substantial research project on the topic. Their project title is "Risk Assessment/Management and its Implications for Marginalized Women in Canadian Corrections."

References

American Correctional Association. 1992. *The Female Offender*. Laurel, Maryland: American Correctional Association.

American Friends Service Committee. 1971. *Struggle for Justice: A Report on Crime and Punishment in America*. New York: Hill and Wang.

Andrews, D. 1989. Recidivism is Predictable and Can Be Influenced: Using Risk Assessments to Reduce Recidivism. *Forum on Corrections Research.* 1,2:11-18.

————. 1996. Criminal Recidivism is Predictable and Can be Influenced: An Update. *Forum on Corrections Research.* 8:3:42-44.

Andrews, D., J. Bonta, and R. Hoge. 1990. Classification for Effective Rehabilitation: Rediscovering Psychology. *Criminal Justice and Behavior.* 17:19-52.

Andrews, D., I. Zinger, D. Hoge, J. Bonta, P. Gendreau, and F. Cullen.1990a. Does Correctional Treatment Work? Clinically Relevant and Psychologically Informed Meta-Analysis. *Criminology.* 28:369-404.

Arbour, The Hon. L. 1996. *Commission of Inquiry into Certain Events at the Prison for Women in Kingston.* Ottawa: Public Works and Government Services.

Bashevkin, S. 1998. *Women on the Defensive: Living Through Conservative Times.* Chicago: University of Chicago Press.

Bittner, E. 1967 Police Discretion in Emergency Apprehension of Mentally Ill Persons. *Social Problems.* 14:278-292.

Bloom, B. 1998. Beyond Recidivism: Perspectives on Evaluation of Programs for Female Offenders in Community Corrections. Presentation to the ICCA conference (*see* the chapter in this book).

Bonta, J., B. Pang, and S. Wallace-Capretta.1995. Predictors of Recidivism Among Incarcerated Female Offenders. *The Prison Journal.* 75:3:277-294.

Carlen, P. 1990. *Alternatives to Women's Imprisonment.* Milton Keynes: Open University Press.

Cayley, D. 1998. *The Expanding Prison: The Crisis in Crime and Punishment and the Search for Alternatives.* Toronto: House of Anasi.

Chan, J. and R.V. Ericson. 1981. *Decarceration and the Economy of Penal Reform.* Toronto: Centre of Criminology, University of Toronto.

Chesney-Lind, M. 1998. What to do About Girls? Thinking About Programs for Young Women. Presentation to the ICCA conference (*see* the chapter in this book).

Chesney-Lind, M. and B. Bloom. 1997. Feminist Criminology: Thinking About Women and Crime. In B. D. MacLean and D. Milanovic, eds. *Thinking Critically About Crime.* Vancouver: Collective Press.

Christie, N. 1977. Conflicts as Property. *British Journal of Criminology.* 17:1-4.

————. 1982. *Limits to Pain.* Oxford: Martin Robertson.

————. 1994. *Crime Control as Industry: Towards Gulags Western Style.* London: Routledge.

Cicourel, A. V. 1968. *The Social Organization of Juvenile Justice.* New York: John Wiley and Sons.

Cohen, S. 1985. *Visions of Social Control.* Cambridge: Polity.

Comack, E. 1996. *Women in Trouble: Connecting Women's Law Violations to their Histories of Abuse.* Halifax: Fernwood.

Conrad, J. P. 1973. Corrections and Simple Justice. *Journal of Criminal Law and Criminology.* 64:208-217.

Cooper, D. 1998. Female Delinquency in Chile. Presentation to the XIV World Congress of Sociology. Montreal (July).

Covington, S. S. 1998. Helping Women Recover: Creating Gender-Specific Treatment for Substance-Abusing Women and Girls in Community Correctional Settings. Presentation to the ICCA conference.

Cullen, F. T. and K. Gilbert. 1982. *Reaffirming Rehabilitation.* Cincinnati: Anderson.

Currie, E. 1998. *Crime and Punishment in America: Why the Solutions to America's Most Stubborn Crisis Have Not Worked—and What Will.* New York: Metropolitan Books.

Dash, L. 1997. *Rosa Lee.* London: Profile Books.

Downes, D. 1988. *Contrasts in Tolerance: Post-war Penal Policy in the Netherlands and England and Wales.* Oxford: Clarendon.

Downes, D. and P. Rock. 1998. *Understanding Deviance: A Guide to the Sociology of Crime and Rule Breaking,* 3rd edition. Oxford: Oxford University Press.

Emerson, R. 1969. *Judging Delinquents.* Chicago: Aldine.

Ericson, R. V. and K. D. Haggerty. 1997. *Policing the Risk Society.* Toronto: University of Toronto Press.

Faith, K. 1993. *Unruly Women: The Politics of Confinement and Resistance.* Vancouver: Press Gang.

Faludi, S. 1991. *Backlash: The Undeclared War Against American Women.* New York: Doubleday.

Federally Sentenced Women Programme. 1995. *Security Management System*. Ottawa: Correctional Service of Canada.

Feeley, M. and J. Simon. 1992. The New Penology: Notes on the Emerging Strategy of Corrections and its Implications. *Criminology*. 30:4:49-74.

Foucault, M. 1977. *Discipline and Punish: The Birth of the Prison*. New York: Pantheon.

Frankel, M. L, 1972. *Criminal Sentences: Law Without Order*. New York: Hill and Wang.

Garland, D. 1985. *Punishment and Welfare: A History of Penal Strategies*. Aldershot: Gower.

Gaylin, W. 1974. *Partial Justice: A Study of Bias in Sentencing*. New York: Vintage.

Gendreau, P. 1996. The Principles of Effective Intervention With Offenders. In A. Harland, ed. *Choosing Correctional Options that Work: Defining the Demand and Evaluating the Supply*. Thousand Oaks, California: Sage.

Glover Reed, B. and M.. E. Leavitt. 1998. Modified Wraparound and Women Offenders: A Community Corrections Continuum. Presentation to the 1998 ICCA conference (*see* the chapter in this book).

Goffman, E. 1961. *Asylums*. Garden City, New York: Doubleday.

Greenberg, D. F. 1970. *The Problem of Prisons*. Philadelphia: National Peace Literature Service.

Hannah-Moffat, K. 1991. Creating Choices or Repeating History: Canadian Female Offenders and Correctional Reform. *Social Justice*. 18:3:184-203.

———. 1995. Feminine Fortresses: Women-Centred Prisons. *The Prison Journal*. 75:2:135-164.

———. 1997. *From Christian Maternalism to Risk Technologies: Penal Powers and Women's Knowledges in the Governance of Female Prisons*. Ph.D. Thesis, Toronto: University of Toronto, Centre of Criminology.

———. 1999. Moral Agent or Actuarial Subject: Risk and Canadian Women's Imprisonment. *Theoretical Criminology*. 3:1:71-94.

Harland, A., ed. 1996. *Choosing Correctional Options That Work: Defining the Demand and Evaluating the Supply*. Thousand Oaks, California: Sage.

Howe, A. 1994. *Punish and Critique: Toward a Feminist Analysis of Penality*. London: Routledge.

Ignatieff, M. 1978. *A Just Measure of Pain: The Penitentiary in the Industrial Revolution*. London: Macmillan.

Kendall, K. 1994. Therapy Behind Prison Walls. A Contradiction in Terms? *Prison Service Journal*. 96:2-11.

Kittrie, N. N. 1971. *The Right to be Different: Deviance and Enforced Therapy*. Baltimore: John Hopkins University Press.

Lemert, E. 1951. *Social Pathology*. New York: McGraw-Hill.

———. 1967. H. *Human Deviance, Social Problems and Social Control*. Englewood Cliffs, New Jersey: Prentice-Hall.

———. 1971. *Instead of Court: Diversion in Juvenile Justice*. Chevy Chase, Maryland: Center for Studies of Crime and Delinquency.

Mannheim, H. 1960. *Pioneers in Criminology*. London: Stevens and Sons.

Mannheim, K. 1936. *Ideology and Utopia*. London: Routledge and Kegan Paul.

Martinson, R. 1974. What Works? Questions and Answers About Penal Reform. *The Public Interest*. 35.22-54.

McMahon, M.. 1987. Review of Stanley Cohen's "Visions of Social Control: Crime, Punishment and Classification." *Canadian Journal of Sociology*. 12:1-2:175-178.

———. 1988. Police Accountability: The Situation of Complaints in Toronto. *Contemporary Crises*. 12:301-327.

———. 1990. Net-Widening: Vagaries in the Use of a Concept. *British Journal of Criminology*. 30:121-149.

———. 1992. *The Persistent Prison? Rethinking Decarceration and Penal Reform*. Toronto: University of Toronto Press.

———. 1995. *Crime, Justice and Human Rights in the Baltics*. HEUNI Papers #5. Helsinki: The European Institute for Crime Prevention and Control, affiliated with the United Nations.

———. 1996. Critical Criminology and the Problem of Power. *Chronicles/Chroniques/Xponika [Greek Journal of Criminology]*. 9:1-20.

———. 1998. Control as Enterprise: Some Recent Trends in Privatization and Criminal Justice. In S. Easton, ed. *Privatizing Correctional Institutions*. Vancouver: The Fraser Institute.

————. 1999. *Women on Guard: Discrimination and Harassment in Corrections.* Toronto: University of Toronto Press.

————. 1999a/in press. *Everyday Life After Communism: Some Observations From Lithuania.* Pittsburgh: Carl Beck Monograph Series on Eastern Europe, University of Pittsburgh.

Mitford, J. 1973. *Kind and Usual Punishment: The Prison Business.* New York: Alfred A. Knopf.

Motiuk, L. and K. Blanchette. 1998. Assessing Women Offenders: What Works. Presentation to the ICCA conference (*see* the chapter in this book).

O'Dwyer, J., J. Wilson, and P. Carlen.1987. Women's Imprisonment in England, Wales, and Scotland. In P. Carlen and J. Worrall, eds. *Gender, Crime and Justice.* Milton Keynes: Open University Press.

Ohlin, L.E. 1956. *Sociology and the Field of Corrections.* New York: Russell Sage Foundation.

O'Malley, P. 1992. Risk, Power and Crime Prevention. *Economy and Society.* 21:3:252-275.

Penal Reform International. 1998. War on Tuberculosis in Russian Prisons. *Newsletter, Penal Reform International, Eastern Europe and Central Asia.* 3:1-2.

Ponomarev, L. In Quest of the Quantum. Quoted in B. Edwards. 1979. *Drawing on the Right Side of the Brain: A Course in Enhancing Creativity and Artistic Confidence.* Los Angeles: J. P. Tarcher.

Radzinowicz, L. 1961. *In Search of Criminology.* London: Heinemann.

Ritzer, G. 1996. *The McDonaldization of Society: An Investigation into the Changing Character of Contemporary Social Life.* Revised edition. Thousand Oaks, California: Pine Forge Press.

Rosenhan, D.L. 1973. On Being Sane in Insane Places. *Science.* 179:250-258.

Rothman, D. 1980. *Conscience and Convenience: The Asylum and Its Alternatives in Progressive America.* Boston: Little, Brown.

Scheff, T. 1966 *Being Mentally Ill: A Sociological Theory.* Chicago: Aldine.

Scull, A.T. 1984. *Decarceration: Community Treatment and the Deviant—A Radical View.* 2nd edition. Cambridge: Polity Press.

Simon, J. 1987. The Emergence of a Risk Society: Insurance, Law and the State. *Socialist Review.* 95:1:93-108.

Skolnick, J. H. 1966. *Justice Without Trial: Law Enforcement in Democratic Society.* New York: Wiley.

Skotnicki, A. 1998. Continuity and Change in the Pursuit of Criminal Justice. Presentation to the ICCA conference.

Smith, D. 1999. *Writing the Social: Critique, Theory, and Investigations.* Toronto: University of Toronto Press.

Sommers, E. K. 1995. *Voices from Within: Women Who Have Broken the Law.* Toronto: University of Toronto Press.

Stern, V. 1998. *A Sin Against the Future: Imprisonment in the World.* London: Penguin.

Sudnow, D. 1965. Normal Crimes: Sociological Features of the Penal Code in a Public Defender Office. *Social Problems.* 12:225-276.

Task Force on Federally Sentenced Women. 1990. *Report of the Task Force on Federally Sentenced Women.* Ottawa: Ministry of the Solicitor General.

Third International Congress of Criminology. 1955. *General Reports.* London. September.

van Swaaningen, R. 1997. *Critical Criminology: Visions from Europe.* London: Sage.

Vold, G. B. 1958. *Theoretical Criminology.* New York: Oxford University Press.

———. 1979. *Theoretical Criminology.* 2nd edition, prepared by T. J. Bernard. New York: Oxford University Press.

Walklate, S. 1995. *Gender and Crime: An Introduction.* London: Prentice-Hall.

Weber, M.. 1921/1968. *Economy and Society.* New Jersey: Beminister Press.

———. 1949. *The Methodology of the Social Sciences.* New York: Free Press.
Wiebe, R. and Y. Johnnson. 1998. *Stolen Life: The Journey of a Cree Woman.* Toronto: Alfred A. Knopf Canada.

Young, P. 1983. Sociology, the State, and Penal Relations. In D. Garland and P. Young, eds. *The Power to Punish.* London: Heinemann.

1998 Margaret Mead Award Address: Rational Policies for Reforming Offenders

8

Paul Gendreau, Ph.D.
Director
Center for Criminal Justice Studies
University of New Brunswick
Saint John, New Brunswick, Canada

Thank you so very much for honoring me with this prestigious award. Indeed, there have been some dark days in the United States during the last two decades or so regarding the rehabilitative agenda. Everyone is familiar with Martinson's "nothing works" pronouncement and its legacy of "get tough," which is still felt today. The first counterattacks launched against this ethos were Jerome Miller's "reaffirming rehabilitation" conferences held in Arlington, Virginia in the mid-1980s. Given the political climate of the times, Miller deserved a great deal of credit for going against the tide. And, thank goodness, the International Community Corrections Association has carried on the fight, beginning with the legendary conference—almost of Woodstock proportions—in Philadelphia. I had the good fortune to participate in that one as well as the subsequent one in Seattle. So here we are in 1998, and ICCA continues to do a yeoman's job by encouraging practitioners/policymakers to provide a quality service to offenders based on the research evidence.

Getting from Here to There

I became involved in corrections in 1961 through the time-honored tradition of nepotism. After I received my B.A., during which my specialization in university was golf team captain and basketball forward (who never played defense), I signed on as an assistant professional at an Ottawa golf club. My father, who was deputy commissioner of penitentiaries at the time, was not amused at this development, and he and my mother gently (using reinforcement, not punishment, I should add) steered my career into graduate school. Meanwhile, dad engineered a succession of internships for me in the Canadian penitentiary system, where, doing my best James Dean imitation, I blotted my copybook several times and vowed never to work in the system after I received my doctorate.

Oh well, another mistaken prediction about my career, which as we shall see, was prescient. As one of my mentors, a colorful forensic psychiatrist named George Scott, told me "Paul, we are paid to make mistakes." I took his advice quite literally.

When I was a graduate student, I thought I would quickly establish a reputation by generating research that would attract people's attention. Back in the sixties, there was a well-regarded theory called "the addiction prone theory." I jumped into the fray, did some research at Kingston Penitentiary where I worked at the time, and published a series of articles that were highly critical of the concept of "addiction proneness." I stated that scholars who supported this theory had committed four major errors in reasoning. Shortly thereafter, to my delight, my publications were included in a text entitled *Classic Contributions in the Addictions*. Then, I realized that I committed three of the four logical errors in my own work. No one noticed. It slowly dawned on me that my career in corrections had something in common with many offenders' lives: immediate gratification with no punishment. No wonder their lifestyle can be so appealing.

Then, I thought the time was propitious to clarify recidivism research in Canada. I headed up the largest recidivism prediction study ever, which led to the development of a recidivism index for Canada. I was very proud of it. But a year after its publication, I noticed that the scale was upside down. When researchers look at recidivism data in Canada using my index, they must wonder why the Canadian data are out of sorts with everybody else.

Bear with me for one more example. It is the career path of a typical administrator. In 1972, I became an administrator in corrections. We were really proud of some exciting programs that we were delivering at Rideau

Correctional Centre, some of which were developed by last year's International Community Corrections Association award winner, Don Andrews. I helped initiate a successful token economy for highly disruptive inmates. The institution was much safer as a result, and some of the inmates benefitted tremendously. The talented staff, who conducted the hands-on administration, were otherwise occupied for a couple of weeks on another task. It was up to me to take over the program. As you may know, a token economy is an economic system. Within two weeks, I introduced 300 percent inflation and almost brought it to its knees. What was the consequence of this behavior? About a month later I was "promoted" to a position of more responsibility and status.

There is a lesson to be learned from all of this (although I am not too sure what it is at times). Well, yes, I am, that is, corrections can be a forgiving career if you are lucky; stay the course, and sooner or later you can "get it right," and make a contribution. There are so many exciting things to do and discover. Lately, I think, we have been "getting some of it right."

Respect for Evidence

I joined the Martinson debate in the mid-1970s. I am a psychologist and, of course, psychologists in my specialty are trained to help people. One of our mandates is to deliver human services that are effective. So, when a colleague made me aware of Martinson's pronouncement that offender's treatment were a failure, I was flabbergasted. Nothing worked with offenders? Were offenders some kind of strange genetic mutation whose behavior was immutable while all the rest of the people on this planet were not? It was just an absurdity. So, along with others at the time such as Don Andrews, William Davidson, Ted Palmer, and Bob Ross, I started generating evidence to counter the "nothing works" credo.

Indeed, so much evidence has accumulated that now we have to use statistical syntheses of the literature to make sense of it. While I still do primary studies, essentially I have been working as a quantitative librarian (in other words, meta-analysis), summarizing the literature for the benefit of practitioners and policymakers.

Treatment Efficacy

What kind of success rates—reductions in recidivism—can we expect in corrections? I am not too sure what our collective criminal justice IQ is at times; an empirical study might prove to be embarrassing. Frankly, I find the criminal justice field to be unduly xenophobic and parochial. There is not enough curiosity (one aspect of intelligence) about what goes on in other fields. If one has a relativistic view, then we can make much more sense of what we are about.

Let me give you examples of this. Before we start flagellating ourselves over our so-called failures in offender treatment, let us ask ourselves how well treatment works in medicine. Do professionals in medicine routinely achieve 50 to 100 percent success? Thanks to people like Mark Lipsey, Robert Rosenthal, and Morton Hunt, psychologists are aware that various medical treatments such as coronary bypass, AZT for AIDS, drug treatment for arthritis, ECT for depression, chemotherapy for breast cancer, and so forth are not automatic cure-alls. Treatment reductions for these "diseases" are modest, albeit highly cost effective, in the range of 5 to 30 percent. Let us turn to the recent evidence from the field of psychology. Two thumbs up to Lipsey and Wilson, who summarized the results emanating from 20,000 studies and 2 million subjects that covered 37 content areas. They reported that the average effect size for psychological treatments is about a 25 percent reduction in the problem behavior in question. Mindful of this background, I now turn to our success in reforming offenders.

First, I am going to talk about "get tough" approaches. The following information will be published in the near future by Claire Goggin, Don Andrews, Francis Cullen, and myself. Prisons, according to liberal dogma, are considered to be cruel and unusual punishment. Offenders presumably become more psychologically disabled (for example, more anxious, depressed, and cognitively impaired) as a result of doing time. Prisons even may be "schools of crime." On the other hand, if you approach prisons from a "conservative" perspective, prisons are a great thing. The misery of prison life should encourage offenders to "straighten up and fly right" and not come back. I expect many of your politicians might believe in that approach.

The facts of the matter are as follows. Some people here will not like this comment, but the available evidence indicates that prisons are not necessarily cruel and unusual punishment. It is very hard to find that prisons, on the assumption they are managed in a humane fashion, have produced deleterious psychological effects in offenders.

I have always felt, however, that prisons presented a different sort of problem. A social-learning point of view would predict that prisons should be "schools of crime." On the reasonable assumption there are few treatment programs in place in most prisons, the prison culture should reinforce procriminal sentiments. In my view, this iatrogenic effect should be most pronounced for lower-risk offenders. They have the most negative things (antisocial attitudes) to learn.

Based on studies since the 1950s, we uncovered 325 comparisons of offenders who either have spent longer time in prison than their counterparts or have gone to prison for brief periods of time versus those who remained in the community (for example, probation). The results were 0 to 7 percent increases in recidivism, depending on the comparisons made and the outcomes measured. Given the costs of incarceration and future crimes committed, this may be a substantial burden on taxpayers. The magnitude of this result, by the way, is similar to some medical treatments that physicians have considered to be meaningful. In addition, we found that the length of time an individual is incarcerated in prison was associated with increases in recidivism of about 3 percent. This result, contrary to my prediction, applied to *both* lower and higher risk offenders, with the problem marginally worse for lower risk offenders.

I now address another form of "getting tough." There has been a fascinating revolution in community corrections in the last fifteen years in the United States, which, of course, is the use of intermediate sanctions. Remember Billie Jean Erwin's famous comment, which was highlighted in the *New York Times* and the *Washington Post* in 1986, that is, the new panacea for reforming offenders would be to put the heat on probationers and parolees by punishing them for their misdeeds. Let us spy on them every minute of the day, make them pay restitution, put them into a boot camp before release on parole, give them a quick taste of jail, scare them, do drug testing and electronically monitor them so the story goes.

We assessed the effectiveness of these strategies by gathering 158 comparisons of "getting tough" in community corrections versus control groups (for example, regular probation, which is usually two-to-three times less costly). Our database encompasses about 55,000 offenders. The average effect is no effect on recidivism—none at all. Folks, this intermediate sanction turkey is not going to fly as a cost-effective intervention!

As a matter of fact, some of these community "get-tough programs" seemed to have made things worse. Scared straight programs produced about a 6 percent *increase* in recidivism. Interestingly, when I was sifting through the intermediate sanction programs, I uncovered a fascinating result. Those few intermediate sanction programs that made an attempt at providing some treatment, although it was not their primary goal (but they provided more treatment than did the regular probation control group) reduced recidivism by 10 percent. The ones that did not include treatment increased recidivism by 1 percent. The best intermediate sanction program in terms of reducing recidivism in the whole literature came from Mario Paparozzi's (the president of the American Probation and Parole Association) New Jersey Intermediate Sanction Program. It had a treatment emphasis and monitored the quality of supervision by parole officers.

This latter result provides a nice segue to what does work. Guess what; it's treatment! There have been many summaries of this literature. The latest comes from Don Andrews, Craig Dowden, and me. When all the treatment comparisons are added up (n=374), whether they be behavioral, nondirective, or psychodynamic treatment programs, on average, they reduced recidivism by 8 percent.

More important, when those programs that followed the principles of effective treatment, which Don Andrews and I have written about extensively over the years (for example, programs that target criminogenic needs, of higher risk cases, and are behaviorally oriented) were examined, the average effect size was a 26 percent reduction in recidivism. There were, regrettably, just sixty such instances in the literature. Also, there have been relatively few effective interventions of recent vintage (one exception being Scott Henggeler's exciting work with high-risk juveniles) because we are still in the era of "get tough" and restorative justice programs.

So there it is—an average reduction of 26 percent. These are useful outcomes compared to the medical and psychological literature. And the cost savings can be enormous. Please consult Mark Cohen's 1998 article in the *Journal of Quantitative Criminology*. Some programs need only a 2 to 3 percent success rate to show substantial cost benefits.

Cynics might say there is little support for rehabilitative policies in the public body. Dead wrong! Francis Cullen and colleagues at the University of Cincinnati have produced compelling evidence that there is still strong support for rehabilitative practices, even in "conservative parts" of your country. Some of their conclusions have included the following.

(a) Polls have presented a misleading picture of public crime by assessing only surface views. In fact, the public's opinion is fairly complex. They favor a balanced approach to crime. Offenders, particularly high-risk ones, merit punishment, yet it is also important to rehabilitate most offenders.

(b) Community corrections is considered worthwhile if something constructive (in other words, quality treatment/supervision) is provided.

(c) Rehabilitation for juveniles is advocated as well as early intervention, even favoring using tax dollars for these programs rather than building more prisons.

Knowing, however, what programs work or do not and the extent of public support is one matter; implementing rational policies is another. There are several barriers in this regard. Unless we attempt to scale them, correctional quackery will remain alive and well.

Correctional Quackery

Medical analogies are tired ones, but they still can be illustrative. A few years ago, I had an endocrine problem, partially genetic in nature. Actually, it was a useful disease to have; I could be perfectly miserable to people (particularly ones I disliked) and they had no recourse but to grudgingly excuse my behavior. In any case, I had to seek out treatment. I went to a hospital. I was treated by an endocrinologist. All the"policies" centering about my health over a two-year period were generated and monitored by medically qualified people. Now, if my medical problem were treated in the way we are all too often are accustomed to doing things in the criminal justice system, I likely would have been referred to a university humanities department, assessed and treated by people of vague, uncertain, or no relevant qualifications such as a deconstructionist, or someone with just plain old common sense. Would that be acceptable to anyone here? I hope not; it is quackery. Lately, I have been trying to document this phenomenon. For those interested, see an article of mine in *Criminal Justice and Behavior*, 1996, 23: 144-161; and a paper with Claire Goggin and Paul Smith (which has just been published in *Corrections Management Quarterly*, 2000, Vol. 4, No. 2). My examples of quackery will focus on correctional treatment staff, academics, and policymakers/ administrators. I only have sympathy for the former.

It is one thing to demonstrate that certain types of treatment services, as reported in the literature, can be effective. But what is the situation "in the real world"? I always have suspected the reality is bleak. In fact, I am sure of it, having worked in the field for years. The Correctional Program Assessment Inventory (CPAI), now the CPAI 2000, was developed partly to assess this assumption. Surveys of programs using the CPAI that have been conducted by Claire Goggin, Don Andrews, Alan Leschied, Ed Latessa, and myself found that the vast majority of programs received a failing grade.

Here are some of the most frequent defects as reported in our surveys. When it comes to implementing correctional treatment programs, thorough literature reviews often were missing and program designers' credibility was suspect. Assessments were based on the clinical approach, and some of the factors targeted for treatment were weak predictors of criminal behavior. Sometimes we found an inverse relationship between what we know works and what was used in many clinical settings, similar to the classic research of alcohol treatment practices by William Miller. The responsivity issue was ignored. That is a very powerful modality where a number of ethnic, gender, and other individual differences can be addressed effectively within treatment paradigms.

In some instances, program manuals were mimeographed sheets of five-to-six pages, scribbled notes or "manuals" consisting mainly of the usual rules and regulations. No one, no matter how talented a clinician, could take these types of manuals and conduct a useful therapeutic session.

We must confront the staffing issue if we are going to make substantial progress. Too many treatment staff, let alone other corrections experts, simply do not know their basic criminological theory and, more important, the psychological theory and practice regarding the why's and how's of reinforcing and punishing behavior. Thus, I now propose to you a fundamental test that should be mandatory for all future hiring of researchers, policymakers, and clinicians in corrections who will be involved with developing offender-intervention strategies.

It is the Skinner box test. If you really think you know how to change behavior, put a rat in the box and shape its behavior so it learns a simple contingency (for example, to press a lever for a food reinforcer). Our undergraduates, who have taken a course in learning, can do it in about one-to-two hours. Can you imagine the results if we asked the typical corrections policymaker and criminologist, many of whom eschew treatment and are ignorant of the psychology of learning, to pass this test? After about a day, I predict, the poor rat either would be catatonic, shredding paper (an administrator's delight) or standing on its head.

Well, we can have a little laugh about this scenario, but it really is a crucial issue because what often passes for therapy in the field are nice little friendly or, in the case of intermediate sanction programs, not so friendly, chats, where the reinforcers and punishers (usually threats which are useless for modifying behavior) are delivered almost randomly to the offenders. No wonder so many programs are ineffective.

At least these problem can be remedied. The majority of correctional treatment staff I have met want to be effective and augment their skills.

The problem is providing the training, and, unfortunately, such venues are rare.

The next two examples of quackery, in my opinion, have much less of a chance of being resolved. The first is the paradigm passion and ethnocentrism of academics. Here is how it works.

Academics' graduate training, by necessity, is narrowly defined. Most of us associate with very few colleagues, and those we associate with are mainly from the same speciality area and in agreement on various professional matters. Our work settings often impose filters on our professional perspectives. We do not get reinforced for embracing knowledge that is contrary to the accepted ways we view issues in our area of expertise. Ethnocentrism evolves out of paradigm passion. Once it is taken for granted that our disciplinary boundaries and the sociopolitical context we live in adequately define the nature of things, then it is a small step to tacitly assume intellectual hegemony.

I have examples galore of the disastrous effects of this state of affairs. Suffice it to say, sociologists and criminologists do not read psychologists' work and vice versa. Moreover, there is also not enough technology transfer within disciplines. Evidence from other cultures/countries is looked upon suspiciously. I could go on, but let me close with one example of the anti-intellectual consequences of staggering proportions.

One would think that program designers and evaluators of "get-tough" programs would pay some attention to the vast experimental and human behavior modification literature on punishment and the social psychological research on persuasion and coercion, which provide a convincing rationale as to why punishing-smarter programs would not work. I counted about 30,000 references on these latter two topics. Just two of these references were cited in the entire "get-tough" literature, and even in these two instances it was a questionable call.

Finally, we have the fartcatcher syndrome. I am not being scatological. It is a legitimate American word (*see* Bill Bryson's book, *Made in America*) common to the last century. It referred to footmen. Now it refers to those political toadies one commonly finds in the Prime Minister's office, premiers, and various ministers, officers, senior government administrative positions, and so on. Notice, I am using Canadian terminology because it is possible fartcatchers do not exist in your country. The job of a fartcatcher is a legitimate one. It is to glory in the wafts emanating from the great one and effectuate and empower (these are words they love to use) political agendas of various sorts.

Who are these people? First, they are content free, having been trained in the MBA management mold of the generic administrator (*see* Mintzberg on Management, 1989, Free Press, for a withering critique of MBA training). You know the prototypical fartcatchers; transportation one year, fisheries the next, then corrections. They never stay in a job long enough to learn it or suffer the consequences. But they sure as heck can "manage." Or they have been trained in one of our academic disciplines that is suspicious of "science," after all, knowledge is political, socially constructed, partial, and so forth. One's own peculiar ideology and moral superiority is all that is needed to know "things." They all have good political connections, if you did not know.

Obviously, I should cheer up, maybe my medication needs altering. Can the situation be that bad? There are, admittedly, "good" fartcatchers. They are those that stay at the highest level ensuring their political masters' success and those that have a thorough knowledge of the field they are administering. There are precious few in the latter group, and they are worth their weight in gold. But ask yourself, how many correctional administrators could pass a senior undergraduate course on the theories of criminal behavior, its assessment, prediction, and treatment, know how prisons work, and so on? These are not trivial issues as they are central to deriving rational policies about how to manage corrections. Recall my medical analogy. My point is not a brain teaser. My goodness, even in academia, notorious for abysmal management, we can get it right. Even though I can manage the usual business affairs of the university required of faculty, they do not allow me to teach physics or anthropology—yet.

Well, if I continue in this vein I can see that I will get gonged and my award rescinded. In closing, we now are at a stage in our development in corrections where we have a solid knowledge base in some areas. I realize, as one legendary bluesman said, "It's a mean old world." To expect that our society is truly experimenting and implementing our hard earned knowledge routinely is to be frightfully naive. I am hopeful, however, that we can have a "hit rate" of 20 to 40 percent regarding respecting evidence that leads to rational policies. That will be progress. It is never too late to start.

Subject Index

Name Index

A

Abbott, A.A., 92, 93
Abbott, B., 59, 92, 173, 198, 202, 222
Abram, K., 73, 176, 233
Abram, K. M., 105
Acoca, L., 74, 75, 76, 93, 147, 165
Adams, L., 220, 225
Adams, P.F., 144t, 160, 165
Adams, R., 165
Agranoff, R., 10, 13, 93
Agular, M., 158, 165
Albrecht, L., 118, 134
Alder, C., 148, 149, 159, 165
Alexander, B., 60, 155, 165
Alexander, M., 222
Allen, E., 232
Allgood-Merten, B., 148, 165
Alonso, A., 210, 222
Amaro, H., 158, 165, 223
Anderson, S.C., 5, 77, 106
Andrews, D. A., 109, 110, 111, 122, 123, 127,
    128, 134, 136, 138, 236, 238, 248, 249, 251,
        264, 265, 266, 291, 308, 311, 323, 331,
            332, 334, 335
Anetra, N, 164
Anglin, D., 113, 138
Anglin, M. D., 20, 73, 74, 93, 99, 106, 174, 233
Anthenelli, R., 193, 223
Arbiter, N., 186, 232

Arbour, L., 177, 223, 280, 318, 323
Arella, L., 150, 165
Aries, E., 209, 210, 223
Arminen, I., 230
Arnold, R., 116, 134, 160, 166, 181, 223
Artz, S., 143, 156, 158, 159, 162, 166
Austin, C. D., 92, 93
Austin, G., 174, 178, 179, 180, 182, 224
Austin, J., 16, 147, 165
Austin, J. B, 112–113, 127, 128, 133, 134, 173,
    184, 223
Axon, L., 75, 93, 184, 223

B

Bachman, R., 73, 93
Bailey, D., 46, 63, 65, 93
Bailey, J., 94
Baird, S.C., 236, 264
Barajas, E., 7, 93
Barkwell, L., 236, 265
Baron, L., 145, 167
Barrett, M., 201, 223
Barrey, E. M., 75, 93
Barthwell, A.G., 74, 94
Bartollas, C., 142, 166
Bashevkin, S., 295, 323
Baskin, D., 179, 232
Bebout, R.R., 2, 100
Beckett, L., 200, 226

ABOUT THE AUTHORS

Kelley Blanchette received her Masters of Arts in psychology in 1996 and is currently a doctoral candidate at Carleton University. Presently, Ms. Blanchette is a senior research officer at the Research Branch, Correctional Service of Canada. Ms. Blanchette has supervisory experience at the Ottawa detoxification center and at a shelter for homeless women. Her research experience includes studies on sex offenders, violent and dangerous offenders, and offenders in segregation. Her primary focus, however, is women offenders. Current research initiatives include a national evaluation of programs for women offenders, and the development of an actuarial security reclassification instrument for federally sentenced women.

Barbara Bloom, is a criminal justice consultant, academic, and researcher with more than twenty years of experience working with local, state, and national criminal justice agencies. She specializes in the development and evaluation of programs serving girls and women under criminal justice supervision. Dr. Bloom holds a master's degree in social work from San Francisco State University and a Ph.D. in Sociology from the University of California, Riverside. She is an Assistant Professor in the Department of Criminal Justice Administration at Sonoma State University and recent past president of the Western Society of Criminology. Among Dr. Bloom's publications are several national studies: Why Punish the Children? A Reappraisal of the Children of Incarcerated Mothers in America, and a National Institute of Corrections-sponsored study, Female Offenders in the Community: An Analysis of Innovative Strategies and Programs. She is currently the project director of a National Institute of

Corrections project, "Gender-Responsive Strategies: Research, Practice and Guiding Principles for Women Offenders."

Meda Chesney-Lind, Ph.D. is Professor of Women's Studies at the University of Hawaii at Manoa. She has served as Vice President of the American Society of Criminology and president of the Western Society of Criminology. Nationally recognized for her work on women and crime, her books include *Girls, Delinquency and Juvenile Justice* which was awarded the American Society of Criminology's Michael J. Hindelang Award for the "outstanding contribution to criminology, 1992" and *The Female Offender: Girls, Women and Crime* published in 1997 by Sage. Her most recent book, an edited collection entitled *Girls and Gangs in America*, has just been published by Lakeview Press. She was named a fellow of the American Society of Criminology in 1996 and also has received the Distinguished Scholar Award from the Women and Crime Division of the American Society of Criminology and the Herbert Block Award for service to the society and the profession from the American Society of Criminology. She also has received the Donald Cressey Award from the National Council on Crime and Delinquency, the Paul Tappan Award for "outstanding contributions to the field of criminology," the Founders award for "significant improvement of the quality of justice" from the Western Society of Criminology, and the University of Hawaii Board of Regent's Medal for "Excellence in Research." She is an outspoken advocate for girls and women, particularly those who find their way into the criminal justice system. Her work on the problem of sexism in the treatment of girls in the juvenile justice system was partially responsible for the recent national attention devoted to services to girls in that system. More recently, she has worked hard to call attention to the soaring rate of women's imprisonment and the need to vigorously seek alternatives to women's incarceration.

Stephanie S. Covington, Ph.D., L.C.S.W., is a clinician, organizational consultant, and lecturer recognized for her pioneering work on women's issues. She has more than twenty years of experience in the design and implementation of treatment services for women. She is recognized for her work in both the public and private sectors. Her twelve years of experience in the criminal justice system includes training, speaking, writing, and consulting with the National Institute of Corrections, Center for Substance Abuse Treatment, Correctional Services of Canada, Federal Bureau of Prisons, and various state and local jurisdictions. The focus of this work is on gender-responsive services. She has published extensively and authored three books: *Leaving the Enchanted Forest: The Path from Relationship Addiction to Intimacy*, *Awakening Your Sexuality: A Guide for Recovering Women*, and *A Woman's Way Through the 12-Steps*. Her most recent publication is a women's treatment curriculum entitled *Helping Women Recover* with a special edition for the criminal justice system. Educated at Columbia University and the Union Institute, Dr. Covington has served on the faculty of the California School of Professional Psychology and has conducted seminars in the United States, Mexico, Europe, Africa, and New Zealand. Dr. Covington maintains a private practice in La Jolla, California, where she is the Co-Director of the Institute for Relational Development.

Dr. Paul Gendreau is Professor of Psychology and Director of the Criminal Justice Studies Center, University of New Brunswick, Saint John. He began working in corrections in 1961. Throughout the years, he has been an administrator in corrections and has held various academic positions. In 1987-88, he was president of the Canadian Psychological Association, and the International Community Corrections Association awarded him the Margaret Mead Award in 1998. The main thrust of his research is concerned with the assessment of treatment and deterrence programs, establishment of guidelines for the optimal use of prediction tools for clinicians and managers in prisons and community corrections, the effects of prison life, and the transfer of knowledge to practitioners and policymakers. Currently, he is involved in developing a state of the art Intensive Parole and Probation service with a rehabilitative emphasis.

Maureen (Marnie) Leavitt, M.S.W., is a therapist and court advocate for First Step, an agency serving victims of sexual and domestic violence, including women in the community corrections system. She also works as a research associate at University of Michigan with Beth Glover Reed, principal investigator of the fifty-state Policy Research on Women and Drugs Project. Her special interest is in the field of programming for women's alcohol and other drug dependencies.

Maeve McMahon, Ph.D., the editor of this volume, is an associate professor in the Department of Law at Carleton University, in Ottawa. Her publications include *The Persistent Prison? Rethinking Decarceration and Penal Reform*, *Crime, Justice and Human Rights in the Baltics*, and *Everyday Life After Communism: Some Observations from Lithuania*. Her current interests include privatization and corrections, criminal justice reform in Lithuania, and activist intellectuals in criminology.

Larry Motiuk is Director General, Research, at the Correctional Service of Canada and Adjunct Research Professor at Carleton University in Ottawa. Dr. Motiuk has a doctorate degree in psychology from Carleton University and a master's degree in clinical psychology from the University of Ottawa. As an employee of the Correctional Service of Canada for the past ten years, Dr. Motiuk has supervised and evaluated operational research projects on a national scale. These include: National Standards for Conditional Release Supervision, Mental Health, Sex Offenders, Day Parole, Risk Assessment, and Management. He is known to be the principal architect of the Community Risk/Needs Management scale (implemented in 1990) and the Offender Intake Assessment Process (implemented in 1994) which are used by field staff in the Correctional Service of Canada to allocate supervision resources. In collaboration with others, he designed and developed a National Parole Board Risk Assessment Training Curriculum. Dr. Motiuk is widely published in literature and has spoken at numerous criminal justice forums. He is also the Editor of *Forum on Corrections Research* that is published three times a year. Current research interests include special risk/need groups, reintegration potential, and offender profiling.

Beth Glover Reed has a Ph.D. in Community and Clinical Psychology and is a faculty member at the School of Social Work and the Program in Women's Studies at the University of Michigan. Her scholarly work focuses broadly on the impact of gender, race, ethnicity and class on and within social systems, with a major emphasis on stigmatized women. She has published broadly on service models and issues, co-edited a two-volume book on treatment services for drug-dependent women, and is engaged in several policy and program-level research projects designed to assess the effectiveness of particular policies and program changes. She also assists several types of community-based agencies to work together more effectively and to incorporate program evaluation into their work.

Andrew Skotnicki is a Carmelite priest. He has been a Visiting Professor at Georgetown University and is currently professor of Catholic Social Ethics at St. Patrick's Seminary in Menlo Park, California. He has done chaplaincy work in numerous correctional facilities and now serves as a part-time chaplain in the Santa Clara County Department of Corrections, serving San Jose, California.